★ **ABOUT THIS BOOK**

This year's edition is set in Myriad Pro, a beautifully proportioned and highly readable humanist *sans serif* typeface designed in the early 1990s by Robert Slimbach and Carol Twombly (both USA). Humanist fonts are those that embody the cleanness and purity of a modern, "grotesque" typeface with the natural, organic feel of hand-drawn letters; *sans serif* refers to the lack of serifs, or flourishes – such as the small feet on a seriffed n or i – common to the "roman" typefaces.

The cover is composed of around 205 different lenses arranged in a vortex pattern over a foil base laminated to paper. It was designed in London, UK, and California, USA, specially for this year's book and took more than one year's development.

Inside, the glow-in-the-dark fold-out sections are printed with phosphorescent ink that absorbs light and remains luminescent even in the dark. For maximum effect, hold the pages to a strong light source for as long as possible.

British Library Cataloguing-in-Publication Data:
a catalogue record for this book is available from the British Library

ISBN: 978-1-904994-18-3

For a complete list of credits and acknowledgements, turn to p.278

If you wish to make a record claim, find out how on p.10. **Always contact us before making a record attempt**.

Check the official website **www.guinnessworldrecords.com** regularly for record-breaking news, plus video footage of record attempts. You can also sign up for the official GWR mobile phone services.

Sustainability
The trees that are harvested to print *Guinness World Records* are carefully selected from managed forests to avoid the devastation of the landscape. For every tree harvested, at least one other is planted.

★**Paper world record!**
This year's paper (Finesse Matt 110 gsm) is a record breaker in its own right. The off-machine coater of the UPM Kymi wood-free coated production line set a new 24-hour speed world record for off-machine coated paper production on 7–8 May 2007. During the record run, the paper was made at an average speed of 1,877 metres/minute (112.6 km/h; 70 mph).

*Pictured opposite is Tony Hawk (USA), who shares the record for the **most X Games medals won** (16) with Andy Macdonald (USA).*

HiT entertainment

EDITOR-IN-CHIEF
Craig Glenday

DEPUTY EDITOR
Ben Way

EDITORIAL TEAM
Rob Dimery, Marcus Hardy, Carla Masson, Matthew White

PROOFREADERS
Harry Boteler, Jeff Probst, Gary Werner

DESIGN CONCEPT AND CREATION
Keren Turner, Lisa Garner at Itonic Design Ltd, Brighton, UK (www.itonicdesign.com)

INDEX
Chris Bernstein

VP, PUBLISHING
Patricia Magill

PRODUCTION EXECUTIVE
Jane Boatfield

PRINTING & BINDING
Printer Industria Gráfica
Barcelona, Spain

TECHNICAL CONSULTANTS
Esteve Font Canadell, Salvador Pujol; Roger Hawkins

COLOUR ORIGINATION
Resmiye Kahraman at Colour Systems, London, UK

COVER FOIL
Designed by Yeung Poon (www.yeungpoon.com); created by Spectratek Technologies, Inc., USA

PICTURE EDITOR
Michael Whitty

DEPUTY PICTURE EDITOR
Laura Jackson

PICTURE RESEARCH TEAM
Karen Gordon
Caroline Thomas

ORIGINAL PHOTOGRAPHY
Richard Bradbury, Drew Gardner, Paul Michael Hughes, Ranald Mackechnie, Joe McGorty, Scott Miller, John Wright

ARTISTS
Ian Bull, Trudi Webb

SENIOR CONSULTANTS
Earth, Science & Technology: David Hawksett
Life on Earth: Dr Karl Shuker
Human Body: Dr Eleanor Clarke (medicine, anatomy); Robert Young (gerontology)
Engineering: Hein Le Roux
Adventure/Exploration: Ocean Rowing Society
Weapons & Warfare: Stephen Wrigley
Arts & Entertainment: Michael Flynn (arts); Thomasina Gibson (TV/movies);
Computer Games: Walter Day (Twin Galaxies)
Music: Dave McAleer; *British Hit Singles & Albums*
Sports & Games: Christian Marais; David Fischer (US sports); International Game Fishing Association (fishing); Wild West Arts Club
General: Stuart Claxton, Kim Lacey

HEAD OF RECORDS MANAGEMENT
Marco Frigatti

RECORDS MANAGEMENT TEAM
Andrea Bánfi
Scott Christie
Laura Hughes
Kaoru Ishikawa
Pamela Schoenhofer
Amanda Sprague
Sophie Whiting
Wu Xiaohong

RECORDS ASSISTANT
Sarah Wagner

GUINNESS WORLD RECORDS 2008

CONTENTS

GLOW IN THE DARK

From fireflies and octopi to pigs
and scorpions, discover a wealth
of creatures that will brighten your
day… and your night.

Mouldy feet, stretchy skin, bulging
eyes, and fearsome fingernails.
These record breakers are bad
enough with the lights *on* – just
wait 'til the lights are *off*!

EDITOR'S INTRODUCTION

AN ELEPHANT WITH A WOODEN LEG... A MAN PULLING A TRUCK WITH HIS EYELIDS... AN APPLE THE SIZE OF YOUR HEAD... IT'S JUST ANOTHER YEAR AT GUINNESS WORLD RECORDS!

The best thing about working on each new edition of the world's biggest-selling copyright book is the incredible variety we encounter on a daily basis. In the past year, for example, the Records Management Team and I have travelled the world, adjudicating records as diverse as the ★ **most people on space hoppers** (England), the ★ **most expensive cocktail** (Northern Ireland), the ★ **largest human wheelbarrow race** (Singapore), the ★ **largest underwater dance class** (Australia), and the ★ **deepest concert** (somewhere in the North Sea!).

We were also invited to take part in some fantastic events over the past year – the X Games (see pp.264–65), the Royal International Air Tattoo, the Wild West Arts Club Convention (see pp.260–61), Children in Need, Comic Relief and the Flora London Marathon (see p.9) are just a few of the highlights. And we were asked to appear on countless TV shows, such as *The Paul O'Grady Show, Sunrise TV, Sattitude, Blue Peter, Newsround, Loose Women, This Morning* and *The Daily Show with Jon Stewart*. (See strip below for some of the records set on TV.)

Many thanks to everyone who treated us so well on these occasions – we're certainly looking forward to returning to your screens again soon.

We were no strangers to radio, either. As well as featuring regularly on London's Capital Radio, Records Manager Scott Christie and I were honoured to set a new Guinness World Record for the ★ **most radio interviews in a day**, pulling off a gruelling 54 interviews in 24 hours with the help of our press agent, TNR, and the BBC (see opposite).

DID YOU KNOW?
This year's language editions: American English, Arabic, Brazilian, Portuguese, Chinese, Croatian, Czech, Danish, Dutch, English, Finnish, French, German, Greek Hebrew, Hungarian, Icelandic, Italian, Japanese, Norwegian, Portuguese, Russian, Slovakian, Spanish, Swedish and Turkish.

CAPITAL RADIO

As part of GWR Day 2006, we spent time on the roof at Capital Radio in London to ratify the record for the ★ **most consecutive passes of a giant volleyball**. Paddy "Sports Monkey" Bunce and guest listener Vanessa Sheridan managed 582 passes during Johnny Vaughan's Capital Breakfast show. Pictured (left to right) is Johnny with Paddy, Vanessa and GWR's Kim Lacey.

CUT ABOVE THE REST

We were honoured this year to welcome two very striking record holders to our London offices: Lee Redmond (USA), the owner of the **longest female fingernails** at 7.51 m (24 ft 7.8 in), and Aaron Studham (USA), who boasts the **tallest mohican** at 53 cm (21 in)!

Aaron coped well with the flight over here – he could easily tie up his hair – but Lee fared less well. She kept stepping on her nails and couldn't manoeuvre into the toilet cubicle! Once in the office, though, she proved herself fully capable by making us all cups of tea... and even doing the washing-up afterwards!

★ **NEW RECORD**
★ **UPDATED RECORD**

BLUE PETER
★ **Most people tossing pancakes**
The record for the largest pancake toss was 108, achieved by The Scout Association on *Blue Peter* for Pancake Day at the BBC Television Centre, London, UK, on 20 February 2007.

SATTITUDE
★ **Most Brussels sprouts eaten in one minute**
GWR's Katie Forde adjudicated as Liam McCormack (Ireland) ate 21 sprouts on RTE 2's *Sattitude* in Cork, Ireland, in February 2007.

EMMERDALE
In March 2007, last year's edition of the Guinness World Records book featured in a storyline in the famous soap opera, when Belle Dingle set her heart on breaking a record...

DANCING IN THE STREET
We were pleased to act as adjudicators – and co-hosts – for this BBC national dancing extravaganza in July. Find out more about records set on the show on pp.182–83.

LOOSE WOMEN
We turned up on the lunchtime show to adjudicate a (failed!) attempt by actress Denise Welch (UK) on the record for the **most bras strapped on in a minute**.

07

BBC RADIO – MOST INTERVIEWS IN A DAY

Here's me (left) with GWR's Record Manager Scott Christie during our arduous attempt at the ★ **most radio interviews in a day**. Scott and I sat in a small, hot radio booth in north London and patched through to a grand total of 54 different BBC radio studios across the UK. We're not keen on giving ourselves records, of course, but we did this to kickstart Guinness World Records Day 2006 and to prove that anyone could do it – it's all about making the effort! Thanks to all the hosts who had us on their show – you'll find a full list of participants on p.279.

The radio marathon was attempted as part of the annual **Guinness World Records Day**. This event has grown into an international phenomenon, and we played host to a multitude of weird and wonderful record challenges everywhere from the northernmost wilds of Scotland (★ **narrowest street**) to the southernmost beaches of Africa (★ **longest bra chain**). Find out more about this great day – and some of the other amazing global events we've visited – on the special fold-out feature on pp.52–54.

> "Hi, this is Michael Jackson's assistant. Michael wants to visit your offices. Is 2 p.m. today okay?"

We've had a really fun year meeting and greeting record holders. For me, the highlight was probably meeting the King of Pop himself, Michael Jackon (see above right). Who else? Elijah Wood, star of *The Lord of the Rings* trilogy (**most Oscars won by a movie**) received his certificate in person, as did *Lost* star Jorge Garcia (**most expensive TV pilot**).

And we happily turned up at various movie premieres – my favourite being the new James Bond movie, *Casino Royale* (US/UK 2006), to present stunt driver Adam Kirley with his certificate for the

KING OF POP

One of the highlights of our year was undoubtedly a visit from the King of Pop, Michael Jackson. A long-term fan of the book, Michael popped into our London headquarters in November to pick up an array of certificates for his incredible musical achievements. He also insisted that he be awarded his record for the **best-selling album** (*Thriller*) at the World Music Awards the following day (with the help of Beyoncé), an honour we were more than happy to oblige!

★ **most cannon rolls** (see p.173) – and numerous dinners, most recently the Ocean Rowing Society's black-tie affair to celebrate those hardy souls who've rowed an ocean (see p.94).

Of course, you don't have to be a famous face or an accomplished explorer to be a record holder. If you want to get *your* name in next year's edition, find out how to get your idea registered on p.10.

This page will also tell you a little bit about what our adjudicators do – and how they do it.

DOCTOR WHO
★ **LONGEST RUNNING SCI-FI TV SERIES**
David Tennant took "time" out of his busy schedule to accept the certificate for *Doctor Who*'s 749 record-breaking episodes!

THE PAUL O'GRADY SHOW
Our favourite show of the year was Paul's – in the last 12 months we've set lots of records, such as ★ **fastest escape from a straitjacket** and ★ **fastest time to pop 100 balloons**.

THIS MORNING
★ **Fastest omelette-making**
Howard Helmer (USA) made an omelette in 49 seconds on the set of *This Morning* (ITV) at the London Studios (UK) on 11 October 2006.

X FACTOR
Talent show runner-up Ray Quinn (UK) became the ★ **youngest male artist to enter the UK album chart without releasing a single** with the release of his debut album, *Ray Quinn*.

FLYING HIGH WITH JAY KAY & JAMIROQUAI

Not only did we get to spend a day at 303 m (994 ft) below sea level with Katie Melua as she performed the ★**deepest concert** (see p.183), Sony Ericsson and Jamiroquai invited us onboard their specially modified aircraft in February 2007 for the ★**highest concert** – at 11,277 m (37,000 ft) and 1,017 km/h (632 mph). Thanks to both bands for their audacious achievements – and for inviting us along to adjudicate!

BEDLAM-ANIA

GWR would like to thank Hamleys (London) for hosting a Bedlam cube challenge on Guinness World Records Day. A Bedlam cube is a 3-D puzzle comprising 13 shapes that fit together to form a solid cube (there are 19,186 solutions!). The fastest time to build the cube was 11.03 seconds, set by Danny Bamping (UK).

No one ratifies such a diverse range of records as GWR, so whether your skill is marathon joggling, tea-cosy collecting or pogostick jumping, tell us about it by logging on to **www.guinnessworldrecords.com**.

Talking of the net, this year we've totally revamped our website. Check back regularly for record-breaking updates, events news, competitions and the latest additions to our new online store! (Yes, you've read the book, broken the record – now wear the T-shirt!) And find out more about some of our exciting new interactive services.

THIS YEAR'S BOOK

Back to the book, I'm pleased to reveal some exciting new record categories and topics. Fans of TV show *CSI* – currently the world's **most popular TV show** (see p.184) – will no doubt spend hours analysing our **Forensic Science** records on p.152, and space cadets will want to check out the major changes that have occurred recently in our Solar System on **Planets** (p.20).

The news has been dominated by climate change lately, so stay abreast of new record developments by turning to **Environment** on p.30. And this year, we've organized our **Life on Earth** chapter (pp.36–51) by continent, making it even easier for you to find our what's breaking records in your neighbourhood.

On the human front, we've included an extended chapter on **Epic Endeavours** (pp.92–103), and gathered together the most intriguing human achievements – from the mad to the momentous – in **Fantastic Feats** (pp.72–91). We're also not afraid to investigate some of the more unsavoury aspects of our modern world by reporting on **Terrorism & Conflict** (p.132) and **Politics** (p.130).

PAULO COELHO & UK'S TALLEST MAN

At the 2007 London Book Fair, two very high-profile visitors paid a visit to our stand: the literary giant Paulo Coelho (Brazil), the ★**most translated living author**, and the *actual* giant Neil Fingleton, the ★**UK's tallest living man**. Thanks to both for their continuing support!

SPAMALOT!

Guinness World Records made its West End stage debut in *Spamalot the Musical* in May after we were asked to help organize the **largest coconut orchestra**. Here's me on stage with Monty Python's Terry Jones and Terry Gilliam along with the cast at the curtain call on the night they broke the record!

SUNRISE TV: MOST BODY SKIPS

Australian TV star Grant Denyer is no stranger to Guinness World Record-breaking. The *Sunrise* presenter not only holds three records – for the **highest altitude tandem bungee jump** (300 m; 984 ft), the **most kisses received in one minute** (62) and the **most underpants pulled on in a minute** (19 pairs) – but this year he welcomed on to his show Brittany Boffo (Australia), who broke the record for **most body skips in one minute** (60).

Finally this year, we're excited to feature the first ever GWR **glow-in-the-dark** features. Check out the gatefolds on pp.55–58 and pp.139–42. Where you see the lightbulb symbol, hold the page up to a lightbulb – or run a torch over the images – for about a minute and then turn off the lights to reveal a hidden, fluorescent world! The more you "charge" the page, the stronger and more impressive the effect will be.

So, that's mountain climbing, polar exploring, scorpion eating, warfare, singing and dancing, celebrity gossip, talented pets, movie stars

and glow in the dark… all between the covers of just one book!

Guinness World Records 2008 is truly a fascinating snapshot of the world we live in today. I hope you enjoy reading about these inspiring, crazy, impressive, humbling record-breaking people, pets and places just as much as everyone here at Guinness World Records has enjoyed bringing it all together.

Craig Glenday,
Editor-in-Chief

THE MIRROR TAKES ON GWR

Congratulations to the *Daily Mirror*'s Damien Fletcher. Determined to get his name in our famous book, he tried his hands at various records. And he didn't do too badly, either!

FASTEST TIME TO DRESS A DUVET
1 min 2 sec – still the official record time!

MOST JELLY EATEN WITH CHOPSTICKS
In one minute, Damien ate a record 180 g (6.34 oz)!

MOST EGGS HELD IN THE HAND
Although Damien broke the record, with 12 eggs, it's since been "beaten" – with 19!

LONGEST BRA CHAIN

The women of South Africa proved they were game for some record-breaking fun by having a go at the world's **longest chain of bras** for GWR Day 2006. If you've got an idea for a record, why not attempt it on the next GWR Day – it's held on the second Thursday in November each year.

LONDON MARATHON

Of all the many charity record attempts we visit each year, perhaps the closest to our hearts is the Flora London Marathon – indeed, GWR's own Kim Lacey ran the 2007 race (in a time of 4 hr 56 min 41 sec). And she had some inspired company…

• Oliver Holland and 17 friends dressed as convicts (**most linked runners to finish a marathon**)

• David "Batman" Green (**fastest marathon in superhero costume [male]**, 5 hr 8 min 39 sec)

• Ian Sharman (**fastest time dressed as Elvis**, 2 hr 57 min 44 sec)

• Gary Speakman (**fastest time in fireman's uniform**, 7 hr 10 min 7 sec)

• Angus Macfadyen (**fastest time on crutches**, 7 hr 13 min 59 sec)

• Susie Hewer (**longest scarf knitted while running a marathon**, 1.2 m; 4 ft)

• Sally "Supergirl" Orange (**fastest time in superhero costume [female]**, 4 hr 8 min 13 sec)

HOW TO BE A RECORD BREAKER

GUINNESS WORLD RECORDS IS THE GLOBAL AUTHORITY ON RECORD-BREAKING ACHIEVEMENT. SO IF YOU WANT TO GET YOUR RECORD APPROVED BY OUR ADJUDICATORS, HERE'S HOW...

REGISTER ONLINE

This year, we've completely redesigned our website, making it **even easier to register** your Guinness World Record claim.

You'll find us at www.guinnessworldrecords.com. Log on now and click on **"Break a World Record"** to find out more – including how to monitor your application as it progresses through our claims system.

Guinness World Records is a unique organization – no one else ratifies record-breaking achievement across such a wide range of subjects, and with the same degree of authority. That's why we get over 1,000 record claims sent to us every week!

We have over 50 years' experience of judging and collecting world record facts, helping us produce this, the world's **biggest-selling copyright book**. A record is not a Guinness World Record until our team of experts has examined the claim and given the official stamp of approval.

On the next page, you'll find out how to register your record. If you want your record assessed on the day you attempt it, you can apply for one of our trained adjudicators. Pictured right are judges Anthony and Kim with some of the equipment they may use at a record attempt. If you're successful, they will also present you with your official certificate there and then.

VIDEO CAMERA
We ask all claimants to video-record their attempts, just in case we need to go back and double-check any aspect of the claim.

LASER RANGE FINDER
To measure distances, we might consider using laser technology: by timing the returning pulse of a laser beam, these handheld devices can provide exact distance measurements.

ENVIRONMENTAL GAUGE
For measuring air temperature, humidity, altitude, wind speed and so on.

LASER THERMOMETER
We use high-tech, non-contact, infra-red temperature meters, which help us measure heat at a distance. They work by measuring an object's infra-red energy radiation.

SOUND-LEVEL METER
Got a loud snore or deafening belch? To measure it accurately and objectively, we use a peak sound meter, which tells us in decibels the relative loudness of a sound.

TALKING YOUR LANGUAGE
Guinness World Records has multilingual adjudicators who travel around the globe. Here, judge Sarah Wagner is inspecting the **longest line of pizzas** (186.3 m; 611 ft 2 in) in Treviso, Italy.

INTRODUCTION

GUINNESS WORLD RECORDS ADJUDICATORS

DIGITAL CAMERA
We expect you to take as many photos as possible of your attempt – indeed, the best option is to get a professional along to do the snapping. We use handy pocket digital cameras as well as larger, SLR-style digitals.

TWO-WAY RADIO RECEIVER
May be used at larger attempts to stay in touch with other adjudicators or the record organizers.

DIGITAL STOPWATCH
The most basic piece of equipment for an adjudicator is a stopwatch accurate to 1/100 of a second.

BINOCULARS
Binocular telescopes give three-dimensional (stereo) views of distant images.

TRUNDLE WHEEL
If we need to measure something that's too long for a tape measure – or something that doesn't follow very straight lines – then we use this simple device. It houses a clicker that counts every metre as the wheel turns.

TAPE MEASURE
A tough fabric waterproof tape measure (metric and imperial).

1. GO ONLINE

If you want to break a record you've seen in the book or on television – or you want to set a new one – **the first thing you must do is contact us**. The easiest way is via our website (see opposite page).

2. FOLLOW THE GUIDELINES

Use the website to tell us as much as possible about your idea. If it's an existing record category, or a new idea that satisfies our basic record requirements, **we will send you the official Guinness World Records guidelines** that you must follow in order to achieve the record.

3. GATHER THE EVIDENCE

You don't need a Guinness World Records official at your attempt, although you can apply for one if you wish. Just be sure to **collate all the evidence we ask for**. The minimum we ask for is video footage, photographs and two independent, signed witness statements. You find details of all the evidence we need in the guidelines. Please note that it can take up to six weeks to have your evidence assessed professionally.

Finally, if you didn't request an adjudicator, you'll find out if you're a new Guinness World Record holder when your certificate is mailed to your home. Welcome to the gang!

ANY TIME, ANY PLACE, ANYWHERE...

Guinness World Records travels the globe in our endless quest for exciting new records. Above, adjudicator Michael Whitty visits the Azteca Stadium in Mexico City, Mexico, to measure up the **largest football shirt** (51 m; 168 ft long!).

SIZE MATTERS

No job is too large – or too small – for our adjudicators. If you think you've got the **largest glitter ball**, for example, and it beats Nigel Burrows's (UK) 5 m wide (16-ft) ball being measured here by GWR's Laura Hughes, let us know!

MOST POPULAR RECORDS

★ NEW RECORD ★ UPDATED RECORD

★ TALLEST LIVING MAN

Many people claim to be giants but will not let GWR measure their height officially. In 2006, Leonid Stadnyk (Ukraine) was measured by endocrinologist and gigantism expert Professor Michael Besser (UK) and found to be 2.57 m (8 ft 5.5 in) tall. GWR has now accepted Professor Besser's measurement but hopes to assess Stadnyk formally soon.

TALL TALE?

You can find out more about the tallest living man in the world – and about GWR's stringent rules for establishing the height of contenders for that title – on p.64.

★ MOST PEOPLE DRIBBLING BASKETBALLS

This extremely popular record was broken twice in 2006 (although the most times it has been broken in one year was five, back in 2003). The first successful attempt of the year was on 31 March 2006, when a group of 910 people dribbled basketballs simultaneously at Meadowbank Sports Centre in Edinburgh, Scotland, UK.

Just four and a half months later, 1,111 people beat the record at Flora Hill Secondary College in Bendigo, Victoria, Australia, on 16 August.

★ LONGEST RADIO DJ MARATHON

On average, this record is beaten every four months! Current holder, Stefano Venneri (Italy), DJ'd for an incredible 125 hours on Radio BBSI in Alessandria, Italy, from 26 April to 1 May 2006.

★ LONGEST KEYBOARD MARATHON

Charles Brunner (Trinidad and Tobago) played piano for 64 hours at the Hilton Hotel in Port of Spain, Trinidad and Tobago, from 7 to 9 December 2006.

LONGEST DRUMMING MARATHON

Multiple record holder – and GWR Hall of Fame entrant – Suresh Joachim Arulanantham (Australia) became the 13th person since 2000 to hold the solo drumming marathon record. He played for 84 hours (1–4 February 2004) at the Magic Factory in Zurich, Switzerland.

★ LONGEST LESSON

From 20 to 23 October 2005, Sanjay Kumar Sinha (India) taught a 73-hr 37-min lesson on English grammar to 59 pupils at the Bay City Club in Bandra, India. Two other people briefly held the title in 2005: David Specchio (China) for a 72-hour lesson, also on English, and Tomasz Marczak (Poland) for his 69-hour effort on language.

MOST PHONE BOOKS
TORN IN THREE MINUTES

This record has been broken eight times since 2001. The current holder is a newcomer to the event, Ed Shelton (USA), who ripped 55 telephone directories – each with 1,044 pages – from top to bottom in three minutes in Reno, Nevada, USA, on 18 November 2005.

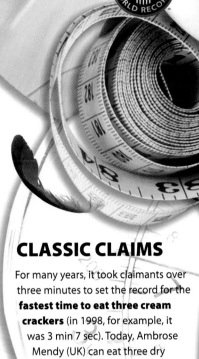

LONGEST ICE HOCKEY ENDURANCE MARATHON

The ice hockey endurance marathon is usually beaten two or three times a year, although the last successful attempt – a 240-hour marathon staged by Brent Saik and friends (all Canada) at Saiker's Acres in Strathcona, Alberta, Canada, in February 2005 – has yet to be beaten. This is the longest time that this record has remained unbroken for at least 10 years!

★ LARGEST GAME OF LEAPFROG

We have received, on average, a leapfrog record claim once a month for the past 10 years!

The most recent successful claim came on 4 July 2006, when 1,197 participants leapfrogged at the UNESCO World Youth Festival in Stuttgart Degerloch, Germany.

CLASSIC CLAIMS

For many years, it took claimants over three minutes to set the record for the **fastest time to eat three cream crackers** (in 1998, for example, it was 3 min 7 sec). Today, Ambrose Mendy (UK) can eat three dry cream crackers in 34.78 seconds!

In 2001, the record for the **most doughnuts eaten in three minutes** stood at just three. However, in six years the record has been doubled to six, by a number of claimants!

Eating too much? Careful, you'll end up like Robert Earl Hughes (USA, 1926–58). He had the **largest chest measurement** at 3 m 15 cm (124 in, or 10 ft 4 in)! Robert was so large when he died that he needed a coffin the size of a grand piano case!

LARGEST PILLOW FIGHT

A total of 3,648 participants gathered at the University at Albany, Albany, New York, USA, on 17 April 2005 to battle it out with feather pillows.

CLAIMS WE *DON'T* WANT TO SEE

"I can lick my elbow" – we don't care: it's not a record.

"Fattest cat" – it's cruel, so please don't overfeed your pets.

"Fastest surgery" – no, please take your time when operating, doctor – it's not a race.

"Longest french fry" and **"Largest potato chip"** – there's no merit in these claims, so thanks but NO!

★ MOST CANDLES ON A CAKE

Every year, this record gets bigger and bigger. Ten years ago, it stood at 900; now, thanks to Ashrita Furman and members of the Sri Chinmoy Centre (all USA), it stands at 27,413 lit candles, which were placed on a cake to mark the 74th anniversary of the foundation of the centre in New York, USA, on 27 August 2005. The cake measured 81.28 cm (32 in) by 14.02 m (46 ft)!

★ FASTEST BALLOON SCULPTING

Two men often come to "blows" over this record! John Cassidy (USA, below) and Salvatore Sabbatino (Germany, inset) have been battling for years to claim this title. The current holder is John, who created 654 balloon sculptures in one hour in New York City, USA, on 21 November 2005.

★ LONGEST HOTDOG

South Africans, Icelanders and now Japanese have laid claim to this not-quite-all-American record! The All-Japan Bread Association made a 60.3-m-long (197-ft 1-in) wiener in Toyama-Ken, Japan, on 4 August 2006.

CONTENTS

★ PLANET WITH THE GREATEST RING SYSTEM

Jupiter, Uranus and Neptune all have ring systems, but none is on the scale of Saturn's. This stunning image was taken by the NASA/ESA *Cassini* spacecraft in 2006, with the planet directly between the spacecraft and the Sun. The dark side of the planet is lit by sunlight reflecting from ring particles. These observations led to the discovery of two new faint rings, formed by micro-meteorite impacts on the tiny moons Janus, Epimetheus and Pallene. The total mass of the ring system is estimated to be around 4×10^{19} kg (9×10^{19} lb) – roughly equivalent to 30 million Mount Everests.

DEEP SPACE

★ MOST COMMON FORM OF MATTER

Observations of the way that galaxies of stars move through space suggest that some 80–85% of the total mass of the universe is actually invisible and does not even interact with light and radiation in the way that stars and planets do. Many scientists believe this "dark matter" may be made up of a new type of undiscovered Weakly Interacting Massive Particle – or WIMP.

The image below shows the first ever 3D map of the distribution of dark matter in the universe, based on observations by the Hubble Space Telescope.

★ SMALLEST STELLAR DISC

Observations by NASA's Spitzer Space Telescope have revealed a disc of material surrounding the brown dwarf star OTS 44 that has a mass just 15 times that of Jupiter (4,770 times that of Earth, or 0.01 times the mass of the Sun).

Over millions of years, this will eventually form a miniature planetary system containing perhaps one small gas giant and a few small rocky planets.

SMALLEST STARS

First discovered in 1967, neutron stars are the remnants of stars that have self-destructed in a spectacular explosion known as a supernova. They may have a mass up to three times that of the Sun, but diameters of only 10–30 km (6–19 miles).

Neutron stars also have the distinction of being the densest stars in the universe. A sand-grain size of neutron star material would have the mass of a skyscraper.

★ LARGEST NEARBY GALAXY

The largest galaxy in our galaxy cluster, the Local Group, is the Andromeda spiral galaxy M31. Results announced in January 2007 suggest Andromeda is five times larger than previously thought, with the discovery of stars orbiting its centre at a distance of at least 500,000 light years (compare image above left with more recent photograph, above right).

At 2.2 million light years from Earth, Andromeda is also the **most distant object visible to the naked eye**.

The left-hand photograph of the Andromeda Galaxy above is actually a mosaic of images taken by amateur astronomer Rob Gendler (USA), with a total exposure time of 90 hours. At 21,904 X 14,454 pixels, this constitutes the ★ **largest image of any spiral galaxy** to date.

FIRST SPIRAL GALAXY DISCOVERED

The Whirlpool Galaxy (M51) was the first celestial object ever to be identified as being a spiral. The discovery was made by William Parsons, Third Earl of Rosse (Ireland) in 1845.

★ YOUNGEST GALAXY

Observations of the galaxy I Zwicky 18, 45 million light years away, by the Hubble Space Telescope reveal that it only began forming stars around 500 million years ago. By way of comparison, our own galaxy, the Milky Way, began star formation around 12 billion years ago.

★ GREATEST GRAVITATIONAL INFLUENCE

Our Local Group of around 30 galaxies is hurtling through space at a speed of approximately 2 million km/h (1.2 million mph), towards a huge agglomeration of mass located some 500 million light years away.

Hidden from view by the bulk of our own Milky Way galaxy, this mass, dubbed The Great Attractor, is believed to be an enormous supercluster of approximately 100,000 galaxies.

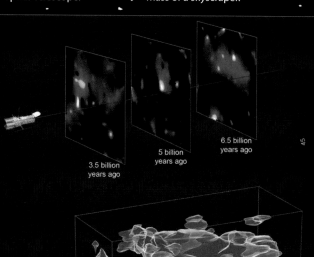

3.5 billion years ago

5 billion years ago

6.5 billion years ago

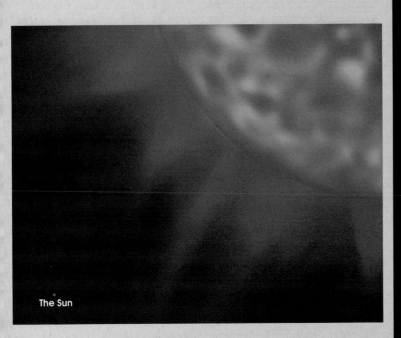

The Sun

MOST LUMINOUS STAR

The latest observations of LBV 1806-20, located 45,000 light years from Earth, indicate it is between 5 million and 40 million times more luminous than the Sun. It has a mass of at least 150 times the mass of the Sun and its diameter is at least 200 times that of the Sun.

BRIGHTEST SUPERNOVA

SN 1006, noted in April 1006 near the star Beta Lupi, flared for two years and reached a magnitude of -9.5. This titanic cosmic explosion was bright enough to be seen with the naked eye for 24 months and, at its most intense, was 1,500 times more luminous than Sirius, the brightest star in the night sky. The supernova took place around 3,260 light years away from Earth.

WINDIEST EXTRASOLAR PLANET

The gas giants 51 Pegasi, HD179949b and HD209458b are all orbiting different stars within 150 light years of Earth. Each orbits its star within around 8 million km (4.9 million miles) – far closer than Mercury orbits the Sun. Results released in January 2007 show that the temperature difference between day and night on these

planets is tiny, suggesting that supersonic winds of up to 14,500 km/h (9,000 mph) are constantly transferring heat from their day sides to their night sides.

LEAST DENSE EXTRASOLAR PLANET

HAT-P-1b, located 450 light years away from Earth, is a gas giant around 1.38 times the diameter of Jupiter, but with only half the mass. This gives HAT-P-1b a density of around one quarter that of water.

If there was an ocean large enough to accommodate it, HAT-P-1b would float in it, just as Saturn would, but at around three times higher than the famous ringed planet.

DENSEST OBJECTS IN THE UNIVERSE

Black holes are the remnants of stars that ended their lives as supernovae. They are characterized by a region of space in which gravity is so strong that not even light can escape. The boundary of this region is known as the "event horizon" and, at the centre of the black hole, is the "singularity", where the mass of the dead star is compressed to a single point of zero size and infinite density. It is this singularity that generates the powerful gravitational field of a black hole.

LARGEST VOID IN THE UNIVERSE

The large-scale structure of the universe looks spongy in nature, with filaments of galactic clusters enclosing bubbles of relatively empty intergalactic space. largest such bubble is the Bootes Void, whose centre is some 700 million light years away. The existence of several dozen galaxies in a rough tube shape through the centre of the void supports theories that the Bootes Void is the result of a mergence between smaller voids.

Below is a computer simulation of the early universe, clearly showing the forming voids and filaments of galaxy clusters.

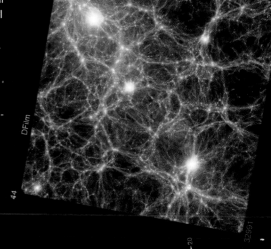

LARGEST GALACTIC COLLISION

Observations of the galactic cluster Abell 754 by the XMM Newton X-ray space telescope indicate it is actually the product of a collision between two smaller clusters of galaxies. The collision, which began around 300 million years ago, was between a cluster of around 300 galaxies and a larger cluster of around 1,000 galaxies, resulting in a turbulent giant cluster around 1 million light years across. Turbulence caused by the collision is expected to last around 1 billion years (1,000,000,000 years), and the combined energy released from this event will be second only to the Big Bang.

The images below are a computer simulation of the collision, spaced around 100 million years apart.

★ NEW RECORD
★ UPDATED RECORD

GREATEST IMPACT ON EARTH

Most astronomers now believe that, 4.5 billion years ago, a planet the size of Mars collided with the young Earth. Some of the debris from this cataclysm went into orbit around the Earth and collected together under its own gravity to form the Moon.

Earth's entire crust would probably have been blasted off into space, leaving behind a planet whose entire surface was an ocean of molten magma.

HOTTEST PLACE

Although no one has ever visited it, the very centre of the Sun is the hottest place in the Solar System, with an estimated temperature of 15,600,000°C (28,080,000°F).

The pressure in the core is around 250 billion times the pressure at sea level on Earth. It is here that around 600 million tonnes of hydrogen are fused into helium every second. This ongoing nuclear reaction is what makes the Sun shine.

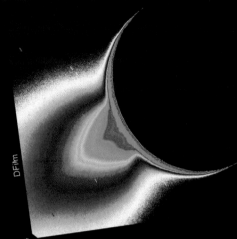

★ HIGHEST CLOUDS

In August 2006, European scientists reported their discovery of faint clouds some 90–100 km (55–62 miles) above the surface of Mars. The clouds, detected by an instrument on the European Space Agency's (ESA) *Mars Express* orbiter, are made up of carbon-dioxide ice crystals.

★ LARGEST DUST STORMS

Mars is the only world other than Earth where dust storms have been observed. In 1971 and 2001, dust storms grew to immense proportions, covering 100% of the planet and obscuring its surface from telescopes and spacecraft.

★ STRONGEST MAGNETIC FIELD

Generated by the liquid metallic hydrogen in its interior, Jupiter's magnetic field is around 19,000 times stronger than Earth's and extends several million kilometres towards the Sun and almost all the way to Saturn in the direction away from the Sun.

If it was visible to the naked eye, Jupiter's magnetic field would appear at around the same size that the full Moon does from Earth.

★ LARGEST DC ELECTRICAL CIRCUIT

Gases spew from the volcanoes of Jupiter's moon Io, forming a huge cocoon that surrounds the planet. As Io orbits through this electrically charged gas, a massive electrical current flows between Jupiter and Io, carrying around two trillion watts of power.

SMALLEST GEOLOGICALLY ACTIVE BODY

In December 2005, the Cassini team announced their discovery of plumes of icy material erupting into space from the surface of Saturn's frozen moon, Enceladus. (The image to the left was processed to bring out weak signals – highlighting contours in the plumes – and strengthen the colours.)

This moon, which measures 256.3 x 247.3 x 244.6 km (159.2 x 153.6 x 151.9 miles) in radius, joins a small club of worlds known to be geologically active: Earth, Jupiter's moon Io and Neptune's moon Triton.

DID YOU KNOW?
Between 16 and 22 July 1994, over 20 fragments of comet Shoemaker-Levy 9 collided with Jupiter. The largest of these fragments was around 3–4 km (2 miles) across.

The greatest impact was caused by the "G" fragment, which exploded with the energy of roughly 600 times the world's nuclear arsenal, or around 6 million megatons of TNT. This represents **the largest recorded impact in the Solar System**.

This is roughly equivalent to all the manmade power produced on Earth.

FASTEST WINDS

When observed in 1989 by NASA's *Voyager 2* probe, the winds on Neptune were measured at around 2,400 km/h (1,500 mph), almost five times faster than the highest known wind speed for a tornado on Earth.

COLDEST OBSERVED GEOLOGICAL ACTIVITY

Active geysers of frigid nitrogen gas erupt several kilometres high into the thin atmosphere of Neptune's moon Triton. With a surface temperature of -235°C (-391°F), Triton is so cold that lakes of water are frozen as hard as steel and show retain impact craters that are millions of years old.

LARGEST CANYON

The Valles Marineris on Mars (seen as a long "scar" on the planet's surface, left, and in detail, inset) is around 4,500 km (2,800 miles) long. At its widest, the canyon measures 600 km (370 miles) across and up to 7 km (4.3 miles) deep. It is named after the *Mariner 9* spacecraft that first discovered it in 1971.

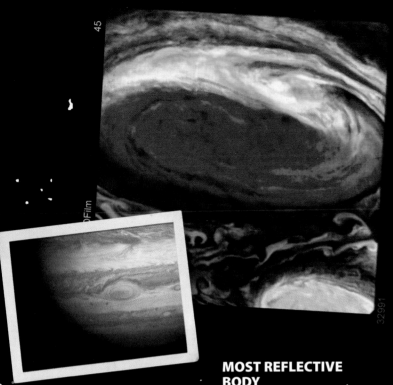

LARGEST CYCLONE

The Great Red Spot on the planet Jupiter (visible as an oval shape on the planet's surface, above, and in closer detail, above right) is the largest cyclone in the Solar System.

The spot varies in size, but can be up to 40,000 km (24,800 miles) long and 14,000 km (8,700 miles) wide. Three planets the size of Earth would fit along its length.

★ LARGEST CHAOTICALLY ROTATING OBJECT

Saturn's misshapen moon Hyperion measures 410 x 260 x 220 km (254 x 161 x 136 miles) across and is the largest highly irregularly shaped body in the Solar System (see box, bottom right).

Hyperion is one of only two bodies in the Solar System discovered to have chaotic rotation, meaning that it is randomly tumbling in its orbit around Saturn. The other body is the asteroid 4179 Toutatis, which measures 4.5 x 2.4 x 2.9 km (2.7 x 1.5 x 1.8 miles) across.

★ CLOSEST MOONS TO EACH OTHER

Janus and Epimetheus share the same average orbit some 91,000 km (56,500 miles) above Saturn. As their orbital paths are only 50 km (31 miles) apart, one of the moons is always catching the other up.

Every four years the two moons come within 10,000 km (6,200 miles) of each other and swap orbits, before drifting apart until their next encounter four years later.

MOST REFLECTIVE BODY

Saturn's small moon Enceladus reflects some 90% of the sunlight that illuminates it, making it more reflective than freshly fallen snow. Its surface is composed of icy material.

DARKEST OBJECT

The surface of the 8 km-long (5-mile) nucleus of Comet Borrelly reflects less than 3% of the sunlight it receives. Its low albedo (ratio of light reflected to light received) is caused by a coating of dark dust.

Borrelly has about half the albedo of the Moon, which is as dark as an asphalt car-park surface. By way of comparison, Earth reflects around 30% of the sunlight it receives.

MOST VOLCANICALLY ACTIVE BODY

When NASA's *Voyager 1* probe passed by the giant planet Jupiter in 1979, its camera imaged the moon Io. The photographs revealed enormous volcanic eruption plumes, some reaching several hundred kilometres into space. Io's activity is driven by tidal energy inside it.

This tidal energy is a result of gravitational interactions between Jupiter, Io and one of the other moons, Europa.

MOST POWERFUL VOLCANO

Loki, an active volcano on Jupiter's moon Io discovered by *Voyager 1* in 1979, emits more heat than all of Earth's active volcanos together.

The volcano has an enormous caldera (volcanic crater) over 10,000 km^2 (4,000 miles^2) in area that is regularly flooded with molten lava.

HIGHEST MOUNTAIN

Located on the planet Mars, Olympus Mons is the highest mountain in the Solar System. Its peak is 25 km (15 miles) above its base – making the mountain nearly three times the height of Mt. Everest.

Olympus Mons is more than 20 times wider than it is high and, despite its great height, it has a very gentle slope. Because of its shape, Olympus Mons is designated a shield volcano.

> **The Solar System is around 4,540 million years old. It will probably last another 5,000 million years**

★ TALLEST EYE-WALL CLOUDS

A massive vortex of clouds, similar to a hurricane, was discovered at Saturn's south pole in 2006. Unlike Jupiter's Great Red Spot (see left), this feature exhibits the classic eye wall of a hurricane on Earth.

The discovery of this south polar vortex represents the only time an eye wall has been detected on another planet. With heights of 35–70 km (18–46 miles), this cloud vortex is roughly five times higher than those in terrestrial hurricanes.

SATURN'S MISSHAPEN MOON

Some scientists believe that Hyperion was involved in a large collision with a comet or asteroid millions of years ago, which broke off part of the moon and brought about its irregular shape.

★ LARGEST EXTRATERRESTRIAL LAKES

In January 2004, scientists released data from the NASA/ESA *Cassini* mission revealing what look like lakes of liquid methane on the surface of Saturn's largest moon, Titan. Cloud-penetrating radar images show around 75 lakes, in a region near Titan's north pole, the largest of which are around 110 km (68 miles) across.

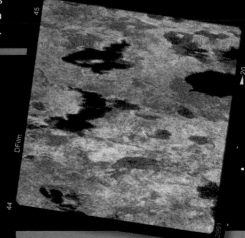

PLANETS

★ OUTERMOST MAJOR PLANET

Since the demotion of Pluto as a planet in 2006 (see opposite page), Neptune is now the farthest major planet from the Sun. At 4.5 billion km (2.7 billion miles) from the Sun, it orbits at 5.45 km/sec (3.38 miles/sec), taking 164.79 years to make one orbit.

★ SMALLEST MAJOR PLANET

Since the reclassification of Pluto as a dwarf planet, Mercury is now the smallest major planet in the Solar System. At 4,879 km (3,031 miles) across, it is less than one and a half times the diameter of Earth's Moon.

Being the closest planet to the Sun, it also has the **fastest orbit**, at 48.87 km/sec (30.36 miles/sec).

MOST EARTH-LIKE PLANET

With surface temperatures ranging from -140°C to 20°C (-220°F to 68°F), and a day lasting 24.6 hours, Mars is the planet that would be easiest to colonize. Spacesuits would still be required, however, as the carbon-dioxide atmosphere is thin and poisonous. Some scientists have suggested "terraforming" Mars – gradually changing the planet's atmosphere so that humans could walk on its surface with minimal protection.

LARGEST PLANET

Jupiter has an equatorial diameter of 143,884 km (89,405 miles) and a polar diameter of 133,708 km (83,082 miles). Its mass is 317.828 times that of the Earth. It also has the **shortest period of rotation**, resulting in a Jovian day of only 9 hr 55 min 29.69 sec.

HOTTEST PLANET

Often referred to as the closest place to hell in the Solar System, Venus has the **thickest atmosphere of any planet**, with a pressure nearly 100 times that of Earth's at sea level. The gases in its atmosphere cause a greenhouse effect and the surface temperature can reach 480°C (896°F).

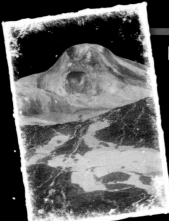

FASTEST PLANET

Mercury, which orbits the Sun at an average distance of 57.9 million km (35.9 million miles), has an orbital period of 87.968 days, giving a highest average speed in orbit of 172,248 km/h (107,030 mph) – almost twice as fast as the Earth's orbiting speed.

Mercury is also the **closest planet to the Sun** (see below).

BRIGHTEST PLANET

Viewed from Earth, the brightest of the five planets normally visible (Jupiter, Mars, Mercury, Saturn and Venus) is Venus, which has a maximum magnitude of -4.4. Indeed, with the exception of the Sun and the Moon, Venus is the brightest object visible to us in the night sky.

VENUS
Hottest surface of any planet in the Solar System, with an average temperature of around 480°C (896°F).
Diameter: 12,104 km (7,521 miles)
Mass: (Earth = 1) 0.81
Mean distance from Sun: 108,200,600 km (67,232,700 miles)
Orbital period: 224.70 days

EARTH
Densest planet: average density 5.517 times that of water.
Diameter: 12,756 km (7,926 miles)
Mass: 5.976 x 10²⁴ kg
Mean distance from Sun: 149,600,000 km (92,955,900 miles)
Orbital period: 365.25 days

MARS
Home to Olympus Mons, the **highest mountain in the Solar System**, with a peak 25 km (15 miles) above base.
Diameter: 6,787 km (4,217 miles)
Mass: (Earth = 1) 0.107
Mean distance from Sun: 227,940,000 km (141,634,800 miles)
Orbital period: 686.98 days

MERCURY
Innermost planet.
Diameter: 4,879 km (3,032 miles)
Mass: (Earth = 1) 0.055
Mean distance from Sun: 57,910,100 km (35,983,000 miles)
Orbital period: 87.97 days

JUPITER
Largest major planet.
Diameter: 143,884 km (89,405 miles)
Mass: (Earth = 1) 318
Mean distance from Sun: 778,330,000 km (483,632,000 miles)
Orbital period: 11.86 years

NEIL DEGRASSE TYSON

Dr Neil DeGrasse Tyson is Director of the Hayden Planetarium at the American Museum of Natural History in New York City, USA. In 2001, he opened a new exhibition of the Solar System in which he controversially relegated Pluto from a planet to just one of the many small icy bodies beyond the orbit of Neptune. In August 2006, Pluto was demoted from planetary status, as Dr Tyson explains:

It's official. Pluto is no longer a planet, as voted in August 2006 by the General Assembly of the International Astronomical Union, the world body of professional astrophysicists. Pluto's planethood must now endure the modifier "dwarf".

But why is Pluto no longer deemed to be a planet?

Frontier science, which is driven by data, is not normally determined, or even guided by, democratic vote. So this decision remains controversial, not only with the professional researchers but also in the hearts and minds of the general public. Yet the reasons for it are clear. According to a new criterion, a planet must have cleared its orbit of debris. Pluto fails this test – badly.

Beginning in 1992, hundreds of small icy bodies have been discovered in the outer Solar System that looked and behaved a lot like Pluto. Like the 19th-century discovery of the asteroid belt – itself a swarm of craggy chunks of rock – a new swath of populated real estate had

been discovered. And this region of the Solar System cor Pluto, one of its largest members. No other planet is so crowded in its orbit.

Combine this with Pluto's other oddball properties – including its diminutive size (six moons are larger, including Earth's Moon), mass (Pluto is less than 1/20th the mass of Mercury, the next smallest planet) and its high ice content (more than half its volume) – and a new understanding of the outer Solar System emerges. We did not lose a planet. We gained perspective.

MOONS

PLANET WITH THE MOST MOONS

As of January 2006, the planet in the Solar System with the most satellites is Jupiter, with 63. Saturn comes second, with 47, and Uranus and Neptune have 27 and 13 respectively.

Of Jupiter's moons, four are large enough to be considered planets in their own right:

GANYMEDE

The **largest satellite** is Ganymede, which is 2.017 times as heavy as the Earth's Moon and has a diameter of 5,267 km (3,273 miles). Ganymede is larger than the planet Mercury.

CALLISTO

The outermost of Jupiter's four large moons, Callisto is an ancient relic whose surface is completely covered with impact craters, making it the **most heavily cratered moon**.

IO

The active volcanoes of Io create eruption plumes reaching several hundred kilometres into space, making it the **most volcanically active world** in the Solar System. The moon is squeezed by tidal interactions with Jupiter and another of its moons – Europa – vigorously heating its interior and causing the activity.

EUROPA

Jupiter's large, icy moon Europa has the **smoothest surface of any solid body in the Solar System**. The only prominent relief on its surface are ridges a few hundred metres in height.

☆ DWARF PLANET WITH THE MOST MOONS

In 2005, two tiny moons of Pluto were discovered using the Hubble Space Telescope. Named Nix and Hydra, they are around 140 km (87 miles) and 170 km (105 miles) across respectively.

This discovery raises the total number of Pluto's moons to three.

☆ LARGEST DWARF PLANET

The icy world Eris was discovered in January 2005. It has an elliptical orbit, its distance from the Sun ranges from 5.6 billion km to 14.6 billion km, and it has a diameter

of around 2,400 km (1,490 miles) – larger than Pluto. Before the reclassification of Pluto as a dwarf planet, Eris was regarded by many astronomers as the tenth planet.

Eris has a small moon, Dysnomia, which is approximately 350 km (217 miles) across.

MOST TILTED PLANET

The planet Uranus has a greater axial tilt than any of the other planets in the Solar System. Its axis of spin is tilted 97.86 degrees from the plane of its orbit. By way of comparison, the Earth has an axial tilt of only 23.45 degrees.

The reason for this extreme tilt is unknown, although one theory suggests that it was struck by an Earth-sized planet during the violent formation of the Solar System, and that the impact of the collision knocked Uranus over on its side.

☆ LARGEST MOON COMPARED TO ITS PLANET

At 3,474 km (2,159 miles) across, Earth's Moon has a diameter 0.27 times that of Earth.

The Moon is the largest of the three moons in the inner Solar System and the only other world to have been visited by humans.

☆ **NEW RECORD**
★ **UPDATED RECORD**

NEPTUNE
Fastest winds in the Solar System: measured at around 2,400 km/h (1,500 mph) in 1989.
Diameter: 49,528 km (30,775 miles)
Mass: (Earth = 1) 17
Mean distance from Sun: 4,504,300,000 km (2,800,000,000 miles)
Orbital period: 164.79 years

▸ GOODBYE PLUTO... HELLO NEPTUNE

On 24 August 2006, an assembly of the International Astronomical Union (IAU) in Prague, Czech Republic, voted to remove Pluto's planetary status. Henceforth, it is classified as a "dwarf planet". The Solar System now officially comprises eight major planets.

First discovered in 1930 by Clyde Tombaugh (USA), Pluto was initially thought to be larger than it actually is (it is smaller than many moons in the Solar System). Later research revealed objects that rivalled Pluto in size, but were not classified as planets.

As a result, Neptune is now regarded as the most distant major planet.

DID YOU KNOW?

Mercury and Venus are the only planets in the Solar System that do not have moons. Earth, with its single moon, has the next fewest.

Our Moon is actually moving away from the Earth at a rate of around 4 cm (1.6 in) per year.

SATURN
Least dense planet: mostly hydrogen and helium, the two **lightest elements**.
Diameter: 120,536 km (74,898 miles)
Mass: (Earth = 1) 95
Mean distance from Sun: 1,429,400,000 km (888,200,000 miles)
Orbital period: 29.45 years

URANUS
Most tilted planet: its axis of spin is tilted 97.86 degrees from the plane of its orbit.
Diameter: 51,118 km (31,763 miles)
Mass: (Earth = 1) 15
Mean distance from Sun: 2,870,990,000 km (1,784,000,000 miles)
Orbital period: 84.01 years

PLANET EARTH

CONTENTS

HIGHEST
ATMOSPHERIC
PHENOMENA

Of all the phenomena visible in our skies, the very highest are the aurorae, also known as the northern and southern lights. Often visible at night from low and high latitudes, these beautiful coloured, shimmering lights are the result of charged particles from the Sun interacting with the upper atmosphere. The lowest aurorae occur at altitudes of around 100 km (62 miles), while the highest extend up to around 400 km (248 miles). Pictured is the aurora borealis at the Great Slave Lake area, Northwest Territories, Canada.

ATMOSPHERE

LAYERS OF THE ATMOSPHERE

Staring up into our atmosphere is like standing on the ocean floor, looking up through the sea. As you ascend through the atmosphere, its density decreases until it eventually merges with space. There are four distinct layers, nearest Earth: stratosphere; mesosphere; and thermosphere, which gradually merges with space. Note: the diagram is not to scale.

THERMOSPHERE: HOTTEST PART OF THE ATMOSPHERE

The thermosphere starts at around 50 miles (80 km) above the Earth and continues up to the exosphere, at around 310 miles (500 km). In this extremely rarefied gas, the temperature rises with altitude, where it can reach 3,632°F (2,000°C) when the Sun is particularly active.

MESOSPHERE: COLDEST PART OF THE ATMOSPHERE

The mesosphere exists between around 30 and 50 miles (50 and 80 km) above Earth. Here, the temperature drops with altitude, reaching a minimum of around -148°F (-100°C).

STRATOSPHERE: HIGHEST OZONE CONCENTRATION

O_3, or ozone, can form at ground level as a pollutant, but over 90% of the Earth's total resides in the stratosphere, where it forms the ozone layer. At around 15 miles (25 km) above the Earth, it reaches its highest concentration of just a few parts per million, but this is enough to absorb almost all the high-frequency ultraviolet light from the Sun.

HIGHEST ATMOSPHERIC PHENOMENA

Also known as the northern and southern lights, aurorae are beautifully coloured, shimmering lights that are the result of charged particles from the Sun interacting with the upper atmosphere. The lowest aurorae occur at altitudes of around 100 km (62 miles), while the highest extend up to around 400 km (248 miles).

FASTEST ANNUAL METEOR SHOWER

The Leonid meteor shower which occurs between 15 and 20 November each year, enters Earth's atmosphere at around 71 km (44 miles) per second and begins to glow at an altitude of around 155 km (96 miles).

WIND SPEED (SURFACE)

• The highest wind speed at a low altitude was registered on 8 March 1972 at the USAF base at Thule (altitude: 44 m; 145 ft) in Greenland, when a peak speed of 333 km/h (207 mph) was recorded.

• The highest surface wind speed at a high altitude peaked at 371 km/h (231 mph) at Mount Washington (altitude: 1,916 m; 6,286 ft) in New Hampshire, USA, on 12 April 1934.

★ STRONGEST MICROBURST

On 1 August 1983, at Andrews Air Force Base in Maryland, USA, a "microburst" of wind was recorded at 240.5 km/h (149.5 mph). This rare phenomenon, characterized by a brief downdraft of hurricane-force winds, can be a threat to aircraft during take-off or landing.

STRONGEST JET STREAM

The fastest jet-stream velocity ever measured is 656 km/h (408 mph). It was recorded by instruments onboard a Skua rocket above South Uist, Outer Hebrides, UK, at an altitude of 47,000 m (154,200 ft) on 13 December 1967.

WIND SPEED (NON-SURFACE)

Scientists using the "Doppler on Wheels" mobile weather observatory, based at the University of Oklahoma, USA, recorded a 486 +/-32 km/h (302 +/- 20 mph) wind speed associated with a large tornado near Bridge Creek, Oklahoma, USA, on 3 May 1999.

★ LARGEST SOLITON CLOUD

Soliton clouds are rare, solitary forms that maintain their shape while moving at a constant velocity. The longest regular occurrence of this is known as the Morning Glory, which forms in the Gulf of Carpentaria, Australia. This backward-rolling cloud formation may be 1,000 km (620 miles) long, 1 km (3,280 ft) high and can travel at up to 60 km/h (37 mph). The Morning Glory regularly attracts gliders, who catch the updraft on the leading edge of the cloud.

CLOUDS WITH THE GREATEST VERTICAL RANGE

The cloud form with the greatest vertical range is cumulonimbus, which has been observed to reach a height of nearly 20,000 m (65,600 ft) – nearly three times the height of Mount Everest – in the tropics.

GREATEST DISPLAY OF SOLAR HALOES

On 11 January 1999, at least 24 types of solar halo were witnessed at the South Pole. Solar halos are formed by sunlight being reflected and refracted (bent) by ice crystals in the atmosphere, causing what looks like rings around the Sun and brightly coloured patches in the sky.

★ NEWEST MATHEMATICAL CONSTANT

The study of turbulent weather and water, and other chaotic phenomena, has revealed the existence of a new universal constant, the Feigenbaum number, first calculated by Mitchell J. Feigenbaum (USA). It is approximately equal to 4.66920160910299.

BEAUFORT SCALE

British Navy Commander Francis Beaufort devised a scale – from Force 0 to Force 12 – in 1805 to quantify wind force. Force 13 to 17 were added in 1955 by the US Weather Bureau, but are not in international use. Force 0 is calm, with no wind. After that, things start to get a bit blustery…

1. LIGHT AIR 1–5 KM/H

2. LIGHT BREEZE 6–11 KM/H

3. GENTLE BREEZE 12–19 KM/H

4. MODERATE BREEZE 20–28 KM/H

5. FRESH BREEZE 29–38 KM/H

6. STRONG BREEZE 39–50 KM/H

7. NEAR GALE 51–61 KM/H

8. GALE 62–74 KM/H

9. STRONG GALE 75–87 KM/H

10. STORM 88–101 KM/H

11. VIOLENT STORM 102–117 KM/H

12. HURRICANE OVER 118 KM/H

★ LONGEST SERIES OF CLOUD VORTICES OF

Cloud streets are parallel rows of marine stratocumulus clouds that form along the direction of wind flow. Here the cloud street has formed a series of vortices, in the wake of Jan Mayan Island, Norway extending for over 300 km (around 186 miles). The above image was captured by NASA's *Terra* satellite in June 2001.

TROPOSPHERE: ★ MOST TURBULANT PART OF THE ATMOSPHERE

The troposphere begins at ground level and reaches up to 16 km (10 miles) at the equator and 8 km (5 miles) at the Poles. This region contains some 75% of the atmosphere's mass, and it is here where almost all of Earth's weather occurs. Air molecules can move from the ground right up to the top of the troposphere and back down in just a few days. Beyond the troposphere is the stratosphere, which is much more stable.

LOWEST CLOUDS

Stratus formations are patches or sheets of shapeless low grey cloud, often thin enough to see the Sun through. They give rise to light drizzle and, in winter, snow.

HOTTEST PLACE ON EARTH

The hottest place on Earth is the air around a lightning strike. For a fraction of a second, the air is heated to around 30,000°C (54,032°F), or roughly five times hotter than the visible surface of the Sun.

EARTH

FASTEST MOVING TECTONIC PLATE
The fastest moving tectonic plate is the Tonga microplate, near Samoa, which is moving at a rate of 24 cm (9.4 in) per year.

LARGEST REGION OF THE EARTH'S INTERIOR
The Earth's mantle is 2,900 km (1,800 miles) thick and makes up around 70% of the Earth's volume.

LARGEST LIQUID BODY
The outer core is a layer of liquid with a thickness of 2,259 km (1,403 miles), representing 29.3% of the Earth's mass.

LARGEST CRYSTAL
The Earth's inner core is a sphere of mostly iron at around 5,000–6,000°C (9,000–10,000°F). Differences in the behaviour of seismic waves passing through it mean that many geologists now believe that this molten metal ball is actually a single crystal.

★ FASTEST ROTATING
PART OF THE EARTH

Precise measurements in earthquake timings have revealed that the Earth's inner core – a solid ball of iron and nickel around 2,442 km (1,517 miles) across (see artwork above) – is spinning slightly faster than the outer liquid core and the rest of the Earth. Each year, the inner core moves ahead of the Earth's surface by around 0.3–0.5 degrees – a rate of around 50,000 times the speed that the continental plates move.

★ THICKEST CRUST

The Earth's crust is the cold, solid, outermost layer of the lithosphere, which sits above the hot, convecting asthenosphere. Its thickest point is found at the Himalaya mountains in China at around 75 km (46 miles).

The ★ **thinnest part of the Earth's crust** is just 6 km (3.7 miles) thick and occurs in parts of the Pacific Ocean. The **thinnest continental crust** is around 15 km (9 miles) thick and is located in the Great Rift Valley of northeast Africa.

★ LARGEST ISLAND CREATED BY VOLCANIC ERUPTIONS

The largest volcanic island is Iceland, the entirety of which was formed from volcanic eruptions from the mid-Atlantic Ridge, upon which it sits. Measuring 103,000 km² (39,768 miles²) in area, it is essentially ocean floor exposed above the ocean surface.

TALLEST SEA STACK

The world's tallest sea stack is Ball's Pyramid (pictured above) near Lord Howe Island, Australia, in the Pacific Ocean. It is 561 m (1,843 ft) high, but has a base axis of only 200 m (660 ft).

★ HIGHEST MOUNTAIN TABLETOP

Monte Roraima, on the border of Brazil, Venezuela and Guyana, is a sandstone plateau with vertical sides measuring 2,810 m (9,220 ft) in height. Its harsh environment has resulted in around one third of its plant species being unique to the mountain. Monte Roraima is believed to have been the inspiration for Arthur Conan Doyle's (UK) 1912 novel *The Lost World*.

★ LARGEST MUD VOLCANO

Azerbaijan is home to the world's largest mud volcano, measuring 1 km (0.6 miles) across the base and reaching several hundred metres in height. Mud volcanoes are little-known relatives of the regular, magmatic variety and can be as dynamic, if cooler. Azerbaijan is home to more than half the world's total, although the majority of mud volcanoes are small, temporary landforms.

TALLEST MOUNTAIN FACE

The Rupal face of Nanga Parbat (pictured below) in the western Himalayas, Pakistan, is a single rise of some 5,000 m (16,000 ft) from the valley floor to the summit. Nanga Parbat – the 8th highest mountain in the world and the highest in Pakistan at 8,126 m (26,660 ft) – is also the world's **fastest rising mountain**, growing taller at a rate of 7 mm (0.27 in) per year.

LARGEST ISLAND WITHIN AN ISLAND

Samosir in Lake Toba, Sumatra, Indonesia, has an area of 630 km² (245 miles²). Formed between 30,000 and 100,000 years ago, it is the original home of the Toba Batak people.

★ LOWEST ISLAND

The world's lowest island is in the Ye'ch'ew Hayk lake in Ethiopia – it is 103 m (338 ft) below sea level.

LARGEST ISLAND

Greenland, with an area of about 2,175,000 km² (840,000 miles²) is the largest island in the world.

★ NEW RECORD
  UPDATED RECORD

★ FLOWSTONE CASCADE WITH THE GREATEST VERTICAL EXTENT

Flowstone cascades are sheet-like deposits of calcite that form as limestone-saturated water runs down cave walls and floors, leaving deposits that build up over time. The flowstone cascade with the greatest vertical extent is 150 m (492 ft) in length and is located in the Neverland to Dead Sea Lechuguilla Cave in New Mexico, USA.

LARGEST GEODE

A geode discovered by geologist Javier García-Guinea (Spain) near Almería, Spain, in May 2000 forms a mineral-lined cave 8 m (26 ft) long, 1.8 m (6 ft) wide and 1.8 m (6 ft) high.

A geode is a rock cavity filled with minerals and is usually small enough to fit in the palm of a human hand.

HIGHEST...

• Mount Everest, in the Himalayas, has been measured to a height of 8,848 m (29,028 ft), making it the world's *highest* mountain – that is, the peak is the highest point on Earth.

• The world's *tallest* mountain is Mauna Kea (White Mountain) on the island of Hawaii, USA. Measured from its submarine base in the Hawaiian Trough to its peak, it has a combined height of 10,205 m (33,480 ft), of which 4,205 m (13,796 ft) is above sea level.

• Monte Pico in the Azores, Portugal, has an altitude of 2,351 m (7,711 ft) above sea level and extends a record 6,098 m (20,000 ft) from the surface to the sea floor, making it the **highest underwater mountain face**.

• The **highest cliffs** are the sea cliffs on the north coast of east Molokai, Hawaii, near Umilehi Point. They descend 1,010 m (3,300 ft) to the sea at an average inclination of more than 55 degrees and an average gradient of more than 1 in 1.428.

• The Ojos del Salado on the border between Chile and Argentina is the world's **highest active volcano** at 6,887 m (22,595 ft) high.

• Excluding its ice shelves, Antarctica has an average elevation of 2,194 m (7,198 ft) above the OSU91A Geoid (similar to, and more accurate than, sea level), making it the **highest continent**.

• The Salto Angel in Venezuela, located on a branch of the Carrao River (an upper tributary of the Caroni River), is the **highest waterfall** (as opposed to vaporized "bridal veil") in the world. It has a total drop of 979 m (3,212 ft), with the longest single drop being 807 m (2,648 ft).

• The red sandstone Rainbow Bridge in Lake Powell National Monument, Utah, USA, is the **highest natural arch**. It is only 82.3 m (270 ft) long, but rises to a height of 88.4 m (290 ft).

EARTH

LAND MOST REMOTE FROM THE SEA

The world's most distant point from open sea is the Dzungarian Basin, which is in the Xinjiang Uygur autonomous region of far northwest China. It is at a great-circle distance of 2,648 km (1,645 miles) from the nearest open sea.

The **most remote city from the sea** is the region's capital, Urumqi (below), at about 2,500 km (1,500 miles) from the nearest coastline.

REMOTEST SPOT FROM LAND

There is a point in the South Pacific 2,575 km (1,600 miles) from the nearest land. The closest land can be found on Pitcairn Island, Ducie Island and Peter I Island.

LOWEST EXPOSED BODY OF WATER

The Dead Sea lies at an average of 400 m (1,312 ft) below sea level. The waters in the deepest parts are so salty and dense that they are effectively fossilized, resting on the sea floor since a few centuries after Biblical times. Any fish washed into it die instantly, and no other life aside from bacteria survives in its waters.

Running along the Israeli (western) shore is the **lowest road**, at 393 m (1,290 ft) below sea level.

REMOTEST ISLANDS

The **remotest inhabited island** in the world is Tristan da Cunha (pictured with its capital, Edinburgh of the Seven Seas). It was discovered in the South Atlantic by Tristão da Cunha, a Portuguese admiral, in March 1506, and has an area of 98 km² (38 miles²). After evacuation in 1961 (owing to volcanic activity), 198 islanders returned in November 1963. The nearest inhabited land to the group is the island of St. Helena, 2,435 km (1,315 nautical miles) to the north-east.

Bouvet Island, discovered in the South Atlantic by J.B.C. Bouvet de Lozier (France) on 1 January 1739, is the **remotest uninhabited island** in the world. A Norwegian dependency, it is about 1,700 km (1,050 miles) north of the nearest land – the coast of Queen Maud Land, which is also uninhabited, in Antarctica.

FLATTEST COUNTRY

The country with the lowest high point is the Republic of Maldives; its loftiest peak is just 2.4 m (8 ft) high. (Unconnected is the fact that it is also the country with the **highest divorce rate**, with 10.97 divorces per 1,000 inhabitants!)

★ LEAST FLAT COUNTRY

From the Gangetic plain to Mount Everest, Nepal is the least flat country in the world. Within just 100 miles, the altitude of Nepal varies from 100 m (328 ft) above sea level to 8,848 m (29,028 ft).

★ LARGEST GRASSLANDS

The Great Plains of North America are sandwiched between the Rockies and the Mississippi, and run from the southern provinces of Canada through the midwest USA to Mexico, a total area of around 3 million km² (1.2 million miles²). Bison – at up to 1 tonne (2,204 lb) in weight, the heaviest land animal on the North American continent – are a common feature of these grasslands (below): their grazing goes some way to preserving the open prairies.

LARGEST PINGO

Pingoes are isolated conical mounds that have a core of ice. They form when lakes in permafrost regions drain. As the residual water in the ground under the lake freezes, it expands, pushing up a mound of land. Ibyuk Pingo (above), in the Tuktoyaktuk Peninsula on the western Arctic coast of Canada, is the world's largest. It measures around 50 m (160 ft) high and 300 m (990 ft) around its base.

MOST FORESTED COUNTRY

The country with the highest percentage of forested land is the Cook Islands in the South Pacific Ocean. As of 2000, a total of 95.7% of the country was covered.

In 2005, Brazil was the **most forested country by area**, with a cover of 477,698,000 hectares (1,844,400 miles²), representing 57.2% of the total area. Next was the Democratic Republic of Congo, with 133,610,000 hectares (515,871 miles²) – 58.9% of the country's area.

LARGEST TROPICAL FOREST

The Amazon rainforest is the largest of its kind, covering 6.475 million km² (2.5 million miles²). Served by the Amazon basin, the world's **largest river basin**, it crosses nine different countries: Brazil, Colombia, Peru, Venezuela, Ecuador, Bolivia, Guyana, Suriname and French Guiana.

LARGEST TROPICAL FOREST RESERVE

The largest tropical forest reserve is the Tumucumaque National Park, in the northern Amazonian state of Amapá, Brazil. Measuring some 38,875 km² (15,010 miles²) in area – over 600 times the size of Manhattan in New York, USA – the reserve contains many endangered species of plant and animal. The creation of the park was announced on 22 August 2002 by Brazilian president Fernando Henrique Cardoso. Tumucumaque means "rock at the top of the mountain", in reference to the granite rocks rising above the forest canopy.

LARGEST SWAMP

The world's largest tract of swamp is the Pantanal in the states of Mato Grosso and Mato Grosso do Sul in Brazil. It is about 109,000 km² (42,000 miles²) in area – larger than Denmark and the Netherlands combined!

★ LARGEST TUNDRA

Lying along the Arctic Circle, between the northernmost tree limit and the lower fringes of the ice cap, is the tundra, a vast tract of barren, treeless land that remains frozen for most of the year. The largest swathe of tundra in the world is that found in North America – an area of permafrost (that is, land frozen for over two years) 5.3 million km² (2 million miles²) across northern Alaska, USA, and Canada.

★ MOST COMMON CROP

In terms of global production, maize is the world's most common crop, with 600 million tonnes harvested annually. Rice and wheat are the next most common, at just under 600 million tonnes each. All three form the planet's primary food staples.

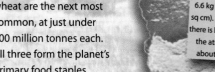

THE EARTH AT A GLANCE

- The Earth is **over 4.6 billion years old**.

- The **diameter of the Earth at the Equator** is 12,756.2726 km (7,926.5966 miles), but…

- The **diameter at the Poles** is 12,713.5032 km (7,900.0205 miles).

- The distance between the **centre of the Earth and the North Pole** is 44 m (144 ft) *longer* than the distance from the **centre to the South Pole**.

- So, the Earth is clearly **not a perfect sphere** – in fact, it has pear-shaped asymmetry.

- It has a **mass** of (deep breath!) 5,976,000,000,000,000,000,000,000 kg (that's 5.9 septillion kg).

- The mass is being added to all the time as the planet picks up about **40,000,000 kg of cosmic dust** each year!

- The **atmosphere** – the air above us – weighs 5,517,000,000,000,000,000 kg (5.517 quintillion kg).

> At sea level, the weight of the air pressing down on this square inch is about 6.6 kg (14.7 lb, or 1 kg per sq cm). At the top of Everest there is less air above you, so the atmosphere weighs about one third of this.

- The **weight of the ocean's water** is 1,390,000,000,000,000,000,000 kg (1.39 sextillion kg).

- The **volume of the Earth** is about 1,083,207,000 km³ (259,875,300 miles³).

- The **temperature at the centre of the Earth** is estimated to be 5,000–6,000°C (9,032–10,832°F).

- The **Earth's crust** is an average of 21 km (13 miles) thick, but the **deepest we've ever drilled down** is just over 12 km (7.6 miles).

ENVIRONMENT

★ LARGEST ARTIFICIAL REEF

The US Navy's attack aircraft carrier USS *Oriskany* (aka the "Mighty O", laid 1944) was decommissioned in 1976 after a long, illustrious service. It was scheduled for scrapping until it was decided to be sunk as an artificial reef in the Gulf of Mexico, 38 km (24 miles) off Pensacola, Florida, USA. It was finally sunk on 17 May 2006, using 226 kg (500 lb) of C4 explosives, taking just 37 minutes to reach the sea bed. At 350.5 m (1,149 ft) tall and 270 m (888 ft) long, it attracts an abundance of marine life rarely seen in the northern Gulf of Mexico.

★ HIGHEST LEVELS OF CARBON DIOXIDE

According to the World Meteorological Organization, the atmospheric abundance of carbon dioxide, a powerful greenhouse gas, was 377.1 parts per million in 2004. This is the highest in recorded history and represents a 35% increase of CO_2 in Earth's atmosphere since the pre-industrial era of the 18th century.

★ LARGEST PRODUCER OF CARBON DIOXIDE (COUNTRY)

In 2004, nearly 6 billion tonnes of carbon dioxide emissions resulted from the consumption and flaring of fossil fuels in the USA. China is second, with 4.7 billion tonnes, and Russia third, with 1.7 billion tonnes.

★ LARGEST FLEET OF "SPY BINS" (COUNTRY)

In 2006, officials in the UK secretly fitted bugs to around half a million household rubbish bins in order to monitor the weight of rubbish thrown out by British people.

The UK has the third worst recycling rate in Europe, and this scheme may eventually lead to fines for people who exceed a certain weight of rubbish thrown out each week.

★ LARGEST PROGRAMME OF CLOUD SEEDING

In order to artificially increase the amount of rainfall over arid regions in China, around 37,000 peasants armed with rockets and anti-aircraft guns regularly fire munitions containing silver iodide particles at passing clouds. These tiny particles artificially increase a cloud's likelihood of producing rain by encouraging water droplets to coalesce and pull moist air up into the clouds. Pictured are cloud-seeding aircraft bearing racks of silver iodide flares that are dropped into clouds as the aircraft flies through.

★ WARMEST YEAR ON RECORD

A NASA report from January 2006 revealed that 2005 was the warmest year on record. By including data from the Arctic, where there are few weather stations, NASA estimates that 2005 very slightly beats 1998, when the Earth suffered an increase of 0.2°C (0.4°F). Experts have already forecasted 2007 to be even warmer.

★ LARGEST ENVIRONMENTAL PRIZE

In February 2007, Sir Richard Branson (UK) announced a prize of $25 million (£12.7 million) to be awarded to the person or group that provides the best solution to the removal of carbon dioxide from the Earth's atmosphere. Claimants need to devise a system that will rid the atmosphere of at least 1 billion tonnes of carbon dioxide every year for a decade. The deadline for Branson's "Earth Challenge" is 8 February 2010.

★ HIGHEST AND LOWEST
ENVIRONMENTAL PERFORMANCE

In Environmental Performance Index (EPI) research findings presented to the World Economic Forum in January 2006 by scientists from Yale and Columbia Universities in the USA, the country (out of 133 investigated using 16 key indicators) with the best environmental performance was New Zealand (above right), with a score of 88.0. The country with the ★ **worst environmental performance** was Niger (above) with 25.7.

★ LONGEST-SURVIVING GREENHOUSE GAS

Of all the gases emitted by mankind that are understood to contribute to global warming, the longest surviving is the refrigerant gas tetrafluromethane, CF_4. The strong carbon-fluorine bonds mean that once it enters the atmosphere, the gas can last in excess of 50,000 years.

★ LARGEST REFORESTATION PROJECT

In May 2002, the Chinese State Forestry Administration announced the beginning of a 10-year reforestation project to plant up an area of land the size of Sweden.

The replanted region will measure about 440,000 km² (169,884 miles²), representing 5% of China's landmass. It is hoped that this audacious scheme will offset some of the environmental problems caused by excessive logging in China over the past century.

DID YOU KNOW?
The top 10 highest-ranking countries in the Environmental Performance Index 2006 are:
1. NZ 88.0
2. Sweden 87.8
3. Finland 87.0
4. Czech Rep. 86.0
5. UK 85.6
6. Austria 85.2
7. Denmark 84.2
8. Canada 84.0
9.=Malaysia 83.3
9.=Ireland 83.3

GREATEST DISTANCE COVERED BY CAMPAIGN VESSELS

Rainbow Warrior 1 and *Rainbow Warrior 2*, the flagships of environmental pressure group Greenpeace, are estimated to have covered 926,592 km (500,000 nautical miles). *Rainbow Warrior 2* covered 193,524.29 km (104,428 nautical miles) from 1996 to 1999. Greenpeace, founded in 1971, is also the **longest-running environmental campaign group**.

★ LARGEST LIGHT BULB BAN

On 20 February 2007, Australia announced that incandescent light bulbs would be banned by 2009 to help cut an estimated 800,000 tonnes of greenhouse gas emissions.

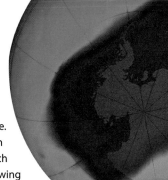

LARGEST OCEAN LANDFILL SITE

The North Pacific Central Gyre is a vast vortex of slowly revolving ocean water, which naturally concentrates floating litter in its centre. In 2002, environmental studies revealed that the centre of the Gyre contained around 6 kg (13 lb) of waste plastic for every 1 kg (2.2 lb) of plankton.

WORST RIVER POLLUTION

On 1 November 1986, firemen fighting a blaze at the Sandoz chemical works in Basel, Switzerland, flushed 30 tonnes (66,150 lb) of agricultural chemicals into the river Rhine, killing half a million fish.

★ LARGEST HOLE IN THE OZONE LAYER

On 2 October 2006, the European Space Agency (ESA) revealed that the hole in the ozone layer above Antarctica was large enough to hold 40 million tonnes (88 billion lb) of ozone.

The image (right) has been created from satellite data, with the blue and purple colours showing the areas of least ozone in the atmosphere.

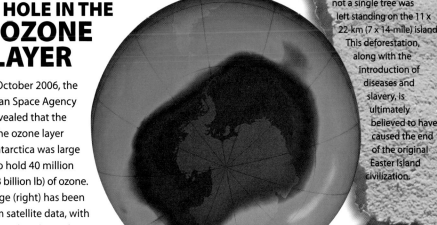

DEFORESTATION

• Of the 44 countries that, combined, represent 90% of the world's forests, Indonesia has the **highest annual rate of deforestation**, with 1.8 million ha (4,447,896 acres) of forest lost annually between 2000 and 2005. This equates to 2% of the country's forest per year.

• The **largest deforestation by area** occurred in Brazil, which contains 14% of the world's forest, where 2,309,000 ha (5,705,663 acres) of tropical forest were lost between 1990 and 2000. In 2004 alone, Brazilian ranchers, soybean farmers and loggers cut down 26,127 km² (10,088 miles²) of rainforest.

• The ★ **oldest deforestation disaster caused by humans** occurred when Polynesians first settled Easter Island in the Pacific, around AD 700. The islanders' obsession with building huge stone figures required the use of trees for their transportation. By 1722, not a single tree was left standing on the 11 x 22-km (7 x 14-mile) island. This deforestation, along with the introduction of diseases and slavery, is ultimately believed to have caused the end of the original Easter Island civilization.

FRIGID EARTH

LONGEST ICE CORE

An ice core measuring 3,623 m (11,886 ft) in length was drilled from the ice above the subglacial Lake Vostok in Antarctica in 1998. Drilling stopped around 150 m (492 ft) above the surface of the lake in order to avoid contamination of the lake's pristine environment.

COLDEST DESERT

The McMurdo Dry Valleys in Antarctica receive less than 100 mm (4 in) of precipitation per year and have a mean annual temperature of -20ºC (-4ºF). With an area of around 4,800 km^2 (1,850 miles^2), they are the largest ice-free zone on the continent. Despite the inhospitable conditions – and a complete lack of sunlight for much of the year – this polar desert can support life in the form of algae, nematode worms, phytoplankton and bacteria.

LARGEST ICE SHELF

The Ross Ice Shelf covers an area of around 472,000 km^2 (182,240 miles^2) of the Ross Sea, an indentation into the western edge of Antarctica. At nearly twice the area of the UK, it is the largest piece of floating ice in the world. *For a map of Antarctica, see p.97.*

★ FASTEST GLACIAL SURGE

In 1953, the Kutiah Glacier in Pakistan advanced more than 12 km (7.4 miles) in three months – averaging some 112 m (367 ft 5 in) per day.

★ THICKEST ICE

On 4 January 1975, a team of US seismologists measured the depth of the ice at Wilkes Land in eastern Antarctica and found it to be 4,776 m (15,669 ft) – equivalent to 10 Empire State Buildings!

LARGEST SUBGLACIAL LAKE

As a result of analysing radar imagery in 1994, scientists discovered the subglacial Lake Vostok in Antarctica buried under 4 km (2.5 miles) of the East Antarctic Ice Sheet. It is the **oldest** and **most pristine lake** on Earth, having been completely isolated from the rest of the world for at least 500,000 years and perhaps much longer. Covering an area of 14,000 km^2 (5,400 miles^2), it is the 18th largest lake in the world and has a depth of at least 100 m (330 ft).

★ LARGEST TROPICAL GLACIER

The Quelccaya Ice Cap lies at an average elevation of 5,470 m (17,946 ft) in the Peruvian Andes and covers an area of around 44 km^2 (16.9 miles^2). Studies have shown that the glacier is melting and retreating by 60 m (196 ft 10 in) per year.

★ COLDEST LIQUID WATER DROPLETS

On 13 August 1999, Dr Daniel Rosenfeld (Israel) and Dr William Woodley (USA) reported their discovery of tiny water droplets that remained liquid for several minutes at temperatures as low as -37.5ºC (-35.5ºF) in clouds over west Texas, USA. Their results were published in the journal *Nature* in May 2000.

Colder droplets have also been reported, but these 17-micron (0.017-mm; 0.00066-in) droplets are the coldest ever found that remain stable for several minutes.

COLDEST PERMANENTLY INHABITED PLACE

In the Siberian village of Oymyakon (population 4,000; 63°16'N, 143°15'E) in Russia, the temperature reached -68°C (-90°F) in 1933. An unofficial figure of -72°C (-98°F) for this region has been published more recently.

LONGEST GLACIER

The Lambert Glacier was discovered by an Australian aircraft crew in Australian Antarctic Territory in 1956–57.

Draining about a fifth of the East Antarctic ice sheet, it is up to 64 km (40 miles) wide and, with its seaward extension (the Amery Ice Shelf), it measures at least 700 km (440 miles) in length – longer than the state of Florida, USA. It is also the **largest glacier** in the world.

DID YOU KNOW?
The -68°C (-90°F) recorded in Siberia represents the coldest temperature ever recorded outside of Antarctica.

★MOST PRODUCTIVE ICE FLOE

Disko Bay in northern Greenland, 300 km (185 miles) north of the Arctic Circle, produces an average of 20 million tonnes of ice and icebergs a day. The glacier that creates the ice advances at around 2,530 m (8,298 ft) per day and produces icebergs from a front 10 km (6 miles) long.

LARGEST AREA OF SEA ICE

The largest area of ocean covered by sea ice is in the Southern Ocean. During the winter, 17–20 million km² (6.5–7.7 million miles²) of this ocean is covered by sea ice, which decreases in size to around 3–4 million km² (1.1–1.5 million miles²) during the warmer summer months.

The Arctic Ocean, by comparison, is covered by 14–16 million km² (5–6 million miles²) of sea ice in the winter, decreasing to 7–9 million km² (2.7–3.5 million miles²) in the summer.

★LARGEST BODY OF FRESH WATER

The Antarctic ice cap holds some 30 million km³ (7.1 million miles³) of fresh water – around 70% of the world's total. By contrast, the Caspian Sea – the world's **largest lake**, situated between Russia and Iran – contains only about 78,000 km³ (18,713 miles³) of fresh water.

★ NEW RECORD
UPDATED RECORD

LARGEST PANCAKE ICE

Sea ice covers 7% of the world's oceans and is mostly found in the polar regions. This ice formation is usually seasonal, but in very cold places – such as the Weddell Sea in Antarctica – the ice can last for two, three or more summers. When this occurs, "pancake ice" forms – large, rounded discs of ice that can range from 30 cm (1 ft) to 3 m (10 ft) in diameter and may grow up to 10 cm (4 in) thick. The "pancakes" have raised edges from continually bumping into each other.

LOWEST TEMPERATURE ON EARTH

A record low of -89.2°C (-128.6°F) was registered at Vostok, Antarctica (altitude 3,420 m; 11,220 ft), on 21 July 1983. The Vostok research station (pictured below) was established on 16 December 1957 by the Soviets, but is now operated by American, French and Russian scientists.

ICE AGE

Geological evidence suggests that the Earth endured several severe ice ages early in its history. The **longest ice age** was between 2.3 and 2.4 billion years ago, and lasted around 70 million years. During this period, the entire planet was probably covered in ice, possibly to a depth of 1 km (0.6 mile), as illustrated in this artist's impression, left.

GLACIATED AREAS*

REGION	AREA
South Polar Region	**12,588,000 km²**
Antarctic Ice Sheet	12,535,000 km²
Other Antarctic glaciers	53,000 km²
North Polar Region	**2,070,000 km²**
Greenland Ice Sheet	1,726,000 km²
Other Greenland glaciers	76,200 km²
Canadian archipelago	153,200 km²
Svalbard (Spitzbergen)	58,000 km²
Other Arctic islands	55,700 km²
Asia	**115,800 km²**
Alaska/Rockies	**76,900 km²**
South America	**26,500 km²**
Iceland	**12,170 km²**
Alpine Europe	**9,280 km²**
New Zealand	**1,010 km²**
Africa	**10 km²**

*all figures are approximate

BLUE PLANET

DEADLIEST LAKE

The lake responsible for the most deaths in the world, excluding drowning, is Lake Nyos in Cameroon, west Africa, where toxic gases have claimed nearly 2,000 lives in recent decades. On just one night, in August 1986, between 1,600 and 1,800 people and countless animals were killed by a large natural release of carbon-dioxide gas.

★ OLDEST LAKE

Lake Baikal in Siberia, Russia, is between 20 and 25 million years old. It was formed by a tectonic rift in the Earth's crust, which still causes Baikal to widen by about 2 cm (0.78 in) per year. It holds more water than all of North America's Great Lakes combined and has a wealth of biodiversity, including the world's only freshwater seal.

★ LARGEST MARINE RESERVE

The Northwestern Hawaiian Islands Marine National Monument covers 356,879 km^2 (137,791 miles^2) of the Pacific Ocean surrounding the northwestern Hawaiian islands. The coral reefs are home to more than 7,000 marine species, a quarter of which are unique to the area. The region was designated a marine reserve in June 2006.

SMALLEST OCEAN

The Arctic Ocean has an area of 9,485,000 km^2 (3,662,000 miles^2), making it the smallest ocean in the world. It has a maximum depth of just 5,450 m (17,880 ft). The ocean's waters are frozen for up to 10 months a year, with any surrounding landmass usually covered in snow and ice. Up to 50 cm (19 in) of ice covers the frozen waters in the coldest months of March and April.

★ FASTEST OCEAN CURRENT

The current of warm water that originates in the Gulf of Mexico and then crosses the Atlantic Ocean is responsible for the climate in some parts of Europe being a few degrees warmer than it would be otherwise. The southwest of England, for example, has a very mild climate. With peak speeds of up to 7.2 km/h (4.4 mph), the current is the fastest found anywhere in the global circulation of the oceans.

★ OLDEST OCEAN

The Pacific Ocean has the oldest of the current ocean basins, with the earliest rocks found on its floor being around 200 million years old. The world's oceans are constantly changing in size as tectonics make the great plates of the Earth's crust slowly move around. One effect of this plate movement is that the Pacific Ocean is gradually shrinking in size by a few centimetres each year, just as the Atlantic Ocean is gradually expanding.

★ HIGHEST RAISED BEACH

The High Coast in Västernorrland, Sweden, has a shingle beach some 260 m (853 ft) above sea level. Its high elevation is a result of land rising after the last ice age, when the vast weight of the icesheets was lifted. The region is still rising, at a rate of around 1 cm (0.39 in) per year, and will continue rising for around another 10,000 years.

LARGEST...

★ UNTAPPED FOSSIL FUEL RESOURCE

Gas hydrates are molecules of methane, which are trapped inside a lattice of water molecules, forming a solid similar to water ice. They occur as vast deposits under the sea floor, where the overlying pressure means that they are kept in the form of a stable solid.

Occasionally, undersea landslides and earthquakes can cause these hydrates to release their methane, which bubbles to the surface. The bizarre phenomenon of "burning water" happens on rare occasions when lightning ignites the methane at the ocean surface. It is estimated that around 10,000 billion tonnes of gas hydrates exist globally, around twice the amount of all other fossil fuels combined.

TOP 10 DEEPEST OCEAN TRENCHES

TRENCH	OCEAN	DEPTH (M)	DEPTH (FT)
1. Mariana	Western Pacific	10,911	35,797
2. Tonga-Kermadec	Southern Pacific	10,882	35,702
3. Kuril-Kamchatka	Western Pacific	10,542	34,587
4. Philippine	Western Pacific	10,497	34,439
5. Idzu-Bonin	Western Pacific	9,810	32,185
6. Puerto Rico	Western Atlantic	9,220	30,249
7. New Hebrides	Southern Pacific	9,165	30,069
8. New Britain (Solomon)	Southern Pacific	9,140	29,988
9. Yap	Western Pacific	8,527	27,976
10. Japan	Western Pacific	8,412	27,599

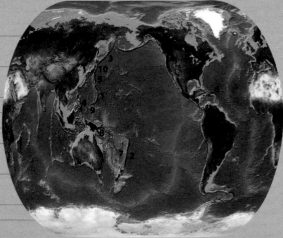

LARGEST WHIRLPOOLS

There are several large, permanent whirlpools around the world, usually caused by merging tides, narrow straits or fast-flowing water. The most powerful are the Saltstraumen and Moskstraumen whirlpools (both Norway), whose currents have been measured at 40 km/h (24.8 mph) and 28 km/h (17.3 mph) espectively. The "Old Sow" (USA) and Naruto (Japan, pictured) whirlpools have been measured at 27.8 km/h (17.2 mph) and 20 km/h (12.4 mph) respectively.

OCEAN
The Pacific – named from the Latin *Mare Pacificum*, or "peaceful sea" – is the largest ocean (and largest body of water) in the world. Excluding adjacent seas, it represents 45.9% of the world's oceans, with an area of 166,241,700 km^2 (64,186,000 miles^2). The average depth of the Pacific is 3,940 m (12,925 ft).

RIVER BASIN
Drained by the Amazon, the largest river basin in the world covers about 7,045,000 km^2 (2,720,000 miles^2) – an area roughly 13 times the size of France. Countless tributaries run from it, including the Madeira, the world's longest (see opposite for more).

ICEBERG
The largest tabular iceberg ever was over 31,000 km^2 (12,000 miles^2). It was 335 km (208 miles) long and 97 km (60 miles) wide and was sighted 240 km (150 miles) west of Scott Island in the Southern Ocean by the USS *Glacier* on 12 November 1956.

BAY
The Hudson Bay in Canada, has a shoreline of 12,268 km (7,623 miles) and covers an area of 1,233,000 km^2 (476,000 miles^2). The Bay of Bengal, in the Indian Ocean, is much larger, at 2,172,000 km^2 (839,000 miles^2), but only if measured by area rather than shoreline length.

★ RIVER WITH ITS ENTIRE DRAINAGE SYSTEM IN ONE COUNTRY
The Chang Jiang river in China measures 6,300 km (3,915 miles) long, making it the third longest river in the world and the longest in Asia. Its entire drainage system is contained within Chinese territory. The Yangtze, as it is also known, has its headwaters in the glaciers of the Qinghai-Tibetan plateau, heads east across China and empties into the East China Sea.

★ RIVER TRIBUTARY
The Madeira tributary of the Amazon is the longest in the world, stretching 3,380 km (2,100 miles). It is surpassed in length by only 17 other rivers.

ESTUARY
The world's longest estuary is that of the Ob river, in northern Russia, at 885 km (550 miles). In places it is up to 80 km (50 miles) wide. It is also the world's widest river that is able to freeze solid in winter.

FJORD
The Nordvest Fjord arm of Scoresby Sund in Greenland extends inland 313 km (195 miles) from the sea.

WATER WATER EVERYWHERE . . .

• The **highest wave**, dependent on weather or climate, was calculated at 34 m (112 ft) from trough to crest. It was measured by Lt Frederic Margraff, USN, from the USS *Ramapo* proceeding from Manila, Philippines, to San Diego, California, USA, on the night of 6–7 February 1933 during a hurricane that reached 126 km/h (78 mph).

• The **highest tsunami wash** ever reported was 524 m (1,719 ft) high and occurred alon the fjord-like Lituya Bay, in Alaska, USA, on 9 July 1958. It was caused by a giant landslip and moved at 160 km/h (100 mph).

• The **highest average tides** occur in the Ba of Fundy, which divides the peninsula of Nov Scotia, Canada, from the United States' north-easternmost state of Maine and the Canadian province of New Brunswick. Burncoat Head in the Minas Basin, Nova Scotia, has the greatest mean spring range, with 14.5 m (47 ft 6 in).

• The **highest ocean temperature** recorded is 404ºC (759ºF) for a hydrothermal vent. It was measured by an American research submarine 480 km (300 miles) off the American west coast in 1985.

• The **deepest part of the ocean** was first pinpointed in 1951 by HM Survey Ship *Challenger* in the Mariana Trench in the Pacific Ocean. On 23 January 1960, the manned US Navy bathyscaphe *Trieste* descended to the bottom of the trench for the first time. On 24 March 1995 the unmanned Japanese probe *Kaiko* also reached the bottom, recording a depth of 10,911 m (35,797 ft), the most accurate measur of the trench ever made.

• The world's **clearest sea** is the Weddell Sea, off Antarctica. On 13 October 1986, scientists from the Alfred Wegener Institute in Bremerhaven, Germany, measured the clarity by lowering a standard Secchi disc, measuring 30 cm (1 ft) across, into the water unt it was no longer visible. Ir the Weddell Sea, the disc was visible until it reache a depth of 80 m (262 f) – which means the se has a clarity similar t that of distilled wate

LONGEST RIVER

The Nile, the longest river in the world, extends 6,695 km (4,160 miles) and has two tributaries. The White Nile flows through Lake Victoria in east central Africa and merges with the Blue Nile in Sudan. The river then flows north, through Egypt, until it reaches the Nile Delta on the edge of the Mediterranean Sea.

LIFE ON EARTH

CONTENTS

LOWEST TEMPERATURE ENDURED BY A BIRD

The emperor penguin (*Aptenodytes forsteri*) endures an average temperature of -20ºC (-4ºF) on the Antarctic sea ice, where the windspeed can vary from 25 to 75 km/h (16 to 47 mph). Luckily, penguins have the **highest density of feathers** of all bird species – around 11 to 12 feathers per square centimetre in the emperor (which also has the longest feathers of any penguin), Adelie, yellow-eyed and fairy penguins. The feathers have their own small muscles associated with them to allow control. On land, the feathers stay erect to trap air to insulate them; in the water, they flatten to form a watertight barrier.

TALLEST
LIVING TREE

A coast redwood (*Sequoia sempervirens*) was discovered by Chris Atkins and Michael Taylor (both USA) in the Redwood National Park, California, USA, on 25 August 2006 and named Hyperion, after the Greek god. The tree currently measures 115.5 m (379 ft 1 in) – this is approximately 2.5 times the height of the Statue of Liberty in New York City, USA.

LARGEST LEECH

When fully extended, the Amazonian *Haementeria ghilianii* can attain a maximum total length of 45.7 cm (18 in). In July 2003, however, the first of several mysterious mega-leeches that could break this record was found in New Jersey, USA. The first specimen – and only the second terrestrial species of leech recorded from the USA – was maintained in a tank at Rutgers-Camden University, New Jersey, where it grew to just under 43 cm (17 in) when fully extended. Moreover, James Parks (USA) – who in October 2004 found four more examples of this extraordinary species – had previously seen one measuring 50.1 cm (20 in), curled up in a coil the size of a tennis ball. He did not realize at the time that it was special, so did not collect it. Studies are ongoing to uncover their zoological identity.

LARGEST FLEA

Siphonapterologists (flea experts) recognize 1,830 species of flea, of which the largest known is *Hystrichopsylla schefferi*. Females measuring up to 8 mm (0.3 in) long – roughly the diameter of a pencil – were taken from the nest of a mountain beaver (*Aplodontia rufa*) at Puyallup, Washington, USA, in 1913.

SHORTEST GESTATION PERIOD FOR A MAMMAL

The shortest mammalian gestation period is 12–13 days and is common in a number of species, including the Virginia opossum (*Didelphis virginiana*, pictured) of North America; the rare water opossum, or yapok (*Chironectes minimus*), of central and northern South America; and the short-nosed bandicoot (*Isoodon macrourus*) and the Eastern dasyure, or marsupial native cat (*Dasyurus viverrinus*) of Australia. (The gestation period is the time during which an embryo or fetus develops in the womb – in other words, the length of the pregnancy.)

★ FASTEST SPIDER

An adult female giant house spider (*Tegenaria gigantea*), which is native to North America, attained a maximum running speed of 1.9 km/h (1.18 mph) over short distances during tests undertaken in the UK in 1970. This means that the spider covered a distance equivalent to 33 times her own body length in only 10 seconds.

OLDEST SPIDER

Bird-eating spiders are among the longest lived of all terrestrial invertebrates. A female of the tropical bird-eaters (family Theraphosidae) that was collected in Mexico in 1935 had the oldest recorded age – an estimated 26 to 28 years.

SMALLEST OWL

The elf owl (*Micrathene whitneyi*, pictured) from south-western USA and Mexico has an average height of 12–14 cm (4.75–5.5 in) and weighs less than 50 g (1.75 oz). This record is shared by the least pygmy owl (*Glaucidium minutissimum*) of south-east Brazil and Paraguay; it measures and weighs the same as the elf owl.

LARGEST STARFISH

The very fragile brisingid *Midgardia xandaros* is one of 1,600 known starfish species. In 1968, a specimen measuring an astonishing 1.38 m (4 ft 6 in) from tip to tip was collected in the Gulf of Mexico.

ACTUAL SIZE

★ **NEW RECORD** ☆ **UPDATED RECORD**

HIGHEST RING COUNT

A bristlecone pine (*Pinus longaeva*) known as Prometheus had a record ring count of 4,867 when it was cut down in 1963 on Mount Wheeler, Nevada, USA. The tree grew at an elevation of 3,000 m (10,000 ft) in very harsh conditions. In such a demanding environment, trees grow very slowly and often do not produce a ring for every year, so Prometheus is likely to have been closer to 5,200 years old – the **oldest tree ever documented**.

★ FASTEST-RUNNING FLYING BIRD

The **fastest-running bird** in the world is the flightless ostrich, but the fastest-running flying bird is the North American roadrunner (*Geococcyx californianus*). This predominantly ground-dwelling species of cuckoo is native to the south-western USA. When pursued by a car, the roadrunner has

DID YOU KNOW?
To avoid extreme environmental conditions, certain species of animal enter into a dormant state during the summer months. This is called **aestivation** or summer hibernation.

been clocked at a highly impressive 42 km/h (26 mph) over a short distance.

★ SMALLEST CENTIPEDE

Hoffman's dwarf centipede (*Nannarrup hoffmani*) is only 10.3 mm (0.4 in) long and has

ACTUAL SIZE

41 pairs of legs. In 1998, researchers collected 10 of them in Central Park, New York City, USA, and sent them to Richard Hoffman, curator of invertebrates at the Virginia Museum of Natural History. The centipede was named in his honour in 2002.

GREATEST EATER RELATIVE TO WEIGHT

The caterpillar of the North American silk moth (*Antheraea polyphemus*) eats more food relative to its own body weight than any other animal. Living on the leaves of oak, birch, willow and maple, it eats up to 86,000 times its own weight during the first 56 days of its life. If a human baby

★ SLEEPIEST MAMMALS

The Uinta ground squirrel (*Spermophilus armatus*, pictured) begins aestivating (see left) in July and thereafter directly enters hibernation, not waking until late March to mid-April of the next year. Hence it sleeps for up to nine months of the year.

The Barrow ground squirrel (*Spermophilus undulatus barrowensis*) does not aestivate, but hibernates continuously for up to nine months to avoid the chilly conditions of its Arctic habitat.

weighing 3.2 kg (7 lb) were to equal this feat, it would need to consume 273 tonnes (601,800 lb) of food in the same period.

LARGEST DEER

An Alaskan moose (*Alces alces gigas*) bull shot in the Yukon Territory, Canada, in September 1897, stood 2.34 m (7 ft 8 in) tall and weighed an estimated 800 kg (1,800 lb).

ENDANGERED ANIMALS

• The North American ivory-billed woodpecker (*Campephilus principalis*), America's biggest woodpecker, is also the world's ★ **most endangered bird**. It was believed to have been extinct since the 1940s. But in April 2005, after an intensive year-long search for this species, researchers from Cornell University's Cornell Laboratory of Ornithology and the Nature Conservancy found a single male specimen in the Cache River and White River national wildlife refuges of Arkansas, USA.

• The Devil's Hole pupfish (*Cyprinodon diabolis*) numbers between 200 and 500 and is restricted entirely to an unusual system of waterholes in Nevada, USA, making it the **most endangered fish**. Its main threat comes from the pumping of groundwater for irrigation, desert development and the introduction of exotic fish species into their environment.

• The **rarest bird of prey** is the Californian condor (*Gymnogyps californianus*) of which only 49 are reported to exist in captivity.

★ SMELLIEST MAMMAL

The striped skunk (*Mephitis mephitis*), a member of the mustelid family, ejects a truly foul-smelling liquid from its anal glands when threatened. This defensive secretion contains seven major volatile and stench-filled components. Two of these substances, both sulphur-containing thiols, are responsible for the secretion's strongly repellent odour and are known respectively as (E)-2-butene-1-thiol and 3-methyl-1-butanethiol. They are so potent that they can be detected by humans at a concentration of 10 parts per billion – an incredibly low dilution that is roughly equivalent to mixing a teaspoonful with the water from an Olympic-sized swimming pool!

SOUTH AMERICA

MOST FEROCIOUS FISH

The piranha – especially those of the genera *Serrasalmus* (pictured) and *Pygocentrus*, found in the large rivers of South America – is the most ferocious fish. Attracted to blood and frantic splashing, a school of piranhas can completely strip an animal as large as a horse of its flesh within minutes, leaving only its skeleton.

SMALLEST MONKEY

Pygmy marmosets (*Callithrix pygmaea*) weigh a mere 15 g (0.53 oz) at birth and commonly grow to an adult weight of just 119 g (4.2 oz). On average, they measure 136 mm (5.35 in) excluding the tail, which is usually longer than the body. Despite their size, they can leap up to 5 m (16 ft 5 in) into the air!

They are found in the upper Amazon, the forests of Peru, Ecuador, Colombia, Bolivia and Brazil.

ACTUAL SIZE

★ SMELLIEST FROG

The vile-smelling skin secretion of the suitably named Venezuelan skunk frog (*Aromobates nocturnus*) is released for defence purposes and actually contains the same stink-producing organosulphur compound that is present in the famously foul emissions released by skunks. Yet in spite of its awful stench, this extraordinary frog remained unknown to science until as recently as 1991, when it was finally described and named. Measuring 6.2 cm (2.44 in) long, it is also the largest member of the poison-arrow frog family, Dendrobatidae.

★ RAREST SNAKE

Fewer than 150 Antiguan racers (*Alsophis antiguae*) are now believed to exist, including those in captivity. The snake was once common in Antigua, but disappeared from the island following the introduction of non-indigenous predators, black and brown rats (*Rattus rattus* and *R. norvegicus*) and the Asian mongoose (*Herpestes javanicus*). The racer was

LARGEST RODENT

The capybara, or carpincho (*Hydrochoerus hydrochaeris*), is found in the basins of the Paraná and Uruguay rivers and in the wetlands of Argentina and Brazil. It has a head-and-body length of 1–1.3 m (3 ft 3 in–4 ft 3 in) and can weigh up to 80 kg (174 lb).

thought to be extinct, but was rediscovered in 1989 only on Great Bird Island off the northeast coast of Antigua. Following intense conservation programmes, the species is slowly recovering but remains classified as Critically Endangered on the IUCN (World Conservation Union) Red List 2004.

★ LONGEST COLUMN OF ANTS

Army ants in the genus *Eciton*, from Central and South America (as well as driver ants in the genus *Dorylus* from Africa), have a reputation for travelling in highly organized columns. These can be up to 100 m (328 ft) long and over 1 m (3 ft 4 in) wide and may contain as many as 600,000 individuals, which can take several hours to pass one spot.

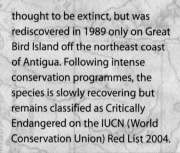

NOISIEST LAND ANIMAL

The fearsome screams of the howler monkey (*Alouatta*) of Central and South America have been described as a cross between the bark of a dog and the bray of an ass increased a thousandfold! The males have an enlarged bony structure at the top of the windpipe that enables the sound to reverberate. Once in full voice, they can be heard clearly up to 5 km (3 miles) away.

FASTEST BIRD

The mean estimated ground speed recorded for a satellite-tagged grey-headed albatross (*Thalassarche chrysostoma*) in level flight was 127 km/h (78.9 mph). The speed was sustained for over eight hours while the bird was returning to its nest at Bird Island, South Georgia, in the middle of an Antarctic storm.

★ SHORTEST SPECIES OF CAMEL

The vicuña (*Vicugna vicugna*) of the Andes, South America, has an average ground-to-shoulder height of 90 cm (35 in) and weighs a maximum of 50 kg (110 lb). The vicuña is an endangered species, as it was hunted to near-extinction in the 1970s; however, this has since prompted extensive attempts by Peru, Chile and Argentina to conserve these animals.

★ LARGEST CENTIPEDE

The giant centipede (*Scolopendra gigantea*) of Central and South America (also known as the Peruvian giant yellowleg centipede) is 26 cm (10 in) long. The jaws on its head trap and deliver venom to its prey, such as mice and frogs. A population discovered hanging from cave roofs in Venezuela feed on bats. The venom is toxic to humans (much like an insect sting) and can cause swelling and fever.

DID YOU KNOW?
The area of the world with the **highest species endemism** is the tropical Andes stretching across Venezuela, Colombia, Ecuador, Peru, Bolivia and part of northern Argentina. So far, scientists have identified 20,000 vascular plants, 677 birds, 604 amphibians, 218 reptiles and 68 mammals endemic to this area of 1,258,000 km² (485,716 miles²).

SMALLEST DEER

The smallest true deer (family Cervidae) is the southern pudu (*Pudu puda*), which is 33–38 cm (13–15 in) tall at the shoulder and weighs 6.3–8.2 kg (14–18 lb). It is found in Chile and Argentina.

SMALLEST CROCODILE

Females of the dwarf caiman (*Paleosuchus palpebrosus*) of northern South America seldom exceed a length of 1.2 m (4 ft). Males rarely grow to more than 1.5 m (4 ft 11 in).

LARGEST WING-SPAN OF A BIRD

The South American teratorn (*Argentavis magnificens*), which lived 6–8 million years ago, had an estimated spread of 7.6 m (25 ft).

★ LONGEST BEETLE

The titan beetle (*Titanus giganteus*, pictured) of South America has a body length of 15 cm (6 in) – the longest species of beetle in terms of body size alone.

★ FASTEST SELF-POWERED PREDATORY STRIKE

The trap-jaw ant (*Odontomachus bauri*) of Central and South America snaps its jaws shut at speeds of 35–64 m/s (114–209 ft/s). Its jaws are employed not only to attack prey but also to escape threat by purposely biting the ground. Its huge head muscles are used to contract its mandibles, hold them in place and then release them with such force that it catapults itself to recorded vertical heights of 8.3 cm (3.2 in), or horizontally through to 39.6 cm (15.5 in) – the equivalent, in human terms, of a 1.67-m (5-ft 6-in) person being propelled 13 m (44 ft) upwards or 67 m (220 ft) horizontally!

LARGEST...

• Since the early 1970s, when it was discovered as a living species (until then it had only been known from Ice Age fossils), the world's ★ **largest species of peccary** has been the Chacoan peccary (*Catagonus wagneri*), native to the Gran Chaco region of South America. It has a head-and-body length of 90–110 cm (3–3 ft 7 in), a tail length of 2.4–10 cm (1–4 in), a shoulder height of 52–69 cm (20–27 in) and a weight of 29.5–40 kg (65–88 lb). In 2004, however, zoologist Dr Marc van Roosmalen (Netherlands) and wildlife cinematographer Lothar Frenz (Germany) encountered a huge, unfamiliar-looking peccary newly captured by some villagers in the Amazon region of Rio Aripuana. It was 1.3 m (4 ft 3 in) long and weighed 40 kg (88 lb), but was killed and eaten by the villagers. Some of its remains were sent for DNA analysis. The results showed that the giant peccary appears to belong to a completely separate species from the three previously known living peccaries. It is awaiting a formal description and scientific name, and is now the largest species of modern-day peccary.

• The giant water bug (*Lethocerus maximus*) is a carnivorous species that inhabits Venezuela and Brazil. Although not as heavy as some of this continent's burly terrestrial beetles and stick insects, it is still the ★ **largest aquatic insect** at 11.5 cm (4.53 in) long.

• *Megaloprepus caeruleata* of Central and South America has been measured at up to 12 cm (4.7 in) in length with a wing-span of up to 19.1 cm (7.5 in) – making it the world's **largest dragonfly**.

EUROPE

★ LARGEST OWL

The European eagle owl (*Bubo bubo*) has an average length of 66–71 cm (26–28 in), a weight of 1.6–4 kg (3–8 lb) and a wing-span of more than 1.5 m (5 ft). It is an active predator, hunting rodents and other small mammals.

SUPER SPAN

The largest prehistoric insect was the dragonfly *Meganeura monyi*, which lived about 280 million years ago. Fossil remains discovered at Commentry, France, indicate that this dragonfly had a wing expanse of up to 70 cm (27.5 in).

★ LARGEST MAMMOTH

The largest extinct elephant was the Steppe mammoth *Paraelephas* (= *Mammuthus*) *trogontherii*, which roamed over what is now central Europe a million years ago. A fragmentary skeleton found in Mosbach, Germany, indicates a shoulder height of 4.5 m (14 ft 9 in). By way of comparison, the largest African elephant recorded had a shoulder height of 3.6 m (12 ft).

LARGEST COLONY OF ANTS

The largest recorded ant colony in the world stretches 6,000 km (3,700 miles) from northern Italy, through the south of France to the Atlantic coast of Spain. It is home to a species of Argentine ant (*Linepithema humile*) introduced into Europe approximately 80 years ago.

OLDEST FOSSILIZED ANIMAL FOOD STORE

In November 2003, a team of scientists led by Dr Carole Gee (Germany) from the University of Bonn, Germany, announced their discovery of a 17-million-year-old fossilized rodent burrow containing more than 1,200 fossilized nuts. The animal responsible was probably a hamster or a squirrel.

★ OLDEST SPIDER WEB WITH TRAPPED PREY

The oldest known example of a spider's web with insects entrapped has been dated back to the Early Cretaceous period of 110 million years ago; it was discovered in San Just, Spain, and reported in June 2006. The sample contains a parasitic wasp (now extinct), a beetle, a mite and a fly trapped within 26 strands of sticky silk, and is preserved in ancient tree sap (amber).

MOST ENDANGERED WILD CAT

The Iberian lynx (*Lynx pardinus*) is restricted to Spain and Portugal, and in 2000 it was estimated that there were only 600 survivors in an extremely fragmented population. It was once widespread across Spain, but has lost much of its territory to agriculture and urban development.

★ FARTHEST JOURNEY BY A CRAB

In December 2006, an American Columbus crab (*Planes minutus*) was discovered washed up but still alive on a beach in Bournemouth, UK – 8,000 km (5,000 miles) away from its home in the Sargasso Sea, east of Florida, USA. The bright orange, 15-cm (6-in) crab (the actual record-holder is pictured above!) is believed to have made its epic journey by clinging to barnacles on a buoy for three months, surviving storms, predators and sharp changes in sea temperature.

★ FURRIEST FISH

The extraordinary but little-known species *Mirapinna esau* ("hairy with wonderful fins") was first discovered in June 1911 – when a specimen was caught at the surface in the middle of the Atlantic Ocean about 880 km (547 miles) north of the Azores – but remained undescribed and unnamed by science until 1956. *Mirapinna* measures 6.35 cm (2.5 in) long, with a humped back and uniquely lobed fins, but its most striking characteristic of all is the fur-like covering on its body. When viewed closer, however, this "fur" is revealed to be a profuse mass of living body outgrowths, the function of which remains unknown.

★ LONGEST BIRD LEGS

While the ostrich has the **longest legs of any living bird**, the bird with the longest legs relative to its body size is the black-winged stilt (*Himantopus himantopus*, right), widely distributed across much of Europe, as well as Africa and Asia. Its long, pink legs measure 17–24 cm (7–9 in), which is up to 60% of its total 35–40 cm (14–16 in) body length.

★ NEWEST ANIMAL PHYLUM

A hitherto neglected genus of small flatworm-like creatures, *Xenoturbella*, was first made known to science when it was dredged up from the Baltic Sea in 1949. At the time it was thought to be a bizarre mollusc. In November 2006, studies revealed that in reality its two species, *X. bocki* and *X. westbladi*, are so different from all other species of animal that they require the creation of an entirely new phylum – the highest category of animal classification – all for themselves.

★ OLDEST INSECT

The fossilized *Rhyniognatha hirsti* lived in what is now Aberdeen, Scotland, UK, approximately 410 million years ago – making it 30 million years older than any other known insect fossil!

DID YOU KNOW?

The **largest extant bird egg** on record weighed 2.519 kg (5 lb 8 oz) and was laid by an ostrich (*Struthio camelus*) on 19 September 2006 at a farm in Borlänge, Sweden.

An average ostrich egg is 150–200 mm (6–8 in) long, 100–150 mm (4–6 in) in diameter and weighs 1.1–1.9 kg (2.4–4.2 lb) – around two dozen hen's eggs in volume. The shell, although only 1.5 mm (0.06 in) thick, can support the weight of an adult person.

The ★ **largest duck egg** ever weighed just over 227 g (8 oz) and was 20 cm (8 in) in circumference and 14 cm (5.5 in) high. It was laid by a White Pekin duck owned by Willie and Kitty Costello (Ireland).

The specimen was first described in 1926 by entomologist Robin John Tillyard (Australia), who regarded it as unremarkable and left it to London's Natural History Museum, UK. It remained in the museum's vaults for approximately 80 years until entomologists David Grimaldi and Michael Engel (both USA) re-studied the fossil using modern microscopes and discovered the creature's classic insect features. They published the results of their research in *Nature* on 12 February 2004.

Although no wings survive, the triangular jaw structure of *R. hirsti* is similar to those of winged insects, suggesting that insect flight is 80 million years older than was previously thought.

★ OLDEST TICK

In April 1999, a team of American scientists unearthed a 90-million-year-old tick that had been preserved in amber. This blood-sucking parasite from the Cretaceous period was found in a vacant lot in New Jersey, USA. Named *Carlos jerseyi*, the tiny insect has unusual hairs on its back, which may have been used to detect vibrations. It is a logical conclusion that many dinosaurs carried parasitic ticks, just like today's animals.

GREATEST TREE GIRTH EVER

A European chestnut (*Castanea sativa*) known as the Tree of the Hundred Horses (*Castagno di Cento Cavalli*) was measured on Mount Etna, Sicily, Italy, in 1770 and 1780. It had a girth of 57.9 m (190 ft).

LARGEST CORK TREE

The Whistler Tree in the Alentejo region of Portugal averages over 1 tonne (2,000 lb) of raw cork per harvest – enough to cork 100,000 wine bottles! Portugal has more cork-oak trees than any other country and is responsible for 51% of global cork production.

LARGEST FORESTS

The **largest coniferous forests** cover 4 million km² (1.5 million miles²) in northern Russia (pictured), between Latitude 55ºN and the Arctic Circle. By way of comparison, the **largest area of tropical forest** is the Amazon rainforest, which covers approximately 6.5 million km² (2.5 million miles²).

ACTUAL SIZE

★ NEW RECORD
UPDATED RECORD

ASIA

LARGEST TREE-DWELLING MAMMAL

Bornean orang-utan (*Pongo pygmaeus*) and Sumatran orang-utan (*P. abelii*) males typically weigh 83 kg (183 lb) and measure 1.5 m (5 ft) tall. They have opposable toes on their feet and use their arm-span of about 2 m (6 ft) to swing between branches and feed off fruit, small leaves and tree bark. Being lighter (37 kg; 81 lb), the females usually build nests in trees, whereas the adult males sleep on the ground.

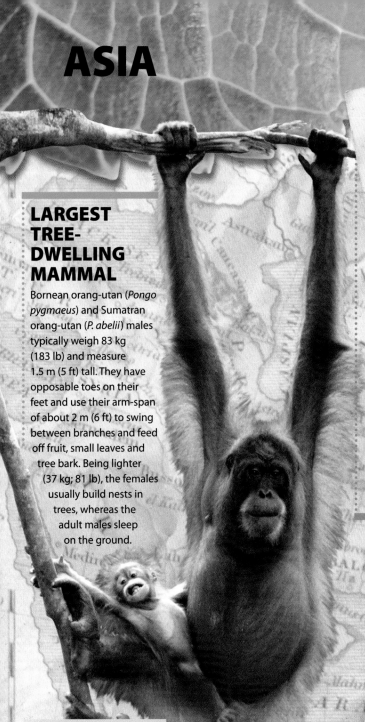

RARE ANIMALS

The Iriomote cat (*Felis iriomotensis*) is confined to Iriomote in the Ryukyu chain of islands, Japan, making it the ★**rarest wild cat**. Fewer than 100 specimens are left, some in Japanese zoos.

The **rarest crocodilian** is the Chinese alligator (*Alligator sinensis*), which can grow to 2 m (6 ft 6 in) and weigh up to 40 kg (88 lb). It is found in the lower Yangtze River, but fewer than 200 were living in the wild in 2002.

SMELLIEST PLANT

Also known as "the corpse flower", the *Amorphophallus titanum* – or titan arum – is believed by many to be the smelliest plant on Earth. When it blooms, it releases an extremely foul odour that smells like rotten flesh and can be detected half a mile away.

CARNIVOROUS PLANT WITH LARGEST PREY

Of all the carnivorous plants, those of the Nepenthaceae family (genus *Nepenthes*) digest the largest prey. They are commonly found in the rainforests of Asia, in particular Borneo, Indonesia and Malaysia. *Nepenthes villosa* (pictured), *N. rajah* and *N. rafflesiana* are known to catch large frogs, birds and even rats.

★ LONGEST FEATHERS IN A WILD BIRD SPECIES

The central tail feathers of Reeves's pheasant (*Syrmaticus reevesii*), native to the mountains of central and northern China, sometimes exceed 2.4 m (8 ft) in length. If thrown up in flight, they act as a brake, causing the bird to drop vertically down into the cover of trees to escape any would-be attacker.

LARGEST LEAF

The largest leaves of any plant are those of the raffia palm (*Raphia farinifera = R. ruffia*) of the Mascarene Islands in the Indian Ocean; and the Amazonian bamboo palm (*R. taedigera*) of South America and Africa. Their leaf blades can measure 20 m (65 ft 7 in) long, with petioles (the stalk by which a leaf is attached to a stem) measuring 4 m (13 ft).

LARGEST BAT

The largest bats in the world are the flying foxes, or fruit bats (family Pteropodidae), particularly those living in south-east Asia. Several species in the genus *Pteropus* have a head–body length of up to 45 cm (17.75 in), a wing-span of 1.7 m (5 ft 7 in) and a weight of 1.6 kg (3 lb 12 oz). The biggest are generally considered to be the large flying fox and the gigantic or Indian flying fox. Although certain other mammals are capable of gliding, bats are the only mammals capable of true flight.

LONGEST INSECT

★ NEW RECORD
UPDATED RECORD

Two stick insects share this record, depending on how they are measured. *Pharnacia kirbyi* (pictured) is a stick insect from the rainforests of Borneo. The longest specimen known had a body length of 32.8 cm (12.9 in) and a total length, including the legs, of 54.6 cm (21.5 in). This makes it the longest insect in the world based on head-plus-body length. A specimen of Malaysia's *Phobaeticus serratipes* had a head-plus-body length of 27.8 cm (10.9 in), but when its outstretched legs were included, it measured a record 55.5 cm (21.8 in).

ACTUAL SIZE

★ MOST AQUATIC SPIDER

The only species of spider that lives entirely under water is *Argyroneta aquatica*, known as the diving bell spider or

air bubble or "bell"

water spider. Large populations are spread across northern Asia (as well as Europe and north Africa). The water spider's legs and abdomen are covered with dense hairs that trap air when it goes under water. Although the spider makes infrequent trips to the surface to replenish the air, oxygen easily diffuses into the bubble from the surrounding water, and, reversely, carbon dioxide diffuses out.

SMALLEST BIRD OF PREY

This record is held jointly by the black-legged falconet (*Microhierax fringillarius*) of south-east Asia and the white-fronted or Bornean falconet

ACTUAL SIZE

(*M. latifrons*) of north-western Borneo. Both species have an average length of 14–15 cm (5.5–6 in) – including a 5-cm (2-in) tail – and a weight of about 35 g (1.25 oz).

OLDEST MARSUPIAL

The oldest known relative of all marsupials is *Sinodelphis szalayi*, a fossil discovered in China's Liaoning Province in 2001 and thought to be 125 million years old. A Sino-American research team, including Ji Qiang and Zhe Xi Luo (both China), named the fossil and concluded that it originally measured 15 cm (5.9 in) long and weighed approximately 30 g (1.05 oz).

DID YOU KNOW?

The world's **rarest seashell** is the white-toothed cowry (*Cypraea leucodon*, left). It is known from just two specimens, the second of which turned up in 1960, and is thus the most coveted species among conchologists. Its only recorded locality is the Philippines' Sulu Sea. The stomach of a fish caught here during the 1960s was later found to contain a white-toothed cowry.

★ MOST MYSTERIOUS NEW ANIMAL

The holy goat or kting voar (*Pseudonovibos spiralis*), named in 1994 and reported by local hunters in southern Vietnam and neighbouring Cambodia, is still only known to scientists as a result of the discovery, in 1993, of several pairs of horns. Each pair was around 45 cm (18 in) in length.

LONGEST SNAKE

The reticulated python (*Python reticulatus*) is found in Indonesia, south-east Asia and the Philippines. A specimen shot and measured in Celebes, Indonesia, in 1912 was 10 m (32 ft 9 in) long.

BIG AND SMALL

• Collected from a depth of 1,425 m (4,675 ft) in the Philippine Sea, a mature adult male of *Photocorynus spiniceps* measured only 0.24 in (6.2 mm) in length. This is the ★**smallest species of fish**. It also holds the record for **smallest vertebrate**.

• Mature males of the pygmy hog (*Sus salvanius*) measure 61–71 cm (24–28 in) long; females are 55–62 cm (21–24 in). This, the ★**smallest species of pig**, was indigenous to the Terai region of India, Nepal and Bhutan, but has been critically endangered since 1996. Isolated populations can still be found in Assam, India, and in wildlife sanctuaries.

• The **largest species of bee** is the king bee (*Chalicodoma pluto*). The females measure a total length of 3.9 cm (1.5 in). The smaller males measure no more than 2.4 cm (0.9 in) long. They are found only in the Molucca Islands of Indonesia.

• The Chinese giant salamander (*Andrias davidianus*) lives in mountain streams in north-eastern, central and southern China. One specimen measured 1.8 m (5 ft 11 in) in length and weighed 65 kg (143 lb), making this the **largest amphibian** of all.

LONGEST VENOMOUS SNAKE

The king cobra (*Ophiophagus hannah*), also called the hamadryad, is found in south-east Asia and India and measures 3.5–4.5 m (12–15 ft) in length. The longest specimen caught, in Negri Sembilan (now Malaysia) in 1937, later grew to 5.71 m (18 ft 9 in) in London Zoo. The head of the king cobra is as big as a man's hand and it can stand tall enough to look an adult human being in the eye. The venom from a single bite from a king cobra is enough to kill an elephant or 20 people.

★ NEW RECORD

☆ UPDATED RECORD

ACTUAL SIZE

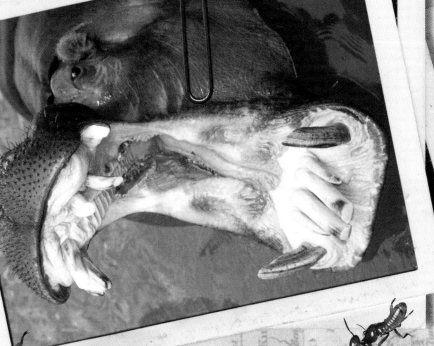

AFRICA

SMALLEST CHAMELEON

The tiny leaf chameleon (*Brookesia minima*, pictured) of Madagascar is acknowledged to be the smallest of its kind. Another related species, *Brookesia tuberculata*, is also extremely small, measuring an average length of 18 mm (0.7 in) from snout to vent.

ACTUAL SIZE

★ LONGEST LEAF LIFESPAN

The welwitschia (*Welwitschia mirabilis*), native to the Namib Desert of Namibia and Angola, has an estimated lifespan of 400–1,500 years, with some specimens carbon-dated to 2,000 years old. Each plant produces two leaves per century and never sheds them. Ancient individuals sprawl out over 10 m (33 ft) in circumference, with enough foliage to cover a 400-m (1,300-ft) athletic field.

GREATEST ROOT DEPTH

A wild fig tree (*Ficus natalensis*) at Echo Caves, near Ohrigstad, Mpumalanga, South Africa, has roots penetrating a calculated 120 m (393 ft).

LARGEST SEED

The coco-de-mer (*Lodoicea maldivica*) is a rare, very slow-growing palm that can live up to 350 years. It is found wild only in the Seychelles. The fruits can take up to six years to develop and contain one to three seeds, each measuring up to 50 cm (19.6 in) long and weighing up to 25 kg (55 lb).

★ LARGEST PANGOLIN

The giant pangolin (*Manis gigantea*), found from Senegal to Uganda and Angola, is the largest species of pangolin or scaly anteater. It is almost 2 m (6 ft) long and weighs 32 kg (70 lb); because of its size, this species is terrestrial, whereas many other pangolins are at least partly arboreal (tree dwellers).

LOUDEST INSECT

Noise intensity is measured in decibel units (dB), with silence equal to 0 dB. Rustling leaves are 10 dB, a normal conversation 60 dB, busy street traffic 70 dB and a lawn-mower 90 dB. The African cicada (*Brevisana brevis*) produces a calling song with a mean sound pressure level of 106.7 dB at a distance of 50 cm (1 ft 7.5 in) – almost as loud as a car horn at 110 dB! Cicada songs play a vital role in both communication and reproduction of the species.

★ MOST AGGRESSIVE BUTTERFLY

The world's most aggressive butterfly is *Charaxes candiope* of Uganda. This very powerful flier actively dive-bombs animals and people intruding upon its territory.

LONGEST SURVIVAL OUT OF WATER

The four species of lungfish that live in Africa (*Protopterus annectens*, *P. aethiopicus*, *P. dolloi* and *P. amphibius*) live in freshwater swamps that frequently dry out for months or even years at a time. Two of these species are considered to be the real survival experts. As the water recedes, they burrow deep into the ground and secrete mucus to form a moisture-saving cocoon around their bodies. They then build a porous mud plug at the entrance of the burrow – and wait. Abandoning gill-breathing in favour of their air-breathing lungs, they can live for up to four years in this dormant position.

LARGEST GAPE FOR A LAND ANIMAL

The hippopotamus (*Hippopotamus amphibius*) can open its jaws to almost 180° – the greatest angle for a land animal. In a fully grown male, this gives an average gape of 1.2 m (4 ft)!

LONGEST FANGS

The fangs of one specimen of the highly venomous gaboon viper (*Bitis gabonica*) of tropical Africa measured 50 mm (2 in). The gaboon viper is also considered to produce more venom than any other snake. A single adult male may have enough venom to inject lethal doses into 30 adult men. Not only do they produce more venom than any other snake, but they also inject more deeply.

GREATEST TRANSIENT MASCULINIZATION BY A FEMALE MAMMAL

The only known female mammal in the world that temporarily changes sex is the juvenile female fossa (*Cryptoprocta ferox*), the largest carnivore species in Madagascar. Research carried out by Dr Clare Hawkins and supported by Dr Paul Racey (both UK) of Aberdeen University, UK, has shown that young, female fossas have a protrusion resembling male genitalia and secrete a substance found in male fossas. The fossas eventually out-grow this state in adulthood, when they are ready to mate and raise young.

MOST EFFICIENT SCAVENGER

The spotted hyena (*Crocuta crocuta*) utilizes the carcasses of large vertebrates such as zebras and wildebeest more efficiently than any other animal. Its jaw muscles and teeth are strong enough to crush large bones – the teeth exert a pressure of 800 kg/cm² (11,378 lb/in²) – and its powerful digestive system can break down the organic matter of bones, hooves, horns and hides.

★ LARGEST TERMITE

Queen termites of the African *Macrotermes bellicosus* species sometimes measure as much as 14 cm (5.5 in) long and 3.5 cm (1.4 in) across. When she reaches this size, the queen can lay up to 30,000 eggs a day. Pictured is one such queen in Okavango, Botswana, attended by her workers.

★ LARGEST LEMUR EVER

The largest lemur of all time was *Archaeoindris fontoynontii*, known only from incomplete fossil remains found in Madagascar's central highlands. The remains, which suggest a body size near to that of a gorilla, and an estimated weight of 150–250 kg (330–550 lb), have been dated at 8,245 (+/- 215 years) bp (before present day).

LARGEST MILLIPEDE

The largest millipede in the world is a fully grown African giant black millipede (*Archispirostreptus gigas*) that measures 38.7 cm (15.2 in) in length and 6.7 cm (2.6 in) in circumference, and has 256 legs. It is owned by Jim Klinger (USA).

LARGEST SNAIL

The largest known land gastropod is the African giant snail (*Achatina achatina*). The largest recorded specimen of this species measured 39.3 cm (15.5 in) from snout to tail when fully extended, its shell length was 27.3 cm (10.75 in) and it weighed exactly 900 g (2 lb).

OCEANIA

★ LONGEST-GLIDING MAMMAL

The yellow-bellied glider (*Petaurus australis*) of Australia can glide further than any other species of gliding mammal (including other marsupial phalangers, as well as flying squirrels and colugos). It is able to glide up to 115 m (377 ft) through the air and is also highly manoeuvrable while airborne.

★ LARGEST WASP NEST

A wasp nest found on a farm at Waimaukau, New Zealand, in April 1963 was composed of wood scrapings mashed up with saliva into a papier-mâché-like substance. It was so heavy that it fell from the tree in which it had been hanging, then split into two. When whole, it measured 3.7 m (12 ft 2 in) long, and was 1.75 m (5.25 ft) in diameter. It had most probably been built by introduced German wasps (*Vespula germanica*).

RAREST INSECT

Scientists believe that there may be as few as 10 specimens of the Lord Howe Island flightless giant stick insect (*Dryococelus australis*) in existence. The giant stick insect, which can grow up to 15 cm (6 in) long, evolved before the dinosaurs. Presumed extinct for 80 years, it was rediscovered feeding in a tree on the remote island of Lord Howe off Australia in 2001. Several eggs were also found. The insect has since been successfully bred at Melbourne Zoo. Pictured is an adult with new baby.

FASTEST FLYING INSECT

Acceptable modern experiments have established that the highest maintainable airspeed of any insect, including the deer bot-fly (*Cephenemyia pratti*), hawk moths (Sphingidae), horseflies (*Tabanus bovinus*) and some tropical butterflies (Hesperiidae), is 39 km/h (24 mph), rising to a maximum of 58 km/h (36 mph) for the Australian dragonfly *Austrophlebia costalis* for short bursts.

MOST VENOMOUS CENTIPEDE

A peculiarly venomous form of *Scolopendra subspinipes* inhabits the Solomon Islands. So potent is the venom it injects into its victim by a modified pair of front limbs rather than by its jaws that human victims have been known to plunge their bitten hands into boiling water in order to mask the excruciating pain of this centipede's bite!

SMALLEST STARFISH

The smallest known starfish is the asterinid sea star *Patiriella parvivipara* discovered by Wolfgang Zeidler on the west coast of the Eyre peninsula, South Australia, in 1975. It had a maximum radius of only 4.7 mm (0.18 in) and a diameter of less than 9 mm (0.35 in).

MOST VENOMOUS MOLLUSC

The two closely related species of blue-ringed octopus, *Hapalochlaena maculosa* and *H. lunulata*, found around the coasts of Australia and parts of south-east Asia, carry a neurotoxic venom so potent that their relatively painless bite can kill in a matter of minutes. Each individual carries sufficient venom to cause the paralysis (or even death) of 10 human adults. Fortunately, blue-ringed octopuses are not considered aggressive and normally bite only when they are taken out of the water or provoked. These molluscs have a radial spread of just 100–200 mm (4–8 in).

SLEEPIEST MARSUPIAL

Because the koala (*Phascolarctos cinereus*) has a very low-quality diet and subsists almost exclusively upon the leaves of eucalyptus trees, it spends up to 18 hours out of every 24 asleep. It does this in order to conserve energy. A koala typically eats no more than 600–800 g (1.3–1.7 lb) of leaves per day, which is equivalent to a human being living on a single bowl of cereal per day.

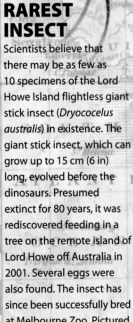

★ LARGEST EEL

A specimen of the yellow-edged moray eel (*Gymnothorax flavimarginatus*) found in the Coomera River in Queensland, Australia, measured 3.7 m (12 ft 2 in) in length and was as thick as a man's thigh. This eel is sometimes also referred to as a leopard moray eel.

LARGEST FRESHWATER CRUSTACEAN

The largest freshwater crustacean is the Tasmanian crayfish or crawfish (*Astacopsis gouldi*), found in the streams of Tasmania, Australia. It has been measured up to 61 cm (2 ft) in length and may weigh as much as 4 kg (9 lb).

MOST COWS KILLED BY LIGHTNING

On 31 October 2005, 68 Jersey cows sheltering under a tree at Warwick Marks's dairy farm near Dorrigo, New South Wales, Australia, were killed by a single bolt of lightning.

YOUNGEST INCUBATOR

The white-rumped swiftlet (*Aerodramus spodiopygius*) lives in Australia and Papua New Guinea and is also found on several Pacific islands. The female of this species lays two eggs, several weeks apart. By the time she has laid the second one, the first has hatched and the young chick is old enough to do the incubating on the mother's behalf.

★ SLIMMEST LIZARD

The world's slimmest lizard is the Australian legless snake lizard (*Lialis burtoni*), which can measure more than 50 cm (20 in) long, but at its mid-body is no thicker than a pencil.

LONGEST LIZARD

The slender Salvadori's or Papuan monitor (*Varanus salvadorii*) of Papua New Guinea has been measured at up to 4.75 m (15 ft 7 in) in length, 70% of which is taken up by the tail.

MOST DANGEROUS LOVE LIFE

The male brown antechinus (*Antechinus stuartii*), a marsupial mouse that inhabits eastern Australia, has an insatiable sexual appetite. For two weeks every year, the entire adult male population tries to mate with as many females as possible. The heightened levels of stress from chasing females and fighting off rival males shuts down the antechinus' immune system, and the entire male population dies within a matter of days as a result of ulcers, infections or exhaustion. Many also die of starvation, as they neglect to eat during this intense mating period!

SMALLEST BUTTERFLY

ACTUAL SIZE

The tiny grass blue (*Zizula hylax*) has a forewing length of 6 mm (0.25 in). Its upper side is steely blue-grey in colour with a light grey and scattered dark speckling underside.

★ **NEW RECORD**
UPDATED RECORD

GREAT GREENERY

• New Zealand's tree nettle (*Urtica ferox*, right) is the **most dangerous stinger**. Its stinging hairs inject potent toxins into the skin and has been known to kill dogs and horses.

• The record for the **longest distance travelled by a drift seed** belongs to Mary's Bean (*Merremia discoidesperma*). It has the widest known drift range for any seed or tropical fruit, travelling over 24,140 km (15,000 miles) from the Marshall Islands in the north Pacific Ocean to the beaches of Norway.

• An inflorescence is a cluster of flowers on the branch of a plant. The ★ **largest inflorescence** ever recorded was found on a specimen of *Furcraea gigantea* (also known as *F. foetida*) – a type of agave – measured by Elwyn Hegarty and Hans Meyer in May 2000 in Indooroopilly, Australia. The inflorescence, which took 25 years to grow, reached the remarkable height of 12.18 m (40 ft)!

LARGEST SPECIES OF CAMEL

The dromedary, or one-humped camel (*Camelus dromedarius*), is the largest member of the Camelidae family. Although native to the Middle East, it survives today as a feral animal only in Australia and Spain and as a domestic animal elsewhere. (A feral animal or plant is one that has escaped from domestication and returned, partly or wholly, to its wild state.)

Next 92 km

AT THE POLES

LARGEST NOSE

The nose of the blue whale (*Balaenoptera musculus*, above) measures 5 m (16 ft) long – up to 33% of its total body length. It is the largest mammalian nose, and indeed the largest nose of any animal species.

HEAVIEST BRAIN

The brain of the sperm whale (*Physeter macrocephalus*) weighs up to 9 kg (19 lb 13 oz) – six times heavier than a human's. Despite its size, the whale's brain accounts for just 0.02% of its total body weight.

★ **NEW RECORD**
   UPDATED RECORD

★ LARGEST ANTARCTIC LAND ANIMAL

Other than humans working in various research stations, the largest solely land animal in Antarctica is a number of species of midge (gnat-like flies) no more than 12 mm (0.47 in) long.

★ FIRST RECORDED ANTARCTIC DINOSAUR

Found on Antarctica's Ross Island in 1986, the first species of Antarctic dinosaur to be discovered was *Antarctopelta oliveroi*, an ankylosaurid. Ankylosaurids were heavily armoured from head to tail.

★ MOST SOUTHERLY BIRD

Few Antarctic birds nest inland on the continent's ice-sealed interior. The snow petrel (*Pagodroma nivea*), however, nests up to 240 km (150 miles) inland, among rocky peaks poking up through the ice, and have been spotted at the South Pole.

DEEPEST DIVE BY A BIRD

Professor Gerald Kooyman (USA) of California's Scripps Institution of Oceanography recorded a 534-m (1,751-ft) dive by an emperor penguin (*Aptenodytes forsteri*) at Coulman Island, Antarctica, in 1993.

★ MOST EXCLUSIVE FAMILY OF POLAR BIRDS

The sheathbills, who belong to the Chionidae family, are confined exclusively to the subantarctic-Antarctic zone. They are the only entire family of birds endemic to this faunal region and live on or near to the shores of subantarctic-Atlantic and Indian Ocean islands, often in association with penguin colonies.

SOUTHERNMOST PLANT

Lichens resembling *Rhinodina frigida* were found in Moraine Canyon at latitude 86°09'S, longitude 157°30'W in 1971 and in the Horlick Mountain area of Antarctica at latitude 86°09'S, longitude 131°14'W in 1965.

The **southernmost flowering plant** is Antarctic hair grass (*Deschampsia antarctica*), found on Refuge Island, Antarctica, in 1981.

MOST FATTY DIET

The diet of the polar bear (*Ursus maritimus*) in spring and early summer consists of recently weaned ringed seal pups, which can be up to 50% fat. From April to July, the seals are in such plentiful supply that the bears sometimes feed only on the fat below the skin and leave the rest of the carcasses untouched.

ACTUAL SIZE

MOST REMOTE TREE

The nearest companion of a solitary Norwegian spruce on Campbell Island, Antarctica, is more than 222 km (137.9 miles; 119.8 nautical miles) away on the Auckland Islands.

★ LOWEST TEMPERATURE-TOLERANCE FOR INSECTS

The insect with the greatest tolerance of low temperatures is the woolly bear caterpillar of the Greenland tiger moth (*Gynaephora groenlandica*), native to the high Arctic. For up to 10 months of the year, its caterpillar can spend its time frozen solid at temperatures as low as -50ºC (-58ºF) – and possibly even lower! – and suffer no ill effects.

NORTHERNMOST PLANT

The yellow poppy (*Papaver radicatum*, pictured) and the Arctic willow (*Salix arctica*) survive at latitude 83°N, although the latter exists there in an extremely stunted form.

★ MOST NORTHERLY LIZARD

The common (viviparous) lizard (*Lacerta vivipara*) lives as far north as the northern extremes of mainland Norway, and therefore high above the Arctic Circle.

★ MOST NORTHERLY BIRD

On average, the most northerly breeding range of any species of bird is that of the ivory gull (*Pagophila eburnea*). It occurs almost exclusively north of 70ºN and its principal breeding grounds can be found on Svalbard, Franz Josef Land, Novaya Zemlya, northern Canada and northern Greenland.

★ GREATEST CONCENTRATION OF LARGE MAMMALS

A herd of northern fur seals (*Callorhinus ursinus*) that breeds mostly on St George and St Paul (two islands in Alaska's Pribilof group) currently number just under one million. This herd reached a peak of approximately 2.5 million animals during the late 1950s, but extensive hunting has reduced their numbers significantly.

SHORTEST LACTATION PERIOD FOR A MAMMAL

Hooded seals (*Cystophora cristata*) breed on ice flows and their pups are born between mid-March and early April, weighing about 20 kg (44 lb). Their lactation period is a mere three to five days.

★ MOST SOUTHERLY BIRD TRACKS

The most southerly bird tracks ever recorded were those of an emperor penguin (*Aptenodytes forsteri*), discovered by chance by a team of Antarctic explorers on 31 December 1957 – more than 400 km (248 miles) from the nearest sea! Pictured is an emperor on Snow Hill Island on the Antarctic peninsula.

THE BEAR FACTS

• The **largest of all carnivores on land** is the polar bear (*Ursus maritimus*). Adult males typically weigh 400–600 kg (880–1,320 lb) – up to twice that of a tiger – and have an average nose-to-tail length of 2.4–2.6 m (7 ft 10 in–8 ft 6 in). The **largest specimen** was a bear estimated at around 900 kg (1,984 lb) – it was shot in the Chukchi Sea, west of Kotzebue, Alaska, USA, and reportedly measured 3.5 m (11 ft 5 in) over the body contours from nose to tail.

• A home range is the area where animals typically eat, sleep and interact. The **largest indigenous home range of any land-based mammal** belongs to the polar bear. It can typically tramp over Arctic areas of 30,000 km² (11,500 miles²) – the size of Italy – in a single year. Polar bears can also swim vast distances – up to 100 km (62 miles).

• Polar bears have the **most sensitive noses of all land mammals**. They can detect prey such as seals over 30 km (18 miles) away, often under thick ice.

• An adult male polar bear has a stomach capacity of approximately 68 kg (150 lb) and it is known to kill animals as large as walruses weighing 500 kg (1,100 lb) and beluga whales at 600 kg (1,322 lb). This makes the polar bear the animal with the **largest prey**.

GUINNESS WORLD RECORDS DAY 2006

★ NEW RECORD ★ UPDATED RECORD

USA
★ MOST RATTLESNAKES HELD IN THE MOUTH

Jackie Bibby (USA) once again proved he is the most fearless snake handler on the planet by holding 10 live rattlesnakes in his mouth by their tails, without any assistance, for 10 seconds in New York City, USA!

USA
SMALLEST WAIST

Cathie Jung (USA) paid a visit to our US office to have her tiny waist measured. Despite her regular height (1.72 m; 5 ft 8 in), her corseted waist is just 38.1 cm (15 in).

Canada
★ LONGEST LINE OF DANCERS

The record for the longest single line of dancers consisted of 1,681 participants and was organized by The Hummingbird Centre, Breakfast Television and the Radio City Music Hall Rockettes in Toronto, Canada, on 9 November 2006, as part of Guinness World Records Day.

MORE GWR DAY FUN

RECORD	HOLDER	DETAILS
★ Most underpants pulled on in a minute	Grant Denyer (Australia)	Denyer pulled on 19 pairs of pants in the Sunrise TV studio (Seven Network), Sydney, Australia.
★ Most passes of a giant volleyball	Vanessa Sheridan & Paddy Bunce (both UK)	The pair made 582 passes of a giant volleyball on *Capital Breakfast with Johnny Vaughan* in London, UK.
★ Fastest time to pop 100 balloons	Dermot O'Leary & Alan Conely (both UK)	The duo took just 25 seconds to pop the lot on *The New Paul O'Grady Show* (Channel 4) in London, UK.
★ Most skips in a minute	Philip Sutcliffe (Ireland)	Sutcliffe completed 241 skips on the set of *Ireland AM* (TV3) in Dublin, Ireland.
★ Most shoelaces tied in a minute	Andy Akinwolere (UK)	14 shoes laced on the set of *Blue Peter* (BBC) in London, UK.
★ Most people sport-stacking	World Sport Stacking Association (USA)	An incredible 81,252 participants took part in a multiple-venue mass cup-stack.

Canada
★ HIGHEST WINE CELLAR

The CN Tower's Cellar in the Sky, recognized on 8 November 2006 as part of Guinness World Records Day, stands 351 m (1,151 ft) above ground in Toronto, Ontario, Canada.

Brazil
TALLEST MAN

Xi Shun Bao, until recently the tallest living man at 2.36 m (7 ft 8.9 in), was welcomed with open arms in Brazil, where he visited Corcovado mountain and stood alongside the 38-m-tall (125-ft) statue of Christ the Redeemer.

Germany
LONGEST SINGING MARATHON

The longest singing marathon by an individual was 59 hr 12 min by Hartmut Timm (Germany) at Alt Waren in Waren, Müritz, Germany, between 9 and 11 November 2006 as part of Guinness World Records Day. (*This record has since been broken twice.*)

Scotland
★ SHORTEST STREET

Ebenezer Place in Wick, Caithness, Scotland, measured just 2.05 m (6 ft 9 in) long when verified for Guinness World Records Day. The street has a postal address (No.1), a doorway and even a stone street sign.

England
★ MOST SYNCHRONIZED SWIMMING BALLET LEG SWITCHES IN 1 MINUTE

Members of Aquabatix (UK, above) executed 71 ballet leg switches in a minute in the Trafalgar Square fountains, London, UK.

Norway
MOST CONCRETE BLOCKS SMASHED

Narve Læret (Norway) had a smashing time on GWR Day 2006 – using just his bare hands, he broke 90 concrete blocks in only a minute on the set of *Senkveld* (TV2) in Oslo, Norway.

France
★ MOST PEOPLE KISSING SIMULTANEOUSLY

A total of 594 amorous couples puckered up and kissed at an event organized by OPHA at La Défense in Paris, France.

Sweden
GWR AT GALLERIAN

Lots of records, including the ★ **longest hair extensions**, the most ★ **continuous six-step break moves**, the **longest time controlling a football while lying down,** and the ★ **most yo-yos spinning simultaneously**, were set at the Gallerian shopping centre, in Stockholm, Sweden, as part of GWR Day.

Ireland
★ FASTEST ACCORDION PLAYER

Liam O'Connor (Ireland) proved he has the world's fastest fingers by playing *Tico Tico* at a speed of 11.67 notes a second on the Rick O'Shea radio show on 2FM in Dublin, Ireland.

Portugal
★ MOST WIDELY SUPPORTED FOOTBALL CLUB

The most widely supported football club is Sport Lisboa e Benfica, Portugal, which has 160,398 paid-up members. The record was acknowledged on 9 November 2006 during the celebrations for Guinness World Records Day.

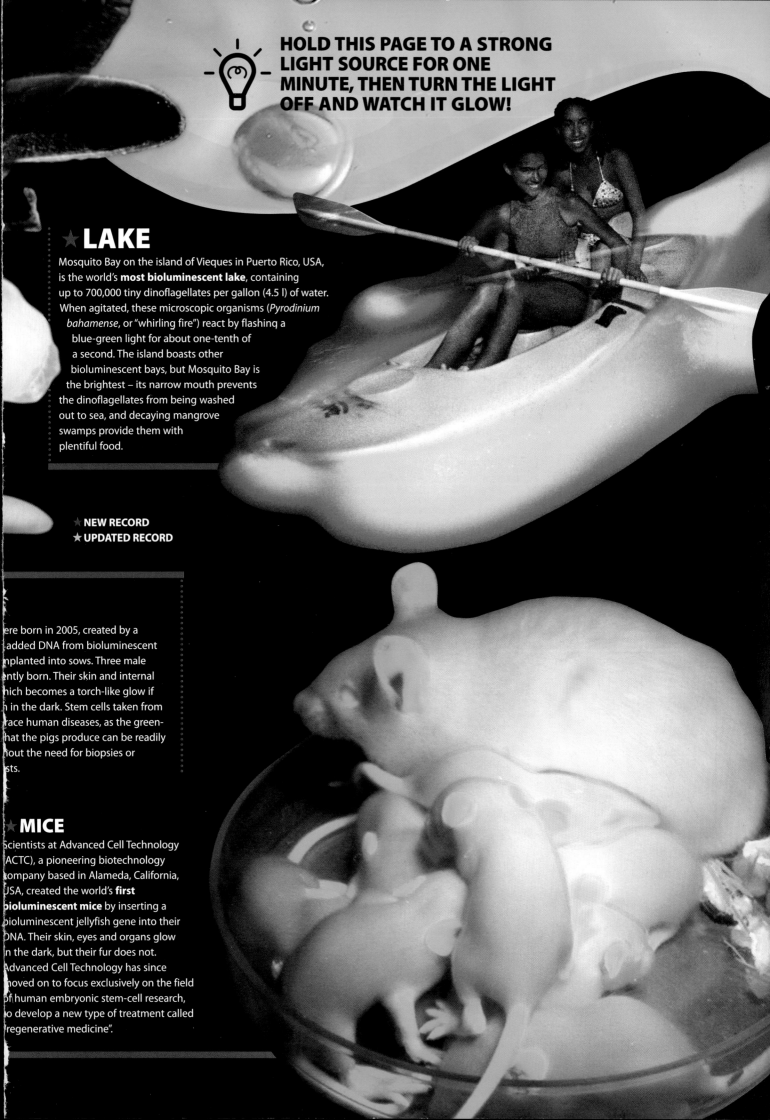

HOLD THIS PAGE TO A STRONG LIGHT SOURCE FOR ONE MINUTE, THEN TURN THE LIGHT OFF AND WATCH IT GLOW!

★ LAKE

Mosquito Bay on the island of Vieques in Puerto Rico, USA, is the world's **most bioluminescent lake**, containing up to 700,000 tiny dinoflagellates per gallon (4.5 l) of water. When agitated, these microscopic organisms (*Pyrodinium bahamense*, or "whirling fire") react by flashing a blue-green light for about one-tenth of a second. The island boasts other bioluminescent bays, but Mosquito Bay is the brightest – its narrow mouth prevents the dinoflagellates from being washed out to sea, and decaying mangrove swamps provide them with plentiful food.

★ **NEW RECORD**
★ **UPDATED RECORD**

...ere born in 2005, created by a ...added DNA from bioluminescent ...mplanted into sows. Three male ...ntly born. Their skin and internal ...hich becomes a torch-like glow if ...h in the dark. Stem cells taken from ...race human diseases, as the green-...hat the pigs produce can be readily ...hout the need for biopsies or ...sts.

★ MICE

Scientists at Advanced Cell Technology (ACTC), a pioneering biotechnology company based in Alameda, California, USA, created the world's **first bioluminescent mice** by inserting a bioluminescent jellyfish gene into their DNA. Their skin, eyes and organs glow in the dark, but their fur does not. Advanced Cell Technology has since moved on to focus exclusively on the field of human embryonic stem-cell research, to develop a new type of treatment called "regenerative medicine".

LIGHT FANTASTIC

FIREFLY

The **most bioluminescent insect** is the firefly (*Pyrophorus noctilucus*), which has been documented as having a surface brightness of 45 millilamberts. The light emitted by fireflies (which are actually beetles, not flies) is unique as almost 100% of the energy is given off as light. In a lightbulb, for example, only 10% of the energy is light, while the other 90% is given off as heat.

★ PIGS

The world's **first bioluminescent pigs** w
scientific team from Taiwan University. They
jellyfish to pig embryos, which were then i
bioluminescent piglets were subsequ
organs have a greenish tinge, w
blue light is shone on ther
them will be used to
glowing protein
observed wit
invasive t

Find out about GWR DAY 2007 at
www.guinnessworld records.com/ gwrday07

China
★ LARGEST GAME OF CHINESE WHISPERS

The largest game of Chinese whispers involved 1,083 people from the Cycling Club of Chengdu City Sports Association for Oldster and was set in Chengdu City, Sichuan Province, China.

International
★ LARGEST GLOBAL NEWSPAPER

A total of 71 editions of the *Metro* newspaper are published in over 100 cities, 21 countries and 19 languages across Europe, the Americas, and Asia, attracting a daily readership of 18.5 million. Pictured is GWR Editor-in-Chief Craig Glenday (left) with *Metro's* founder, Pelle Tornberg (Sweden).

Australia
★ LARGEST UNDERWATER DANCE CLASS

An underwater dance class consisting of 74 students and instructors, who danced for 13 min 30 sec, was held at the Sydney Olympic Park Aquatic Centre, New South Wales, Australia.

Qatar
★ LARGEST FOOTBALL

The largest football made from artificial leather measures 9.07 m (29 ft 9 in) in diameter. The record was set by Doha Bank, Doha, Qatar, and the football displayed in Doha, Qatar, on 9 November 2006.

New Zealand
★ FARTHEST ZORB ROLL

The greatest distance travelled by a zorb ball in one roll is 570 m (1,870 ft), by Steve Camp (South Africa) in Paengaroa, New Zealand. A zorb ball weighs around 89 kg (198 lb) and keeps the "zorbonaut" inside in an air cushion about 60 cm (2 ft) off the ground.

ADRENALINE JUNKIES

★ FIRST FLIGHT WITH ROCKET-POWERED WINGS

The first person to successfully achieve horizontal human flight is Yves Rossy (Switzerland), who flew for four minutes at an altitude of 1,600 m (5,250 ft) and at a speed of 180 km/h (111 mph) above Yverdon airfield near Lake Neuchâtel in Switzerland on 24 June 2004. The former military pilot created his "jet-man" project by adding two kerosene-powered jet engines to 3-m-long (10-ft), foldable carbon wings.

HIGHEST ALTITUDE BALLOON SKYWALK

Mike Howard (UK) walked on a beam between two hot-air balloons at an altitude of 6,522 m (21,400 ft) over Yeovil, Somerset, UK, on 1 September 2004, as part of a recording for the *Guinness World Records: 50 Years, 50 Records* TV show. In doing so, he broke his own record of 5,791.2 m (19,000 ft), which he set in 1998 over Marshall, Michigan, USA, without using a parachute!

OLDEST PERSON TO
ABSEIL DOWN A BUILDING

Doris Long (UK, b. 18 May 1914) abseiled down Millgate House – 60 m (197 ft) from the roof to the ground – in St George's Square, Portsmouth, UK, on 10 June 2006, aged 92 years and 24 days.

★ LARGEST VESSEL
WATERSKIED BEHIND

Dirk Gion (Germany) waterskied for five minutes at 17 knots (32 km/h; 20 mph) behind MS *Deutschland*, a 175-m (575-ft), ocean-going cruise liner, on 12 June 2006. Gion was brought up to speed behind the liner by a small motorboat, then jumped with his skis on, line in hand, and began waterskiing at full speed.

HIGHEST
COMMERCIAL DECELERATOR

The highest commercial decelerator descent facility is Sky Jump at Macau Tower Convention and Entertainment Centre in Macau (China) – the 10th tallest building in the world. The descent starts from level 61 of the tower, at a height of 233 m (764 ft 4 in) from ground level, and each descent takes 17–20 seconds to complete. The inaugural jump was completed by multiple Guinness World Record holder A. J. Hackett (New Zealand) on 17 August 2005.

FIRST BACK FLIP ON A KICK SCOOTER

Using a ramp with a height of 5.48 m (18 ft), stuntman and action-sports expert Jarret Reid of Anaheim, California, USA, performed a back flip – landing with both feet on the scooter – at Van Nuys Airport, California, USA, for *Guinness World Records: Primetime* on 21 January 2001.

★ KITE BUGGY
LONGEST JOURNEY

Pete Ash, Kieron Bradley and Brian Cunningham (all UK) used a kite to propel a kite buggy 1,015 km (630.7 miles) across the Gobi Desert in China and Mongolia between 5 and 21 September 2004.

★ **NEW RECORD**
★ **UPDATED RECORD**

★ MOST BUILDINGS CLIMBED (UNASSISTED)

Alain "Spiderman" Robert (France) has climbed 70 towers, monuments and skyscrapers without ropes, suction devices or safety equipment. A dedicated solo urban climber (who suffers from vertigo), Alain uses pipes, window frames, cables and the gaps between brickwork to scale structures that often measure over 400 m (1,300 ft). He has been arrested and imprisoned at locations all over the world for his unannounced and illegal ascents. He is pictured here climbing the Investment Authority building in Abu Dhabi on 23 February 2007.

LONGEST KITE SURF (FEMALE)

Andreya Wharry (UK) kite-surfed 115.4 nautical miles (213.72 km; 132.80 miles) between Watergate Bay, Cornwall, UK, and Dungarven, Ireland, on 7 September 2005.

HUMAN BEINGS

CONTENTS

HAIRIEST FAMILY

Victor "Larry" Ramos Gomez, pictured here, and his brother Gabriel "Danny" (both Mexico) suffer from a rare condition characterized by excessive facial and bodily hair. They are two of a family of 19 that span five generations and all suffer from congenital generalized hypertrichosis. The women are covered with a light to medium coat of hair while the men of the family have thick hair on approximately 98% of the body, apart from the hands and feet.

ANATOMICAL ANOMALIES

★ HEAVIEST LIVING MAN

When work began working on *Guinness World Records 2008*, Mexico's Manuel Uribe weighed an estimated 560 kg (88 st; 1,235 lb), heavier than any known living person. Uribe appeared on Mexican television, making an impassioned plea for help with his extraordinary weight, which he received in the form of surgeon Giancarlo De Bernardinis (Italy). He offered Uribe a gastric bypass, on condition that he lose some weight first. Uribe obliged and began a successful high-protein diet.

As we went to press, Uribe was making his first foray outdoors in five years (below, on a flatbed truck driving around Monterrey), and now weighs around 381 kg (60 st; 840 lb).

★ TALLEST LIVING HUMAN BEING

Leonid Stadnyk (Ukraine, pictured with his mother Galina) was measured in 2006 by endocrinologist and gigantism expert Professor Michael Besser (UK) and found to be an incredible 2.57 m (8 ft 5.5 in) tall. Stadnyk, a certified veterinarian in Podoliansky, Ukraine, suffers from acromegalic gigantism caused by a tumour on his pituitary gland that stimulated the over-production of growth hormone.

★ MOST FINGERS AND TOES (POLYDACTILISM)

Pranamya Menaria (India) has 25 digits in total (12 fingers and 13 toes), as does Devendra Harne (India), who also has 12 fingers and 13 toes.

★ LARGEST APPENDIX REMOVED

The appendix removed from 72-year-old Safranco August (Croatia) during an autopsy at the Ljudevit Jurak University Department of Pathology in Zagreb, Croatia, on 26 August 2006, measured 26 cm (10.2 in) long.

DID YOU KNOW?

The discovery of Leonid Stadnyk (see above) leaves Guinness World Records in a quandary. Without yet having had the chance to measure him six times in a day, as our rules require, we would not normally ratify the record. The tallest man we have fully verified is Xi Shun (China), at 2.361 m (7 ft 8.95 in). But, because of the 20-cm (7.8-in) difference in height between the two men, and the testimony of Prof. Besser, we have accepted the claim.

★ HEAVIEST FIBROID

The heaviest fibroid – a benign fibrous tumour usually found in the uterus – weighed 10.36 kg (22 lb 13 oz) and belonged to Indira Khetan (India). The fibroid was removed by a team of surgeons led by Dr Archana Baser (India) at the Suyash Hospital, Indore, India, on 20 January 2007. This was over three times heavier than the previous record holder, removed in an operation in India on 25 December 2000.

★ WIDEST TOOTH EXTRACTED

Nine-year-old Shane Russell (Canada) had a tooth measuring 1.52 cm (0.6 in) wide excised on 28 June 2000. The average width of a maxillary central incisor is 0.762 mm (0.3 in). The ★ **longest tooth extracted** measured 2.53 cm (0.997 in). It was removed from 12-year-old Philip Puszczalowski (Canada) in 1993.

★ LONGEST HAIR

• **Nipple** Simon Mould (UK) has a nipple hair that was measured at 11.4 cm (4.5 in) on 13 November 2005.

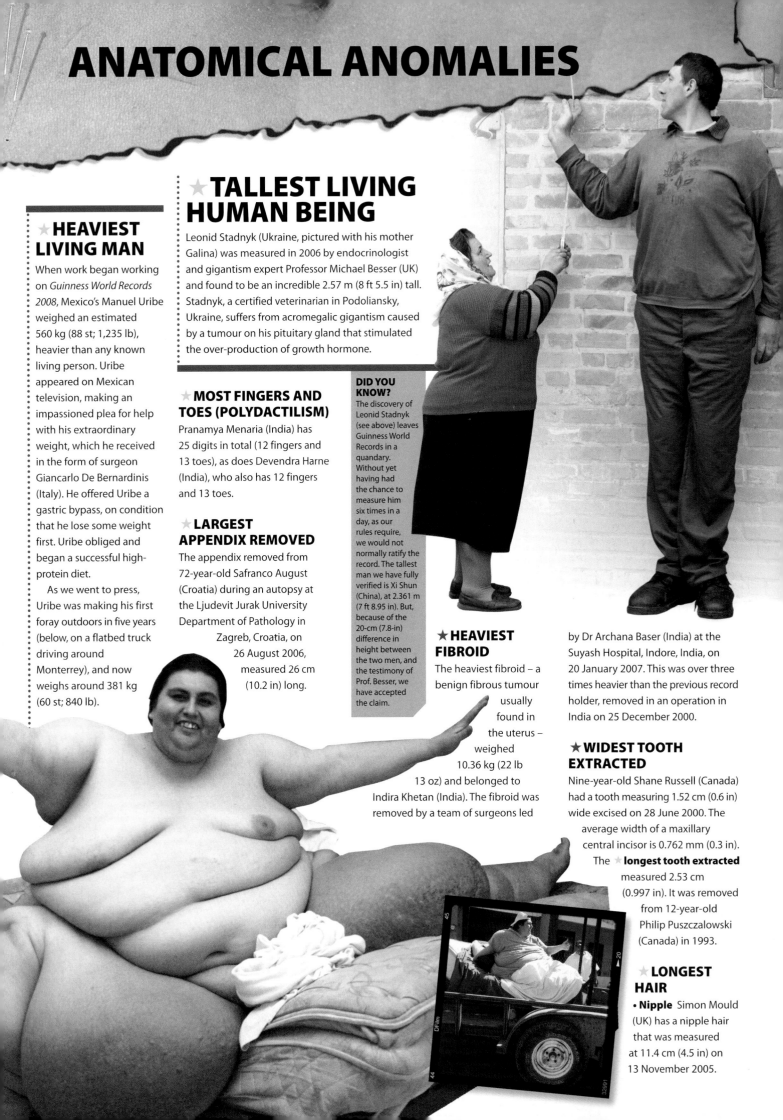

LONGEST BEARD (FEMALE)

Vivian Wheeler (USA) began shaving her face aged seven, but in 1993, after four marriages and the death of her mother, she finally stopped the daily trimming and grew a full beard. The longest strand from the follicle to the tip of the hair was measured at 27.9 cm (11 in) in 2000. She prefers to tie the beard up, to allow her to continue with her day-to-day routines.

"It really helped to have a Guinness World Record," said Wheeler. "It showed me I could be proud of being me. It made me feel like I had a chance in society."

★ **Eyelash** On Jolie Matzes' (USA) right upper lid is an eyelash measuring 6.4 cm (2.5 in) long.

★ **Eyebrow** Ji Yang (China) had an eyebrow hair that was measured at 11.5 cm (4.5 in) on the set of the *Guinness World Records* presentation ceremony in Beijing, China, on 17 January 2006.

★ **Arm** Robert Starrett (USA) had an arm hair with a length of 13.5 cm (5.3 in) when measured in Mequon, Wisconsin, USA, on 7 December 2006.

★ **NEW RECORD**
★ **UPDATED RECORD**

★ LONGEST FINGERNAILS
ON BOTH HANDS (MALE)

Melvin Feizel Boothe of Pontiac, Michigan, USA, hasn't cut his fingernails for 25 years. As a result, he now has a total nail length of 931 cm (346 in) for both hands – the longest nails of anyone on the planet.

For the female with the longest nails, see p.141.

LIFE STORIES

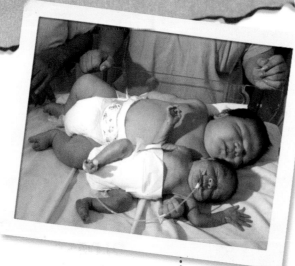

MOST FETUSES

The highest number of fetuses in a single confinement was reported by Gennaro Montanino (Italy). On 22 July 1971, he removed the fetuses of ten girls and five boys from a 35-year-old housewife. A fertility drug was responsible for this unique instance of quindecaplets.

☆ OLDEST PERSON TO GIVE BIRTH

The oldest mother is Maria del Carmen Bousada Lara (Spain, b. 5 January 1940), who gave birth by Caesarean section to twin boys, Christian and Pau, aged 66 years 358 days at the Sant Pau hospital, Barcelona, Spain on 29 December 2006.

HEAVIEST BIRTHS

The world's **heaviest twins**, with an aggregate weight of 12.58 kg (27 lb 12 oz), were born to Mary Ann Haskin (USA) on 20 February 1924.
• The **heaviest triplets**, weighing 10.9 kg (24 lb), were born to Mary McDermott (UK) on 18 November 1914.
• The **heaviest quadruplets** (2 girls, 2 boys), weighing 10.426 kg (22 lb 15.75 oz), were delivered by Tina Saunders (UK) on 7 February 1989.
• Two cases have been recorded of the **heaviest quintuplets**. Both had a weight of 11.35 kg (25 lb) and were delivered on 7 June 1953 by Liu Saulian (China) and, on 30 December 1956, by Mrs Kamalammal (India).

INTERVALS BETWEEN BIRTHS

The record for the **longest interval between the birth of twins** goes to Peggy Lynn (USA), who gave birth to a baby girl, Hanna, on 11 November 1995. She delivered the other twin, Eric, on 2 February 1996, 84 days later at the Geisinger Medical Center, Danville, Pennsylvania, USA.

★ HEAVIEST NEWBORN BABIES

The heaviest baby delivered in the past 12 months was Antonio Cruz (b. 28 January 2007, pictured left with an average newborn to show his size), who was born in Cancun, Mexico, weighing 6.4 kg (14 lb 1.4 oz). Despite his size, he was a kilogram lighter than Ademilton dos Santos (b. 18 January 2005, above right), a boy from Salvador, Brazil, who weighed 7.57 kg (16 lb 11 oz)! The **heaviest newborn** ever was born to Anna Bates (Canada) in Ohio, USA, on 19 January 1879 and weighed 10.8 kg (23 lb 12 oz). He lived for only 11 hours. The **heaviest newborn to survive** was a boy weighing 10.2 kg (22 lb 8 oz), born to Carmelina Fedele (Italy) in Italy in 1955.

• The record for the ★ **longest interval between the birth of quadruplets** goes to Jackie Iverson of Saskatoon, Canada, who gave birth normally to a boy, Christopher, on 21 November 1993 and a girl, Alexandra, eight days later on 29 November 1993. She then went on to deliver another boy and girl, Matthew and Sarah, by Caesarean section on 30 November 1993, a full nine days after the first child was born.

> *Twins Iris Johns and Aro Campbell (b. 1914) were reunited after a record 75 years' separation!*

LARGEST GATHERING OF TWINS

On 12 November 1999, 3,961 pairs of twins gathered at Taipei City Hall (right) in Taiwan.
The ★ **largest gathering of opposite-sex twins**, organized by the Taipei Twins Association, was of 806 pairs of opposite-sex fraternal twins at Chung-Shan Hall, Taipei, Taiwan, on 10 November 2002.

WORLD'S OLDEST LIVING PEOPLE

NAME	NATIONALITY	AGE	DATE OF BIRTH
Yoneko Minagawa (f)	Japan	114	4 Jan 1893
Edna Parker (f)	USA	113	20 Apr 1893
Maria de Jesus (f)	Portugal	113	10 Sep 1893
Helen Stetter (f)	USA	113	18 Nov 1893
Bertha Fry (f)	USA	113	1 Dec 1893
Florence Finch (f)	UK	113	22 Dec 1893
Shitsu Nikano (f)	Japan	113	1 Jan 1894
Arbella Ewing (f)	USA	112	13 Mar 1894
Marie-Simone Capony (f)	France	112	14 Mar 1894
Gertrude Baines (f)	USA	112	6 Apr 1894
Tsuneyo Toyonaga (f)	Japan	112	21 May 1894

Source: Gerontology Research Group (www.grg.org) as of 3 March 2007   f = female, m = male

FAMILY TREES

• The record for the **most generations born on the same day** is four and is held by five families: Ralph Betram Williams (USA, b. 4 July 1982), Veera Tuulia Tuijantyär Kivistö (Finland, b. 21 March 1997), Maureen Werner (USA, b. 13 October 1998), Jacob Camren Hildebrandt (USA, b. 23 August 2001) and Mion Masuda (Japan, b. 26 March 2005) all share their birthday with a parent, grandparent and great-grandparent.

• The Rollings family (UK) and the Taylor family (USA) have given birth to the **most consecutive generations of twins**, with four sets each.

• The **most albino siblings** were born to two families: the four eldest sons born to George and Minnie Sesler (USA), and all four children of Mario and Angie Gaulin (Canada).

• The **most twin siblings born on the same day** were born to two women: Laura Shelley (USA) bore Melissa Nicole and Mark Fredrick Julian Jr in 1990, and Kayla May and Jonathan Price Moore in 2003, on 25 March. Caroline Cargado (USA) bore Keilani Marie and Kahleah Mae in 1996 and Mikayla Anee and Malia Abigail in 2003, on 30 May.

• The **tallest female twins** are Ann and Claire Recht (USA, b. 9 February 1988), who, on 10 January 2007, were both found to have an average overall height of 2.01 m (6 ft 7 in). The **tallest male twins** are Michael and James Lanier (USA, b. 27 November 1969), who both have an average overall height of 2.23 m (7 ft 3 in).

• The record for the **youngest great-great-great-great grandmother** was set by Augusta Bunge (USA, b. 13 October 1879) on 21 January 1989 at the age of 109 years 97 days, when her great-great-great-granddaughter gave birth to a son, Christopher John Bollig.

• The ★ **shortest interval between the birth of twins in a single confinement** is two minutes and was set by Ellen Louise Brown (UK), who gave birth to Thomas at 16:54 and Niall at 16:56 at Dryburn Hospital in Durham, UK, on 10 July 1995.

PREMATURE BIRTHS

The world's **most premature twins**, Devin and Dorraine Johnson, were born on 8 April 1996 at the Elizabeth Blackwell Hospital, Riverside, Ohio, USA, 119 days premature.

• The **most premature triplets**, Guy, Kathryn and Marcus Humphrey (UK), were born on 28 February 1992 at St Mary's Hospital, Manchester, UK, 108 days early.

DID YOU KNOW?
Conjoined twins derive the name "Siamese" from the **first Siamese twins**, Chang and Eng Bunker, born at Meklong on 11 May 1811 of Chinese parents. They were joined by a cartilaginous band at the chest. Both married and fathered children and they died within hours of each other on 17 January 1874, aged 62 years 251 days.

• The **most premature quadruplets** were delivered by Kathryn Tepper (Australia) on 20 February 1997, 15 weeks early. Ben Stewart (790 g; (1 lb 10.3 oz), Hannah Elise (680 g; 1 lb 6.9 oz), Ryan Colin (780 g; 1 lb 10 oz), and Lisa Nicole (735 g; 1 lb 8.5 oz) were born at the Royal Women's Hospital, Melbourne, Australia.

MOST OFFSPRING

The **most children delivered at a single birth to survive** is seven, born to three women: to Bobbie McCaughey (USA), on 19 November 1997 at Blank Children's Hospital, Des Moines, Iowa, USA, and to 40-year-old Hasna Mohammed Humair (Saudi Arabia) on 14 January 1998 at Abha Obstetric Hospital, Aseer, Saudi

★ OLDEST LIVING PERSON

Yoneko Minagawa (Japan, b. 4 January 1893), became the world's oldest living person aged 114 years 24 days, following the death of Emma Faust Tillman (USA) on 28 January 2007.

Arabia. Eight children were born to Nikem Chukwu (USA), one on 8 December, seven on 20 December, 1998, at St Luke's Hospital, Houston, Texas, USA. The lightest, Odera, died on 27 December, 1998.

• The greatest **officially recorded number of children born to one mother** is 69, to the wife of Feodor Vassilyev (1707–82), a peasant from Shuya, Russia. Over the course of 27 confinements, she gave birth to 16 pairs of twins, seven sets of triplets and four sets of quadruplets.

★ LIGHTEST TWINS

The lowest combined birth weight for surviving twins is 847 g (1 lb 13.57 oz), recorded for Hiba and Rumaisa, born by Caesarean section to Mahajabeen Shaik (India) at Loyola University Medical Center, Maywood, Illinois, USA, on 19 September 2004 (pictured).

The **lightest surviving triplets** – Peyton, Jackson and Blake Coffey (all USA), born by Caesarean at the University of Virginia Hospital, Charlottesville, Virginia, USA, in 1998 – had a combined weight of 1,385 g (3 lb 0.8 oz).

MEDICAL MIRACLES

★ MOST KIDNEY STONES REMOVED

On 27 January 2004, it took surgeons three hours to remove 728 kidney stones from the right kidney of Mangilal Jain (India). The ★ **most kidney stones passed naturally** is 5,704 (as of August 2006) by Donald Winfield (Canada).

★ MOST CORONARY STENT IMPLANTS

Between 8 August 2000 and 30 March 2006, Emil Lohen (USA) had a total of 34 coronary stents implanted. Until then, the most implants carried out at any one time had been six. A stent is a thin tube fed into a blood vessel in order to support or widen it.

★ MOST TUMOURS REMOVED

The most tumours removed in one surgical procedure is eight from Kamala Devi (India), who had a total of 13 tumours in her brain. Dr Krishan Bansal and his team (all India) performed the surgery at the Himalayan Institute Hospital Trust in Dehradun, India, on 22 April 2004.

DID YOU KNOW?
We introduced the **longest time to live with a bullet in the head** record in 2003, following a claim of 53 years from Satoru Fushiki (Japan). Each year since the record was published, a new, older claimant has stepped forward to break it.

YOUNGEST HEART SURGERY PATIENT

A team of 10 doctors at the Childrens Hospital in Boston, Massachusetts, USA, carried out heart surgery on a 23-week-old premature baby named Jack, who was born six weeks early in November 2001 at Boston's Brigham and Women's Hospital.

FIRST SELF-CONTAINED MECHANICAL HEART IMPLANT

Surgeons from the University of Louisville, Kentucky, USA, performed the first self-contained mechanical heart implant on an unnamed American patient at the Louisville Jewish Hospital on 2 July 2001.

★ LONGEST TIME TO LIVE WITH A BULLET IN THE HEAD

William Lawlis Pace (USA) was accidentally shot in October 1917, aged eight. As of September 2006, the bullet remains lodged in the back of his head, 89 years later.

★ YOUNGEST PERSON TO HAVE GALLSTONES AND GALLBLADDER REMOVED

On 1 April 1993, Lindsay Owen (Canada, b. 25 September 1983) was admitted with abdominal pains to Saskatoon City Hospital, Saskatchewan, Canada, to have her gallbladder removed. She was aged just 9 years 189 days.

★ LARGEST OBJECT REMOVED FROM THE SKULL

On 15 August 2003, construction worker Ron Hunt (USA) fell off a ladder and landed face first on a still-revolving 46-cm-long (18-in) drill bit. It passed through his right eye and exited through his skull above his right ear. Surgeons at Washoe Medical Center in Nevada, USA, found that it had pushed his brain tissue aside rather than penetrating it, therefore saving his life.

ACTUAL SIZE

LARGEST
BLADDER STONE REMOVED

A bladder calculus – a stone formed by a build-up of mineral salts – weighing 1.9 kg (4 lb 2 oz) and measuring 17.9 x 12.7 x 9.55 cm (7 x 5 x 3.7 in) was removed from José de Castro da Silva (Brazil) at the Instituto do Câncer Arnaldo Vieira de Carvalho, São Paulo City, Brazil, on 25 August 2003.

★ GREATEST DISTANCE THROWN IN A CAR ACCIDENT

Matt McKnight (USA), a paramedic helping at an accident scene on 26 October 2001, was struck by a car travelling at 112.6 km/h (70 mph) and thrown a distance of 35.9 m (118 ft) along Route 376 in Monroeville, Pennsylvania, USA. He broke his legs and ripped his thigh open to the bone, dislocated both shoulders, suffered a collapsed lung and fractured his pelvis, but made a full recovery and returned to work a year later!

The undiscovered twin of Hisham Ragab (Egypt) was found in 1997... it had been growing inside his own abdomen for a record 16 years!

★ LARGEST TUMMY TUCK OPERATION

Surgeons at the Hospital de Cruces in Barakaldo, Spain, removed an "apron" of fat weighing 60 kg (132 lb) from a woman in March 2006. During the nine-hour operation, small cranes were used to help remove the fat from her stomach, which hung over her waist on to her legs. The amount of weight removed is equivalent to that of an average 17-year-old girl, and had an energy content of 462,000 calories!

FIRST SEPARATION OF CONJOINED TWINS

The earliest successful separation of Siamese twins was performed on xiphopagus (joined at the sternum) girls at Mount Sinai Hospital, Cleveland, Ohio, USA, by Dr Jac Geller on 14 December 1952.

★ FIRST BIONIC ARM RECIPIENT (FEMALE)

The first female to be fitted with a bionic arm is Claudia Mitchell (USA), who lost her left arm at the shoulder in a motorcycle accident. Her new arm was fitted on 14 September 2006 and allows Mitchell to control parts of the limb by thought. She is pictured here with fellow bionic recipient Jesse Sullivan (USA).

★ MOST BLOOD DONATED

Lionel Lewis (South Africa) donated his 376th unit of blood on 29 August 2006. Lewis has high blood pressure and so can donate every six weeks, whereas normal donation is every eight weeks.

HIGHEST BODY TEMPERATURE

Willie Jones (USA) was admitted to hospital on 10 July 1980 with heatstroke on a day when the temperature reached 32.2°C (90°F). His temperature was found to be 46.5°C (115.7°F).

The **highest dry-air temperature endured by heavily clothed men** was measured during US Air Force experiments held in 1960 at 260°C (500°F). Temperatures of 140°C (284°F) can be found in saunas.

★ NEW RECORD
★ UPDATED RECORD

LONGEST...

• ★**Ambulance ride with patient** Ambulix Fire & Rescue (Denmark) delivered a patient a distance of 3,269 km (2,031 miles) in a Mercedes Benz Sprinter 312 Diesel ambulance from Lisbon (Portugal) to Copenhagen (Denmark) on 14–16 October 2004.

• **Ectopic pregnancy** Marina Hoey (UK) gave birth to Sam on 22 May 2002 at the Royal Jubilee Maternity Service, Belfast, after an ectopic pregnancy lasting a record 233 days (33rd week).

• **Iron-lung patient** June Middleton (Australia) has relied on an iron lung to keep her alive since contracting polio in April 1949.

• **Stay in hospital** Martha Nelson (USA) was admitted to the Columbus State Institute for the Feeble-Minded in Ohio, USA, in 1875. She died in January 1975 at the age of 103 years 6 months in the Orient State Institution, Ohio, USA, after spending more than 99 years in various hospitals.

• ★**Kidney dialysis** Brian Tocher (UK) began haemodialysis on 13 June 1966 and continues to be dialysed three times a week. He has undergone two kidney transplants during this time. In total, he has received dialysis for a record total of 33 years.

• **Porcine aortic valve replacement** As of 11 May 2007, Harry Driver of Wetherby, West Yorkshire, UK, was the oldest survivor of a porcine (pig) aortic valve replacement, at the age of 76 years 214 days.

HEALTH & FITNESS

★ LONGEST TIME WITH ILL HEALTH

On average, Mexican women spend 15.3% of their lives in ill health. The world average for women is 12%, according to the Organization for Economic Co-operation and Development (OECD).

Hungarian males are ill for 13.8% of their lives, on average. The world average is 9.8%.

WORLD'S HEAVIEST SMOKERS

This chart is taken from figures published in the OECD's *Health Data 2005* report and shows the top 10 heaviest-smoking nations, based on the number of people who smoke at least one cigarette a day. Austria has the highest number of smokers, with 36.3% of the population – more than 1 in 3.

The world's **largest consumer of cigarettes**, however, is China, where 1,690,000,000,000 are sold every year – one third of all cigarettes consumed annually!

%	Country
28%	DENMARK
28.1%	SPAIN
30.3%	JAPAN
30.4%	SOUTH KOREA
32%	NETHERLANDS
32.1%	TURKEY
33%	LUXEMBOURG
33.8%	HUNGARY
35%	GREECE
36.3%	AUSTRIA

HIGHEST LIFE EXPECTANCY

The country with the highest life expectancy in 2005 – the most recent year for which figures have been recorded – is Andorra, with an average of 83.51 years: 80.6 years for males and 86.6 years for females.

AGEING POPULATION

The country with the ★**largest population of centenarians** (people aged 100 years or above) is Japan, with 25,606 centenarians by the end of September 2005. Evidence suggests that it will extend to 1 million by 2050.

★ LOWEST LIFE EXPECTANCY

Life expectancy in Swaziland has fallen in recent years owing to a combination of poverty and HIV. The average is just 30.8 years, for both men and women.

HEALTH BUDGETS

According to a World Health Organization (WHO) report, the USA has the ★ **highest health budget**. On average, each US citizen received $5,274 (£3,480) of health care in 2002.

North Korea has the ★ **lowest health budget**; on average, its citizens received the equivalent of just $0.30 (£0.19) of care in the same year.

PATIENT-DOCTOR RATIOS

On average, there are 71,958 patients for every doctor in Kinshasa, Congo, the ★ **highest patient-to-doctor ratio**. African nations dominate the chart of patient-doctor ratios, holding the top 13 places.

By contrast, the ★ **lowest ratio of patients to doctor** is in Cuba, where there are just 170 patients per doctor.

DEATH RATES

Swaziland has the ★ **highest rate of death** of any country, with 31.2 deaths per 1,000 population per year, as of 2005. The United Arab Emirates has the ★ **lowest rate of death**, with 1.3 per 1,000.

POPULATION INCREASES

The country with the **highest natural population increase** (births minus deaths) is Somalia, with an estimated increase of 32 per 1,000 people in 2002. The world average for the same year was 12 per 1,000 people.

The countries with the **lowest natural population increase** (i.e. the fastest rate of a decreasing population) were Latvia and Ukraine, both with an increase of -6 per 1,000 people in 2002.

FERTILITY RATES

The country with the **highest fertility rate** – measured in terms of most children per woman – is Niger, with eight in 2004.

Niger is expected to have the world's fastest-growing population later this century, with a predicted increase of 41 million from 12 million (2004) to 53 million (2050).

Hong Kong (China) has the **lowest fertility rate**, with one baby per mother in 2004.

★ MOST PROSTHETICS DONATED

The Prostheses Foundation (Thailand) donated and fitted 664 artificial legs, the most donated by a single organization, in Sanamluang, Bangkok, Thailand, on 16–26 July 2006. The charity was set up in 1992 with a brief to provide free artificial limbs to the poor, regardless of their nationality or religion.

★ HAPPIEST COUNTRY

In a poll by the World Values Survey to establish levels of happiness around the world, people were asked, "Would you say you are very happy, quite happy, not very happy or not at all happy?" The results showed that the world's happiest country was Venezuela – 55% of Venezuelans questioned said they were "very happy". By contrast, just 3% of Latvians thought themselves "very happy", making Latvia the world's ★ **unhappiest country**.

★ NEW RECORD
☆ UPDATED RECORD

GREATEST CONSUMERS OF FAT

The French have the highest average consumption of fat. On average, each person eats 170.8 g (6 oz) daily – the equivalent of more than 10 blocks of lard (pictured) every month!

HIGHEST RATE OF DEATH FROM CANCER

A 2004 OECD report lists the Netherlands as the country with the highest rate of cancer death, with 433 deaths per 100,000.

★ HIGHEST INCIDENCE OF DIABETES

The country with the most type-II diabetes in the population is the United Arab Emirates, where 20% of people aged 20 to 79 years are affected. Two other Gulf states are in the top 10: Kuwait (12.8%) and Oman (11.4%). At joint second are Cuba and Puerto Rico (13.2%).

HIGHEST INCIDENCE OF BREAST CANCER

According to the WHO, Iceland has the highest incidence of breast cancer, with 39.4 women out of 100,000 undergoing treatment.

INFANT MORTALITY RATES

Sierra Leone has the ★ **highest infant mortality rate**, with 159.8 deaths per 1,000 live births, as of 2005.
   Singapore has the ★ **lowest infant mortality rate**, with just three deaths per 1,000 live births.

★ HIGHEST RATE OF ABORTIONS

In Russia, in 2004, there were 1.6 million registered legal abortions. Not only is this the highest figure for any country, and the highest figure per capita, it is also higher than the number of live births in Russia in the same year (1.5 million). According to the federal Statistics Service, Russia's population could plummet dramatically – to just 77 million – by the middle of the 21st century.

★ HIGHEST RATE OF DEATH FROM HEART DISEASE

The country with the most deaths from heart disease is Ukraine, where 686 deaths per 100,000 population are associated with the illness.

★ HIGHEST RATE OF DEATH FROM HIV/AIDS

In Swaziland in 2005, HIV/AIDS was responsible for killing 1,455 people per 100,000 of the population.

★ HIGHEST RATE OF OBESITY

The South Pacific island nation of Nauru (population 13,287) has more obese people per capita than any other country, with 80.2% of men and 78.6% of women totalling a body mass index greater than 30. Neighbouring islands Tonga and Samoa have the next largest populations of obese citizens.

WHO CONSUMES THE MOST...?

Calories On average, US citizens consume 3,774.1 calories every day, the highest in the world. The recommended daily requirement for men is 2,700, and for women, 2,500.

Protein Israel consumes more protein than any other country, according to the United Nations, with every Israeli eating 128.6 g (4.53 oz) every day on average. The world average for protein consumption is 75.3 g (2.65 oz).

Alcohol The country that drinks the highest amount of alcohol per capita is Luxembourg. In 2003, each citizen consumed an average of 12.6 litres (2.8 gal) of pure alcohol. Russia has the **highest consumption of spirits per person**, with every Russian drinking on average 6.2 litres (1.4 gal) of pure alcohol in 2003.

Food Each citizen of Argentina eats, on average, 183% of the UN Food and Agriculture Organization (FAO) minimum daily recommendation.

FANTASTIC FEATS

CONTENTS

LARGEST SCORPION HELD IN THE MOUTH

In August 2006, Guinness World Records travelled to Castaic, California, USA, to meet Dean Sheldon (USA), who held a scorpion measuring 17.78 cm (7 in) in his mouth for a record-breaking 18 seconds!

The journey to the photoshoot was… eventful, shall we say. En route, the emperor scorpion (*Pandinus imperator*) you see here escaped and began scuttling around inside the car – at which point everyone went very quiet. Luckily, it was soon recaptured, so there's no sting in this tale.

YOUNG ACHIEVERS

GAMEKEEPER

On 9 November 2005, at the age of 11 years 312 days, Robert Mandry (UK, b. 1 January 1994) led his first professional shoot at his family's estate on Holdshott Farm, Hampshire, UK. Mandry dedicates most after-school evenings and weekends to gamekeeping, including rearing young birds, controlling vermin and preparing for the next season's shoots.

★ HOLE-IN-ONE GOLFER (FEMALE)

Rhiannon Linacre (UK) was 9 years 75 days old when she scored a hole-in-one at the par-3 17th hole at Coxmoor Golf Club, Sutton-in-Ashfield, Nottinghamshire, UK, on 18 June 2006.

★ FOOTBALL REFEREE

Aged 10 years 358 days, Martin Milkovski (USA) officiated at a football match between Avanza and Orchard Valley in Redwood City, California, USA, on 3 June 2006.

★ FILM DIRECTOR

The youngest director of a professionally made feature-length film is Kishan Shrikanth (India, b. 6 January 1996), who directed *C/o Footpath* (India, 2006) – a movie about an orphaned boy who wants to go to school – when he was nine years old.

★ TOP-FLIGHT NATIONAL LEAGUE FOOTBALLER

The youngest footballer to play in a top-flight national league is Nicolás Millán (Chile, b. 17 November 1991), who competed in Chile's leading division aged 14 years 297 days. He came on as a substitute (in the 79th minute) for his Colo Colo team-mate, Felipe Mella (Chile), in their match against Santiago Wanderers on 10 September 2006.

★ OCEAN ROWER (TEAM)

The youngest person to row an ocean is Martin Adkin (UK, b. 7 January 1986), who rowed the craft *All Relative* across the Atlantic (east to west) with team-mates Justin Adkin, Robert Adkin and James Green (all UK). Martin was aged 19 years 327 days when he left the Canary Islands on 30 November 2005; he and his crewmates finished their trip in Antigua on 8 January 2006.

★ YOUNGEST PERSON TO VISIT THE NORTH POLE

Alicia Hempleman-Adams (UK, b. 8 November 1989) stood at the geographic North Pole at the age of 8 years 173 days on 1 May 1998, the youngest person ever to have done so. She flew to the pole to meet her father, the well-known adventurer David Hempleman-Adams (UK), at the end of his successful trek to the pole.

★ LAURENCE OLIVIER AWARD WINNER

On 26 February 2006, Liam Mower (UK, b. 30 May 1992, above right) became the youngest person to win a Laurence Olivier Award for his performance as Billy Elliot in *Billy Elliot the Musical*, aged 13 years 272 days. Mower shared the award for Best Actor in a Musical with the other two actors who rotated the role: 15-year-olds James Lomas (above left) and George Maguire (centre); it was the first time that such an accolade has been shared. The musical is based on the film *Billy Elliot* (UK, 2000) about a young boy learning ballet.

★ OCEAN ROWERS (TEAM)

The crew of *All Relative* (see opposite page) also set a record for the youngest team of four to row any ocean. Justin Adkin (UK, b. 28 May 1979), James Green (UK, b. 16 February 1981), Robert Adkin (UK, b. 4 June 1982) and Martin Adkin (UK, b. 7 January 1986) rowed the Atlantic east to west between 30 November 2005 and 8 January 2006, with a combined age of 94 years 249 days at the start.

★ TRAVELLER TO EVERY CONTINENT

The youngest person to have travelled to all seven continents is Imogen Grace Barnes (Australia, b. 25 May 2004), who completed her journey at the age of 1 year 240 days on 20 January 2006 in Bangkok, Thailand. She was accompanied by her parents Gregory and Katherine Barnes (both Australia).

ASTRONAUTS

Major Gherman Stepanovich Titov (USSR, b. 11 September 1935) was aged 25 years 329 days when he was launched into orbit in *Vostok 2* on 6 August 1961.

The **youngest woman in space** was Valentina Tereshkova (USSR, b. 6 March 1937), who was 26 years 102 days old when she also became the **first woman in space** on 16 June 1963 in *Vostok 6*.

AUTHORS

The **youngest commercially published author** is Dorothy Straight (USA, b. 25 May 1958), who wrote *How the World Began* in 1962, aged four. Her book was published in August 1964.

Adauto Kovalski da Silva (Brazil) is the ★ **youngest commercially published male author.** His book *Aprender é Fácil* was released on 15 October 2005, when the author was 5 years and 302 days old.

★ ATLANTIC SAILOR (SOLO)

Michael Perham (UK, b. 16 March 1992) left Gibraltar in his boat *Cheeky Monkey* on 18 November 2006, aged 14 years 247 days, and sailed via the Canary Islands and Cape Verde, before heading west, arriving in Nelson's Dockyard, Antigua, on 3 January 2007.

(For more about his amazing trip, see box top right.)

★ NEW RECORD
☆ UPDATED RECORD

JUDGE

At the age of 18 years 11 months, John Payton of Plano, Texas, USA, was elected as a Justice of the Peace. He assumed the post in January 1991.

SKIER ON EVERY CONTINENT

Timothy Turner Hayes (USA, b. 29 July 1991) started skiing at the age of two in Stratton, Vermont, USA. By the age of 13 years 205 days, he had skied on all seven continents: North America (Stratton, Vermont, USA) at the age of two; Europe (Courmayer, Italy) at 10; Oceania (Thredbo, New South Wales, Australia), Antarctica (Argentine Station) and Africa (Oukaimeden, Morocco) at 12; South America (Chile) and Asia (Nagano, Japan) at 13.

MICHAEL MAKES WAVES!

Fourteen-year-old Michael Perham spent six weeks sailing the Atlantic and, when not battling the elements, kept himself busy by catching up on his school homework.

At one point during the journey, rope became entangled in the boat's steering mechanism and he had to jump overboard with a knife between his teeth to clear the obstruction!

His father, Peter – an experienced yachtsman – sailed 3.2 km (2 miles) behind his son throughout the crossing and kept in regular radio contact. They spent Christmas apart, but each released flares to celebrate the occasion.

BODY-PIERCING

Charlie Wilson and Kam Ma (both UK) underwent a total of 1,015 body piercings in 7 hr 55 min at Sunderland Body Art, Sunderland, Tyne and Wear, UK, on 4 March 2006.

BOUNCY-CASTLE

On 7–8 July 2006, a team of seven members of the Executive Committee of the Newman Trust Charity carried out a marathon bouncy-castle session that lasted for 19 hr 45 min at Priory Woods School, Middlesbrough, UK.

CANOEING (24 HOURS)

The greatest distance canoed (or kayaked) on flat water in 24 hours is 241.95 km (150.34 miles) by Carter Johnson (USA) on Lake Merced, San Francisco, California, USA, on 29–30 April 2006.

CARD-PLAYING

Hiebaum Klaus, Arno Krautner, Mellacher Franz, Flucher Friedrich, Finster Ferdinand and Zmugg Manfred (all Austria) played the card game Bauernschnapsen for 109 hr 20 min in Feldkirchen bei Graz, Austria, from 25 to 29 October 2006.

CARROM-PLAYING

On 30–31 July 2005, Atul Kharecha, Narayan Paranjape, Prakash Kagal and Pramod Shah (all USA) played the board game Carrom for a total of 32 hr 45 min at the Indian Association Office, Richardson, Texas, USA.

CELLO-PLAYING

The longest cello marathon lasted 24 hours and was performed by Shamita Achenbach-König (Austria) in Dachau, Munich, Germany, on 5–6 November 2005.

TATTOO SESSION

Stephen Grady and Melanie Grieveson (both Australia) underwent a tattoo session that lasted for a total of 43 hr 50 min, between 26 and 28 August 2006.

The marathon skin-inking was staged at the Twin City Tattoo And Body Piercing, Wodonga, Victoria, Australia.

During her record-breaking achievement, Achenbach-König played a selection of music by Indian composer Sri Chinmoy Kumar.

CONCERTS (24 HOURS)

N. Karthik (India) performed an unprecedented 50 concerts in a 24-hour period at venues in and around Bangalore, India, on 29–30 November 2005.

CRICKET

The longest cricket marathon lasted 33 hr 30 min, and was set by Citipointe Church/Global Care (Australia) at Griffith University, Brisbane, Queensland, Australia, on 10–11 June 2006.

FULL-BODY ICE-CONTACT

Gilberto da Silva Cruz (Brazil) spent a bone-chilling 1 hr 9 min in direct, full-body contact with ice on the set of *Funniest Video Awards* at the Fuji Television Studios, Tokyo, Japan, on 4 February 2006.

LADDER CLIMBING

On 3–4 December 2005, 10 men from The Professional Firefighters of New Zealand recorded the ★ **farthest distance climbed on a ladder by a team in 24 hours**, with a distance of 109.5 km (68.1 miles). On the same date, Shaun Cowan (New Zealand), from the same organization, climbed 12.8 km (7.9 miles) on a ladder, the ★ **farthest distance climbed on a ladder in 24 hours by a man**. The ★ **farthest distance climbed on a ladder in 24 hours by a woman** is 11.5 km (7.1 miles) by Barbara Nustrini (New Zealand), also from the same organization, on the same date. All record breakers achieved their feats in Auckland, New Zealand.

Kym Coberly's (USA) record-breaking hula-hoop marathon lasted 72 hours, from 17 to 20 October 1984

YOUNGEST WOMAN TO COMPLETE A MARATHON ON EACH CONTINENT

On 26 February 2006, aged 26 years 244 days, Karen Zacharias (USA) became the youngest person to complete a marathon on all seven continents.

★ BOARD-GAME

Marcus Stahl, Sascha Walner, Leszek Bajorski and Frank Riemenschneider (all Germany) played the board game Carcassonne for 42 hr 48 min, from 8 to 10 September 2006 in Herne, Germany.

★ KARAOKE (MULTIPLE PARTICIPANTS)

A group karaoke session lasted for 142 hours at an event organized by Karaoke Club Austria. The session ended on Vienna World Records Day, in Austria, on 16 September 2006.

KEYBOARD

Charles Brunner (Trinidad and Tobago) played piano for 64 hours at the Hilton Hotel in Port of Spain, Trinidad and Tobago, from 7 to 9 December 2006.

★ LACROSSE

The Orange and Green teams from MetroLacrosse (USA) played a lacrosse game that lasted 8 hr 16 min at Saunders Stadium, Boston, Massachusetts, USA, on 26 June 2005.

★ MARBLES

Michael Gray and Jenna Gray (both Australia) played a 26-hour game of marbles at First Fleet Park, The Rocks, Sydney, Australia, on 11–12 February 2006.

PEDAL-BOATING

Kenichi Horie (Japan) pedalled a boat 7,500 km (4,660 miles) when crossing the Pacific Ocean between Honolulu, Hawaii, USA, and Naha, Okinawa, Japan, from 30 October 1992 to 17 February 1993. This represents the **greatest distance covered in a pedal-powered boat**.

On 7 May 2005, the Trieste Waterbike Team (Italy) pedalled 177.3 km (110.2 miles) in a boat in Trieste, Italy, the ★ **greatest distance covered in a pedal-powered boat in 24 hours**.

★ ROLLER-COASTER

Stefan Seemann (Germany) rode the Boomerang roller coasters at Freizeit-Land Geiselwind in Geiselwind, Germany, for 221 hr 21 min from 10 to 19 August 2006.

★ SCUBA-SUBMERGENCE

The longest scuba submergence in a controlled environment is 220 hours by Khoo Swee Chiow (Singapore) at Tampines Central, Singapore, from 16 to 25 December 2005.

★ TREADMILL IN 48 HOURS (FEMALE)

Martina Schmit (Austria) covered 309.8 km (192.5 miles) in 48 hours on a treadmill at the Fitness Company, Gitty City, Stockerau, Austria, from 10 to 12 March 2006.

★ TABLE FOOTBALL

Paul Pickering, Patrick Polius, Edward Polius and Luke Smith (all UK, pictured) played table football for 36 hours at Harpars Bar in Horncastle, Lincolnshire, UK, on 26–27 August 2006.

The record equalled that of Jens Rödel, Kalle Krenzer, Steffen Krenzer and Raphael Schroiff (all Germany), who had also achieved a time of 36 hours for a table-football marathon at the YMCA building in Bielefeld, Germany, on 25–26 May 2006.

★ **NEW RECORD**
★ **UPDATED RECORD**

★ LONGEST SKATEBOARD JOURNEY

Dave Cornthwaite (UK) left Perth, Australia, in late August 2006 and arrived in South Bank, Brisbane, Australia, on 22 January 2007, having completed an epic 5,823-km (3,618-mile) trip on his skateboard *Elsa*.

PUSH-UPS

MOST PUSH-UPS	NUMBER	HOLDER	DATE
One year	1,500,230	Paddy Doyle (UK)	Oct 1988–Oct 1989
Five hours (one arm)	8,794	Paddy Doyle (UK)	12 Feb 1996
Five hours (fingertips)	8,200	Terry Cole (UK)	11 May 1996
One hour	3,416	Roy Berger (Canada)	30 Aug 1998
One hour (one arm)	1,868	Paddy Doyle (UK)	27 Nov 1993
One hour (back of hands)	1,781	Doug Pruden (Canada, pictured)	8 Jul 2005
One hour (one arm, back of hand)	677	Doug Pruden (Canada)	9 Nov 2005
One minute (one arm)	126	Jeremiah Gould (USA)	30 Mar 2006
Consecutive, one finger	124	Paul Lynch (UK)	21 Apr 1992
One minute (back of hands)	123	John Morrow (USA)	5 May 2006

FASTEST IRON BAR BENDING

On 17 July 2004, Les Davis (USA) managed to bend a 6-m-long (19-ft 8-in) iron bar with a diameter of 12 mm (0.47 in) and fit it into a suitcase with dimensions 50 x 70 x 20 cm (19.6 x 27.5 x 7.8 in). He achieved this incredible feat of strength in a record 29 seconds at Dothan, Alabama, USA.

GREATEST WEIGHT BALANCED ON THE HEAD

The greatest weight ever balanced on the head and held for 10 seconds is 188.7 kg (416 lb), by John Evans (UK) using 101 bricks at BBC Television Centre, London, UK, on 24 December 1997.

★ HEAVIEST MILK-CRATE STACK BALANCED ON THE CHIN

On 16 June 2006, Ashrita Furman (USA) balanced 17 milk crates – stacked on top of each other and with a total weight of 42.4 kg (93 lb 7 oz) – on his chin for 11.23 seconds in Jamaica, New York City, USA.

★ GREATEST WEIGHT SUPPORTED ON THE SHOULDERS

Franz Müllner (Austria) supported an average of 550 kg (1,212 lb) on his shoulders for 30 seconds while a helicopter landed on a frame which he was partly lifting. The record was achieved during Vienna World Records Day in Vienna, Austria, on 16 September 2006.

★ HEAVIEST CONCRETE BLOCK BREAK ON A BED OF NAILS

Chad Netherland (USA) had 26 concrete blocks weighing a total of 384.65 kg (848 lb) placed on his chest and then broken with a 7.25-kg (16-lb) sledgehammer while he lay on a bed of nails in St Louis, Missouri, USA, on 14 July 2006.

★ MOST CONCRETE BLOCKS BROKEN IN A SINGLE STACK

On 20 January 2007, Narve Læret (Norway) smashed a stack of 21 concrete blocks by hand in Oslo, Norway.

★ HEAVIEST EYELID PULL

On 26 September 2006, Dong Changsheng (China) pulled a 1.5-tonne (3,300-lb) car for about 10 m (32 ft) using ropes hooked on to his lower eyelids. Dong pulled off this feat in a park in Changchun, Jilin Province, China, and attributed his success to Qigong (pronounced "chi-kong", which means "energy cultivation"), a system of deep-breathing exercises.

★ MOST PANES OF SAFETY-GLASS RUN THROUGH

Martin Latka (Germany) ran through a total of 10 panes of safety glass in one minute on 9 September 2006. He set this record on the set of *Guinness World Records: Die größten Weltrekorde* (RTL, Germany) in Cologne, Germany.

★ HEAVIEST DEADLIFT WITH THE LITTLE FINGER

On 11 July 2006, Lu Zhonghao (China) lifted 91.6 kg (201 lb 14 oz) with his little finger in the Tanggu district of Tianjin, China.

★ LONGEST TIME TO RESTRAIN TWO CARS

On 10 October 2006, Tomi Lotta (Finland) succeeded in restraining two cars for a time of 17.36 seconds on the set of *La Nuit Des Records*, Paris, France.

★ VEHICLE PUSHING

Ashrita Furman (USA) pushed a van weighing 2,023 kg (4,460 lb) a distance of one mile (1.6 km) in 21 min 8 sec in Long Island, New York, USA, on 5 October 2006, the ★ **fastest time for an individual to push a car for a mile**.

Krunoslav Budiselic and Mario Mlinaric (both Croatia) hold the record for the ★ **greatest distance to push a car in 24 hours by a pair**.

They pushed a 970-kg (2,138-lb 7-oz) Citroën a distance of 81 km (50.33 miles) around a track at RŠC Jarun, Zagreb, Croatia, on 24–25 September 2006.

★ HEAVIEST VEHICLE PULLED BY RICE-BOWL SUCTION ON THE STOMACH

By pressing a rice bowl on his abdominal muscles, Zhang Xingquan (China) was able to create enough suction to pull a 3,305.5-kg (7,287-lb) vehicle for 10 m (32 ft) on the set of *Zheng Da Zong Yi – Guinness World Records Special* in Beijing, China, on 16 December 2006.

★ MOST PINE BOARDS BROKEN (ONE MINUTE)

Glenn Coxon (Australia) broke 359 pine boards on the set of *Guinness World Records* at Seven Network Studios, Sydney, New South Wales, Australia, on 16 August 2005.

★ GREATEST DISTANCE FIRE-WALKED

Scott Bell (UK) walked 100 m (328 ft) over embers with a temperature of 653–671ºC (1,209–1,241ºF) at Wuxi City, Jiangsu Province, China, on 28 November 2006.

★ MOST KNEE BENDS ON A SWISS BALL

Ashrita Furman (USA) performed 30 knee bends in one minute while standing on a Swiss ball at the Sound One Corporation recording studio, New York City, USA, on 11 September 2006.

★ FARTHEST WASHING-MACHINE THROW

Bill Lyndon (Australia) tossed a washing machine weighing 45.3 kg (99 lb 12 oz) a distance of 3.36 m (11 ft 0.2 in) at the studios of *Guinness World Records*, Sydney, New South Wales, Australia, on 26 June 2005.

★ MOST WEIGHT SQUAT-LIFTED IN ONE HOUR

Stuart Burrell (UK) squat-lifted 8,400 kg (18,519 lb) in one hour at George's Gym in Rayleigh, Essex, UK, on 29 May 2005.

★ MOST WATERMELONS CRUSHED BY FOREHEAD

In one minute, John Allwood (Australia) smashed 40 watermelons with his head in Chinchilla, Queensland, Australia, on 17 February 2007.

FITNESS FANATIC

The **GWR Multi-Discipline Fitness Challenge** requires you to complete as many repetitions as you can of four different exercises, within a time limit of 15 minutes per discipline. Strongman Paddy Doyle (UK), who set the record on 10 April 1994, remains unbeaten with:

• 429 one-arm push-ups
• 400 squat thrusts
• 323 burpees
• 592 alternative squat thrusts.

★ NEW RECORD
★ UPDATED RECORD

SURVIVAL INSTINCT

HIGHEST FALL SURVIVED...

WITHOUT A PARACHUTE

On 26 January 1972, Vesna Vulović (Yugoslavia) was working as an air hostess when the DC-9 she was aboard blew up. She fell inside part of the tail section, which helped her to survive a drop of 10,160 m (33,333 ft; 6.3 miles) over Srbská, Kamenice, Czechoslovakia (now Czech Republic). She broke numerous bones, spent 27 days in a coma, and was hospitalized for 16 months.

WHILE SKIING

In April 1997, at the World Extreme Skiing Championships in Valdez, Alaska, USA, Bridget Mead (New Zealand) fell a vertical distance of nearly 400 m (1,312 ft 9 in), incurring only bruises and concussion.

DOWN A LIFT SHAFT

Betty Lou Oliver (USA) survived a plunge of 75 storeys (over 300 m; 1,000 ft) in a lift in the Empire State Building in New York City, USA, on 28 July 1945, after an American B-25 bomber crashed into the building in thick fog.

HIGHEST PERCENTAGE OF BURNS SURVIVED

David Chapman (UK) became the first person to survive 90% burns to his body after a fuel canister exploded and drenched him with petrol on 2 July 1996. He was taken to St Andrew's Hospital in Essex, UK, where surgeons spent 36 hours removing dead skin. After having skin grafts for nine months in a UK hospital, the 16-year-old flew to Texas, USA, for specialist treatment.

FASTEST MOTORCYCLE CRASH SURVIVED

Ron Cook (USA) crashed a 1,325cc Kawasaki at 322 km/h (200 mph) on 12 July 1998 during time trials at El Mirage Dry Lake in California, USA.

HIGHEST G FORCE ENDURED (NON-VOLUNTARY)

Racing driver David Purley (UK) survived a drop from 173 km/h (108 mph) to zero in 66 cm (26 in) in a crash at the Silverstone Circuit in Northamptonshire, UK, on 13 July 1977. He endured 179.8 g – along with 29 fractures, three dislocations and six heart stoppages.

★ **NEW RECORD**
☆ **UPDATED RECORD**

YOUNGEST CAR-CRASH SURVIVOR

On 25 February 1999, Virginia Rivero from Misiones, Argentina, went into labour at her home and walked to a nearby road in order to hitchhike to hospital. She was offered a lift by two men, but so advanced was her pregnancy that before long she gave birth to a baby girl on the back seat.

When Rivero told the men she was about to have a second baby, the driver overtook the car in front, only to collide with another vehicle. Rivero and her newborn daughter were ejected through the back door of the car, suffering minor injuries, but she was able to stand up and flag down another car, which took them to the hospital. Once there, she gave birth to a baby boy.

MOST LIGHTNING STRIKES SURVIVED

The only person to survive being struck by lightning seven times was ex-park ranger Roy C. Sullivan (USA), the "human lightning conductor".

The history of his lightning liaisons runs as follows: 1942, lost big toe nail; 1969, lost eyebrows; July 1970, left shoulder seared; 16 April 1972, hair set on fire; 7 August 1973, new hair re-singed and legs seared; 5 June 1976, ankle injured; 25 June 1977, chest and stomach burned.

Sullivan died in 1993 – not killed by lightning, but by his own hand, reportedly rejected in love.

★ FASTEST CAR CRASH SURVIVED

In September 1960, during speed trials at Bonneville Salt Flats, Utah, USA, Donald Campbell (UK) crashed his car *Bluebird* while travelling at a speed of 579 km/h (360 mph).

The vehicle rolled over and Campbell fractured his skull, yet against all the odds he survived.

YOUNGEST *TITANIC* SURVIVOR

Millvina Dean (UK, b. 2 February 1912) was just 69 days old when she sailed on the cruiseliner *Titanic* with her parents and 18-month-old brother. Along with her mother and brother, she survived when the ship sank on 14 April 1912, but her father perished.

LONGEST CARDIAC ARREST

Fisherman Jan Egil Refsdahl (Norway) fell into the icy waters off Bergen, Norway, on 7 December 1987 and suffered a four-hour cardiac arrest. He was rushed to nearby Haukeland Hospital after his body temperature fell to 24°C (75°F) and his heart stopped. He later made a full recovery.

MOST...

★ ASSASSINATION ATTEMPTS SURVIVED

In 2006, Fabian Escalante (Cuba), a bodyguard assigned to protect Cuba's president Fidel Castro, announced that there had been 638 assassination attempts on the communist leader.

HANGINGS SURVIVED

Joseph Samuel (Australia) was due to hang for murder in Sydney, Australia, on 26 September 1803, but at the first attempt the rope broke. A second attempt failed when the rope stretched and the victim's feet touched the ground. At the third try, the rope broke again. Samuel was then reprieved.

John Lee (UK) also survived three hangings in Exeter, Devon, UK, in 1885. On each occasion, the trapdoor failed to open. The Home Secretary of the time commuted the sentence to life imprisonment.

LONGEST SURVIVAL...

★ AT SEA IN A ROWBOAT

The longest collective time spent at sea in an ocean rowboat is 940 days, covering 34,238 km (21,275 miles), by Peter Bird (UK) during his rows across the Atlantic (east to west), the Pacific (east to west) and the Pacific (west to east) between 1974 and 1996.

The **longest known time that anyone has survived adrift at sea** is approximately 484 days, by Captain Oguri Jukichi and one of his sailors, Otokichi (both Japan). After their ship was damaged in a storm off the Japanese coast in October 1813, they drifted in the Pacific before being rescued off California, USA, on 24 March 1815.

WITHOUT A PULSE

The longest time anyone has survived without a pulse in their vascular system is three days. Julie Mills (UK) was at the point of death due to severe heart failure and viral myocarditis when, on 14 August 1998, cardiac surgeons at the John Radcliffe Hospital, Oxford, UK, used a blood pump to support her for one week, while her heart recovered.

WITH HEART OUTSIDE THE BODY

Christopher Wall (USA, b. 19 August 1975) is the longest-known survivor of the condition *ectopia cordis*, in which the heart is not located within the chest cavity – in Wall's case, his heart lies outside his body. Most people with this condition do not live beyond 48 hours.

Wall now wears a chest guard to protect his heart from potentially fatal knocks.

★ HIGHEST DEATH TOLL FROM A LIGHTNING STRIKE

Few survival stories are more dramatic than that of Juliane Koepcke (Germany, left), the sole survivor out of 92 passengers after LANSA Flight 508 was struck by lightning and crashed in the Amazon rainforest on Christmas Eve 1971. Several passengers survived the 3-km (2-mile) fall to earth, but only Koepcke was able to leave the crash site to seek help.

Her story was later told in the film *Wings of Hope* (Germany, 2000) directed by Werner Herzog (Germany), who had almost caught the ill-fated flight himself.

OUT OF HELL

Having been taught by her father that settlements may be found by tracking along a water source, Koepcke (see above) followed a stream until she stumbled upon a canoe and shelter that belonged to some local lumbermen. When the men returned and discovered Koepcke, they treated her injuries as best they could before taking her downriver to Tournavista, Peru. From there she was flown to a hospital in Pucallpa, where she was reunited with her father.

UNUSUAL SKILLS

MOST...

LONGEST TIME TO HOLD ONE'S BREATH

On 5 January 2006, Tom Sietas (Germany) held his breath for 14 min 12 sec under 3.05 m (10 ft) of water in Milan, Italy.

★ APPLES CUT IN THE AIR BY SWORD

Kenneth Lee (USA) cut 23 apples in half while they were in the air, in one minute, using a samurai sword, on the set of *Live With Regis & Kelly* in New York City, USA, on 14 September 2006.

★ GRAPES CAUGHT BY MOUTH IN ONE MINUTE

On 21 June 2006, in Jamaica, New York, USA, Ashrita Furman (USA) caught 77 grapes in his mouth in a minute at a distance of 4.57 m (15 ft).

★ ARROWS CAUGHT BY HAND IN TWO MINUTES

Standing at a distance of 8 m (26 ft) from two archers, Anthony Kelly (Australia) caught 36 arrows in two minutes in Beijing, China, on 15 December 2006.

★ BALLS JUGGLED

Tim Nolan (USA) juggled 11 balls simultaneously at the Old Dominion University Fieldhouse in Norfolk, Virginia, USA, on 11 March 2006.

★ HULA-HOOP SPINS IN ONE MINUTE

Leah Black (UK) completed 162 hula revolutions in one minute in London, UK, on 10 April 2006. The **most spins of a giant hula hoop in one minute** is 62 by Laura Rico Rodriguez (Spain) using a 3.5-m-wide (11-ft 6-in) hoop.

★ NAILS BALANCED ON THE HEAD OF ONE NAIL

Daniel Urlings (Luxembourg) balanced 216 nails on the head of a single nail in Walferdange, Luxembourg, on 26 April 2006.

★ RANDOM OBJECTS MEMORIZED

Nischal Narayanam (India) recalled 225 random items in the order that they were read to him at the Hotel Taj Krishna, Hyderabad, India, on 20 August 2006.

★ MOST BRAS UNDONE IN ONE MINUTE

Thomas Vogel (Germany) unfastened 56 bras – using just one hand, as per the rules – in one minute on the set of *Guinness World Records: Die größten Weltrekorde* (RTL, Germany) in Cologne on 9 September 2006. He beat the previous record by 24!

★ YO-YOS SPUN AT ONCE

Eric Lindeen (Sweden) kept nine yo-yos spinning simultaneously, on hooks, at the Gallerian shopping centre in Stockholm, Sweden, on 4 November 2006.

★ TENNIS BALLS HELD IN THE HAND

Arnaud Deschamps (France) held 19 tennis balls in his left hand for 10 seconds in Epône, France, on 22 October 2005.

★ HIGHEST JUMP ON A POGO STICK

On 9 March 2006, Brian Spencer (USA) achieved a jump of 182.88 cm (6 ft) in Mission Viejo, California, USA, using a pneumatically driven "Vurtego Pro" pogo stick.

★ NEW RECORD
★ UPDATED RECORD

MOST MILK CRATES BALANCED ON THE CHIN

Frank Salvatore (USA) balanced 18 milk crates stacked on top of each other with a total weight of 40.3 kg (89 lb) on his chin for 11.53 seconds at Wells Fargo Arena, Tempe, Arizona, USA, on 5 January 2003.

WHISTLE FOR IT!

The ★ **lowest note ever whistled** is the F below middle C, and was achieved by Jennifer Davies (Canada) at the Impossibility Challenger Games in Dachau, Germany, on 6 November 2006.

Davies also holds the record for the ★ **highest note ever whistled** – the third E above middle C – which she set at the same event and on the same date.

★ TIME TO COMPLETE THE GWR THROWING ACCURACY CHALLENGE

Robert Lambert (UK) completed the Guinness World Records throwing accuracy challenge in 1.4 seconds at the Royal International Air Tattoo Show in Swindon, UK, on 16 July 2006.

The challenge involves throwing objects across a distance of 3 m (10 ft) into holes of varying sizes.

★ KNITTER

The fastest knitter is Miriam Tegels (Netherlands), who hand-knitted 118 stitches in one minute at the Swalmen Townhall in the Netherlands on 26 August 2006.

FASTEST...

★ EGG-AND-SPOON MILE

Jonathan Kehoe (USA) ran a mile in 7 min 30 sec while balancing an egg on a spoon in Summerville, South Carolina, USA, on 4 November 2006.

★ METAL DETECTORIST

Sergei Teplyakov (USA) achieved a National Metal Detecting League (NMDL) score of 11 (20 tokens found in 30 minutes) during the 2002 championships in Connecticut, USA.

★ TIME TO BEND 10 NAILS

Chad Netherland (USA) bent 10 nails by hand in 21.13 seconds at the Millennium Hotel and Convention Center in St Louis, Missouri, USA, on 14 July 2006.

DID YOU KNOW?
The message used in the **fastest text message** record is: The razor-toothed piranhas of the genera Serrasalmus and Pygocentrus are the most ferocious freshwater fish in the world. In reality they seldom attack a human.

★ TEXT MESSAGE

Ben Cook (USA) typed a 160-character SMS message (see box, left) on his mobile phone in 42.22 seconds in Denver, Colorado, USA, on 29 July 2006.

The ★ **fastest text sent blindfold** – again, using 160 characters – took Andrea Fantoni (Italy) 1 min 23.5 sec in Milano Marittima, Italy, on 2 September 2006.

★ GREATEST WEIGHT LIFTED BY HUMAN BEARD

Antanas Kontrimas (Lithuania) lifted a girl weighing 63 kg 10 g (138 lb 14 oz) to a height of 10 cm (3.93 in) from the ground on the set of *Guinness World Records – El Show De Los Récords* in Madrid, Spain, on 25 May 2006.

★ FASTEST TIME TO PLACE SIX EGGS IN EGG CUPS USING THE FEET

Contortionist Leslie Tipton (USA) managed to transfer six eggs into six egg cups using her feet in 57 seconds, a feat achieved on the set of *Guinness World Records – El Show de los Récords* in Madrid, Spain, on 11 June 2006.

TRIVIAL PURSUITS

★ MOST SNAILS ON THE FACE

Thomas Vincent (UK) managed to keep seven snails on his face at one time on the set of *Guinness World Records: A Few Records More* (ITV2, UK) at the London Television Studios, London, UK, on 11 September 2004.

FASTEST TIME TO TYPE ONE TO ONE MILLION

Les Stewart (Australia) has typed the numbers one to one million manually, in words, on 19,990 quarto sheets. Stewart began his marathon type-athon in 1982. His target to become a "millionaire" became a reality on 7 December 1998.

Partially paralysed after a tour of duty in Vietnam, he typed with just one finger.

FASTEST TIME TO...

★ ARRANGE A DECK OF PLAYING CARDS

Zheng Taishun (China) arranged a shuffled deck of cards in order (Ace through to Ten, Jack, Queen, King for all suits), using just his hands, in 39.28 seconds in Fuzhou City, Fujian Province, China, on 10 June 2006.

★ COVER 50 M AS A HUMAN WHEELBARROW

Basil and Kerwin Miller (both Barbados) completed 50 m (164 ft) in 15.56 seconds as a human wheelbarrow during the Barbados World Record Festival at the Barbados National Stadium, St Michael, Barbados, on 25 March 2006.

★ PAINT 10-M² WALL

Wilhelm Probst (Austria) painted a 10-m² (107-ft²) wall in 4 min 40 sec on Vienna World Records Day, in Vienna, Austria, on 16 September 2006, in an event organized by bauMax AG.

★ WALK 50 M ON CAN-AND-STRING STILTS

Ashrita Furman (USA) covered 50 m (164 ft) walking on can-and-string stilts in 17.78 seconds on 6 August 2006.

★ PAPER AIRCRAFT ACCURACY

Jon Lewis and Fraser Greenhalgh (both UK) each flew three consecutive paper aircraft into a bucket from a distance of 3 m (9 ft 10 in) at RAF Fairford, Gloucestershire, UK, on 17 July 2004.

★ DRESS A DUVET

Damien Fletcher (UK) put a duvet into its cover – and secured all the press studs in order – in 1 min 2 sec at the Daily Mirror Studios, London, UK, on 4 October 2006.

★ TIE A WINDSOR KNOT

Zvi Dubin (USA) tied a Windsor knot with a necktie, in a professional manner, in 32 seconds, in Teaneck, New Jersey, USA, on 20 August 2006.

> *Thomas Schuster (Germany) snapped 81 bananas in one minute in Flensburg, Germany, on 13 August 2005*

MOST...

★ BIRTH DATES MEMORIZED

Biswaroop Roy Chowdhury (India) memorized 14 birth dates at the Le Meridian Hotel in New Delhi, India, on 20 July 2006.

★ CARTWHEELS PERFORMED IN ONE HOUR

Don Claps (USA) carried out a total of 1,297 cartwheels in one hour outside the set of ABC's *Live With Regis & Kelly* in New York City, USA, on 13 September 2006.

FARTHEST DISTANCE TO SQUIRT MILK FROM THE EYE

Ilker Yilmaz (Turkey) squirted milk from his eye a distance of 279.5 cm (9 ft 2 in) at the Armada Hotel, Istanbul, Turkey, on 1 September 2004. The choice of milk is important to Yilmaz – full-fat milk clogs the tear ducts, so he uses semi-skimmed or skimmed!

★ LONGEST SOCK LINE

A line of socks measuring 1.3 km (0.8 miles) was organized by Wolfgang Zwerger (Germany) in Hechingen, Germany, on 27 May 2006.

★ NEW RECORD
★ UPDATED RECORD

★ PEOPLE TOSSING PANCAKES

A total of 108 members of the Scout Association tossed pancakes simultaneously on *Blue Peter* for Pancake Day on 20 February 2007. The record attempt took place at the BBC Studios, London, UK.

★ ROCK'N'ROLL WINDMILL SPINS IN ONE MINUTE

David Felipe Verche and Monica Martinez Chust (both Spain) performed 49 rock'n'roll "windmills" in one minute on the set of *Guinness World Records – El Show de los Records* in Madrid, Spain, on 4 June 2006.

★ SHEETS OF GLASS PIERCED WITH NEEDLES IN ONE MINUTE

Jiang Zhan (China) pierced 21 sheets of glass with needles in a minute on the set of *Zheng Da Zong Yi – Guinness World Records Special* in Beijing, China, on 15 December 2006.

★ SOAP BUBBLES BLOWN INSIDE ONE LARGE BUBBLE

Sam Sam (aka Sam Heath, UK) from Bubble Inc., blew 49 bubbles inside a larger soap bubble on the set of *Blue Peter* at the BBC Studios, London, UK, on 23 May 2006.

★ COCONUTS SMASHED IN ONE MINUTE

On 13 August 2005, Muhamed Kahrimanovic (Bosnia and Herzegovina) smashed a grand total of 65 coconuts in one minute, using only his hands. The attempt took place at the Tummelum Festival in Flensburg, Germany.

DID YOU KNOW?
The **greatest number of socks worn on one foot** is 74, by Alastair Galpin (New Zealand). He performed his superlative sock-stuffing on 7 November 2006, during Guinness World Records Day in Auckland, New Zealand.

★ KICKS TO THE HEAD IN ONE MINUTE (SELF)

The record for the most consecutive kicks to one's own head in one minute is held by Cody Warden (USA), who kicked himself in the forehead 77 times in succession at Bonifay, Florida, USA, on 29 November 2006. Warden's record is an impressive 20 kicks greater than the record attained by the previous holder!

★ MOST EGGS BALANCED BY AN INDIVIDUAL

Ashrita Furman (USA) balanced 700 eggs vertically on one end at the Rhode Island School of Design, Providence, USA, on 29 October 2006.

★ ORIGAMI CRANES MADE IN FIVE MINUTES

The greatest number of origami cranes created in five minutes is six and was achieved by Eng Tze Hwee (Singapore) at the National University of Singapore on 22 August 2006.

★ LARGEST BALL OF STICKY TAPE

The largest sticky-tape ball weighed 844.59 kg (1,862 lb) and had a circumference of 7.23 m (23 ft 9 in).

It was made by Tim and Ryan Funk (both Canada) and measured in the City of Langley, British Columbia, Canada, on 18 June 2006. The used tape with which the pair created the ball was collected from various ice-hockey teams across the country.

EXCEPTIONAL EXPLOITS

★ NEW RECORD
★ UPDATED RECORD

★ HEAVIEST VEHICLE PULLED BY HOOKS THROUGH THE SKIN

Using two hooks inserted through the skin in the small of his back, Hannibal Helmurto (Germany) pulled a 4-tonne (8,818-lb) van a distance of 91.4 m (300 ft) in Croydon, London, UK, on 24 October 2006. Quite a contrast to his previous job – he was a tax inspector!

FASTEST TIME TO PUSH AN ORANGE ONE MILE USING ONLY THE NOSE

Ashrita Furman (USA) pushed an orange with his nose for a mile (1.6 km) in 24 min 36 sec in Terminal 4 of JFK Airport, New York, USA, on 12 August 2004. He used one green, unripe orange for the attempt, as it was perfectly round and rolled far better than a ripe orange.

HEAVIEST MANTLE OF BEES

On 21 July 1998, at Fair Oaks, California, USA, Mark Biancaniello (USA) was covered by a mantle of bees weighing 39.6 kg (87 lb 6 oz) and comprising an estimated 350,000 bees.

★ LARGEST GAME OF HEAD, SHOULDERS, KNEES AND TOES

To raise money for The Rainbow Trust Children's Charity, 255 participants from Emap Advertising (all Spain) took part in a game of Head, Shoulders, Knees and Toes on 5 May 2006.

★ LARGEST FREE-FLOATING SOAP BUBBLE

The largest free-floating soap bubble had a volume of 2.98 m³ (105.4 ft³) and was made using a wand. It was produced by XTREME Bubbles LLC in Farmington, Minnesota, USA, on 9 October 2005.

GREATEST ALTITUDE REACHED USING HELIUM-FILLED PARTY BALLOONS

Using 1,400 helium-filled toy balloons, Mike Howard (UK, pictured) and Steve Davis (USA) rose to a height of 5,580 m (18,300 ft) near Albuquerque, New Mexico, USA, on 4 August 2001.

★ LONGEST GUM-WRAPPER CHAIN

Gary Duschl (USA) has been making a gum-wrapper chain since 1965. It now measures 15,515 m (50,905 ft) long and features 1,192,492 wrappers.

MOST CONSECUTIVE JUMPS ON A POGO STICK

Gary Stewart (USA) managed 177,737 consecutive pogo jumps at Huntington Beach, California, USA, on 25–26 May 1990.

FARTHEST...

★ DISTANCE BY WATER SLIDE IN FOUR HOURS

On 23 July 2005, Doug Mercer (USA) covered 20,848 m (68,400 ft) in four hours on a water slide at Surf Coaster USA water park, New Hampshire, USA.

★ DISTANCE MOONWALKED IN ONE HOUR

On 10 September 2006, Krunoslav Budiselic (Croatia) moonwalked for 5.255 km (3.265 miles) at the Athletic Stadium Mladost, Zagreb, Croatia.

The **farthest distance moonwalked in 24 hours** is 49.252 km (30.60 miles), by Arulanantham Suresh Joachim (Australia) at The Fregata Restaurant & Night Club, Ontario, Canada, on 11 January 2006.

MOST...

★ AIRCRAFT FLOWN IN AS A PASSENGER

Edwin A. Shackleton (UK) had flown in 841 different types of aircraft as of January 2007. Shackleton made his first flight in 1943 in a De Havilland DH 89 Dominie and has subsequently travelled in balloons, airships, helicopters and microlights.

★ BOOKS TYPED BACKWARDS

Using a computer and four keyboards, Michele Santelia (Italy) typed 57 books in reverse in their original languages (a total of 3,194,024 words) – without looking at the screen – beginning in 1992. The titles Santelia typed include *The Odyssey*, *Macbeth*, *The Vulgate Bible* and the 2002 edition of *Guinness World Records*!

P686 OLH

★LONGEST DISTANCE WALKING OVER HOT PLATES

Rolf Iven (Germany) walked 19.1 m (62 ft 8 in) over hot plates while barefoot on the set of *Guinness World Records: Die größten Weltrekorde* (RTL, Germany) in Cologne, Germany, on 9 September 2006.

BOWLING BALLS STACKED

Dave Kremer (USA) stacked 10 bowling balls vertically on the set of *Guinness World Records: Primetime*, Los Angeles, California, USA, on 19 November 1998.

CHERRY STEMS KNOTTED IN THREE MINUTES

Al Gliniecki (USA) knotted 39 cherry stems in three minutes, using only his tongue at the Guinness World Records Experience in Orlando, Florida, USA, on 26 January 1999.

Gliniecki also holds the record for the **most cherry stems knotted in one hour**, with 911, a feat he achieved on the set of *The Ricki Lake Show* on 4 September 1997.

★CUSTARD PIES THROWN IN ONE MINUTE (TWO PEOPLE)

Kelly Ripa (USA) threw 24 custard pies at Wilma Valderrama (USA), star of *That 70s Show*, on the set of *Live with Regis and Kelly* (ABC) in New York City, USA, on 15 September 2006.

★FASTEST TIME TO CRAWL ONE MILE

Ashrita Furman (USA) – the man who holds the most Guinness World Records, with 54 as of March 2007 – crawled a mile (1.6 km) in 24 min 44 sec at the Beardsley Park in Bridgeport, Connecticut, USA, on 18 October 2006.

★FISH SNORTED IN ONE MINUTE

In fish snorting, the participant sucks a fish up through the back of the mouth and ejects it from a nostril. India's G. P. Vijayakumar is a yoga instructor who honed his fish-snorting skills by practising with peas before graduating to small fish. On 21 July 2005, he managed to snort eight fish in one minute at the Town Hall in Cuddalore, India.

Vijayakumar also holds the record for ★ **most fish snorted in one hour**, with 509.

★KITES FLOWN AT ONCE (INDIVIDUAL)

Ma Qinghua (China) flew 43 kites off a single string in Weifang City, Shandong Province, China, on 7 November 2006.

★PEOPLE SKIPPING ON THE SAME ROPE

On 26 February 2006, 292 participants skipped on the same rope at the College of Engineering, Pune, India.

★POGO-STICK JUMPS IN A MINUTE

Ashrita Furman (USA) performed a total of 234 jumps on a pogo stick in one minute at Chelsea Piers, New York City, USA, on 28 March 2006.

★FARTHEST DISTANCE TO BLOW A MALTESER WITH A STRAW

Using a straw, Wayne Iles (UK) blew a malteser 336 cm (11 ft 0.2 in) on 5 May 2006. The feat took place as part of an event in support of The Rainbow Trust Children's Charity in Barcelona, Spain.

KILLER SNAKE

Jackie Bibby (left) was not alone in his record-breaking attempt. At the same time Rosie Reynolds-McCasland (USA) also sat in a bathtub with 75 live western diamondback rattlesnakes (*Crotalus atrox*), which can grow to 1.98 m (6 ft 6 in). The snake's venom can kill small mammals in minutes.

SHARING A BATH WITH THE MOST RATTLESNAKES

Jackie Bibby (USA) shared his bath with 75 live western diamondback rattlesnakes on 24 September 1999 in Los Angeles, California, USA. The western diamondback is one of the more aggressive species found in North America, and has a toxic venom.

TEAMWORK

★ MOST PEOPLE CRAMMED INTO A MINI

On 17 June 2006, 21 students of INTI College Subang Jaya in Selangor, Malaysia, crammed into an "old style" Mini (below).

The record for the ★ **most people crammed into a "new style" Mini** is 22. It was organized by Ignacio Sáchez Díaz-Calderón for 22 of his friends (all Spain) on the set of *Guinness World Records – El Show de los Records* in Madrid, Spain, on 11 June 2006.

★ LARGEST UNDERWATER DANCE CLASS

A group of 74 students and their instructors conducted an underwater dance class (while wearing weighted scuba equipment) for 13 min 30 sec at the Sydney Olympic Park Aquatic Centre in Sydney, New South Wales, Australia, on 27 October 2006.

★ LARGEST SNOWBALL

Rolled by students of Michigan Technological University in Houghton, Michigan, USA, the world's largest snowball measured 6.48 m (21 ft 3 in) in circumference on 10 February 2006.

★ LARGEST URBAN SCAVENGER HUNT

The largest scavenger hunt game consisted of 116 participants at The Great Gator Hunt, Gainesville, Florida, USA, on 19 November 2005.

★ LARGEST CLAPPERBOARD

A movie clapperboard measuring 3.11 m x 4.00 m (10 ft 2 in x 13 ft 1 in) was created by a team of 10 people for *Une Semaine Chrono* in Vendôme, France, on 29 July 2006.

★ TALLEST STACK OF POPPADOMS

A team from Manchester Confidential, UK – Andrew Mullet, Jayne Robinson, Georgina Hague, Tristan Welch (all UK) – stacked poppadoms to a height of 1.37 m (4 ft 6 in) at an event organized by Scope in Albert Square, Manchester, UK, on 13 October 2006.

★ LONGEST CIGAR

A cigar measuring 41.2 m (135 ft 2 in) – about the length of 515 regular cigarettes – was hand-rolled by Patricio Peña (Puerto Rico) and his team from Don Ray Cigars in Fort Buchanan, Puerto Rico, between 13 and 15 February 2007.

★ LONGEST INLINE SKATING CHAIN

A chain of 280 participants in Padang, Singapore, skated at an event organized by Samsung Asia Pte Ltd (Singapore) on 6 August 2006.

LONGEST...

★ BRA CHAIN

On 30 April 2006, the Cyprus Cancer Patients Support Group in Paphos Harbour, Cyprus, created a bra chain that included 114,782 bras fastened together, which stretched for 111 km (68.9 miles).

★ DISTANCE SPINNING ON STATIC CYCLES BY 100 TEAMS IN 24 HOURS

The record for the farthest distance covered spinning on static cycles by 100 teams in 24 hours stands at 64,524 km (40,093.27 miles) and was set during the CentrO Festival in Oberhausen, Germany, between 30 September and 1 October 2006.

★ HUMAN TEDDY-BEAR CHAIN

A total of 431 people and 430 teddy bears linked hands and paws at an event organized by Unilever GmbH during the Vienna World Records Day in Vienna, Austria, on 16 September 2006.

★ LARGEST COCONUT ORCHESTRA

To celebrate St George (the patron saint of England) and the first anniversary of the UK production of *Spamalot* – the musical "ripped off" from *Monty Python and the Holy Grail* (UK, 1975) – a total of 5,567 fans formed a coconut "orchestra" on 23 April 2007 to accompany "Always Look on the Bright Side of Life". Above is the show's cast with Pythons Terry Jones (left of certificate) and Terry Gilliam (right).

★ JOURNEY ON AN ELECTRIC MOBILITY VEHICLE (TEAM)

John Duckworth, Simon Parrott, David Benham and Geoff West (all UK) travelled from Land's End anticlockwise around mainland UK and back to Land's End on a Horizon Mayan electric mobility scooter from 5 May to 5 August 2004, covering a distance of 5,491 km (3,412 miles).

★ CONCERT BY MULTIPLE ARTISTS

Over 700 solo and group musicians, organized by piano teacher Kuniko Teramura (Japan), took turns playing live music for a total of 184 hours in Hikone, Shiga, Japan, from 23 to 31 March 2007.

★ STRAW CHAIN

Made up of 50,000 drinking straws, the longest straw chain measured 8,582.59 m (28,158 ft). The chain was made by Brad Mottashed, Evgueni Venkov and 18 fellow students (all Canada) of Waterloo University, Ontario, Canada, on 1 April 2006.

MOST...

★ PEOPLE INSIDE A SOAP BUBBLE

Ana Yang (Canada) managed to fit 26 people inside a soap bubble on the set of *Zheng Da Zong Yi* in Beijing, China, on 16 December 2006.

★ DOMINOES TOPPLED

It took a team of 90 builders about two months to set up 4,400,000 dominoes for Domino Day 2006 in Leeuwarden, the Netherlands, on 17 November. In all, a record 4,079,381 "stones" fell.

★ SIBLINGS TO COMPLETE A MARATHON

The 12 Irwin siblings – Frank, Martin, Barry, Margaret, Maria, Geraldine, Patricia, Katrina, Josephine, Veronica, Cecilia and Rosemary (all Ireland) – ran the Dublin City Marathon on 31 October 2005. All completed the marathon in under eight hours.

★ FACES PAINTED IN AN HOUR (TEAM)

A team of five painted a total of 405 different faces, using a minimum of three colours per face, as part of The Rainbow Trust Children's Charity "Day of 1,000 Lions" event held at Longleat House, Wiltshire, UK, on 3 June 2006.

On 17 November 2006, five face painters drew a total of 1,071 different faces, using a minimum of three colours per face, as part of a Children in Need fundraiser held at BBC Birmingham, The Mailbox, Birmingham, UK. This represents the ★ **greatest number of faces painted in four hours by a team**.

★ HEADS SHAVED IN AN HOUR (TEAM)

The greatest number of heads shaved in one hour by a team of 10 hairdressers was 229 at the "Short Cut to the Cure" event at Drill Hall in Wetaskiwin, Alberta, Canada, on 17 June 2006.

★ MOST PEOPLE FIRE-BREATHING

To celebrate the 2006 Burning Man festival in Black Rock City, Nevada, USA, a total of 82 fire-breathers amassed to form "Ocean of Fire II" – the largest simultaneous breathing of fire. The gathering, on August 31, beat the previous attempt – held at Stonehenge in the UK in 2004 – by 12 fire-breathers.

SPEED FREAKS

The ★ **fastest time to hang three strips of wall paper by a team of two** is 2 min 34 sec, and was achieved by Del Dervish and Pas Tullio (both UK) at the BBC Studios, London, on 12 April 2006.

The ★ **fastest time to run 100 miles on a treadmill by a team** (of 12) is 9 hr 47 min 15 sec. The record was set at the Fitness First health club in Luton, UK, on 4 February 2006.

On the same day, and at the same venue, the record for the ★ **fastest time to run 100 km on a treadmill by a team** (of 12) was set, with a time of 6 hr 4 min 30 sec.

RULES FOR MASS RECORDS

• Attendance numbers must be accurately confirmed.
• The two overall independent witnesses must confirm the final figure of total participants.
• Sufficient stewards must be involved to ratify that all the contestants fully participate in the attempt.

★ LONGEST FOOTBALL TABLE

Made by workers of the sheltered workshop at the St John of God's Establishment in Gremsdorf, Germany, the longest table-football table measures 12.26 m (40 ft 2 in) long and can accommodate 40 participants. The game has 80 poles, 234 football figures and 30 balls, and was displayed on 8 June 2006.

MASS PARTICIPATION

LARGEST SMURF GATHERING

On 21 May 2006, the Bay to Breakers Footrace in San Francisco, California, USA, was overrun with 290 people dressed as Smurfs. Each Smurf had a blue-painted face and white hat, as per official Guinness World Records rules.

MOST PEOPLE...

★ NORDIC WALKING
On 22 September 2006, 1,026 people Nordic-walked a minimum of 3 km (1.8 miles) in Lidingöloppet, Sweden.

★ SCUBA DIVING
On 25 February 2006, 958 people scuba dived at Sunlight Thila in Male, Maldives.

★ SHAKING HANDS
A total of 596 couples shook hands for 30 seconds at Lincoln-Way High School, New Lenox, Illinois, USA, on 30 September 2005.

★ TOASTING (SINGLE VENUE)
A total of 13,500 participants toasted in the New Year on 31 December 2005 at the Fremont Street Experience, Las Vegas, Nevada, United States at an event organized by Beaulieu Vineyard (USA).

★ WEARING BALLOON HATS
On 16 August 2006, 1,876 people wore balloon hats at an event organized by United Way and Intel Oregon as part of a Celebrate Hillsboro event in Hillsboro, Oregon, USA.

★ LARGEST GAME OF BINGO

As part of their 20th Anniversary celebrations, the San Manuel Indian Bingo and Casino organized a game of bingo with 53,991 players – all of them spectators at Dodger Stadium in Los Angeles, USA – on 7 July 2006. The stadium was turned into a temporary open-air bingo hall and everyone in attendance received a bingo card to play for three prizes of $10,000, $6,000 and $4,000.

★ WEARING GROUCHO MARX GLASSES
The most people simultaneously wearing Groucho Marx-style glasses, nose and moustache at one location was 1,463 by visitors to the Gorham, Maine Family Festival in Maine, USA, on 30 July 2006.

LARGEST...

★ CAR HORN ENSEMBLE
A cacophony of 19 cars tooted and honked in time during the Vienna World Records Day in Vienna, Austria, on 16 September 2006.

★ CHEERLEADING CHEER
On 7 November 2004, a group of 884 cheerleaders performed a cheer in Baltimore, Maryland, USA.

★ GROUP HUG
On 25 September 2005, a total of 6,623 people gathered in Juárez, Mexico, for a group hug.

★ LANGUAGE LESSON
Thomas Bug and Bastian Sick (both Germany) taught 6,287 participants at the Kölnarena in Cologne, Germany, on 13 March 2006.

★ MASS HANDSTAND
At an event organized by the Braderie Comity of Wevelgem in Wevelgem, Belgium, on 17 September 2006, 399 people stood on their hands.

★ MASS HEADSTAND
On 12 March 2006, 159 people performed a simultaneous unassisted headstand in Mechelen, Belgium.

★ MOST WOMEN BREAST FEEDING SIMULTANEOUSLY

At an event organized by Children for Breastfeeding, Inc. and the City of Manila in partnership with Nurturers of the Earth, a total of 3,541 women breast-fed their children in Manila, Philippines, on 4 May 2006.

★ MOST PEOPLE BRUSHING TEETH SIMULTANEOUSLY

A total of 33,628 people gathered for the Aquafresh Minty Mouth Challenge as part of the BT Giant Sleepover in more than 1,000 locations around the world, on 18 June 2006. The record for the ★ **most people brushing their teeth at a single venue** is 13,380, at the Cuscatlán Stadium (pictured), City of San Salvador, El Salvador, on 5 November 2005.

★ STAND-UP (MULTIPLE VENUE)

On 15–16 October 2006, a staggering 23,542,614 participants in 11,646 events around the globe took part in the United Nations' Millennium Campaign "Stand Up Against Poverty".

★ TUG-BOAT FLOTILLA

A flotilla of 68 tug boats assembled for the ITS Tug Parade in Rotterdam, the Netherlands, on 26 April 2006.

★ PARADE OF BICYCLES

In total, 641 people cycled together for 3.5 km (2.17 miles) in Leiden, the Netherlands, on 29 March 2006.

★ PUB CRAWL

A pub crawl of 2,237 "crawlers" visited 17 pubs in Maryborough, Queensland, Australia, on 11 June 2006 in an event arranged by the World's Greatest Pub Crawl Committee (Australia).

★ LONGEST LINE OF FLOATING AIR BEDS (LILOS)

A continuous line of 863 air beds – each with a participant on board – was assembled as part of the Coogee Arts Festival at Coogee Beach, Sydney, Australia, on 26 January 2006.

LATEST GREATEST GATHERINGS

EVENT	PARTICIPANTS	COUNTRY	DATE
★ Tree planting (24 hours) (total planted: 254,464) (picture 1)	300	India	1–2 Oct 2005
★ 5-km run (2)	101,246	UK	4 Jun 2006
★ Longest drawing (3) (length: 3,839 m; 12,595 ft)	900	Japan	1 Oct 2005
★ Pumpkin carving (4)	118	USA	28 Oct 2006
★ Golf cart parade (5)	3,321	USA	4 Sep 2005
★ Skipping (6)	7,632	UK	24 Mar 2006
★ Snow angels (7)	8,962	USA	17 Feb 2007
★ Drum ensemble (8)	7,951	India	28 Oct 2006
★ Bunny hop (9)	1,879	USA	15 Apr 2006
★ Music lesson (10)	539	Switzerland	12 May 2006
★ Sing-along	293,978	UK	9 Dec 2005
★ Champagne cork-popping	410	Germany	16 Jul 2005
★ Game of musical bumps	137	UK	17 Sep 2006
★ Game of musical statues	265	Spain	5 May 2006
★ Quiz	1,263	Australia	14 Jun 2006
★ Hora dance	13,828	Romania	24 Jan 2006
★ Didgeridoo ensemble	238	UK	5 Aug 2006
★ Longest line of footprints (length: 4,484 m; 14,711 ft)	15,200 prints	Australia	10 Dec 2005
★ Longest line of hand prints (length: 35,502.5 m; 116,478 ft)	119,537 prints	Germany	6 Oct 2005

★ **NEW RECORD**   ★ **UPDATED RECORD**

EPIC ENDEAVOURS

CONTENTS

LONGEST SWIM
UNDER ICE
WITH BREATH HELD

The ultimate sub-zero swimming champion is Wim Hof (Netherlands). Without using any special equipment, and wearing only bathing trunks and goggles, Hof has managed to swim 57.5 m (188 ft 7 in) under ice in just 1 min 1 sec. To do so, he endured a "bracing" water temperature of -6ºC (21.2ºF).

CROSSING THE SEAS

★ FIRST OCEAN FOUR TO ROW THE ATLANTIC WEST TO EAST

The first Ocean Four to row the Atlantic West to East from the USA was the crew of *Vopak Victory*: Gijs Groeneveld, Robert Hoeve, Jaap Koomen and Maarten Staarinnk (all Netherlands). They achieved this feat on 27 June 2005, and in doing so achieved the **fastest recorded time** for this route: 60 days 16 hr 19 min.

★ FIRST MOTHER-AND-DAUGHTER TEAM TO ROW ACROSS ANY OCEAN

Sarah and Sally Kettle (both UK) rowed across the Atlantic East to West in *Calderdale – Yorkshire Challenger* between 20 January and 5 May 2004.

FIRST PERSON TO ROW AN OCEAN TWICE IN A YEAR

Michael Perrens (UK) crossed the Atlantic East to West in *Carpe Diem* between 20 January and 8 March 2004 and again in *Britannia Endeavour* between 12 November and 23 December 2004.

★ SMALLEST ROWING BOAT TO CROSS AN OCEAN

The smallest ocean rowing boat to successfully cross any ocean is *Alison May*, which measured 4.87 m (16 ft) long, and was rowed by Matthew

FIRST MOTHER-AND-SON TEAM TO ROW ACROSS ANY OCEAN

Between 12 October 1997 and 21 January 1998, Jan Meek and Daniel Byles (both UK) rowed the Atlantic East to West. They started their journey in Los Gigantes in the Canary Islands and rowed to Barbados, West Indies, in *Carpe Diem*.

Boreham (UK) across the Atlantic East to West solo between 20 January and 13 April 2004.

FIRST WOMAN TO ROW ANY OCEAN

Sylvia Cook rowed the Pacific East to West along with John Fairfax (both UK) in *Britannia II* between 26 April 1971 and 22 April 1972, becoming the **first ever to row across the Pacific**.

★ OLDEST FEMALE TO ROW AN OCEAN

The oldest female ocean rower – and the first British woman to row any ocean solo – is Diana Hoff (UK, b. 1 May 1944), who rowed the Atlantic East to West solo in *Star Atlantic II* between 13 September 1999 and 5 January 2000. She was 55 years 152 days old at the outset.

FASTEST ROWING ACROSS THE ATLANTIC

• The **fastest row ever recorded for crossing the Atlantic in any direction land to land** is 35 days 8 hr 30 min, a record held by the 11-man crew of *La Mondiale*. The French team rowed East to West from Santa Cruz de la Palma in the Canary Islands to Martinique, West Indies, between 25 March and 29 April 1992.

• The **★fastest Ocean Four to row across the Atlantic West to East from Canada** was the crew of Naturally Best – George Rock, Robert Munslow, Nigel Morris and Steve Dawson (all UK) – in a time of 39 days 22 hr 10 min 30 sec between 31 May and 10 July 2005. They were also the **★first Ocean Four to row the Atlantic West to East from Canada**.

★ FARTHEST MONOHULL SAILING IN A DAY

ABN Amro Two, skippered by Sebastien Josse (France), sailed 562.96 nautical miles (1,042.6 km; 647.8 miles) in 24 hours at an average speed of 23.45 knots during the second leg (Cape Town to Melbourne) of the Volvo Ocean Race in the Southern Ocean on 11 January 2006.

SOLO OCEAN ROWERS

FIRST PERSON TO ROW...	RECORD HOLDER	DATE
Any ocean (Atlantic East to West)	John Fairfax (UK)	20 Jan–9 Jul 1969
Pacific East to West	Peter Bird (UK)	23 Aug 1982–14 Jun 1983
Pacific West to East	Gerard d'Aboville (France)	11 Jul–21 Nov 1991
Atlantic West to East from USA	Gerard d'Aboville (France)	10 Jul–20 Sep 1980
Atlantic West to East from USA land to land	Oliver Hicks (UK, pictured)	27 May–28 Sep 2005
★ Atlantic West to East from Canada land to land	Robert Munslow (UK)	27 Jun–30 Aug 2006
★ Atlantic East to West, Europe to South America	Stein Hoff (Norway)	10 Aug–14 Nov 2002
★ Atlantic East to West, Spain to West Indies	Leven Brown (UK)	26 Aug 2005–26 Jan 2006

★ FASTEST OVERALL TRANSATLANTIC SAILING

Bruno Peyron (France) and the crew of *Orange II* crossed the Atlantic in 4 days 8 hr 23 min 54 sec, reaching Lizard Point, Cornwall, UK, from Ambrose Light Tower, New York City, USA, on 7 July 2006. *Orange II* also set a new 24-hour sailing record of 766 nautical miles (1,420 km; 882 miles).

★ FASTEST SOLO ROW ACROSS THE ATLANTIC WEST TO EAST

Emmanuel Coindre (France) rowed from Cape Cod, Massachusetts, USA, to Île d'Ouessant, France, in 62 days 19 hr 48 min from 9 July to 10 September 2004 – a distance of around 3,400 nautical miles (6,300 km; 3,900 miles).

• The ★ **first** and ★ **fastest Ocean Four to row across the Atlantic East to West** were Shaun Barker, Jason Hart, Phil Langman and Yorkie Lomas (all UK) on *Queensgate*, in 36 days 59 min between 20 January and 26 February 2004.

• The **first person to row across the Atlantic West to East solo from USA land to land** is Oliver Hicks (UK), who rowed *Miss Olive, Virgin Atlantic* between 27 May and 28 September 2005, aged 23 years 175 days (at the start). He rowed from Atlantic Highlands, New Jersey, USA, to St Mary's, Isles of Scilly, UK, in 123 days 22 hr 8 min. Hicks, pictured above right, is also the **youngest person to row any ocean solo**.

• The **youngest person to row across the Atlantic East to West solo** is Sam Knight (UK, b. 19 June 1980), who rowed *Pacific Pete TNT*, leaving La Gomera, Canary Islands, on 20 January 2004, aged 23 years 214 days, and arriving in Barbados on 19 March 2004.

• The **first Ocean Four to row the Atlantic West to East from USA land to land**, from Liberty Island, New York, USA, to Port Pendennis Marina, Falmouth, UK, were Jordan Hanssen, Dylan Le Valley, Brad Vickers and Greg Spooner (all USA, right), between 10 June and 20 August 2006, in a time of 71 days 3 hr 22 min 35 sec.

OCEAN ROWING SOCIETY

Guinness World Records only accepts ocean-rowing records ratified by the Ocean Rowing Society. Prior to this, we were indebted to Squadron Leader D. H. "Nobby" Clark, DFC, AFC, who began ratifying rowing records for the founders of the book, Ross and Norris McWhirter, in 1967.

Today, Nobby's accumulated facts and statistics on ocean rowing can be found on the ORS's website, www.oceanrowing.com, which continues to monitor attempts at crossing the oceans by rowing boat.

At the time of going to press, at least 21 ocean-rowing attempts were underway or planned for 2007 – look out for potential new records from a team of four British police officers attempting the fastest row across the Atlantic; the first American to row solo from the USA to Europe; the first woman to row solo across the Pacific; and the British women's record for rowing across the Atlantic. Good luck from everyone at Guinness World Records!

REACHING THE POLES

★ FIRST MARRIED COUPLE TO REACH BOTH POLES UNASSISTED

After setting off from Ward Hunt Island, Canada, on 22 March 2002, Thomas and Tina Sjögren (Sweden) walked unassisted to the North Pole, arriving there on 29 May 2002. Only a few weeks earlier, on 1 February 2002, they had also arrived unaided at the South Pole.

★ MOST POLAR EXPEDITIONS

Paul Landry (Canada) has completed seven successful treks to the North and South poles: he visited the magnetic North Pole in April 1998 and the geographic North Pole in April 2000, April 2001 and April 2002. He reached the geographic South Pole in January 2002, January 2003 and January 2005. At the time of going to press (April 2007), he was on his fourth trip to the geographic North Pole.

SOUTH POLE

FIRST PERSON TO REACH THE SOUTH POLE

A Norwegian party of five men led by Roald Engebereth Gravning Amundsen reached the pole at 11 a.m. on 14 December 1911 after a 53-day march with dog sledges.

★ FIRST SOLO JOURNEY

At the age of 29, Erling Kagge (Norway) became the first person to reach the South Pole after a solo and unsupported trek on 7 January 1993. His 1,400-km (870-mile) journey from Berkner Island took 50 days.

FIRST MOTHER AND SON TO REACH A POLE

At 9:15 p.m. local time (GMT 5 a.m.) on 2 May 2007, Daniel Byles and his mother Jan Meek (both UK) reached the magnetic North Pole (N 78° 35.724′, W 104° 11.940′) following a 24-day trek on foot and skis from Resolute Bay in Canada – a journey of around 560 km (350 miles). *Read about the pair's ocean-rowing record on p.94.*

FIRST CROSSING OF THE ANTARCTIC CONTINENT

A party of 12 led by Sir Vivian Ernest Fuchs (UK) completed a crossing of the surface of the Antarctic continent at 1:47 p.m. on 2 March 1958, after a trek of 3,473 km (2,158 miles) lasting 99 days from 24 November 1957. The crossing was from Shackleton Base to Scott Base via the pole.

FASTEST SOLO KITE-ASSISTED JOURNEY

The fastest unpowered journey to the pole (solo) was made by explorer Børge Ousland (Norway), who skied – with assistance from a parafoil kite – in 34 days from 15 November to 19 December 1996. The journey was unsupported – i.e., he received no outside assistance. Ousland also achieved the **fastest** and **first solo and unaided crossing of Antarctica** from 15 November 1996 to 18 January 1997.

FIRST BALLOON FLIGHT OVER THE SOUTH POLE

Balloonist and adventurer Ivan André Trifonov (Austria) floated over the South Pole at an altitude of 4,571 m (15,000 ft) on 8 January 2000.

★ **NEW RECORD**
UPDATED RECORD

FASTEST OVERLAND JOURNEY TO THE SOUTH POLE

The fastest overland journey to the South Pole from Patriot Hills on the Antarctic coastline took 69 hr 21 min on 9–12 December 2005, by a team of five drivers – Jason De Carteret, Andrew Regan, Richard Griffiths, Andrew Moon (all UK) and Gunni Eglis (Iceland) – using a modified 6x6 vehicle.

NORTH POLE

FIRST TO REACH THE NORTH POLE

Explorer Robert Peary (USA) is widely regarded as the first person to have reached the North Pole. Peary set off from Ellesmere Island, Canada, on 1 March 1909 with his close associate Matt Henson (USA), and on 6 April made observations indicating that he had reached his destination. Although rival explorer Frederick Cook (USA) challenged his claim and asserted that he had reached the pole first earlier that month, the US Congress acknowledged Peary's achievement in 1911.

DID YOU KNOW?
The vehicle above had air suspension (metal gets too cold and brittle) and was fitted with huge 111-cm (44-in) tyres that create as much contact with the ground as possible.

★ FIRST UNDISPUTED SURFACE JOURNEY TO THE NORTH POLE

Expedition leader Ralph Plaisted (USA), accompanied by a team of three, reached the North Pole across the sea ice on 19 April 1968 after a 42-day snowmobile trek.

FASTEST SKI JOURNEY TO THE NORTH POLE (FEMALE)

Catherine Hartley and Fiona Thornewill (both UK) skied to the North Pole (supported) in 55 days from 11 March to 5 May 2001, after setting out from Ward Hunt Island, Northwest Territories, Canada.

★ YOUNGEST PERSON TO WALK TO THE NORTH POLE

On 10 April 2006, 14-year-old Jordan Maguire (UK, b. 23 August 1991) set off on foot from the Borneo air base in Russia and walked 178 km (111 miles) to the North Pole, arriving 10 days later.

★ MOST NORTHERLY MARATHON

The North Pole Marathon has been held annually since 2002, and the course at the geographic North Pole has been certified by the Association of International Marathons and Road Races. The fastest men's completion time to date is 3 hr 36 min 10 sec by Thomas Maguire (Ireland) in the 2007 marathon, and the fastest woman is Susan Holliday (UK) in 6 hr 17 min 40 sec, also in 2007.

POLE TO POLE

Marek Kamiński (Poland) completed a solo unsupported walk to the North Pole on 23 May 1995, and an unsupported walk to the South Pole on 27 December 1995, the ★ **first person to trek to both poles unsupported**.

Thomas and Tina Sjögren (Sweden) reached the South Pole on 1 February 2002, and the North Pole by 29 May 2002 – the ★ **shortest time between walking to both poles**.

The **first person to walk to both poles** was Robert Swan (UK). His team reached the South Pole on 11 January 1986; he arrived at the North Pole three years later on 14 May 1989.

★ FASTEST SOLO UNSUPPORTED TREK TO THE SOUTH POLE

Hannah McKeand (UK) skied her way to the South Pole from the Hercules Inlet at the edge of the Antarctic continent in 39 days 10 hr 33 min between 19 November and 28 December 2006. The former marketing manager made the journey – in 24-hour sunshine – without resupplies. She ate noodles for breakfast and freeze-dried meals for dinner, and snacked throughout the day on chocolate, salami and the explorer's favourite, Kendal mint cake.

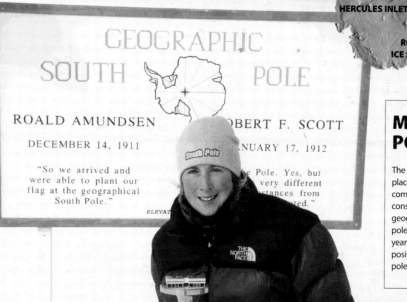

GEOGRAPHIC SOUTH POLE

ROALD AMUNDSEN
DECEMBER 14, 1911

"So we arrived and were able to plant our flag at the geographical South Pole."

ROBERT F. SCOTT
JANUARY 17, 1912

The Pole. Yes, but very different from what was expected.

HERCULES INLET
SOUTH POLE
ROSS ICE SHELF
1909 1931 1952 1962 1990 2005

MAGNETIC POLES

The Earth's magnetic poles are the places towards (and from) which a compass points, and are located a considerable distance from the geographic poles. The magnetic poles "wander" slowly over the years, constantly changing position. (See above for how the poles have shifted since 1909.)

SCALING THE HEIGHTS

MURDEROUS MOUNTAIN

On 13 July 1990, 43 people were killed in a massive ice and snow avalanche on Peak Lenin on the border between Tajikistan and Kyrgyzstan. Only two climbers survived this, the **worst mountaineering disaster** ever.

★ MOST CONQUESTS OF EVEREST

Apa Sherpa (Nepal, centre) reached the summit of Mount Everest for the 16th time on 19 May 2006, the most times anyone has ever successfully climbed the world's **highest mountain**, at 8,848 m (29,028 ft).

EVEREST

FIRST ASCENT

Mount Everest (8,848 m; 29,028 ft) was first climbed at 11:30 a.m. on 29 May 1953, when the summit was reached by Edmund Percival Hillary (New Zealand) and Sherpa Tenzing Norgay (Nepal). The successful expedition was led by Col. (later Hon. Brigadier) Henry Cecil John Hunt (UK).

FIRST ASCENT WITHOUT OXYGEN

Reinhold Messner (Italy) and Peter Habeler (Austria) made the first successful ascent of Mount Everest without supplemental oxygen on 8 May 1978. This feat is regarded by some purist mountaineers as the first "true" ascent of Everest, since overcoming the effects of altitude (i.e. the low oxygen content of the air) is the greatest challenge facing high-altitude climbers.

FIRST SOLO SUMMIT

Reinhold Messner (Italy) was the first to successfully climb Mount Everest solo, reaching the summit on 20 August 1980. It took him three days to make the ascent from his base camp at 6,500 m (21,325 ft), and the climb was made all the more difficult by the fact that he did not use bottled oxygen.

LONGEST STAY ON SUMMIT

Babu Chhiri Sherpa of Nepal completed a stay of 21 hours at the summit of Mount Everest without the use of bottled oxygen in May 1999.

KILIMANJARO

FASTEST ASCENT

Sean Burch (USA) ran the 34 km (21.1 miles) from the base to the summit of Mount Kilimanjaro, Tanzania (altitude 5,895 m; 19,340 ft), in 5 hr 28 min 48 sec on 7 June 2005, the fastest anyone has climbed Africa's highest peak.

WALKING BACKWARDS

From 20 to 23 July 1997, Jurgen Gessau (South Africa) climbed to the summit of Mount Kilimanjaro in 72 hours, walking backwards from Marangu Gate to Ulhuru Peak.

★ YOUNGEST CLIMBER OF EL CAPITAN

At 1,095 m (3,593 ft) tall, El Capitan in Yosemite National Park, California, USA, is the **tallest granite monolith** in the world. A prow between its two faces, known as the Nose, is the most popular choice for climbers wishing to summit "El Cap". On 8–9 September 2001, Scott Cory (USA) became the youngest person to climb the Nose, aged 11 years 110 days. On 2 October 2001, he tackled El Cap again and became the ★ **youngest to ascend in one day**, aged 11 years 133 days. Pictured is Cory in March 2006, bouldering in Red Rock, Nevada, USA.

K2

FIRST ASCENT

K2 is situated in the Karakoram mountain range on the border between Pakistan and China. At 8,611 m (28,251 ft), it is the world's second highest mountain. The first successful ascent of K2 was achieved by Achille Compagnoni and Lino Lacedelli (both Italy) on 31 July 1954. They were members of an Italian expedition led by Ardito Desio (Italy).

FIRST ASCENT BY A WOMAN

Wanda Rutkiewicz (Poland) reached the summit of K2 on 23 June 1986, becoming the first woman to do so.

FASTEST
SEVEN SUMMITS BY A WOMAN

Joanne Gambi (UK, pictured here with her husband, Rob) climbed the highest peak on each continent in 799 days, starting with Mt McKinley, Alaska (North America), on 12 June 2003, and finishing at Puncak Jaya, Indonesia, (Oceania) on 19 August 2005.

The **first person to successfully climb the Seven Summits** was Patrick Morrow (Canada), who completed the last, Ngga Pulu, Indonesia (Oceania), on 7 May 1986.

★ NEW RECORD
UPDATED RECORD

OTHER PEAKS

PEAKS OVER 8,000 M

When Reinhold Messner (Italy) summited Lhotse (8,501 m; 27,890 ft) on the Nepal–Tibet border on 16 October 1986, he became the **first person to climb the world's 14 peaks over 8,000 m** (26,246 ft). His quest had started in June 1970. The difficulty of this feat is illustrated by the fact that by the second half of 2005, only 12 people had achieved it.

Jerzy Kukuczka (Poland) climbed the 14 peaks higher than 8,000 m (26,246 ft) in 7 years 11 months 16 days, starting on 4 October 1979 and finishing on 18 September 1987. This is the **fastest ascent** ever of these peaks.

★ OLDEST EVEREST CLIMBER

Takao Arayama (Japan, b. 4 October 1935) reached the 8,848-m-high (29,028-ft) summit of Everest on 17 May 2006, aged 70 years 225 days. Arayama was only three days older than the previous record-holder.

CANADIAN HIGHPOINTS

Jack Bennet (Canada) climbed the highest points in each of the 13 Canadian provinces and territories, including the new Inuit territory of Nunavut, which is 837 km (520 miles) from the North Pole. It took 5 years 361 days to complete all the climbs, with the final summit reached on 15 June 1998.

EUROPEAN HIGHPOINTS

Rob Baber (UK) reached the highest point in each of the 47 European countries in the 835 days between 2 May 1998 and 14 August 2000. He began with Iceland's highest point, Hvannadalshnúkur, and finished with Mount Ararat, Turkey.

★ LARGEST SIMULTANEOUS CLIMB

During the Big Event on 10 September 2000, a record 600 people simultaneously scaled 112 mountains in the UK and Ireland.

★ FASTEST CLIMB OF EVEREST AND K2 WITHOUT OXYGEN

In 2004, Karl Unterkircher (Italy) became the first mountaineer ever to summit the world's two highest mountains, Mount Everest and K2 (pictured), in the same season without bottled oxygen. He repeated this feat between 24 May and 26 July 2006 – a record of 63 days.

CIRCUMNAVIGATING THE GLOBE

FASTEST SOLO SAILOR

Ellen MacArthur (UK, above) sailed solo and non-stop around the world in 71 days 14 hr 18 min from 28 November 2004 to 7 February 2005 in the trimaran *B&Q*. She set sail from Ushant, France, rounded the Cape of Good Hope, sailed south of Australia and rounded Cape Horn before heading back up to Ushant.

LAND

FASTEST BY CAR

The record for the first and fastest man and woman to have circumnavigated the Earth by car covering six continents under the rules applicable in 1989 and 1991 embracing more than an equator's length of driving (40,075 km; 24,901 road miles), is held by Saloo Choudhury and his wife Neena Choudhury (both India). The journey took 69 days 19 hr 5 min from 9 September to 17 November 1989. The couple drove a 1989 Hindustan "Contessa Classic" starting and finishing in Delhi, India.

FASTEST BY BICYCLE

Steven Strange (UK) cycled around the world in a time of 276 days 19 hr 15 min between 9 May 2004 and 13 February 2005, having cycled a total of 29,651 km (18,424 miles) and travelled over 40,100 km in total (including transfers). His journey started and finished in Vancouver, Canada.

LOWEST FUEL CONSUMPTION

Starting on 17 January 2006, John and Helen Taylor (UK and Australia, respectively) drove an unmodified Volkswagen Golf FSI a minimum distance of 28,970 km (18,000 miles) in 78 days. The couple used just 1,303 litres (286 gal) of petrol, which works out at an incredibly low fuel-consumption rate of 22.2 km per litre (63 miles per gal).

AIR

FASTEST BY HELICOPTER (FEMALE)

Jennifer Murray (UK) piloted her Robinson R44 helicopter around the world in 99 days from 31 May to 6 September 2000, at an average speed of 16.99 km/h (10.55 mph). The journey started and finished at Brooklands airfield in Surrey, UK, and crossed 30 countries.

FASTEST BY MICROLIGHT

Colin Bodill (UK) circumnavigated the globe in his Mainair Blade 912 Flexwing microlight aircraft (above) in 99 days from 31 May to 6 September 2000, starting and landing at Brooklands airfield, Weybridge, Surrey, UK. Bodill flew alongside Jennifer Murray on her successful solo helicopter circumnavigation (see left). The pair covered approximately 35,000 km (21,750 miles), across 30 countries.

FASTEST BY SCHEDULED FLIGHTS

The fastest time to fly around the world on scheduled flights, according to the FAI definition, is 44 hr 6 min by David J. Springbett (UK). His 37,124-km (23,068-mile) route took him from Los Angeles, USA, eastabout via London, Bahrain, Singapore, Bangkok, Manila, Tokyo and Honolulu on 8–10 January 1980.

★ FASTEST NON-STOP WESTBOUND SAIL (SOLO FEMALE)

The fastest female to sail around the world westbound, non-stop, solo and unsupported is Dee Caffari (UK) in *Aviva*, a 22-m (72-ft) monohull. She took 178 days 3 hr 5 min 34 sec to sail back to her starting point in Portsmouth, UK, between 20 November 2005 and 18 May 2006.

★ FASTEST NON-STOP WESTBOUND SAIL (SOLO MALE)

Sailing non-stop, solo and unsupported, Jean-Luc Van Den Heede (France) set off in *Adrien* on 7 November 2003. It took 122 days 14 hr 3 min 49 sec for him to cross the Lizard Point-Ushant finishing line on 9 March 2004.

FASTEST BY AEROPLANE VIA BOTH POLES

The fastest aerial circumnavigation of the Earth via both geographical poles is 54 hr 7 min 12 sec (including refuelling stops) by a Boeing 747 SP piloted by Captain Walter H. Mullikin (USA) between 28 and 31 October 1977. The journey started and finished in San Francisco, USA, stopping off in Cape Town, South Africa, and Auckland, New Zealand.

★ DEEPEST WAVE-PIERCING POWERBOAT

The world's most efficient wave-piercing powerboat – one that cuts through waves rather than riding over the top – is *Earthrace*, a 24-m-long (78-ft) trimaran that can submarine through waves at record depths of 7 m (23 ft). Skippered by Pete Bethune (New Zealand), *Earthrace* set out to break the powerboat circumnavigation world record (using only renewable fuels) on 10 March 2007.

★ FASTEST BY SCHEDULED FLIGHTS WITH A SINGLE AIRLINE

Between 21 and 24 November 2006, Brother Michael Bartlett (UK) circumnavigated the globe on scheduled Air New Zealand flights, taking just 59 hr 58 min.

SEA

FIRST EVER

The first ever world circumnavigation was accomplished when *Vittoria*, under the command of navigator Juan Sebastian de Elcano (Spain), sailed into Seville, Spain, on 9 September 1522. The ship had set out along with four others as part of an expedition led by Ferdinand Magellan (Portugal) in 1519. *Vittoria* was the only ship to survive – of the 239 Europeans who set out, only 17 returned. Magellan had been killed in a squabble in the Philippines in 1521.

> *The only person to circumnavigate the globe solo in a balloon is Steve Fossett (USA) – it took him 13 days 8 hours in 2002*

★ YOUNGEST SOLO SAILOR

The youngest person to circumnavigate the globe, sailing solo, non-stop and unsupported, is Jesse Martin (Australia, b. 26 August 1980), who sailed in *Lionheart* from New South Wales, Australia, on 8 December 1998, aged 18 years 104 days. He returned on 31 October 1999, taking 327 days 12 hr 52 min.

FASTEST (CREW)

A crew of 14 captained by Bruno Peyron (France) sailed around the world in 50 days 16 hr 20 min 4 sec in *Orange II* from 24 January to 16 March 2005. The journey started and finished off Ushant, France.

FASTEST MONOHULL (SOLO MALE)

Vincent Riou (France) circumnavigated the globe in 87 days 10 hr 47 min 55 sec during the 2004 Vendée Globe single-handed yacht race, starting and finishing at Les Sables d'Olonne, France. He covered a distance of 21,760 nautical miles (40,299 km; 25,040 miles) in his yacht *PRB* from 7 November 2004 to 2 February 2005.

★ **NEW RECORD**
★ **UPDATED RECORD**

GUINNESS WORLD RECORDS

★ NEW RECORD
★ UPDATED RECORD

PROBING THE DEPTHS

DEEPEST SCUBA-DIVE BY A DOG

Dwane Folsom (USA) regularly takes his dog, Shadow, scuba-diving off the coast of Grand Cayman Island. The pair usually descend to around 4 m (13 ft). When diving, Shadow wears a specially adapted diving suit made up of a helmet, weighted dog jacket and breathing tube connected to his owner's air tank.

★ LARGEST UNDERWATER PRESS CONFERENCE

A group of 21 journalists dived to a depth of 5 m (16 ft 4 in) to attend the press conference held by Leo Ochsenbauer and Klaus-M. Schremser for the release of their book *Zero-Time, Sex and Depth Intoxication: 333 Answers to Divers' Questions* in Lake Traunsee, Austria, on 17 June 2006.

DEEPEST...

MANNED OCEAN DESCENT

On 23 January 1960, Dr Jacques Piccard (Switzerland) and Lt Donald Walsh (USA) piloted the Swiss-built US Navy bathyscaphe *Trieste* to a depth of 10,911 m (35,797 ft) in the Challenger Deep section of the Mariana Trench – the deepest known point on Earth.

DESCENT INTO AN ICE CAVE

In 1998, the glacier explorer Janot Lamberton (France) descended to a depth of 202 m (662 ft) in a cave in a glacier in Greenland.

UNDERWATER ESCAPE WITHOUT EQUIPMENT

The greatest depth from which an escape has been made without any equipment is 68.6 m (225 ft), by Richard A Slater (USA) from the rammed submersible *Nekton Beta* off Catalina Island, California, USA, on 28 September 1970.

UNDERWATER RESCUE

Roger R Chapman and Roger Mallinson (both UK) were trapped in the mini-sub *Pisces III* for 76 hours after it sank to 480 m (1,575 ft), a distance of 241 km (150 miles) south-east of Cork, Republic of Ireland, on 29 August 1973.

It was hauled to the surface on 1 September by the cable ship *John Cabot* after work by *Pisces V*, *Pisces II* and the remote-control recovery vessel *Curv* (Controlled Underwater Recovery Vehicle).

HALF MARATHON

The deepest half-marathon race took place at a depth of 212 m (695 ft) in Bochnia salt mine, Poland, on 4 March 2004.

The track was 2,438 m (7,998 ft) long, and the 11 runners made approximately 8.5 circuits, covering a total distance of 21,097 m (69,215 ft).

UNDERWATER POSTBOX

The world's deepest underwater postbox is located 10 m (32 ft 8.1 in) beneath the waters of Susami Bay, Japan. Sports divers can post mail in the box, which is officially part of the Susami post office, and the post is collected daily.

The postbox is opened only by authorized employees using post-office keys and the divers use special waterproof plastic postcards. More than 4,273 undersea mails were collected in the postbox's first year of operation.

RECOVERY

The greatest depth at which a salvage operation has been carried out is 5,258 m (17,251 ft), to recover a helicopter that had crashed into the Pacific Ocean in August 1991.

Crew of the USS *Salvor* and personnel from Eastport International raised the wreckage to the surface on 27 February 1992 so that the cause of the accident could be investigated.

DEEPEST-DIVING SUBMARINE IN SERVICE

On 11 August 1989, the Japanese research submarine *Shinkai 6500* (above left) reached a depth of 6,526 m (21,414 ft) in the Japan Trench off Sanriku, Japan.

Shown above is Masanobu Yanagitani, one of the two pilots who steer this deep submergence research vehicle (DSRV) to the bottom of the sea. He is seen sitting inside the cockpit of *Shinkai 6500*.

★ DEEPEST UNDERWATER CYCLING

Vittorio Innocente (Italy) cycled at a depth of 60 m (196 ft 10 in) on the ocean floor off Genoa, Italy, on 13 July 2005. He made minor modifications to his standard mountain bike, such as adding small lead weights and a plastic wing behind the seat and flooding the tyres to reduce buoyancy.

LIVE INTERNET BROADCAST

On 24 July 2001, live footage of HMS *Hood* was broadcast over the internet from a depth of 2,800 m (9,200 ft) at the bottom of the Denmark Strait, where the ship sank in 1941. The broadcast, from a remotely operated vehicle (ROV), followed the discovery of the wreck by David Mearns (UK) of Blue Water Recoveries Ltd (UK), in an expedition organized by ITN Factual for Channel 4.

LIVE RADIO BROADCAST

CBC Radio Points North (Canada) performed the deepest underground live-radio broadcast, at a depth of 2,340 m (7,680 ft), on 24 May 2005. The broadcast was carried out in Creighton Mine, Sudbury, Ontario, Canada.

SCUBA DIVE (FEMALE)

Verna van Schaik (South Africa) dived to a depth of 221 m (725 ft) in the Boesmansgat cave in South Africa's Northern Cape province on 25 October 2004. The dive lasted 5 hr 34 min, of which only 12 minutes were spent descending.

LIVE TV BROADCAST

The world's deepest live TV broadcast was presented by Alastair Fothergill (UK) at an underwater depth of 2.4 km (1.5 miles) on *Abyss Live* (BBC, UK).

The dive was broadcast on 29 September 2002 from inside a MIR submersible, along the Mid-Atlantic Ridge off the east coast of the USA.

DEEPEST SEAWATER SCUBA DIVE

Nuno Gomes (South Africa) dived to a depth of 318.25 m (1,044 ft) in the Red Sea off Dahab, Egypt, on 10 June 2005. While the descent was accomplished in a matter of minutes, the ascent took more than 12 hours to allow for decompression.

FRESHWATER SCUBA CAVE DIVE

On 23 August 1996, Nuno Gomes (South Africa) scuba-dived to a depth of 282.6 m (926 ft 1.6 in) at the Boesmansgat Cave in the Northern Cape province of South Africa. Essentially a very deep sinkhole, the cave at the surface resembles a small lake with vertical sides.

And Gomes breaks records in salt water too – see right...

MODERN SOCIETY

CONTENTS

TALLEST LIVING HORSE

Radar, a Belgian draft horse, measured 19 hands 3.5 in (202 cm; 79.5 in), without shoes, on 27 July 2004 at the North American Belgian Championship in London, Ontario, Canada. Radar is owned by Priefert Manufacturing, Inc., Mount Pleasant, Texas, USA. As of 7 July 2006, the record for the **smallest living horse** was held by Thumbelina, a miniature sorrel brown mare that measures 44.5 cm (17.5 in) to the withers and is owned by Kay and Paul Goessling (both USA), who live in St Louis, Missouri, USA. The two horses were united for the first time by Guinness World Records for this photoshoot on 3 September 2006.

MAN'S BEST FRIEND

★ FIRST CLONED DOG

The first cloned dog to survive birth is Snuppy, an Afghan hound "created" by Hwang Woo-Suk (South Korea) and his team of scientists at Seoul National University (SNU) in South Korea, after which the dog was named. He was born on 24 April 2005.

★ COUNTRY WITH THE HIGHEST RATE OF PET OWNERSHIP

The country with the highest rate of pet ownership per household as of 2003 is Australia, with 66% of households having at least one animal as a companion (typically a cat or dog) and 83% of Australians having owned a pet at some point in their life.

HIGHEST JUMP BY A DOG

Cinderella May a Holly Grey, a greyhound owned by Kate Long and Kathleen Conroy (both USA), jumped a record height of 172.7 cm (68 in). The record was set at the Purina Incredible Dog Challenge National Finals, Gray Summit, Missouri, USA, on 7 October 2006.

★ FASTEST DOG WEAVING

The record for the fastest time for a dog to weave between 60 poles is 12.14 seconds by Zinzan, a German shepherd owned by Kobus Engelbrecht (UK), at the Wallingford agility show in Newbury, Berkshire, UK, on 23 April 2006.

★ LARGEST OBEDIENCE LESSON

The largest dog obedience lesson involved 257 dogs with handlers at Nestlé Purina PetCare's BonzOmerspelen in Arnhem, the Netherlands, on 16 May 2004.

★ LONGEST DOG TUNNEL

Aidee, a border collie owned by Lynn van Beers (New Zealand), successfully ran through a "tunnel" of legs formed by 457 volunteers standing astride. The record was attempted on 27 October 2006 in conjunction with the Otago Canine Training Club (New Zealand) and Anderson's Bay School in Dunedin, New Zealand.

★ LONGEST DOG EARS

Tigger, a bloodhound owned by Bryan and Christina Flessner of St Joseph, Illinois, USA, has a right ear that measured 34.9 cm (13.75 in) and a left ear measuring 34.2 cm (13.5 in) on 29 September 2004.

★ MOST STAIRS CLIMBED WHILE BALANCING WATER ON THE NOSE

Sweet Pea, a border collie-Australian Alsatian cross owned by Alex Rothacker (USA), is able to walk up and down 15 stairs with a glass of water balanced on her nose. She can perform the trick without spilling a drop.

★ LARGEST DOG WALK

The Butcher's Great North Dog Walk, organized by Anthony Carlisle (UK), involved 7,766 dogs going "walkies" together in South Shields, Tyne & Wear, UK, on 18 June 2006.

★ LONGEST DOG LIVING

Mon Ami von der Oelmühle, owned by Jürgen Rösner, Joachim and Elke Müller (Germany), is an Irish Wolfhound measuring 232 cm (91.3 in) from nose to tail tip.

The **longest dog ever** was Aicama Zorba of La-Susa, a 2.544-m-long (8-ft 3-in) Old English mastiff, last measured in 1987.

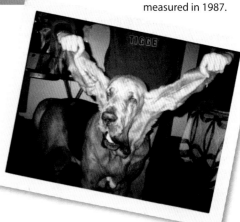

★ LARGEST DOG WEDDING CEREMONY

On 12 February 2006 in Hilversum, the Netherlands, 27 pairs of dogs were "married" in a ceremony organized by Nestlé Purina PetCare Nederland B.V. The dogs had all met during a speed-dating session prior to the mass wedding and were issued with certificates to celebrate the happy day.

TALLEST DOG EVER

Gibson, a harlequin Great Dane, measured 107 cm (42.2 in) tall on 31 August 2004. Millenium's [sic] Rockydane Gibson Meistersinger – as he is more formally known – is owned by Sandy Hall (USA) and works as a therapy dog. When standing on his hind legs, the 77-kg (170-lb) pooch measures more than 2 m (7 ft) tall. By comparison, the smallest dog ever was a dwarf Yorkshire terrier that measured just 7.11 cm (2.8 in) to the shoulder!

★ LARGEST DOG BREED

According to the American Kennel Club, the largest dog breed is the Irish wolfhound, which weighs 47–56 kg (105–125 lb) and stands 76–88 cm (30–35 in) at the shoulder.

The ★ **smallest breed of dog** is the chihuahua, which weighs just 1–3 kg (2–6 lb) and stands 15–23 cm (6–9 in) at the shoulder.

★ MOST DOGS WASHED BY A TEAM IN EIGHT HOURS

A team of 12 people managed to wash 848 dogs in an eight-hour period. Australia's Biggest Dog Wash was organized by The Veterinary Science Foundation of the University of Sydney and held on 14 September 2003 in Sydney, Australia.

★ MOST SKIPS BY A DOG IN ONE MINUTE

Sweet Pea (see above left) also achieved an incredible 65 skipping-rope jumps in a minute. She

performed the trick on the set of the TV show *La Nuit Des Records* filmed in Paris, France, on 10 October 2006.

★ FIRST PET MOVIE STAR

A border collie called Jean, owned by movie director Larry Trimble (USA), became the first doggie star when he appeared in the 1910 feature *Jean and the Calico Doll*. He went on to star in a number of films, including *Jean and the Waif* and *Jean Goes Fishing*.

MOST SUCCESSFUL POLICE DOG

Trepp (short for Intrepid) – a golden retriever owned by Tom Kazo (USA) – has been credited with over 100 arrests and the recovery of illegal drugs worth over $63 million (£28.6 million).

★ HARDIEST DOG

On 15 April 2003, a mixed-breed dog named Dosha slipped out of her owner's home in Clearlake, California, USA, only to be run over by a car. Concerned police officers decided to end her pain and shot her in the head; she was then sealed in a bag and placed in a freezer at an animal centre. She was discovered two hours later by staff – alive and sitting upright!

★ FIRST ANIMAL WHOSE EVIDENCE IS ADMISSIBLE IN COURT

Essentially a nose with a dog attached, the bloodhound is the first animal whose evidence is legally admissible in court.

A typical bloodhound's nose is lined with 230 million scent receptors – around 40 times more than the human nose – which are used in court to match scene-of-crime evidence to criminals.

GUIDE DOGS

- The **longest period of active service for a guide dog** is 14 years 8 months (August 1972–March 1987) in the case of a labrador-retriever bitch named Cindi-Cleo, owned by Aron Barr of Tel Aviv, Israel. The dog died on 10 April 1987.

- The **longest-serving hearing guide dog** is Donna, owned by John Hogan of Pyrmont Point, New South Wales, Australia. She completed 10 years of active service in Australia up to 1995 – and eight years of service prior to that in New Zealand – before her death on 6 May 1995 at the age of 20 years 2 months.

- The Guide Dogs for the Blind Association is the world's **largest breeder and trainer of working dogs**. Around 1,200 would-be guide dogs are born every year in Warwickshire, UK, to breeding stock specially chosen for their intelligence and temperament.

★ MOST POPULAR BREED OF DOG

According to yearly statistics gathered by the American Kennel Club (AKC), out of 153 breeds acknowledged by the AKC for 2006, the most popular purebreed in the USA was the Labrador retriever with 123,760 dogs registered in 2006. The breed has held the US top spot since 1991 and was also the most popular in Canada and the UK.

FOOD & DRINK

NEW RECORD ★ UPDATED RECORD

LARGEST

★ BOWL OF SOUP
Residents of Salonta in Romania cooked up a 5,045-litre (1,109-gallon) goulash soup at their town hall on 3 June 2006.

★ ICE-CREAM CAKE
An ice-cream cake made by Beijing Allied Faxi Food Co., Ltd, for Beijing Children's Art Theater Co., Ltd, weighed in at 8,750 kg (19,290 lb) and was displayed in Beijing, China, on 16 January 2006.

The ★ **largest ice-cream cup** weighed 4,021 kg (8,865 lb) and was made on 13 September 2005 by Baskin-Robbins at their headquarters in Canton, Massachusetts, USA.

★ KEBAB SKEWER
On 16 February 2007, the company Chih'ua Tacos y Cortes of Chihuahua, Mexico, served up a kebab that weighed 3,745.8 kg (8,258 lb).

★ LONGEST BARBECUE

A barbecue measuring 1,290 m (4,232 ft) long was built and fired up by the residents of Hermosillo, Mexico, on 20 November 2006. Over 5,000 kg (11,000 lb) of meat and potatoes were served to a 20,736-strong crowd.

★ LARGEST BURGER

The largest commercially available burger is Big Bob's Texas Belt Buster – a 35.6-kg (78-lb 8-oz) monster available at Bob's BBQ and Grill at Pattaya Beach in Chonburi, Thailand, as of 31 July 2006. It costs $23.95 (£13.42) and anyone who can finish the entire thing within three hours receives a refund, together with their name on a plaque and a gift certificate to use for a future visit. To date, no one has achieved this: the fastest finishing so far is eight hours!

★ PIÑATA
A piñata is a brittle, hollow sculpture that is filled with confectionery and usually smashed to pieces by blindfolded children as a party game. The world's largest piñata measured 12 m (39 ft 8 in) high with a diameter of 12.95 m (42 ft 6 in) and was made by the Cincy-Cinco Latino Festival and displayed in Cincinnati, Ohio, USA, on 5 May 2006.

★ STIR-FRY
A stir-fry weighing 1,052 kg (2,319 lb) was prepared by the Wesvalia High School in Klerksdorp, South Africa, on 22 October 2005.

★ GINGERBREAD MAN
The Gingerbread House in Rochester, Minnesota, USA, baked a biscuit boy weighing 211.5 kg (466 lb 6 oz) on 21 February 2006. Sweet-tooths beware: this works out at something like 750,000 calories!

★ LARGEST SPUN PIZZA BASE

Tony Gemignani (USA, left) spun 500 g (17.6 oz) of dough for two minutes to form a pizza base measuring 84.33 cm (33.2 in) wide at the Mall of America in Minneapolis, Minnesota, USA, on 20 April 2006 during the filming of *Guinness World Records Week* for the Food Network channel.

On the same day, at the same event, Joe Carlucci (USA) set a new record for the ★ **highest pizza-base toss** using 567 g (20 oz) of dough, achieving a height of 6.52 m (21 ft 5 in).

★ LARGEST
CHOCOLATE IGLOO

Marco Fanti (Italy) and his team of builders used a total of 330 chocolate bricks, and worked for 23 hours, to make a chocolate igloo weighing 3 tonnes (6,613 lb) in Perugia, Italy, on 17 October 2006.

DID YOU KNOW?
The white truffle (*Tuber magnum pico*) is the world's **most expensive edible fungus**, usually fetching £1,500 ($3,000) per kg. They can be found only in the Italian regions of Piedmont, Emilia-Romagna, Tuscany and Marches, and because they grow up to 30 cm (12 in) underground, they can only be located with the help of sows or trained dogs.

★ LOAF OF BREAD
A loaf of bread stretching for 1,211.6 m (3,975 ft) was baked during the Bread and Bakers' Party in Vagos, Portugal, on 10 July 2005.

★ PASTA STRAND
On 10 September 2005, Ristorante Hammermühle in Ober-Darmstadt, Germany, created a single strand of pasta measuring 455 m (1,492 ft 9 in) – in other words, longer than six jumbo jets!

★ SALAMI
Salumificio Manuelli s.r.l. made a 564.88-m-long (1,853-ft 3-in) salami in Varallo, Vericelli, Italy, on 14 August 2005.

★ SAUSAGE ROLL
A 111-m (364-ft) sausage roll was made by King Pie in Faerie Glen, South Africa, on 25 June 2005.

'NORMOUS NOSH

If the last few years are anything to go by, the record-breaking public hasn't lost its appetite for creating titanic treats and fantastic feasts:

• The record for **most number of dishes displayed** is 2,007 and was achieved by His Holiness Sri Sri Sri Vasanth Gurudev Shakthipeetadhipathi (above) and Sri Parshva Padmavathi Seva Trust at the Sri Parshva Padmavathi Shakthipeet Temple in Krishnagiri, India, on 3 March 2007.

• If you're vegetarian, look away now! This massive hunk of meat is the world's **largest meatball**! Tipping the scales at 19.6 kg (43 lb 3 oz) – about the same weight as a typical five-year-old boy – it was made by chefs at the SANS Bergmannskroa restaurant in Løkken Verk, Norway, on 24 June 2006.

ACTUAL SIZE

• Still peckish? In 19 November 2005, the Juniorchamber Veenendaal-Rijnvallei in Veenendaal, Netherlands, completed their record for the **largest bag of cookies** with a 3,200-kg (7,054-lb) package measuring 5.5 m (18 ft) wide, 2 m (6 ft 6 in) tall and 3 m (10 ft) deep. The supersize sack contained 207,860 cookies; filling it with baked cookies took 3,600 hours of work!

LONGEST

★ CHILLI-PEPPER STRING
James Johnson (USA) made a chilli-pepper string measuring 316.69 m (1,039 ft) long and consisting of 20,150 chilli pods.

★ DAMPER BREAD
Scouts from the Glimåkra Scout Troop baked a damper bread measuring 125 m (410 ft 1 in) in Glimåkra, Sweden, on 9 September 2006.

★ DRINKS-CAN LINE
The longest line of drinks cans consisted of 84,498 cans in an event organized by Bridge FM Radio and Bridgend County Council in Bridgend, UK, on 26–27 October 2006.

★ GARLIC STRING
A garlic string measuring 124.2 m (407 ft) long was made for the Garlic Festival in Borgholm, Sweden, by a team led by Gunnar Kvarnbäck (Sweden) on 25 September 2005.

★ GINGERBREAD
The record for the longest gingerbread is 23.14 m (75.9 ft) and was achieved by a team of chefs employed at the Langham Place Hotel in Mongkok, Hong Kong, on 3 December 2005.

MOST EXPENSIVE PIE

A pie sold at the Fence Gate Inn in Lancashire, UK, will cost you £8,195 ($14,260) or £1,024 ($1,781) per slice when ordered by eight guests. (Head chef and pricey pie creator Spencer Burge, UK, is pictured.) The pie's expensive ingredients include:

• £500-worth ($870) of Japanese wagyu beef fillet (from cattle that are massaged by hand);
• Chinese matsutake mushrooms (£500 per kg; $420 per lb) – so precious, they are harvested under guard;
• Bluefoot mushrooms (£200 per kg; $175 per lb);
• Gravy made from two bottles of vintage 1982 Chateau Mouton Rothschild wine (£1,000; $1,740 each);
• Edible gold leaf costing £100 ($174) per sheet.

GROSS GASTRONOMY

TABASCO SAUCE
Most drunk in 30 sec:
120 ml (4.2 fl oz)
Andrew Hajinikitas (Australia)
8 May 2005

OYSTERS
Most eaten in 3 min: 187
Rune Naeri (Norway)
6 September 2003

**DOUGHNUTS
(POWDERED)**
Most eaten in 3 min: 4
Shared: Simon Krischer,
Jay Weisberger, Adam
Fenton, Anthony Albelo
(all USA)
12 June 2002

PEAS (CANNED)
Most eaten with cocktail
stick in 3 min: 211
Mat Hand (UK)
8 November 2001

ALE
Fastest time to drink a
yard of ale (1.42 litres;
2.5 pints): 5 sec
Peter Dowdeswell (UK)
4 May 1975

MILKSHAKE
Fastest time to drink
500 ml by straw:
9.8 sec
Osi Anyanwu (UK)
9 November 2005

★**FERRERO
ROCHER**
Most unwrapped and
eaten in 1 min: 5
Matthew Winn (UK)
3 June 2006

★**BANANAS**
Most peeled and
eaten in 1 min: 2
Steve Payne (UK)
5 May 2006

SMARTIES
Most eaten in 3 min
using chopsticks: 170
Kathryn Ratcliffe (UK)
24 November 2004

★ **JELLY**
Most eaten in 1 min
with chopsticks:
180 g (6.34 oz)
Damien Fletcher (UK)
4 October 2006

JAM DOUGHNUTS
Most eaten in 3 min
(without licking lips): 6
Steve McHugh (UK)
28 June 2002

HOT DOGS
Most eaten (with buns and
condiments) in 3 min: 4
Peter Dowdeswell (UK)
27 July 2001

BAKED BEANS
Most eaten with cocktail
stick in 3 min: 136
Nick Thompson (UK)
18 August 2005

★**GARLIC**
Most eaten in 1 min:
4 cloves
Alastair Galpin (Australia)
9 November 2006

RICE
Most eaten with chopsticks
in 3 min: 64 grains
Tae Wah Gooding
(South Korea)
7 November 2000

SWEETCORN (CANNED)
Most eaten with cocktail stick
in 3 min: 236 kernels
Ian Richard Purvis (UK)
27 August 2003

MASSIVE MEALS

LARGEST...	RECORD	WHO	WHEN
Breakfast (uncooked)	27,854 diners	Nutella, Gelsenkirchen, Germany	29 May 2005
Breakfast (cooked)	18,941 diners	Cowboy Breakfast Foundation, San Antonio, Texas, USA	26 Jan 2001
★Risotto	7.5 tonnes (16,556 lb)	Ricegrowers Assoc. of Australia, Sydney, Australia	26 Nov 2004
★Chilli con carne	652.4 kg (1,438 lb)	Keystone Aquatic Club, Harrisburg, Pennsylvania, USA	19 Jul 2003
Fish and chips	35.26 kg (77 lb 12 oz)	Icelandic, USA, Inc., Boston, Massachusetts, USA	15 Mar 2004
Guacamole	1,527.9 kg (3,368.44 lb)	Festival, Con Sabor A Mexico, Dallas, Texas, USA	15 Oct 2005
★Hummus	362 kg (800 lb)	Sabra Mediterranean, New York, USA	6 Mar 2006

KETCHUP
Fastest time to drink a 396-g (14-oz) bottle of ketchup by straw: 33 sec
Dustin Phillips (USA)
23 September 1999

MINCE PIES
Fastest time to eat three: 1 min 26 sec
David Cole (UK)
20 December 2005

★ JALAPEÑO CHILLIS
Most eaten in 1 min: 16
Alfredo Hernandes (USA)
17 September 2006

SAUSAGES
Most eaten in 1 min: 8
Stefan Paladin (New Zealand)
22 July 2001

Most swallowed whole in 1 min: 8
Cecil Walker (USA)
13 March 2003

SHRIMPS
Most eaten in 3 min: 272.1 g (9.6 oz)
William E. Silver (USA)
26 February 2003

STOUT
Fastest time to drink 1 pint: 2.1 sec
Peter Dowdeswell (UK)
24 April 2001

Fastest time to drink 2 pints: 6.1 sec
Ken Robinson (UK)
8 December 2004

GRAPES
Most eaten using a teaspoon in 3 min: 133
Mat Hand (UK)
8 November 2001

BEER
Fastest time to drink...
2 pints: 2.3 sec
Peter Dowdeswell (UK), 11 June 1975

1 pint upside down: 3 sec
Peter Dowdeswell (UK), 16 February 1988

1 litre: 1.3 sec
Steven Petrosino (USA), 22 June 1977

2 litres: 6 sec
Peter Dowdeswell (UK), 7 February 1975

BRUSSELS SPROUTS (COOKED)
Most eaten in 1 min: 21
Liam McCormack (Ireland)
17 February 2007

CREAM CRACKERS
Fastest time to eat three: 34.78 sec
Ambrose Mendy (UK)
9 May 2005

MEATBALLS
Most eaten using a cocktail stick in 1 min: 27
Nick Marshall (UK)
18 November 2002

MILK
Fastest time to drink 2 pints: 3.2 sec
Peter Dowdeswell (UK)
31 May 1975

TOWERING TREATS

• The **tallest champagne fountain** was constructed by Luuk Broos (Germany) and his team during the CentrO Festival in Oberhausen, Germany, on 9 September 2006. The phenomenal fizzy fountain consisted of 61 storeys.

• The ★**tallest chocolate sculpture**, created by Hyatt Regency Chicago pastry chef Alain Roby (France), was a replica of the Rockefeller Center, the Empire State Building and the Chrysler Building. The sky-scraping confectionery measured 6.2 m (20 ft 8 in) and was unveiled at FAO Schwarz toy store in New York City, USA, on 10 October 2006.

• The ★**tallest cooked sugar sculpture** measured 3.91 m (12 ft 10.4 in). It was made in 11 hours by Alain Roby (France) at Mall of America, Minneapolis, Minnesota, USA, on 21 April 2006. As with Roby's record-breaking chocolate sculpture (see above), it was created during the filming of *Guinness World Records Week* for the Food Network channel.

• The record for the ★**tallest pyramid of cookies** is 1.49 m (4 ft 10.7 in) and was achieved by Jan Vinzenz Krause (Germany) and members of the diocese Essen using 12,180 Leibniz butter cookies at the CentrO shopping centre in Oberhausen, Germany, on 16 September 2006.

★ **NEW RECORD**
★ **UPDATED RECORD**

DID YOU KNOW?

- The word "sudoku" is an abbreviation of the Japanese phrase "suji wa dokushin ni kagiru" ("the numbers must be alone" – i.e., appear only once).

- Mathematicians proved that 6,670,903,752,021,072,936,960 different Sudoku boards are possible.

- The ★**first sudoku TV show**, *Sudoku Live*, was broadcast in the UK on 1 July 2005 and hosted by Carol Vorderman.

- The ★**first sudoku world championships** were held in Lucca, Italy, on 10–12 March 2006. The winner was Jana Tylová (Czech Republic).

★ HIGHEST THEORETICAL SINGLE-WORD SCRABBLE SCORE

Which word, according to the World Scrabble Championships website, is the longest feasible word in the game? The board below is set up in such a way that, if you play all the tiles in the rack (HRBYSCZ), you would score 1,790 points. *Note: the word, a 15-letter chemical name, could not be used in a club- or tournament- level game, as it relies on the use of proper nouns, contrary to conventional matchplay practice.**

*Answer at bottom of p.113.

SCRABBLE

★ HIGHEST SCORES

- **Tournament** In a qualifying round of the 1986 British National Championships, Joyce Cansfield (UK) finished with a score of 855 points.
- The highest score in a tournament game using the *Official Scrabble Words International* (OSWI) rules is 785, achieved by Jackie McLeod (UK) in 2002.
- **Club** Under the *US Official Tournament and Club Word List*, Second Edition (OWL2) rules, Michael Cresta (USA) scored 830 points on 12 October 2006.
- Under UK rules, governed by the *Official Scrabble Words* (OSW) book, the highest score achieved was 793 by Peter Preston (UK) in 1993.

★ HIGHEST COMBINED SCORES

- **Tournament** A game played on 13 June 1993 between Mark Landsberg and Alan Stern (both USA) ended 770–338 – a combined record total of 1,108.
- **Club** A game played at club level between Michael Cresta and Wayne Yorra (both USA) resulted in a final score of 1,320 (830–490). Cresta's score of 830 is also an individual world record (see above).

Very easy

1		7				6		8
	8	9			3	4	2	
				5				
7		5		4		1		
		1		9		7		6
			7					
	7	8	9			2	3	
6		3				9		5

Easy

2								3
		1	4			9	5	
			7	8	1			
		7	3	5	6	8		
6	5						4	2
		3	4	2	8	7		
			5	7	9			
	4	2				6	9	
8								1

★ FASTEST TIME TO COMPLETE A "VERY EASY" SUDOKU GRID

The rules of sudoku are simple: every column, every row and every block of nine must contain the numbers 1–9. But how fast can you complete a grid? On the left is a "Very Easy" puzzle – can you solve it faster than the record holder? ★ The **fastest time to complete a "Very Easy" sudoku puzzle** is 1 min 23.93 sec by Thomas Snyder (USA) at BookExpo America, Washington DC, USA, on 20 May 2006. He also holds the record for ★ **fastest "Easy" Sudoku puzzle**, at 2 min 8.53 sec (right).

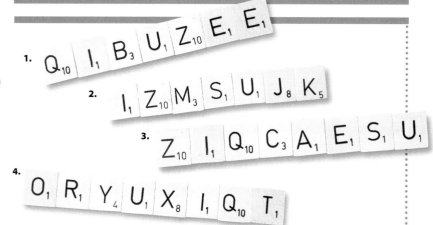

1. Q_{10} I_1 B_3 U_1 Z_{10} E_1 E_1

2. I_1 Z_{10} M_3 S_1 U_1 J_8 K_5

3. Z_{10} I_1 Q_{10} C_3 A_1 E_1 S_1 U_1

4. O_1 R_1 Y_4 U_1 X_8 I_1 Q_{10} T_1

A-LIST ANAGRAMS

Unscramble these record-breaking Scrabble words. (*Answers on p.113.*)

1. ★**Highest-scoring opening word**, 124 points, Sam Kantimathi (USA), 1993: *Noun*, a card game.

2. ★**Highest possible score for an opening word**, 128 points: *Noun* (plural), Russian peasants.

3. ★**Highest-scoring single word**, 392 points, Karl Khoshnaw (Germany), 1982: *Noun (plural)*, tribal chiefs in the Americas.

4. ★**Highest-scoring single word (US rules)**, 365 points, Michael Cresta (USA), 2006: *Noun*, romantic chivalry.

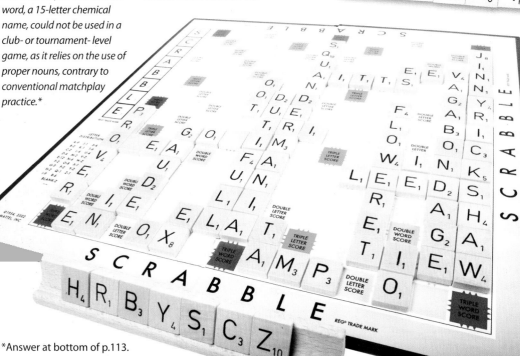

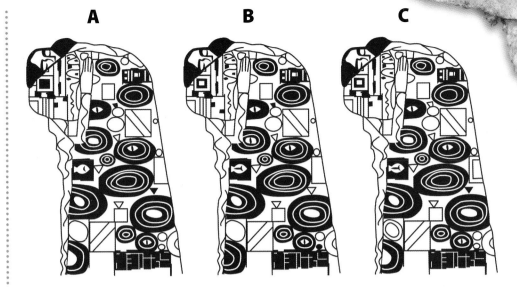

A **B** **C**

★ LARGEST PUZZLE
WORLD CHAMPIONSHIPS

The World Puzzle Championships, organized by the World Puzzle Federation, is the largest event of its kind on the planet. The 15th annual competition was held in 2006 in Borovets, Bulgaria, and attracted a record 200 competitors from 20 countries. Among the challenges set each year are sudokus, logic puzzles and spot-the-differences. Above is a championship-level spot-the-difference.

If you can find all 10 differences in three minutes, you'll be well up to competition standard! Solution on p.286.

TRY ME!
You can attempt some of the puzzles on these pages – and maybe even set some new Guinness World Records along the way. Just take a photocopy of this spread and grab a pencil and stopwatch. If you think you can break a record, find out how to register it with us on p.10.

blocks with 3,200 clues was published by Revistas Coquetel (Brazil) in Rio de Janeiro, Brazil, in March 2006.

LARGEST PUBLISHED CROSSWORD

In July 1982, Robert Turcot (Canada) compiled a crossword comprising 82,951 squares. It contained 12,489 clues across, 13,125 down and covered 3.55 m² (38.21 ft²).

LONGEST WORD IN A CROSSWORD

The Welsh town name Llanfairpwllgwyngyllgogerychwyrndrobwllllantysiliogogogoch is the longest word ever used in a cryptic crossword. Roger F. Squires (UK) used it in the July 1979 edition of the *Telford Wrekin News*.

★ HIGHEST LOSING SCORE

A losing score of 545 was suffered by Kevin Rickhoff (USA) against Mark Milan's (USA) 558 in the 18th round of the 2006 US Open, under *Tournament World List* 2006 (TWL06) rules.

★ LOWEST WINNING SCORE

Rod Nivison (USA) won a game at the 1990 Midwest Invitational in the USA by a score of −8 to −10. This bizarre result was achieved after he and his opponent repeatedly passed turns or changed tiles, and the only word to be placed on the board (DORMINE) was challenged off!

★ MOST POINTS SCORED WITH ONE TILE

In a tournament game in 1999, Tom Kelly (USA) scored 99 by laying an S to form QUIRKS and SMOTHERED.

CROSSWORDS

★ MOST CROSSWORDS COMPILED IN A LIFETIME

Roger F. Squires (UK) compiles an average of 31 puzzles a week. By December 2005, he had compiled 65,000 published crosswords.

★ LARGEST ARROW-WORD PUZZLE

An arrow-word puzzle measuring 1.03 x 3.45 m (4 ft 3 in x 11 ft 3 in) and containing 16,000

FIRST CROSSWORD

The first crossword puzzle appeared in the Sunday "Fun" section of US newspaper *New York World* on 21 December 1913. Created by journalist Arthur Wynne (UK), it was based on a diamond-shaped grid, had no blacked-out squares and featured simple, non-cryptic clues. Try completing the crossword for yourself – the clues are listed in the panel on the right. Solution on p.286.

★ **NEW RECORD**
★ **UPDATED RECORD**

CROSSWORD CLUES

Here are the clues to the crossword below. The solution is given on p.286.

ACROSS

2–3	What bargain hunters enjoy
4–5	A written acknowledgement
6–7	Such and nothing more
8–9	To cultivate
10–11	A bird
12–13	A bar of wood or iron
14–15	Opposed to less
16–17	What artists learn to do
18–19	What this puzzle is
20–21	Fastened
22–23	An animal of prey
24–25	Found on the seashore
26–27	The close of day
28–29	To elude
30–31	The plural of is

DOWN

10–18	The fibre of the gomuti palm
6–22	What we all should be
4–26	A daydream
2–11	A talon
19–28	A pigeon
F–7	Part of your head
23–30	A river in Russia
1–32	To govern
33–34	An aromatic plant
N–8	A fist
24–31	To agree with
3–12	Part of a ship
20–29	One
5–27	Exchanging
9–25	To sink in mud
13–21	A boy

COLLECTIONS

COLLECTING GUIDELINES

• Preference goes to items accumulated personally, over time, rather than those made on behalf of a third party, such as a newspaper appeal.

• The record is based on the number of items of the same type in the collection. Duplicates do not count. For paired items, such as earrings or cufflinks, the number of *pairs* should be given.

• Claims are to be submitted by the owner with a brief history of when and why the collection began. Also of interest is where the collection is housed and if there is a favourite item, and why.

• It is essential that a total count of the items claimed must be taken by some accurate method of counting.

• The number of items in the collection must be included in the witness statements.

• A concise inventory should be submitted for all claims.

• One of the signed statements of authentication should come from a recognized society specializing in collections of the type submitted, if possible.

• Failure to include the required documentation will delay the outcome of a claim or lead to its rejection.

COLLECTIONS A–Z

COLLECTION	NUMBER	HOLDER (NATIONALITY)
★ Armoured vehicles (*picture 1*)	229	Jacques Littlefield (USA)
Bar towels (*picture 2*)	2,372	Robert Begley (USA)
★ Cigarette cases	1,351	Colin Grey (UK)
Dinosaur eggs	10,008	Heyuan Museum (China)
Erasers	19,571	Petra Engels (Germany)
Four-leaf clovers (*picture 3*)	72,928	George J. Kaminski (USA)
Golf clubs	4,393	Robert Lantsoght (Spain)
Handcuffs	843	Stan Willis (USA)
Ice-lolly sticks	449	Poul Lykke Jepsen (Denmark)
Jet-fighters	110	Michel Pont (France)
Keychains	41,418	Brent Dixon (USA)
Letter openers	1,365	Bengt Olsson (Sweden)
Mickey Mouse memorabilia (*picture 4*)	2,143	Janet Esteves (USA)
★ Napkins (*picture 5*)	21,000	Antónia Kozáková (Slovakia)
Owls	18,055	Dianne Turner (USA)
Penguin-related items	2,520	Birgit Berends (Germany)
There are no collections beginning with Q in the Guinness World Records database		
Radios (*picture 6*)	625	M. Prakash (India)
★ Spoon rests	635	Frank Cassa (USA)
★ Teapots	3,950	Sue Blazye (UK)
Uncut banknotes	123 sheets	Leigh Follestad (Canada)
Vintage lawn-mowers	790	Andrew Hall and Michael Duck (both UK)
Whisky bottles	10,500	Alfredo Gonçalves (Portugal)
There are no collections beginning with X in the Guinness World Records database		
Yo-yos	4,251	John Meisenheimer (USA)
There are no collections beginning with Z in the Guinness World Records database		

Do you have a collection of quilts, xylophones or Zippo lighters? Guinness World Records currently has no collections beginning with Q, X or Z, so if you collect anything that starts with these letters, get in touch to see if you can set a new world record. Find out how to register your claim on p.8.

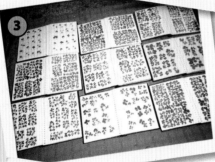

AUTOGRAPHED BOOKS
Michael Silverbrooke and Pat Tonkin (both Canada) have collected 722 books, each signed by their original authors.

★ BARBIE DOLLS
Bettina Dorfmann (Germany) has 2,500 different Barbie dolls.

BOARD GAMES
Since 1992, Linda Ivey (USA) has put together a collection of 868 different board games.

★ BOOKMARKS
Frank Divendal (Netherlands) owns 71,235 bookmarks that he has collected from all over the world. He began his collection in 1982.

★ CAT-RELATED ITEMS
Florence Groff (France) has a collection of 11,717 cat-related items, including 2,118 different cat figurines.

CIGARETTE CARDS (MUSEUM)
Edward Wharton-Tigar (UK, 1913–95) amassed over 1 million cigarette and trade cards in some 45,000 sets. The collection was given to the British Museum, London, UK, after his death.

★ COFFEE POTS
Irma Goth (Germany) started her collection some 20 years ago; she now owns 3,028 different coffee pots.

GNOMES AND PIXIES

Since 1979, artist Ann Fawssett-Atkin (UK) has collected a total of 2,032 garden gnomes and pixies, all of which have gone to live with her in her 1.6-ha (4-acre) Gnome Reserve and Wild Flower Garden at West Putford, Devon, UK. Visitors to the Gnome Garden and Museum are issued with pointy hats when they enter "so as not to embarrass the gnomes that live there!"

★ COINS FROM DIFFERENT COUNTRIES

Justin Gilbert Lopez (India) has a collection of 255 coins, representing 255 different countries. He has been collecting coins since 1986.

★ DRAGONBALL MEMORABILIA

Since 1996, Michael Nilsen (USA) has collected 5,065 unique items of memorabilia relating to *Dragonball*, a popular Japanese animation series.

★ EARRINGS

Carol McFadden (USA) has 37,706 different pairs of earrings, which she has been collecting since 1952.

FOOTBALLS

Roberto A. Fuglini (Argentina) has 861 different footballs that he has collected since 1995.

★ HATS

The record for the largest collection of hats belongs to Roger Buckey Legried (USA). The collection is made up of 82,792 different items that Buckey has accumulated from all over the world. He has been collecting since 1970.

★ MAGIC SETS

Manfred Klaghofer (Austria) has 2,017 different magic sets from all over the world. He started collecting them in 1995, and his oldest set dates back to the 19th century.

★ MODEL TRUCKS

The largest collection of model trucks belongs to Peter and Jens Pittack (both Germany). They have amassed 2,169 different trucks since they began collecting in 1997.

NUTCRACKERS

Uwe and Jürgen Löschner (Germany) have collected 4,334 nutcrackers, all of which are housed at the Nut Cracker Museum in the town of Neuhausen, Germany.

★ POLICEMAN'S PATCHES

Ross Kaiser (USA) has 3,271 policeman's patches, which he started collecting in 2001.

ROYAL MEMORABILIA

Ronny Bragança (Portugal) has collected 2,950 pieces of memorabilia celebrating Diana, Princess of Wales since 1991.

★ SALT AND PEPPER SACHETS

Tim Leigh (UK) has 100 matching pairs of salt and pepper sachets in his collection, each with a different company logo. He has been collecting the sachets since 1998.

★ SHOE-RELATED ITEMS

Darlene Flynn (USA) has 7,765 different shoe-related items, which she has been collecting since 2000.

★ STAMPS FROM DIFFERENT COUNTRIES

Jose Gilbert J. (India) has amassed a total of 192 stamps representing 192 different countries.

TEDDY BEARS

Jackie Miley (USA) has a collection of 4,190 different teddy bears that she has amassed since 2002.

★ TRIBAL AND ETHNIC FOOTWEAR

William Habraken (Netherlands) has 2,322 different pairs of footwear, originating from 155 countries, which he has been collecting since 1968.

★ WATCHES

Franciscus Hendricus Maria Salari (Netherlands) has amassed a collection of 1,366 different watches, depicting various logos, businesses and products.

★ NEW RECORD
★ UPDATED RECORD

LARGEST COLLECTION?

Compiled by Ed Brassard (USA), the largest collection of items currently listed on the *Guinness World Records* database contains a staggering 3,159,119 individual matchbook covers.

DICE

Kevin Cook (USA) has a collection of 11,097 dice that he has amassed since 1977. A member of the Dice Maniacs Club (aka the Random Fandom), Kevin began collecting dice from gaming shops after taking up Dungeons & Dragons. Since 1998, about 80% of his dice have come from eBay, the online auction company.

PLAYTIME

★ CARTWHEELING

The **greatest distance travelled in 24 hours by a team doing cartwheels** is 50 km (31 miles) by 10 gymnasts from Beausejour Gymnos (Canada) at the track in Memramcook, New Brunswick, Canada, from 8 to 9 September 2006.

★ LARGEST GAME OF TUNNEL BALL

In tunnel ball, teams line up and pass a ball along their length, alternately through the legs and over the head. The player at the end then goes to the front and the process repeats. The winner is the first team to get its front player back to the start.

The largest tunnel ball game involved 80 children from Berwick Lodge Primary School in Victoria, Australia, on 19 April 2006. The game took 2 hr 23 min to complete.

DUCKS AND DRAKES

Kurt Steiner (USA) achieved 40 consecutive skips of a stone on water (aka "ducks and drakes") at the Pennsylvania Qualifying Stone Skipping Tournament held at Riverfront Park, Franklin, Pennsylvania, USA, on 14 September 2002.

EGG-AND-SPOON RACING

• The record for the **largest egg-and-spoon race (single venue)** was set by 859 students from Raynes Park High School in Raynes Park, London, UK, on 24 October 2003.

• The **largest simultaneous egg-and-spoon race (multi-venue)** involved 1,277 racers at various venues around Herefordshire, UK, in an event organized by Ready Steady Win, UK, on 30 March 2004.

★ LARGEST ROCK, PAPER AND SCISSORS CONTEST

The fifth Rock Paper Scissors World Championships – organized by the World Rock Paper Scissors Society (RPS) – was staged at the Steam Whistle Brewery in Toronto, Canada, on 11 November 2006 and attracted 500 competitors. Bob Cooper (UK, above left) took the title of world champion, along with a gold medal and CAN$7,000 ($6,000; £3,067) in prize money.

• On 23 April 1990, Dale Lyons (UK) ran the London marathon (42.195 km; 26 miles 385 yd) carrying a spoon with a fresh egg on it in 3 hr 47 min, the **fastest marathon run with an egg and spoon**.

★ HULA DANCE

On 4 June 2005, 122 dancers performed the largest hula dance at an event sponsored by Hicks Lumber (Canada) to support the Help a Child Smile Charity at the annual Rose Festival in Welland, Ontario, Canada.

★ MOST LEAPFROG JUMPS IN ONE MINUTE

The greatest number of leapfrog jumps performed in a minute is 48. The feat was achieved by James Fryer and Nick Jenkins (both UK) from Emap Advertising to raise money for The Rainbow Trust Children's Charity, and was staged in Barcelona, Spain, on 5 May 2006.

★MOST PAPER AIRCRAFT
LAUNCHED SIMULTANEOUSLY

On 17 December 2006, 1,665 paper aircraft were launched simultaneously – and successfully flew a distance of 5 m (16 ft 4 in) or more – at an event organized by The Boys' & Girls' Clubs Association of Hong Kong, in Wan Chai, Hong Kong, China.

SACK-RACE COMPETITION

On 11 October 2002, a group of 2,095 pupils from Agnieton College and primary-school pupils from Zwolle, Wezep and Hattem took part in the largest sack-race competition. The race was staged in Zwolle, the Netherlands.

★SECRET SANTA

The largest game of Secret Santa involved a total of 618 participants and was staged at St Oliver's National School in Killarney, County Kerry, Ireland, on 19 December 2006.

★SIMON SAYS

On 22 April 2006, 1,169 participants played the largest-ever game of Simon Says at Victoria Park in Glasgow, UK.

DID YOU KNOW? The **largest flyable paper aircraft** had a wing-span of 13.97 m (45 ft 10 in). It was built by students from the Faculty of Aerospace Engineering at Delft University of Technology, the Netherlands, and underwent its maiden flight on 16 May 1995.

★SURFING

A record-breaking 44 surfers rode the same wave simultaneously in Lahinch, Ireland, on 13 May 2006.

★TABLE-FOOTBALL TOURNAMENT

The largest table-football contest took place at the Veltins-Arena, Gelsenkirchen, Germany, on 7 May 2006. It was organized by PV Autoteile and FC Schalke 04 and involved 1,564 players.

★TEA PARTY

On 8 October 2006, the city of Nishio, Japan, and the Chamber of Commerce and Industry of Nishio arranged the largest tea party in one venue: 14,718 people drank matcha (powdered green tea) in a traditional Japanese tea ceremony in Nishio City, Aichi, Japan.

FASTEST 10-KM SACK RACE

Ashrita Furman (USA) set the record for the fastest sack race over 10 km (6.2 miles) with a time of 1 hr 22 min 2 sec in Montauk, New York, USA, on 23 August 2001.

SKIP TO IT!

• Alain Trottier (USA) completed a 100-m (328-ft) sprint in 15.3 seconds while skipping rope at Calvary Chapel High School in Santa Ana, California, USA, on 25 October 2003, the ★**fastest time to skip 100 m**.

• The **fastest time to skip 10 miles with a rope** (16 km) is 58 minutes and was achieved by Vadivelu Karunakaren (India) in Madras, India, on 1 February 1990.

• The record for the ★**most skips in 30 seconds** is 152 and was achieved by Megumi Suzuki (Japan) at the Japanese Rope-Skipping Championships in Saitama Prefecture, Japan, on 10 September 2006.

• The **longest skipping marathon (with a rope)** lasted 27 hours and was set by Jed Goodfellow (Australia) at Oasis Shopping Mall, Broadbeach, Queensland, Australia, on 5–6 December 2003.

★LARGEST EASTER-EGG HUNT

On 1 April 2007, an Easter-egg hunt featuring 501,000 eggs was staged at the Cypress Gardens Adventure Park in Winter Haven, Florida, USA.

Altogether, 9,753 children took part in the hunt for the eggs, accompanied by their parents.

GARDEN GIANTS

LONGEST BEETROOT

A beetroot grown by Richard Hope (UK) measured 6.14 m (20 ft 2 in) on 27 September 2003 at the Llanharry Giant Vegetable Championships in Rhondda Cynon Taff, Wales, UK. At the same contest, Richard also presented the ★ **longest parsnip**, a "Gladiator" measuring 5.2 m (17 ft 1 in).

★ TALLEST COTTON PLANT

D. M. Williams (USA) grew a cotton plant (*Gossypium hirsutum*) that was 8.25 m (27 ft 1 in) tall when measured in August 2006.

★ LONGEST CARROT

A carrot grown by Peter Glazebrook (UK) and showcased on BBC TV's *The Great British Village Show* at Highgrove, UK, on 2 October 2006, measured 5.25 m (17 ft 3 in).

LONGEST COURGETTE

In 2005, Gurdial Singh Kanwal (India) grew a courgette measuring 2.39 m (7 ft 10.3 in) long in Brampton, Ontario, Canada.

★ LARGEST BOUQUET

A bouquet made from 156,940 roses was created by NordWestZentrum shopping mall in Frankfurt am Main, Germany, on 29 September 2005.

HEAVIEST FRUIT & VEGETABLES

FRUIT/ VEG	WEIGHT	NAME	YEAR
Apple	1.84 kg (4 lb 1 oz)	Chisato Iwasaki (Japan)	2005
Avocado	1.99 kg (4 lb 6 oz)	Anthony Llanos (Australia)	1992
Beetroot	71.05 kg (156 lb 10 oz)	Piet de Goede (Netherlands)	2005
Blueberry	7 g (0.24 oz)	Brian Carlick (UK)	2005
Broccoli	15.87 kg (35 lb)	John & Mary Evans (both USA)	1993
Brussels sprout	8.3 kg (18 lb 3 oz)	Bernard Lavery (UK)	1992
Cabbage	56.24 kg (124 lb)	Bernard Lavery (UK)	1989
Cabbage (red)	19.05 kg (42 lb)	R. Straw (UK)	1925
Cantaloupe	29.4 kg (64 lb 13 oz)	Scott & Mardie Robb (both USA)	2004
Carrot	8.61 kg (18 lb 13 oz)	John Evans (USA)	1998
Cauliflower	24.6 kg (54 lb 3 oz)	Alan Hattersley (UK)	1999
Celery	28.7 kg (63 lb 4 oz)	Scott & Mardie Robb (both USA)	2003
Cherry	21.69 g (0.76 oz)	Gerardo Maggipinto (Italy)	2003
Cucumber	12.4 kg (27 lb 5 oz)	Alfred J. Cobb (UK)	2003
Garlic head	1.19 kg (2 lb 10 oz)	Robert Kirkpatrick (USA)	1985
Gooseberry	61.04 g (2 oz)	K. Archer (UK)	1993
Gourd	42.8 kg (94 lb 5 oz)	Robert Weber (Australia)	2001
Grapefruit	3.06 kg (6 lb 12 oz)	Debbie Hazelton (Australia)	1995
Jackfruit	34.6 kg (76 lb 4 oz)	George & Margaret Schattauer (both USA)	2003
Kale	26.58 kg (58 lb 9 oz)	David Iles (USA)	2006
Kohlrabi	43.98 kg (96 lb 15 oz)	Scott Robb (USA)	2006
Leek	8.1 kg (17 lb 13 oz)	Fred Charlton (UK)	2002
Lemon	5.26 kg (11 lb 9 oz)	Aharon Shemoel (Israel)	2003
Mango	3.1 kg (6 lb 13 oz)	Tai Mok Lim (Malaysia)	2006
Marrow	62 kg (136 lb 9 oz)	Mark Baggs (UK)	2005
Nectarine	360 g (12 oz)	Tony Slattery (New Zealand)	1998
Onion	7.49 kg (16 lb 8 oz)	John Sifford (UK)	2005
Parsnip	4.78 kg (10 lb 8 oz)	Colin Moore (UK)	1980
Peach	725 g (25 oz)	Paul Friday (USA)	2002
Pear	2.1 kg (4 lb 8 oz)	Warren Yeoman (Australia)	1999
Pineapple	8.06 kg (17 lb 12 oz)	E. Kamuk (Papua New Guinea)	1994
Pomegranate	1.04 kg (2 lb 3 oz)	Katherine Murphey (USA)	2001
Potato	3.5 kg (7 lb 11 oz)	K. Sloane (UK)	1994
Potato (sweet)	37 kg (81 lb 9 oz)	Manuel Pérez Pérez (Spain)	2004
Pummelo	4.86 kg (10 lb 11 oz)	Seiji Sonoda (Japan)	2005
Pumpkin	681.3 kg (1,502 lb)	Ron Wallace (USA)	2006
Quince	2.34 kg (5 lb 2 oz)	Edward Harold McKinney (USA)	2002
Radish	31.1 kg (68 lb 9 oz)	Manabu Oono (Japan)	2003
Zuccini (Courgette)	29.25 kg (64 lb 8 oz)	Bernard Lavery (UK)	1990

HEAVIEST APPLE

On 24 October 2005, Chisato Iwasaki (Japan) picked an apple weighing 1.84 kg (4 lb 1 oz) that he had grown at his apple farm in Hirosaki City, Japan. Chisato may want to consider using his giant fruit to beat the record for the **longest unbroken apple peel**. Kathy Wafler (USA) peeled an apple in 11 hr 30 min with a peel length of 52.51 m (172 ft 4 in), at Long Ridge Mall in Rochester, New York, USA, on 16 October 1976.

★ HEAVIEST
PUMPKIN

The heaviest pumpkin weighed 681.3 kg (1,502 lb) when it was presented by Ron Wallace (USA, left) at the Southern New England Giant Pumpkin Growers Weigh-off, held in Warren, Rhode Island, USA, on 7 October 2006.

★ LONGEST FLOWER BOX

Edgar Ehrenfels made a 323-m-long (1,059-ft 9-in) flower box using flowers from Ralf Plawky (both Germany). It is situated on the bridge between Karlstadt and Karlburg in Germany.

★ LONGEST CUCUMBER

A cucumber grown by Alfred J. Cobb (UK) and presented at the UK National Giant Vegetables Championships in September 2006 measured 89.2 cm (35.1 in). The "big veg" contest forms part of *Amateur Gardening* magazine's annual National Show at the Bath & West Showground in Shepton Mallet, Somerset, UK.

Cobb also produced the **heaviest cucumber** – a 12.4-kg (27-lb 5.3-oz) specimen – for the 2003 championships.

GREAT GARDENS

• The **largest garden** in the world is that created by André Le Nôtre (France) at Versailles, France, in the late 17th century for King Louis XIV. The magnificent formal gardens and parkland were created in what had been a marshland. They cover more than 6,070 ha (15,000 acres) – about the size of 45 regular football fields – of which the famous formal garden covers 100 ha (247 acres).

• Monsieur Le Nôtre would have no doubt made good use of the world's ★ **largest garden** spade. The titanic tool measures 3.16 m (10 ft 4 in) tall, with a blade 53.8 cm (21.1 in) wide, and was made by employees of Joseph Bentley in Barton upon Humber, Lincolnshire, UK. It was measured on 11 May 2005.

• Fans of topiary – the art of sculpting hedges – should pay a visit to Levens Hall in Cumbria, UK, home of the world's **oldest topiary garden**. Initial planting and training was carried out in the 1690s, and some of the designs are over 300 years old.

• The **oldest surviving hedge maze** is located at Hampton Court Palace in Surrey, UK, and was built for King William III and Mary II of England in 1690 using hornbeam (*Carpinus betulus*).

TALLEST PLANTS

PLANT	HEIGHT	NAME	YEAR
Amaranthus	4.61 m (15 ft 1 in)	David Brenner (USA)	2004
Bean plant	14.1 m (46 ft 3 in)	Staton Rorie (USA)	2003
Brussels sprout	2.8 m (9 ft 3 in)	Patrice & Steve Allison (both USA)	2001
Cactus (homegrown)	21.3 m (70 ft)	Pandit S. Munji (India)	2004
Celery	2.74 m (9 ft)	John Priednieks (UK)	1998
Chrysanthemum	4.34 m (14 ft 3 in)	Bernard Lavery (UK)	1995
Coleus	2.5 m (8 ft 4 in)	Nancy Lee Spilove (USA)	2004
Collard	2.79 m (9 ft 2 in)	Reggie Kirkman (USA)	1999
Cosmos	3.75 m (12 ft 3 in)	Cosmos Executive Committee, Okayama, Japan	2003
Cotton	8.25 m (27 ft 1 in)	D. M. Williams (USA)	2006
Daffodil	1.55 m (5 ft 1 in)	M. Lowe (UK)	1979
Dandelion	1 m (3 ft 3 in)	Ragnar Gille & Marcus Hamring (both Sweden)	2003
Eggplant (Aubergine)	5.5 m (18 ft)	Abdul Masfoor (India)	1998
Fuchsia (climbing)	11.40 m (37 ft 5 in)	Reinhard Biehler (Germany)	2005
Herba cistanches	1.95 m (6 ft 4 in)	Yongmao Chen (China)	2006
Papaya tree	13.4 m (44 ft)	Prasanta Mal (India)	2003
Parsley	1.39 m (4 ft 7 in)	Danielle, Gabrielle, & Michelle Kassatly (all USA)	2003
Pepper	4.87 m (16 ft)	Laura Liang (USA)	1999
Periwinkle	2.19 m (7 ft 2 in)	Arvind, Rekha, Ashish, & Rashmi Nema (all India)	2003
Petunia	5.8 m (19 ft 1 in)	Bernard Lavery (UK)	1994
Rosebush (self-supported)	4.03 m (13 ft 3 in)	Paul & Sharon Palumbo (both USA)	2005
Rose (climbing)	27.7 m (91 ft)	Anne & Charles Grant (both USA)	2004
Sugarcane	9.5 m (31 ft)	M. Venkatesh Gowda (India)	2005
Sunflower	7.76 m (25 ft 5 in)	M. Heijms (Netherlands)	1986
Sweet corn (maize)	9.4 m (31 ft)	D. Radda (USA)	1946
Texas Bluebonnet	1.64 m (5 ft 5 in)	Margaret Lipscome & Arthur Cash (both USA)	2005
Tomato	19.8 m (65 ft)	Nutriculture Ltd., Lancashire, UK	2000
Umbrella	8.22 m (27 ft)	Konstantinos Xytakis & Sara Guterbock (both USA)	2002
Zinnia	3.81 m (12 ft 6 in)	Everett Wallace Jr. & Melody Wagner (both USA)	2004

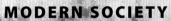

WORK & EMPLOYMENT

★ FASTEST OFFICE

The fastest office is a road-legal desk that can attain a maximum speed of 140 km/h (87 mph). It was created by Edd China (UK) and driven across Westminster Bridge into the City of London, UK, on 9 November 2006 as part of international Guinness World Records Day.

★ **NEW RECORD**
☆ **UPDATED RECORD**

★ LONGEST CAREER IN ONE COMPANY

Lester J. Nichols (USA) started work as a shipping clerk for Malleable Iron Fittings in Connecticut, USA, in 1866. He retired in 1945 having been secretary, assistant, treasurer and director of the company!

LONGEST CAREER

Shigechiyo Izumi (Japan) began work goading draught animals at a sugar mill in Tokunoshima, Japan, in 1872. He retired as a sugar-cane farmer in 1970 – 98 years later – aged 105.

GREATEST DISTANCE WALKED IN A CAREER

Stanley E. Rychlicki (USA) spent 37 years as a pipeline inspector and walked a distance of 220,288 km (136,887 miles), sometimes covering over 32 km (20 miles) per day across Pennsylvania and New York, USA.

LARGEST EMPLOYER

The world's largest commercial or utility employer is Indian Railways, with 1.65 million regular employees as of 2000. This state-owned company is one of the busiest in the world, transporting over six billion people and around 750 million tonnes of freight and cargo every year, covering the entire length and breadth of the country.

OLDEST ASTRONAUT

The oldest astronaut is John Glenn Jr (USA), who was 77 years 103 days old when he was launched into space as part of the crew of *Discovery STS-95* on 29 October 1998.

The **oldest female astronaut** is Shannon Lucid (USA, pictured), who was 53 years 67 days old at the launch of the space shuttle mission *STS-76 Atlantis* on 22 March 1996.

LONGEST WORKING CAREERS

CAREER	HOLDER (NATIONALITY)	WORKING SPAN	YEARS
Accountant	Harilal D Maniar (India)	1929–present	78
Actor	Curt Bois (Germany)	1908–87	79
Actress	Maxine Elliott Hicks (USA)	1914–92	78
Bartender	Angelo Cammarata (USA)	1933–present	74
Builder	Edward William Beard (UK)	1896–1981	85
Butler	Horace Mortiboy (UK)	1937–40, 1945–70, 1987–present	51
Cartoon voiceover	Jack Mercer (USA)	1934–79	45
Clown	Charlie Rivel (Spain)	1899–1981	82
Dance teacher	Tommy Moss (UK)	1929–present	78
Movie director	King Vidor (USA)	1913–80	67
Newspaper boy	Velmore Smith (Canada)	1958–2002	44
Opera singer	Danshi Toyotake (Japan)	1898–1979	81
Pilot	Clarence Cornish (USA)	1918–95	77
Radio DJ	Ray Cordeiro (Hong Kong)	1949–present	58
Santa Claus	Dayton C. Fouts (USA)	1937–97	60
Teacher	Medarda de Jesus Leon de Uzcategui (aka La Maestra Chucha, Venezuela)	1911–present	96
TV naturalist	Sir David Attenborough (UK)	1954–present	53

OLDEST FOOTBALLER

Tércio Mariano de Rezende (Brazil, b. 31 December 1921) plays regularly in the regional Championship as a right-winger for Goiandira Esporte Clube in Goiandira, Goiás, Brazil. The 87-year-old is registered with the Catalao Levindo da Fonseca Soccer League.

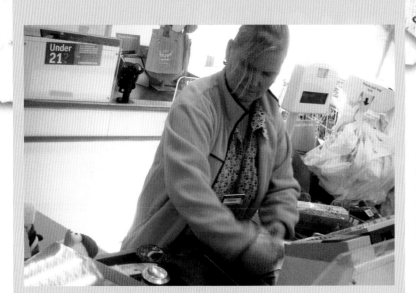

★FASTEST TIME TO SCAN AND BAG 50 SHOPPING ITEMS

In just 3 min 31 sec, checkout operator Debbie O'Brien (UK) scanned and bagged 50 shopping items at the ASDA store in Clapham Junction, London, UK, on 9 November 2006, as part of Guinness World Records Day.

★ HARDEST-WORKING INDUSTRIALIZED NATION

According to the Organization for Economic Co-operation and Development (OECD), the industrialized country with the hardest-working citizens in 2006 was South Korea, whose working population (excluding self-employed labour) clocked up 2,423 hours per employee for 2004.

HIGHEST UNEMPLOYMENT

According to 2003 estimates, the country with the highest rate of unemployment is Liberia, with 85% of its labour force not in paid work.

★LONGEST-SERVING CHIEF OF POLICE

Thomas E. Hawley (USA) served as the Chief of Police in Green Bay, Wisconsin, USA, from 17 August 1897 to 1 June 1946 – a total of 49 years.

★ LONGEST CAREER – RECORDING ARTIST

Kasper Delmar "Stranger" Malone (USA) released recorded music over eight consecutive decades. His first song – "Let Me Call You Sweetheart" – was recorded in 1926; his last was in 2003. Throughout his varied career, he played cornet, clarinet, flute, double bass (including a 10-year spell with the Tucson Symphony Orchestra) and guitar.

He died in 2005, aged 95.

★LONGEST CAREER – MUSIC TEACHER

Charles Wright (USA, b. 24 May 1912) began teaching piano professionally in 1931 and continues to do so.

★ LONGEST CAREER – CONDUCTOR

Juan Garcés Queralt (Spain) has been a conductor in Valencia, Spain, for 67 years. He started leading bands in 1939 and continues to do so at the age of 92.

LONGEST-SERVING EXECUTIONER

William Calcraft (GB, 1800–79) served as public executioner for 45 years. He officiated at nearly every hanging at Newgate Prison, London, UK.

★MOST DURABLE BLOOPER PRESENTER

Denis Norden (UK, b. 6 February 1922) has hosted a TV blooper (out-takes) show for 29 years. He started with *It'll be Alright on the Night* in 1977 and presented his last show – *All the Best from Denis Norden* – in 2006.

WORST JOBS

• **Most feet and armpits sniffed**
Madeline Albrecht (USA) was employed for 15 years at the Hill Top Research Laboratories in Cincinnati, Ohio, USA, where she tested products for hygiene company Dr Scholl. She had the unenviable task of sniffing feet and armpits, and smelled approximately 5,600 feet and an indeterminate number of armpits.

• **Longest-working grave digger**
It is recorded that Johann Heinrich Karl Thieme, sexton of Aldenburg, Germany, dug 23,311 graves during a 50-year career. After his death in 1826, his understudy dug *his* grave!

MOST CRASH TESTS

As of March 2007, W. R. "Rusty" Haight (USA) had driven in 846 crash tests as a "human crash-test dummy". During the tests (right), conducted for research purposes, Rusty and the vehicle are fitted with an array of sensors (accelerometers) for gathering data, which is used by his Collision Safety Institute and others to improve motor vehicle safety.

CULTS, FANS & FOLLOWERS

LONGEST CIVIL DISOBEDIENCE MARCH

In March and April 1930, Mohandas Karamchand Gandhi (India) led 78 followers on a 387-km (241-mile) march between the Gujurat towns of Sabarmati Ashram and Dandi in protest at British India's levy of salt tax.

The protest became known as the Dandi Salt March. Gandhi addressed crowds en route, attracting increasing numbers to the march.

★ LARGEST MASS SUICIDES

In July 1944, the Japanese army was defeated by US soldiers during the Battle of Saipan Island in the Pacific Ocean. About 5,000 islanders jumped off cliffs into shark-infested waters or blew themselves up with grenades rather than face the torture that they thought they would suffer at the hands of their American captors.

Ancient: As reported by the historian Flavius Josephus, some 960 Jewish zealots killed themselves by cutting each other's throats at Masada, Israel, in AD 73, as the palace was being besieged by Romans.

LONGEST STAND-OFF WITH A CULT

In 1993, law-enforcement agencies were engaged in a stand-off with the Branch Davidians, a religious sect led by David Koresh (USA, above), for 51 days at the Mount Carmel Compound in Waco, Texas, USA.

Hostilities began on 28 February, when federal agents tried to enter the compound, and ended on 19 April, when police stormed the main building and fire broke out. In all, 82 Davidians died.

★ LARGEST GATHERING OF ZOMBIES
(OKAY... PEOPLE *DRESSED* AS ZOMBIES)

On 29 October 2006, unsuspecting shoppers at the Monroeville Mall in Pennsylvania, USA, would have been horrified to behold a record-breaking gathering of 894 zombies shuffling through the Mall.

FANS & FAN CLUBS

LOUDEST SCREAM BY A CROWD (INDOORS)

On 6 September 2001, 10,500 fans screamed, cheered and whistled at Wembley Arena on the first London date of UK group Hear'say's national tour, generating a sound-level reading of 128.8 dBA.

★ LARGEST HUMAN NATIONAL FLAG

A "human" flag comprising 18,788 women was organized by Realizar Impact Marketing (Portugal) and unveiled at the National Stadium of Jamor, in Lisbon, Portugal, on 20 May 2006. The national flag was formed to highlight the support for the national soccer team by Portuguese women in the run-up to the football World Cup.

★ MOST ENDURING CARGO CULTS

The oldest so-called "Cargo Cults" appeared in the late 19th century, typically in Melanesia and New Guinea, but many have now died out. The most enduring, however, are those associated with "John Frum" – they worship a mythical World War II American GI of that name (possibly derived from the words "John from America") – and the nearby Yaohnanen tribe (pictured), who, for reasons that remain unclear, worship Britain's Prince Philip, Duke of Edinburgh, as a divine being. *Find out more on p.123.*

★ LARGEST ELVIS GATHERING

The largest gathering of Elvis impersonators (or should that be Elvi, plural?) was created by 109 employees of Maris Interiors (UK), who collectively performed the song "Suspicious Minds" at Gatwick Airport, UK, on 3 December 2006 (pictured). The **longest Elvis singing marathon** lasted 43 hr 11 min 11 sec and was carried out by Thomas "Curtis" Gäthje (Germany) at Modehaus Böttcher, Heide, Germany, on 24–26 June 2004.

CARGO CULTS

The term "cargo cults" was coined in 1945 to describe remote tribes – found mostly in Melanesia – that pray for the return of the various goods that appeared, seemingly miraculously, during occupation of their islands by colonialists.

The two key phases of this occupation were the turn of the 20th century and World War II, during the Allied forces' Pacific campaign. The **earliest known cargo cult** – Fiji's Tuka Movement – is thought to date back to 1885.

MOST FAN MAIL

Although fan mail is traditionally associated with film stars, no actor or actress has received in the course of a career the 3.5 million letters delivered to Charles Lindbergh (USA) following his solo non-stop transatlantic flight in May 1927.

MOST FAN MAIL RECEIVED IN A YEAR

The highest confirmed volume of mail received by any private citizen in one year is 900,000 letters by the baseball star Hank Aaron (USA), as reported by the US Postal Service in June 1974.

Approximately a third of these were hate letters received after Aaron broke Babe Ruth's career record for "home runs".

DID YOU KNOW?

The **largest science-fiction fan club** is Starfleet, the International *Star Trek* Fan Association. Founded in 1974 and based in Independence, Missouri, USA, the organization boasts over 4,100 annual members dedicated to the ideals of the *Star Trek* TV series.

MOST FAN CLUBS FOR A SINGER

As of March 2000, there were over 613 Elvis Presley fan clubs worldwide, with a total membership of 510,489. The oldest is the French *La Voix d'Elvis*, founded in 1956.

★ LONGEST PARADES

• **Fiats** The Fiat 500 Club Italia organized a parade of 500 Fiat cars and their fans from Villanova d'Albenga to Garlenda, Italy, on 9 July 2006.

• **Steam-rollers** The Great Dorset Road Builders arranged for 32 vintage steam rollers to pass over a length of new road at the Great Dorset Steam Fair, UK, on 31 August 2003.

MODERN MASS SUICIDES

GROUP	DEATHS	LOCATION	DATE
The Movement for the Restoration of the Ten Commandments of God	924	Uganda	Mar–Apr 2000
People's Temple	913	Guyana	Nov 1978
Branch Davidians	82	USA	Apr 1993
Order of the Solar Temple	74	Switzerland, Canada and France	Sep 1994– Mar 1997
Heaven's Gate	39	USA	Mar 1997
The Move	11	USA	May 1985
Simbionese Liberation Army	6	USA	May 1974
Source: Cult Information Centre			

★ LARGEST FURRY FAN CLUB

Furry fandom is a fan-club genre for a subculture that enjoys dressing as animals. "Furries", as they are known, meet up at confurences and share their love of animal anthropomorphism – that is, the depiction of animals with human characteristics, such as the rabbits in Richard Adams' novel *Watership Down*. The largest annual furry gathering occurs at Anthrocon in Pittsburgh, Pennsylvania, USA, and on 18 June 2006 a record 2,489 furries attended. Among the trivial "fursuits" on offer were a furries parade, various guests of honour and a charity auction.

FESTIVALS

NEW YEAR

The 2007 New Year celebrations on the island of Madeira were dominated by the world's ★ **largest fireworks display** (below). In just eight minutes, a total of 66,326 fireworks were launched from over 40 sites.
• Incidentally, the ★ **most fireworks launched in 30 seconds** is 56,405, by Dr Roy Lowry (UK) at the 10th British Firework Championship in Plymouth, UK, on 16 August 2006.
• Rod Stewart's free gig at Copacabana Beach in Rio de Janeiro, Brazil, on New Year's Eve 1994, attracted the **largest free concert** audience of 3.5 million.

EASTER

• The **largest Easter egg** on record weighed 4.76 tonnes (10,483 lb) and was made by staff of the Cadbury Red Tulip factory in Ringwood, Victoria, Australia, on 9 April 1992.
• The world's ★ **largest decorated Easter egg** was created by Meisterstammtisch Oberneukirchen, Austria. It measured 8.1 m (26 ft 7 in) long and 5.39 m (17 ft 8 in) in diameter in April 2004.

FOOD & DRINK

The **largest beer festival** in the world is Munich's Oktoberfest. The busiest year was 1999, when 7 million visitors consumed a record 5.8 million litres (1.2 million gallons) of beer in 11 beer tents on a site as large as 50 football pitches.
• The Fellsmere Frog Leg Festival in Fellsmere, Florida, USA, is the **largest frog-leg festival** in the world. From 18 to 21 January 2001, it attracted 75,000 visitors with a taste for amphibians' appendages.
• The three-day Gilroy Garlic Festival, held each summer in Gilroy, California, USA, is the **largest garlic festival**, attracting 130,000 people to try garlic-flavoured food from meat to ice cream.

CHRISTMAS

★ LARGEST SANTA GATHERING

The Liverpool Santa Dash on 4 December 2005 involved 3,921 people dressed as Mr and Mrs Claus running through the streets of Liverpool city centre (above) in the UK.
• The ★ **largest area covered with artificial snow** was 12,462.78 m² (134,148 ft²) of Bond Street in London, UK. Snow Business (UK) showered the street with fake snow to celebrate the switching on of the Christmas lights in November 2006.
• The ★ **largest Christmas stocking** measured 19.25 m (63 ft 2 in) long and 8.23 m (27 ft) wide (heel to toe) on 11 January 2006, and was made by shoppers and staff of the MetroCentre, Gateshead, UK.

• The record for the ★ **most letters to Santa collected** was 410 in an event organized by the Rainbow Trust charity at the Trocadero in London, UK, on 16 December 2006.
• The ★ **longest Christmas cracker** – 63.1 m (207 ft) long – was made by parents of children at Ley Hill School, Chesham, UK, on 20 December 2001.
• A tree adorned with 140,000 lights for the RTL-ChariTree 2005 set the record for the ★ **most lights on a Christmas tree**. The feat was achieved by RTL Television on 26 November 2005 at Cologne Cathedral, Germany.
• The world's **tallest Christmas tree** was a 67-m (221-ft) Douglas fir (*Pseudotsga menziesii*) erected and decorated at Northgate Shopping Center, Seattle, Washington, USA, in December 1950.

• The Rock Creek Lodge Testicle Festival in Clinton, Montana, USA, is the ★ **largest testicle festival** in the world. Every year, around 2.5 tonnes (5,600 lb) of bull testicles (aka "Rocky Mountain oysters") are served to an average of 15,000 visitors.
• The Elmira Maple Syrup Festival held in Elmira, Ontario, Canada, is the world's **largest maple syrup festival**. The busiest event to date was on 1 April 2000, when 66,529 people attended the 36th annual event.

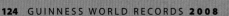

HALLOWEEN

- The **most pumpkins carved in one hour** is 42 by Stephen Clarke (USA, left) for the Halloween celebrations of *The Early Show* (CBS, USA) on 31 October 2002 in New York City, USA.
- Clarke also carved 1 tonne (2,000 lb) of pumpkins in 4 hr 17 min 26 sec at SeaWorld, Orlando, Florida, USA, on 29 October 2005.
- Classroom assistant Jill Drake (UK) registered the **loudest scream** of 129 decibels at the Halloween festivities in the Millennium Dome, London, UK, in October 2000.

LARGEST GATHERING OF...

Centenarians A total of 21 centenarians (people aged over 100) flew on one aircraft between Antwerp, Belgium, and London City Airport, UK, on 15 August 1997.

Clowns In 1991, at Bognor Regis, UK, 850 clowns, including 430 from North America, gathered for their annual convention.

Dancing dragons A total of 40 dragons, with 10 dancers per dragon, amassed at the Taman Jurong Community Club in Taman Jurong, Singapore, on 5 March 2005.

Giant papier-mâché puppets A total of 215 papier-mâché giants made by 88 organizations gathered at Solsona, Catalonia, Spain, on 6 July 2003.

Religious leaders The Millennium World Peace Summit of Religious and Spiritual Leaders involved 1,000 people at the United Nations in New York City, USA, in August 2000.

Test-tube children A group of 579 children born as a result of artificial insemination gathered at the Iscare IVF Assisted Reproduction Centre in Prague, Czech Republic, on 6 September 2003.

MUSIC & DANCE

The Festival de Dança de Joinville in Santa Catarina, Brazil, is the **largest dance festival** in the world. First produced in 1983, the festival is held over a minimum of 10 days and is attended by 4,000 dancers from 140 amateur and professional dance groups, watched by more than 200,000 people annually.

- The **largest rock festival attendance** was 670,000 at Steve Wozniak's 1983 US Festival in Devore, California.
- The **largest international music festival** is WOMAD (World of Music, Arts and Dance), which has presented more than 90 events in 20 different countries since 1982.

DID YOU KNOW?
The **largest gay festival** is the annual MiX Brasil: Festival of Sexual Diversity in São Paulo, Brazil. In its record year, 2005, the festival was attended by 1.8 million people.

- The **largest carnival** is the Rio de Janeiro annual carnival in Brazil, normally held during the first week of March. It attracts approximately two million people each day. In 2004, a record 400,000 foreign visitors attended.

- The world's **largest jazz festival** is the Festival International de Jazz de Montreal in Quebec, Canada, which attracted a record 1,913,868 people for its 25th anniversary, in July 2004.

ARTS

- The Edinburgh Arts Festival in Scotland, UK, is the **largest arts festival** on the planet. Its record year was 2003, when 12,940 artists gave 21,594 performances.
- The world's **longest film festival** is the 25-day-long Fort Lauderdale International Film Festival (FLIFF) held in Fort Lauderdale, Florida, USA.
- The **largest film festival** is the *Festival international du film de Cannes* held in the south of France. The annual event – arguably the most glamorous in the movie calendar – attracts between 40,000 and 50,000 movie industry workers each year, and countless cinephiles flock to the area to catch a glimpse of their favourite stars.

RELIGIOUS RITUALS

The **largest religious crowd** – and the greatest recorded number of people assembled with a common purpose – was an estimated 20 million at the Hindu festival of Kumbh Mela, held at the confluence of the Jamuna, Ganges and mythical "Saraswati" rivers at Allahabad (Prayag), Uttar Pradesh, India, on 30 January 2001. Pictured here is the Ardh (half) Khumn of 2007, a smaller gathering that occurs every six years.

- The **largest annual gathering of women** takes place in February or March each year, when over one million amass at the Attukal Bhagavathy Temple in Kerala, India, for the Pongala offering. The women, from all religions, gather with cooking pots to perform a ritual for health and prosperity. The highest attendance recorded was 1.5 million women on 23 February 1997.

★ NEW RECORD ★ UPDATED RECORD

★ MOST SECURE BANKNOTE

Swiss franc notes have up to 18 security features to deter counterfeiting, 14 of which are visible on the front of the note (see right). In addition, the "paper" is made from the by-products of the cotton-making process, and the notes are printed with special inks that are resistant to 18 different chemicals and machine-washable at high temperatures.

INTAGLIO DIGITS
Denomination of note etched into the paper; feels rough to the touch

KINEGRAM® DIGIT
Moving image of the note's denomination created in foil

WATERMARK DIGITS
Denomination of note printed as a traditional watermark

CHAMELEON DIGIT
Optically variable ink (OVI) changes colour as light hits it from different angles

MICROPERF® DIGITS
Denomination punched into note as tiny perforations

IRIODIN® DIGITS
Denomination of note printed in a shimmering, transparent ink that can only be seen from a particular angle

TILTING DIGIT
Denomination printed in such a way that it can only be seen from an unusual angle

TRANSPARENT REGISTER
A cross printed on each side, one smaller than the other

SYMBOL FOR VISUALLY HANDICAPPED
A raised symbol used to help the blind determine denomination

GUILLOCHES
Fine, entwined lines that change colour as the light changes

SCHWEIZERISCHE NATIONALBANK
BANCA NAZIUNALA SVIZRA

Fünfzig Franken
Tschuncanta Francs

GLITTERING DIGIT
Denomination printed in metal

ULTRAVIOLET DIGIT
Denomination only appears under UV light

MICROTEXT
Text so tiny that it can only be read by magnifying glass

WATERMARK PORTRAIT
Repeat of main portrait

PAY UP!

The ★ **largest payout by an insurer** amounted to $50 billion (£27 billion). It followed the damage by the twin strikes of Hurricanes Katrina and Rita in August and September 2005 in the USA. In 1992, Hurricane Andrew caused $22 billion (£11 billion) worth of damage.

★ MOST EXPENSIVE OFFICE SPACE

According to real-estate managers C.B. Richard Ellis, London (below), UK, is the priciest location for office space. As of June 2006, the cost per square metre per month including rent, taxes and service charges in London's West End was £107 ($201).

LARGEST...

★ ANNUAL TRADE SURPLUS (COUNTRY)

For 2005, boosted by Christmas sales of products in the West, China had a trade surplus of 823 billion Chinese yuan ($102 billion; £57 billion). A country's trade surplus is the difference in value between what it exports and what it imports.

★ NATIONAL DEBT

The largest debtor nation in history is the United States of America. As of 28 March 2007 (at 2 p.m. GMT), the US national debt stood at $8,845,127,059,284.86 (£4.5 trillion). With the US population numbering just over 300 million, each person's share of the debt is $29,357.26.

★ STOCK MARKET CRASH

Stock markets across the world saw their largest ever drop during October 1987, starting with "Black Monday" on the 19th. By the end of the month, the US stock market had dropped 22.68% (the equivalent of $500 billion, or £282 billion, lost), the Canadian stock market 22.5% and the UK stock market 26.4%. Asian markets fared even worse, with the Hong Kong and Australian markets dropping 45.8% and 41.8% respectively in the same period.

Some of the causes of the decline have been attributed to over-valuation and market psychology at the time. However, no exact explanation has ever been found.

★ TAX SCAM

On 3 March 2005, US entrepreneur Walter Anderson was charged with failing to pay more than $200 million (£103 million) in personal income taxes. Eighteen months later, in September 2006, Anderson admitted to two counts of evading taxes and one of fraud, and was sentenced to 10 years' imprisonment. He further pleaded guilty to hiding $365 million (£188 million) of income by using aliases, shell companies, offshore tax havens and secret accounts.

FIRST PAPER MONEY

The use of paper currency can be traced back to the Song dynasty (960–1279) in China, when it was utilized by a group of wealthy merchants and businessmen in Sichuan, the same place where printing was invented. Each banknote issued had printed on it pictures of houses, trees and people. The seals of the issuing banks were then applied and confidential marks were made on each bill in order to prevent counterfeiting.

LARGEST RETAILER BY SALES REVENUE

Sam Walton opened the first Wal-Mart store in 1962. In the fiscal year 2006/07, Wal-Mart Stores, Inc. of Bentonville, Arkansas, USA, had a sales revenue of $348.65 billion (£195.8 billion).

★ TAX DISPUTE

On 11 September 2006, a dispute between the US Internal Revenue Service (IRS) and pharmaceutical giant GlaxoSmithKline (GSK) was finally settled. GSK agreed to pay $3.1 billion (£1.6 billion) in taxes and interest payments after tax accounts dating back 16 years were disputed by the IRS.

★ LEVERAGED BUYOUT

A leveraged buyout involves taking over a company by purchasing a controlling amount of the equity.

On 25 February 2007, a deal was agreed for the leveraged buyout of energy provider TXU Corporation (USA) by a group led by private-equity firms Texas Pacific Group and Kohlberg Kravis Roberts & Co. The deal was valued at $43.8 billion (£22.3 billion).

★ MEDIA CORPORATION

In 2006/07, Time Warner (USA) recorded assets of $131.67 billion (£66.75 billion), according to the *Forbes Global 2000* list.

★ PUBLIC COMPANIES

By profit: Oil and gas giant Exxon-Mobil (USA) made $39.5 billion (£19.7 billion) in profit in 2006/07.
By assets: British bank Barclays currently owns the equivalent of $1,949.17 billion (£988 million) in assets. Source: *The Forbes Global 2000*.

SMALLEST BANKNOTE

ACTUAL SIZE

The smallest national note ever issued was the 10-bani note of the Ministry of Finance of Romania in 1917. Its printed area measured 27.5 x 38 mm (1.08 x 1.49 in). This is roughly one-tenth the size of a $1 banknote.

OLDEST...

FAMILY BUSINESS

Houshi Ryokan (Japan) dates back to AD 717 and is a family business spanning 46 generations. (A ryokan is a traditional Japanese inn.)

★ RECORD SHOP

Spillers Records (Cardiff, UK) was founded in 1894 to sell phonographs, wax cylinders and shellac discs. It has been running as a music and record store non-stop ever since.

LARGEST CHEQUE

The greatest amount paid by a single cheque in the history of banking was £2,474,655,000 ($3,971,821,324). Issued on 30 March 1995 and signed by Nicholas Morris, Company Secretary of Glaxo plc, the cheque represented a payment by Glaxo plc to Wellcome Trust Nominees Ltd. The Lloyds Bank Registrars computer system could not generate a cheque this large and so it was completed by a Lloyds employee using a typewriter. The typist was so overawed by the responsibility that it took three attempts to produce the cheque, numbered 020503.

A cheque for $4,176,969,623.57 (£1,486,466,058.21) was drawn on 30 June 1954, although this was an internal US Treasury cheque.

COLOSSAL COMPANIES

Below is a list of the world's largest companies by sector, based on market value at the end of the 2006/07 fiscal year:

- **Banking:**
  Citigroup (USA)
  $247.42 billion
  (£125.95 billion)

- **Conglomerates:**
  General Electric (USA)
  $358.98 billion
  (£196.49 billion)

- **Consumer durables:**
  Toyota (Japan)
  $217.69 billion
  (£110.82 billion)

- **Household and personal products:**
  Procter & Gamble (USA)
  $200.34 billion (£101.98 billion)

- **Oil and Gas:**
  ExxonMobil (USA)
  $410.65 billion (£209 billion)

- **Retail:**
  Wal-Mart (USA)
  $201.36 billion
  (£102.5 billion)

- **Software:**
  Microsoft (USA)
  $275.85 billion
  (£140.42 billion)

- **Telecommunications:**
  AT&T (USA)
  $229.78 billion
  (£116.97 billion)

SUPER RICH

★ NEW RECORD ★ UPDATED RECORD

★ HIGHEST-EARNING SUPERMODEL

Gisele Bündchen (Brazil, below) earned $30 million (£15.2 million) in 2006 modelling for famous brands such as Dolce & Gabbana, Versace and Ralph Lauren.

★ COUNTRY WITH THE MOST BILLIONAIRES

As of February 2004, the country with the most dollar billionaires is the USA, with 276 according to *Forbes*' Rich List.

YOUNGEST BILLIONAIRE

Aged just 24, his Serene Highness 12th Prince Albert von Thurn und Taxis (Germany, b. 24 June 1983) has an estimated net worth of $2.1 billion (£1.1 billion).

★ HIGHEST ANNUAL EARNERS

- **Author**: *The Da Vinci Code* novelist Dan Brown (USA) earned $88 million (£43.8 million) in 2005–06.
- **Band**: The Eagles earned an estimated $45 million (£26 million) in 2005–06.

LARGEST...

★ BAR OF GOLD

On 11 June 2005, the Mitsubishi Materials Corporation manufactured a pure gold bar weighing 250 kg (551 lb) at the Naoshima Smelter & Refinery, Kagawa Prefecture, Japan.

LARGEST DIAMOND PENDANT

The largest non-religious pendant is the "Crunk Ain't Dead" design owned by hip-hop artist Lil' Jon (USA). With 3,576 white diamonds, alone it weighs 977.6 g (34.4 oz), with its gold chain 2.3 kg (5.01 lb). On 13 December 2006 it was valued at $500,000 (£254,860).

★ NATIONAL LOTTERY JACKPOT

The USA's Powerball jackpot stood at $365 million (£209 million) when drawn on 18 February 2006. It was claimed by eight workers in a meat-processing plant who bought their lucky ticket in Lincoln, Nebraska, USA.

★ BANK (ASSETS)

The Bank of Tokyo-Mitsubishi UFJ opened in Tokyo, Japan, on 1 January 2006. The result of a merger between Mitsubishi Tokyo Financial Group and UFJ Holdings, Inc. on 1 October 2005, the combined estimated assets totalled ¥162,714 billion ($1,440 billion; £816.8 billion).

MOST EXPENSIVE...

★ MOBILE PHONE

The most expensive handset commercially available is the Signature Vertu (a subsidiary of Nokia), launched in Paris, France, on 21 January 2002.

There is a choice of nine different metal finishes, ranging from stainless steel to platinum diamond (decorated with a 0.25-carat solitaire diamond and costing $46,650, or £25,000). Each handset features a sapphire crystal face.

J K ROWLING

J K Rowling's success story began with a tale of a 10-year-old wizard who had a lightning-bolt scar. To date, her Harry Potter books have sold a staggering 325 million copies worldwide, giving her the record for the highest annual earnings by a children's author**. She talked to us about her achievements.**

Of all the things you have been able to buy, which is your favourite?
My favourite material thing is our house in the north of Scotland, where it's very peaceful and we have a lot of fun with family and friends. Probably the very best thing my earnings have given me, though, is absence of worry. I have not forgotten what it feels like to worry whether you'll have enough money to pay the bills. Not to have to think about that any more is the biggest luxury in the world.

Given your fame, how do you keep yourself and your family grounded?
It's one of my top priorities. We try to lead a pretty normal life. We go out to shops like anyone else, walk around town like anyone else. Aside from very special events like premieres or fund-raisers, I tend to keep a fairly low profile and carry on like any other regular person.

Faced with a number of rejections from publishers and having a young daughter to raise, did you ever think of giving up on Harry?
I didn't! Because I really believed in – and really loved – the story. Iris Murdoch, a British writer, once said, "Writing a novel is a lot like getting married. You should never commit yourself until you can't believe your luck." I really couldn't believe my luck having had this idea and I was

determined to press on with it until the last publisher had rejected it, which – at one point – looked likely. What would I be doing if I had given up writing? I'd be teaching!

How do you feel about the series coming to an end?
On the one hand, I think I'm going to feel sad. Harry's been an enormous part of my life and it's been quite a turbulent phase of my life as well... so there will be a sense of bereavement. But there will also be a sense of liberation, because there are pressures involved in writing something so popular. I think that there will also be a certain freedom in escaping that particular part of writing Harry Potter.

MOST VALUABLE POTATO

An exclusive variety of potato – Bonnottes de Noirmoutier, grown on the island of Noirmoutier, France – was sold at auction for £2,000 ($3,050) in April 1996. The bidder took 4.5 kg (10 lb) of potatoes home, worth approximately £33 ($56) each.

★ MOST EXPENSIVE COCKTAIL

The Trader Vic's Original Mai Tai costs £750 ($1,425) and features on the menu of The Bar at the Merchant Hotel, Belfast, Northern Ireland, UK. The high price is due to one particular ingredient: the rare 17-year-old Wray and Nephew Jamaican rum.

★ MOST DIAMONDS SET IN ONE RING

The "Dance of the Angel" ring, made by Lobortas & Karpova jewellery house in Kiev, Ukraine, in 2006, is set with a record 837 diamonds and weighs 5.57 carats.

ACTUAL SIZE

★ KIDNEY STONE

On 18 January 2006, *Star Trek* actor William Shatner (USA) sold a kidney stone for $25,000 (£12,700) to online casino GoldenPalace.com. He donated the money from the sale to charity.

★ MP3 PLAYER

The Presidential MP3 by Douglas J. is available in a choice of a white or yellow gold casing, studded with diamonds. Launched in November 2005 by Meng Duo Ltd, London, UK, it is priced at £25,000 ($43,000).

★ WALL CALENDAR

"To Touch an Angel's Wings", a calendar designed for the Muir Maxwell Trust epilepsy charity, was sold at auction for £15,000 ($26,100) to Stephen Winyard (UK) on 10 December 2005.

MOST VALUABLE...

★ FORTUNE COOKIE

A fortune cookie sold for £10,000 ($17,473) at an auction at the Chinese New Year Gala Dinner in aid of the charity Kids, at the Banqueting House, Whitehall, London, UK, on 8 February 2006.

★ TELEPHONE NUMBER

The most money paid for a number is 10 million QAR ($2.75 million; £1.46 million), by an anonymous Qatari bidder for the mobile telephone number 666-6666 during a charity auction hosted by Qatar Telecom on 23 May 2006.

★ TRUFFLE

Three white truffles weighing a total of 1.51 kg (3 lb 5 oz) sold at auction for €125,000 ($160,572; £84,067) in Hong Kong, China, on 12 November 2006.

★ TOOTH

An upper right canine tooth extracted from the mouth of Napoleon Bonaparte (Napoleon I of France) in 1817 sold for £11,000 ($19,140) at a British auction on 10 November 2005. The tooth is believed to have been extracted in 1816 because of scurvy infection.

RICH LIST

- US oil baron John D. Rockefeller was the **richest person ever**, with an estimated wealth of $900 million (£184 million) in 1913, equivalent to $189.6 billion (£114.3 billion) today.

- William H. Gates III (USA), Chairman and Chief Software Architect of Microsoft Corporation, is the **richest living person** according to *Forbes* magazine, which estimated his wealth at $50.1 billion (£29 billion) in March 2005.

- According to *Forbes*, the **richest woman** is Liliane Bettencourt (France), heiress to the L'Oréal cosmetics fortune, who in 2005 had an estimated net worth of $16 billion (£9 billion).

- The **richest monarch** in the world, as of 2005, is Prince Alwaleed bin Talal Alsaud of Saudi Arabia, with an estimated personal wealth of $20 billion (£11 billion).

- The **youngest non-inherited millionaire** was the American child film actor Jackie Coogan (1914–84). In 1923–24, he was earning $22,000 (£11,936) per week and retained approximately 60% of his films' profits. He was a millionaire in his own right by the age of 13.

★ LARGEST PRIVATELY OWNED YACHT

Golden Star, which measures 160 m (524 ft 10 in) long, is owned by Sheikh Mohammed bin Rashid al-Maktoum, the ruler of Dubai, United Arab Emirates (UAE). The yacht was commissioned in 1996 and launched for sea trials in April 2005; it is presently moored at the Jebel Ali Docks, Dubai. Although precise figures are unobtainable, the price of this "megayacht" is estimated at $300 million (£160.5 million).

POLITICS

COUNTRY WITH THE YOUNGEST VOTING AGE

Universal suffrage – that is, the right of men and women to vote in political elections – is at 15 years of age in Iran.

FIRST COUNTRY TO PASS WOMEN'S SUFFRAGE

The 1893 Women's Suffrage Petition led to New Zealand becoming the first self-governing nation in the developing world to grant women the right to vote. Governor Glasgow signed the Electoral Bill in September 1893.

★ MOST POLITICAL DEMONSTRATIONS IN 24 HOURS

To highlight flaws in the Serious and Organized Crime and Police Act (SOCPA) UK, Mark Thomas (UK) staged 20 demonstrations on 9 October 2006. Ironically, Thomas first had to inform the authorities as, under SOCPA laws, it is illegal to demonstrate outside British Parliament buildings without police permission!

★ MOST CORRUPT COUNTRY

As of 2006, the title of most corrupt country is held by the former French Caribbean colony of Haiti, which scored a record low of 1.8 on Transparency International's Corruption Perceptions Index (CPI). The CPI compares the misuse of public office for private gain in more than 160 countries, as perceived by business and political analysts.

LONGEST SERVING UK LABOUR PRIME MINISTER

At the age of 41, Tony Blair (UK) became the youngest-ever head of the British Labour Party when he was elected as its leader in 1994. In 1997, aged 44 (top), he became the youngest person to become British Prime Minister since Lord Liverpool in 1812. On his 2,838th day in office, on 6 February 2005 (bottom), he became the longest-serving Labour PM.

★ MOST COUNTRIES TO BE HEAD OF STATE SIMULTANEOUSLY

The number of independent nations for which the same person is lawfully Head of State at the same time is 16 and belongs to Her Majesty, Queen Elizabeth II (UK). While the Queen's role is nominal and ceremonial, over 128 million people in 15 Commonwealth states (plus the UK) recognize her as their monarch.

VOTE FOR ME

★ MOST VOTES FOR MR POTATO HEAD IN A POLITICAL CAMPAIGN

In 1985, Mr Potato Head received four postal votes in the mayoral election in Boise, Idaho, USA. However, he failed to win the election – which is just as well, as Mr Potato Head is a toy manufactured by Hasbro (USA).

★ MOST VOTES FOR A PHARMACEUTICAL PRODUCT IN A POLITICAL CAMPAIGN

A brand of foot hygiene powder won a mayoral election in the small Ecuadorian town of Picoazà (population 4,000) in 1967. The pharmaceutical company behind the Pulvapies brand of powder ran a series of election-inspired adverts, such as "Vote for any candidate, but if you want well-being and hygiene, vote for Pulvapies". The advertising campaign coincided with an actual municipal election, and the foot powder was voted in by the electorate on the strength of receiving the most postal votes!

MOST VOTES FOR A CHIMPANZEE IN A POLITICAL CAMPAIGN

In the 1988 mayoral election campaign in Rio de Janeiro, Brazil, the anti-establishment "Brazilian Banana Party" presented a chimp called Tião as their candidate. The chimpanzee came third out of 12 candidates, taking just over 400,000 votes. Known for his moody temper, his campaign slogan was "Vote monkey – get monkey". Tião passed away in December 1996, aged 33, at his cage in Rio zoo.

★ NEWEST INDEPENDENT COUNTRY

In a national referendum held on 21 May 2006, the people of Montenegro – a Balkan nation of 630,548 people – voted for independence from Serbia, thus creating the world's newest state. It will now apply to the European Union, the United Nations and other international institutions in its own right.

KINGS & QUEENS

• The King of Thailand, Bhumibol Adulyadej (Rama IX, b. 5 December 1927), is currently the world's **longest-reigning living monarch**, having succeeded to the throne following the death of his older brother on 9 June 1946.

• The country with the **youngest-reigning monarch** is Swaziland, where King Mswati III was crowned on 25 April 1986, aged 18 years 6 days. He was born Makhosetive, the 67th son of King Sobhuza II.

• The **longest reign of any monarch** is that of Phiops II (also known as Pepi II or Neferkare), a Sixth-Dynasty pharaoh of Ancient Egypt. His reign began *ca.* 2281 BC, when he was six years of age, and is believed to have lasted about 94 years.

★ MOST HANDSHAKES BY A POLITICIAN IN EIGHT HOURS

As part of his campaign to become Governor of New Mexico, USA, Bill Richardson (USA) shook hands with 13,392 visitors to the New Mexico State Fair in Albuquerque, USA, on 14 September 2002. It was clearly worth the trouble – he won the seat!

★ HIGHEST POPULATION OF PRISONERS (DOCUMENTED)

With over 2.1 million people (approximately 25% of the world's prison population) in jail in the United States at any one time, the US prison system is the largest in the world. Its incarceration rate is 737 per 100,000 people; the average rate in most western nations is around 100 per 100,000 people.

★ NEWEST NATO FORCE

The most recent establishment of a force under NATO (North Atlantic Treaty Organization) is the NATO Response Force, or NRF – a technologically advanced force that can be deployed rapidly wherever needed. Its objectives range from combat missions, crisis response, peacekeeping, and counter-terrorist and non-combatant evacuation. It reached its full operational capability of some 25,000 troops in late 2006.

YOUNGEST SERVING PRIME MINISTER

Representing the Dominica Labour Party, the Hon. Roosevelt Skerritt (b. 8 June 1972) was appointed Prime Minister of Dominica on 8 January 2004.

★ SMALLEST AREA TO LAY CLAIM TO NATION STATUS

Founded in international waters 10 km (6 miles) off the Suffolk coast, UK, the Principality (or Duchy) of Sealand is a former World War II sea fort that remained derelict until 1966, when it was declared an independent state by Paddy Roy Bates (UK). Prince Roy I and his family declared themselves hereditary royal rulers and government officials, and have spent years struggling to have their claim recognized. They argue that most major European states and international lawyers have declared that Sealand has fulfilled all the legal requirements for a state.

SEALAND FACTS

• Sealand is just 1,300 m² (13,990 ft²)
• The Sealanders have produced their own constitution, flag, national anthem, currency – the Sealand dollar – and passports (above).
• It's a tax-free zone, and there are no gaming restrictions or customs duties.
• A dramatic take-over was staged in 1978 by the Prime Minister, but Prince Roy launched a helicopter assault and retook Sealand.

TERRORISM & CONFLICT

BLOODIEST BATTLES IN WORLD HISTORY

BATTLE	DATE	FATALITIES
Brusilov Offensive WWI	4 Jun–20 Sep 1916	2,000,000
Battle of Stalingrad WWII (left)	21 Aug 1942–2 Feb 1943	750,000–1,800,000
Siege of Leningrad WWII	8 Sep 1941–27 Jan 1944	850,000–1,500,000
Merv massacre	AD 1221	1,300,000
Urgench massacre	AD 1220	1,200,000
Battle of Moscow WWII	2 Oct 1941–7 Jan 1942	719,000–900,000
Battle of Kiev WWII	Aug–26 Sep 1941	400,000–678,000
Siege of Betar	AD 135	580,000
Battle of Gallipoli WWI	19 Feb 1915–9 Jan 1916	115,000–552,000
Battle of Smolensk WWII	10 Jul–10 Sep 1941	500,000–535,000

★ COUNTRY WITH MOST TROOPS DEPLOYED OVERSEAS

As of May 2005, the country with the highest number of military personnel serving their country overseas is the USA, with approximately 350,000 personnel on active duty. This figure includes those forces normally present in Germany, Italy, the UK and Japan, except when bases at those locations are actively supporting a combat operation.

BLOODIEST ANCIENT BATTLE

Roman losses at the Battle of Cannae in 216 BC, as portrayed in Hans Burgkmair's painting (below), have been estimated at 48,000 to 50,000 dead and 4,500 prisoners out of a force of about 80,000 men. The losses among the opposing forces under Hannibal have been estimated at 5,700. Cannae is considered the greatest battle of annihilation in history.

MOST BOMBED COUNTRY

Between May 1964 and 26 February 1973 some 2.26 million tonnes (5 billion lb) of bombs of all kinds were dropped on Laos along the North to South Ho Chi Minh Trail supply route to south Vietnam.

MOST RECENT MALICIOUS USE OF NERVE GAS

The nerve gas sarin was released with the intention to kill on 20 March 1995 in Tokyo, Japan. Members of the Aum Shinrikyo sect, a Buddhist splinter group, released the gas at several points in the subway system, killing 12 people and injuring more than 5,000.

★ MOST RECENT NUCLEAR BOMB TEST

On 9 October 2006, a nuclear test explosion occurred underground near Kilchu, North Korea. Estimates of the bomb's size range from 550 to 15,000 tonnes (1.2 to 33 million lb) of TNT. As a comparison, the first nuclear bomb ever dropped during conflict – at Hiroshima, Japan, during World War II – had an explosive force of around 12,500 tonnes (27 million lb) of TNT.

★ LARGEST PEACEKEEPING FORCE

The global deployment of United Nations peacekeeping representatives reached an historic high at the end of October 2006, with 80,976 military and police personnel and 15,000 civilians serving in peace operations around the world – the largest present-day peacekeeping force deployed on multiple operations. Pictured is the former UN Secretary General Kofi Annan (Ghana, centre) and French Forces commander General Alain Pellegrini (right) on 29 August 2006 at the UN peacekeeping base in Naqura, Lebanon.

★ LARGEST ORGANIZATION FOR REGIONAL SECURITY

The Organization for Security and Co-operation in Europe (OSCE) has a membership of 56 states from Europe, Central Asia and North America. It spans an area from Vancouver in Canada to Vladivostok in Russia and employs around 450 people in its various institutions and a further 3,000 in its field operations.

DID YOU KNOW?
The country with the **highest military spending per capita** is Israel. In 2005, the Israeli military cost its citizens £828.83 ($1,429.03) each. The country with the **lowest military spend per capita** is Iceland, with $0 spent as of 2005!

★ OLDEST PERSON TO RECEIVE A SERVICE MEDAL

Commander William Leslie King (UK) received the Arctic Emblem at the age of 96 on board HMS *Belfast* in London, UK, on 10 October 2006. The medal, introduced in March 2005, is given in recognition of sailors who served in the Arctic convoys supplying vital aid to the Soviet Union between 1941 and 1945.

★ OLDEST LIVING WORLD WAR I VETERAN

Henry Allingham (UK), the oldest man in the UK, was born in London, UK, on 6 June 1896. He is the oldest surviving member of the armed forces, having served in both World Wars.

★ MOST WANTED TERRORIST

Osama bin Laden (Saudi Arabia), leader of the terrorist organization Al-Qaeda, is the only terrorist on the US Federal Bureau of Investigation (FBI) list of the Ten Most Wanted, and is sought by other nations for his terrorist activities. A reward for his capture of up to $25 million (£13 million) is being offered by the Rewards for Justice Program of the US Department of State, and a further $2 million (£1 million) funded by the Airline Pilots Association and the Air Transport Association.

★ HIGHEST BOUNTY ON A DOG

In 2004, a bounty of $10,000 (£5,100) was placed on Agata, a female golden labrador who is one of Colombia's top drug-sniffer dogs. The bounty was raised by drug traffickers following a very successful string of detections. Luckily, Agata has a 24-hour bodyguard who checks her food for poison.

FIRSTS

• In August 2003, NATO (North Atlantic Treaty Organization) took over command and co-ordination of the International Security Assistance Force (ISAF) in Afghanistan, and in doing so commenced the ★ **first international NATO operation** outside its former Euro-Atlantic area. In Afghanistan, NATO's role includes working closely with UN organizations and the Afghan authorities to prevent Afghanistan falling into the hands of warlords and insurgents.

• Ergot is a type of fungus blight, and ingestion can cause delusions, paranoia, seizures and cardiovascular problems that can lead to death. In the 6th century BC, the Assyrians, who lived in present-day Iraq, used rye ergot to poison enemy wells – the **first incidence of biological warfare**.

• The **first aerial bombardment by aeroplane** occurred on 1 November 1911 during the Italo-Turkish War. Second Lieutenant Giulio Gavotti of the Italian Air Flotilla threw four small 4.5-lb (2-kg) Cipelli grenades over a Turkish camp stationed in Ain Zara, Libya, from his Taube monoplane, which was flying at an altitude of 185 m (600 ft).

WEAPONS

★ NEW RECORD ★ UPDATED RECORD

★ FIRST HEAT-RAY WEAPON

The Active Denial System projects a high-energy microwave beam within a 500-m (1,640-ft) range. On being struck by the beam, human targets feel a burning sensation as the microwave penetrates skin to a depth of 0.5 mm (0.015 in), raising the temperature to 50°C (122°F). The non-lethal beam is designed to disperse hostile crowds.

★ MOST POWERFUL TREBUCHET

A siege trebuchet at Warwick Castle, Warwickshire, UK, gained the record as the ★ **most powerful trebuchet** when, on 26 August 2006, it hurled a 13.2-kg (29-lb 1-oz) projectile over a distance of 249 m (816 ft 11 in). The power output of the trebuchet was 3,286.8 kg/m (23,773.4 lb/ft). It is also the world's ★ **largest trebuchet**, measuring 18 m (59 ft) tall, weighing 22 tonnes (48,500 lb) and able to sling-shot 20-kg (44.1-lb) projectiles up to 25 m (82 ft) high and over a range of 300 m (984 ft).

★ HIGHEST DEATH TOLL FROM AN ATOMIC BOMBING RAID

On 6 August 1945, an atomic bomb was used for the first time against an enemy in war. The bomb, named "Little Boy", was dropped by the USA from a B-29 Superfortress bomber, the *Enola Gay*, on the Japanese city of Hiroshima.

In 1986, the number of identified victims of the explosion was given on the Cenotaph memorial in Hiroshima as 138,890, the **highest death toll from a nuclear explosion** ever.

★ LARGEST NON-NUCLEAR CONVENTIONAL WEAPON IN EXISTENCE

The Boeing Massive Ordnance Penetrator (MOP) weighs a massive 13,600 kg (30,000 lb), including 2,720 kg (6,000 lb) of explosives. The weapon will be used to penetrate targets that might normally be resistant to attack, such as nuclear facilities and weapons bunkers hidden to depths of 61 m (200 ft) – even those buried beneath 8 m (26 ft) of reinforced concrete could be "penetrated" by the device.

The US Air Force are expecting to take delivery of the weapon sometime in 2007, after testing of it was completed in 2006.

★ FIRST TESTS CONDUCTED WITH PILOTLESS FLYING BOMBS

The first flight of the Kettering Aerial Torpedo (later known as the "Kettering Bug") was conducted in the USA on 2 October 1918, during World War I. The bomb was intended to have a range of 80 km (50 miles), but project funding was withdrawn when the war ended. This early form of cruise missile was never used operationally.

HEAVIEST NUCLEAR BOMB

The MK 17, which was carried by US B-36 bombers in the mid-1950s, weighed 19,050 kg (41,998 lb) and was 7.49 m (24 ft 6 in) long. It had a maximum yield of 20 megatons, equivalent to a thousand of the bombs dropped on Hiroshima on 6 August 1945.

★ LARGEST CONTRACT TO EXPORT AN AMRAAM WEAPONS SYSTEM

The largest contract for any advanced medium-range air-to-air missiles (AMRAAM) is the $284-million (£114.6-million) deal by US manufacturer Raytheon to supply the Pakistan Air Force with 200 Sidewinder AIM-9M-8/9 and 500 AIM-120C5 AMRAAM missiles. The contract was announced in January 2007.

SMALLEST NUCLEAR WEAPON

The W54 fission bomb, deployed by the USA in Europe between 1961 and 1971, is the smallest nuclear weapon ever made. With a warhead weighing just 23.13 kg (51 lb) the weapon had a yield of 0.1 kilotons and a maximum range of only 4 km (2.49 miles).

★ FIRST LASER WEAPON TO SHOOT DOWN A ROCKET

The US Army and the Israeli Ministry of Defence destroyed a Katyusha rocket carrying a live warhead using the High Energy Laser/Advance Concept Technology Demonstrator in New Mexico, USA, on 7 June 2000.

FIND OUT MORE
For more about weapons and military hardware see pp.206–7.

MOST ACCURATE HUMAN-PORTABLE ANTI-AIRCRAFT MISSILE

The US-made Stinger missile, introduced in the early 1980s, is 1.5 m (5 ft) long and weighs 9.9 kg (22 lb). It has a range of about 4.8 km (3 miles) and a top speed of about 2,000 km/h (1,300 mph). The Stinger's cryogenically cooled infrared seeker can distinguish between an aircraft's infrared signature and countermeasures that are normally used to disguise an aircraft, such as flares.

★ SMALLEST WORKING CANNON

A fully operational cannon made from wood, brass, iron and steel by Joseph Brooks

★ SMALLEST REVOLVER

The smallest working revolver is the C1ST made by SwissMiniGun (Switzerland), with a calibre of 2.34 mm. It measures 5.5 cm (2.2 in) long, 3.5 cm (1.4 in) high and 1 cm (0.4 in) wide, and weighs just 19.8 g (0.7 oz). It fires the smallest live and blank rimfire ammunition.

ACTUAL SIZE

(USA) measures just 3.175 cm (1.25 in) in length, 2.2 cm (0.86 in) in width and 1.6 cm (0.62 in) in height – an overall scale to the real thing of 1:48. The cannon was fired for the first time ever in Okeechobee, Florida, USA, on 22 October 2006.

★ MOST SYNCHRONIZED TWO-HAND RIFLE SPINS IN ONE MINUTE

Constantine Wilson, Abraham Robbins, Patrick Reed and Valentino Cuba (all USA) completed a total of 168 synchronized two-hand spins – 84 cycles – in one minute at the Navy and Marine Reserve Center, Anacostia Naval Base, Washington, DC, USA, on 28 January 2006.

On the same day and at the same location, the four men also set the record for the ★ **most underhand in-line rifle exchanges in one minute**. Standing in a line formation, they completed 26 exchanges.

HIGHEST CALIBRE

- The **largest-calibre ship guns** were the nine 45.7-cm (18-in) guns installed on the Japanese battleships *Yamato* and *Musashi*. The shells weighed 1,452 kg (3,200 lb) and had a range of 43.5 km (27 miles).

- The **highest-calibre cannon** ever constructed is the "Tsar Pushka" ("Emperor of Cannons"), now housed in the Kremlin, Moscow, Russia, and built in the 16th century. It has a bore of 89 cm (35 in) and a barrel 5.34 m (17 ft 6 in) long.

- The world's **largest bore for a piece of artillery** measures 91.4 cm (36 in) in diameter and belongs to the Mallet mortar, which was designed by Robert Mallet (Ireland) and completed in March 1857.

- The **largest-calibre mortars** ever constructed are Mallet's mortar and the "Little David" of World War II, made in the USA. Each had a calibre of 91.4 cm (36 in), but neither was ever used in action.

ANIMALS & MAN

★ OLDEST PENGUIN IN CAPTIVITY

The oldest ever penguin in captivity was Rocky, one of six rockhopper penguins (*Eudyptes chrysocome*) that arrived at Bergen Aquarium, Norway, in 1974. He lived there until his death in October 2003, aged 29 years 4 months.

★ LARGEST PROSTHETIC LEG

After losing her front left foot in a land mine accident in 1999, Motala was operated on by 30 vets at the Hang Chat Elephant Hospital in Lampang, Thailand – the **most vets involved in one operation**. In September 2006, Motala received a silicon/fibreglass limb big and strong enough to sustain the typical weight of an Asian elephant (3–5 tonnes (6,500–11,000 lb).

OLDEST ANIMALS IN CAPTIVITY

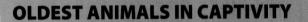

ANIMAL	LOCATION	AGE
★ Salamander	Artis Zoo, Amsterdam, Netherlands	52
★ Grey seal	National Seal Sanctuary, Gweek, Cornwall, UK	43
★ Water buffalo	Tal-Khed, Maharashtra, India	43
Kinkajou	Honolulu Zoo, Hawaii, USA	40
★ Polar bear	Assiniboine Park Zoo, Winnipeg, Canada	40
★ Panda	Wuhan, Hubei Province, China	37
Koala	Lone Pine Sanctuary, Queensland, Australia	23

★ LONGEST JUMP RIDING A LION

Performing for the Russian State Circus Company on 28 July 2006, Askold (pictured) and Edgard Zapashny (Russia) made a jump of 2.3 m (7 ft 6 in) while riding a lion called Michael.

★ LARGEST CINEMA-GOERS

On 6 June 2006, Asian elephants and their handlers (mahouts) were invited to attend a special open-air screening being held in the Ayuthaya Province of Thailand. The main feature was the Thai-animated film *Kan Kluay* (2006) which tells the story of a young elephant who grows up to be a war hero and assistant to the King of Thailand, set 400 years ago. Asian elephants (*Elephas maximus*) can measure up to 3 m (10 ft) in height, with males weighing up to 5 tonnes (11,000 lb).

FASTEST ROBOT JOCKEY

Kamel is a robot jockey designed by K-Team (Switzerland) for racing camels in the Arabian Gulf states. A traditional sport in the region, it has attracted human rights groups who fear for the lives of the jockeys, some as young as four years old, who are forced – often after starvation to keep weight down – to race. To combat this, the ruling sheiks of Qatar are calling for all camel races to be ridden by robot jockeys by the end of 2007. Weighing 27 kg (60 lb), Kamel comes with in-built GPS and shock absorbers, and can be controlled remotely by joystick. The fastest time recorded to date is 40 km/h (25 mph).

★ HIGHEST DEATH TOLL FROM LION ATTACKS

A total of 563 people were killed by lions across Tanzania between 1990 and 2005, including eight fatalities and 16 serious injuries in the region of Sudi and Mingoyo in Lindi, Tanzania, by a pack of four lions in 2001–04 alone. Pictured below is Hassan Dadi (Tanzania), who lost his arm in a lion attack in the village of Usuru, Tanzania.

Another major period of attacks occurred between 1932 and 1947. During these 15 years, 1,500 people were killed by lions (*Panthera leo*) roaming an area of 388.5 km^2 (150 miles^2) in Njombe, Tanzania. This equates to an average of 100 people per year. Lions typically only attack humans when their normal prey and/or habitat is severely compromised by human development.

ANIMAL ATTACKS ON HUMANS

KILLER ANIMAL	LOCATION & DATE	FATALITIES
Long saltwater crocodiles (*Crocodylus porosus*)	Ramree, Burma 19–20 February 1945	980 Japanese soldiers
Tiger	Champawat district, India 1902–07	436 people
Pack of wolves	Darovskoye district, Russia 1948	40 children
"Beast of Gévaudan" (possibly wolf)	Lozère, France 1764–66	Dozens of children and adults

ACTUAL SIZE

★ LARGEST
PANDA CUB

The largest panda cub born in captivity weighed 218 g (7.6 oz) shortly after its birth at the Wolong Giant Panda Research Centre in Chengdu, Sichuan Province, China, on 7 August 2006. The cub is the first offspring of Zhang Ka, who was in labour for 34 hours, itself the ★ **longest recorded labour for a captive panda**. The average weight of new-born pandas is 83–190 g (3–6.7 oz).

★ SMALLEST
POLICE DOG

The smallest dog used for law enforcement is Midge, a chihuahua–rat terrier cross measuring 28 cm (11 in) tall and 58 cm (23 in) long. Midge works as an official "Police K9" with her owner, Sheriff Dan McClelland (USA), at Geauga County Sheriff's Office in Chardon, Ohio, USA.

PANDA FACT FILE

• The giant panda (*Ailuropoda melanoleuca*) is the ★ **most costly of all zoo species**. The entire giant panda population is indigenous to and owned by China. Four zoos in the USA (San Diego, Atlanta, Memphis and Washington) each pay an annual leasing fee of $1 million (£500,000) to the Chinese government for a pair of these creatures. If cubs are born, a payment of $600,000 (£300,000) per offspring must also be made. A panda's upkeep (including bamboo production and security) makes them five times more costly than elephants.

• The ★ **oldest panda ever in captivity** was Dudu, who was born in 1962 and lived for most of her life in Wuhan Zoo, Chengdu, China, until her death on 22 July 1999, aged 37 years.
A male giant panda called Bao Bao was born in China in September 1978 but went to live at Berlin Zoo, Germany, in 1980 at the age of two. He has remained there ever since – the ★ **oldest panda living in captivity**.

• The ★ **longest recorded pregnancy** for a giant panda lasted 200 days for Shu Lan, who gave birth to a healthy male cub on 21 October 2004 at Chengdu Research Base for Giant Pandas, Sichuan Province, China. The average pregnancy for a panda is 95 to 160 days.

OLYMPIC HALL OF FAME

MOST OLYMPIC MEDALS (ATHLETE)

ATHLETE (COUNTRY)	SPORT	GOLD	SILVER	BRONZE	TOTAL
1 Larissa Latynina (USSR, below)	Gymnastics	9	5	4	18
2 Nikolai Andrianov (USSR)	Gymnastics	7	5	3	15
3 Edoardo Mangiarotti (Italy)	Fencing	6	5	2	13
= Takashi Ono (Japan)	Gymnastics	5	4	4	13
= Boris Shakhlin (USSR)	Gymnastics	7	4	2	13
6 Paavo Nurmi (Finland)	Athletics	9	3	0	12
= Birgit Fischer (Germany/ East Germany)	Canoeing/ Kayaking	8	4	0	12
= Sawao Kato (Japan)	Gymnastics	8	3	1	12
= Jenny Thompson (USA)	Swimming	8	3	1	12
= Alexei Nemov (Russia)	Gymnastics	4	2	6	12

JACKIE JOYNER-KERSEE

The **most Olympic heptathlon golds won by an athlete** is two, by Jackie Joyner-Kersee (USA) in 1988 and 1992. She also took gold in the 1988 long jump.

CARL LEWIS

Olympic great Carl Lewis (USA) shares the record for **most men's Olympic gold medals**, with nine: four in 1984 (100 m, 200 m, 4 x 100 m and long jump); two in 1988 (100 m and long jump); two in 1992 (4 x 100 m and long jump); and one in 1996 (long jump). Only two other men have won the same number of Olympic golds: Paavo Nurmi (Finland) and Mark Spitz (USA).

BIRGIT FISCHER

Birgit Fischer (GDR/Germany, left) won four consecutive canoeing golds from the South Korean Olympics in 1988 to the 2000 Sydney Olympics, the **most consecutive Olympic gold medals won by a woman**.

GREG LOUGANIS

Two divers share the record for **most diving medals**, with five each. Greg Louganis (USA, right) won four golds and one silver in 1976, 1984 and 1988. He is seen here in a famous incident in 1988, when his head hit the board mid-dive. Klaus Dibiasi (Italy) also won five diving medals, between 1964 and 1976.

X-REF

• Turn to our sports reference section on p.266 for a wealth of stats from all your favourite sports.

• You'll find all the latest athletics records on p.216–219.

• Crazy about swimming and other water sports? Then dive into p.256.

• If you like your sport to be a little more radical, check out X Games on p.264.

DALEY THOMPSON

At the 1984 Games, Daley Thompson (GB) scored 8,847 points, which remained the **most points scored in the men's Olympic decathlon** for an incredible 20 years. The current record holder is Roman Šebrle (Czech Republic), with 9,026 points.

RAYMOND CLARENCE EWRY

The **greatest number of gold medals won in a men's individual event** is eight, by Raymond Clarence Ewry (USA). He took gold in the standing long, triple and high jumps in 1900 and 1904 and the standing long and high jumps in 1908. (Ewry also won two golds at the 1906 Intercalated Games, but the International Olympic Committee does not officially recognize that event.)

ED MOSES

The **most Olympic gold medals in the men's 400 m hurdles event** won by an individual athlete is two by Ed Moses (USA, below), in 1976 and 1984, and Glenn Davis (USA), in 1960 and 1964.

MICHAEL JOHNSON

Michael Johnson (USA) ran the **fastest men's 200 m sprint** in 19.32 seconds in Atlanta, Georgia, USA, on 1 August 1996. In the same Games, he became the first man to complete the 200 m/400 m "double" in Olympic history.

HEIKE DRECHSLER

The **greatest number of Olympic gold medals won in the women's long-jump event** is two by Heike Drechsler (Germany) in 1992 and 2000.

MOST OLYMPIC MEDALS (COUNTRY)

COUNTRY	GOLD	SILVER	BRONZE	TOTAL
USA	897	691	603	2,191
USSR*	395	319	296	1,010
GB	188	242	237	667
France	184	196	216	596
Italy	182	147	164	493
Germany**	147	153	189	489
Sweden	142	154	171	467
Hungary	156	136	157	449
Germany (East)	153	129	127	409
Australia	117	122	147	386

*1952–92
** 1896–1936, 1956–64, 1992–present

SIR STEVEN REDGRAVE

The **most Olympic rowing gold medals won by a man** is five, by Steve Redgrave (GB), in the coxed fours (1984), coxless pairs (1988, 1992 and 1996) and coxless fours (2000).

JESSE OWENS

One of the greatest Olympians of all time, Jesse Owens (above) was a member of the US quartet that set a time of 39.8 seconds for the **fastest 4 x 100 m relay**, on 9 August 1936 in Berlin, Germany, known to many as the "Hitler Olympics". German premier Adolf Hitler had intended to use the event to prove to the rest of the world the superiority of the "Aryan" race and was visibly annoyed as he watched Owens win four gold medals.

The current record of 37.4 seconds is shared by the US 4 x 100 m teams who competed in Spain, in 1992, and Germany, in 1993.

OLYMPIAN FEATS

• The **earliest celebration of the ancient Olympic Games** of which there is a definite record is that of July 776 BC, when Coroibos, a cook from Elis, won the foot race. It is possible, however, that they date back to *ca.* 1370 BC.

• The total spectator attendance at the Olympic Games held in Los Angeles, California, USA, in 1984 was given as 5,797,923 people, representing the **greatest attendance at an Olympic Games**.

• A total of 201 countries participated in the Summer Olympic Games held in Athens, Greece, between 13 and 29 August 2004. This unprecedented number constitutes the **most countries to attend a Summer Games**.

• A total of 10,651 athletes, of whom 4,069 were women, participated in the Summer Olympic Games celebration held in Sydney, Australia, in 2000. This represents the **most participants at a Summer Games**.

• The USA won 2,191 medals in the Summer Games, 1896–2004, the **most Olympic medals won by a country**. The Winter Olympic Games were first held in 1924. The **most medals won by a country in the Winter Games** is 280, by Norway.

• The USA won 897 gold medals in the Summer Olympic Games, from 1896 to 2004, making it the **country with the most gold medals in the Summer Games**.
The USA also holds the record for the **most gold medals won at a single Summer Olympics**, with a record 83 at the XXIII Olympic Games held at Los Angeles, California, USA, in 1984.

• The **youngest Olympic champion** was Kim Yun-mi (South Korea; b. 1 December 1980), at the age of 13 years 85 days, in the 1994 women's 3,000 m short-track speedskating relay event.
Oscar Swahn (Sweden) was in the winning Running Deer shooting team at the 1912 Olympic Games in Stockholm, Sweden, aged 64 years 258 days, making him the **oldest Olympic gold medallist**.

SCIENCE & TECHNOLOGY

CONTENTS

☆ MOST POWERFUL PARTICLE ACCELERATOR

The Large Hadron Collider (LHC) is an international project designed to study matter by emulating conditions just a few billionths of a second after the Big Bang. It is located in the 27-km-long (16.7-mile) circular tunnel (pictured) at the CERN laboratory in Geneva, Switzerland, that previously housed the Large Electron Positron Collider.

The 38,000-tonne collider will accelerate two beams of matter in opposite directions around the tunnel. Once travelling at nearly the speed of light, the two streams of particles will be allowed to collide, producing showers of exotic subatomic particles, which will be detected by instruments in the tunnel.

The LHC is due for completion in November 2007 and will require 120 MW of power and 91 tonnes of liquid helium to operate. One principle aim of the LHC is to find the theorized but as yet unseen Higgs boson particle – often nicknamed the God Particle.

CUTTING-EDGE SCIENCE

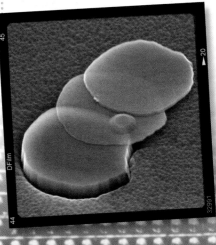

COMPUTERS

In November 2006, IBM's BlueGene/L System, the world's ★ **fastest computer**, retained its number-one spot on the list of top 500 computers with a performance of 280.6 teraflops (trillions of floating-point operations, or calculations) per second.

The world's ★ **smallest external hard drive** is the 4 GB MF-DU204G made by Elecom Japan, at 68 mm x 30 mm x 13 mm (2.6 in x 1.1 in x 0.5 in).

The ★ **smallest USB flash drive** is ATP Taiwan's Petito, released in March 2006. It measures 9.4 mm x 17.6 mm x 36.6 mm (0.37 in x 0.69 in x 1.42 in).

★ NEW RECORD
★ UPDATED RECORD

★ LARGEST FLEXIBLE LCD

Samsung (Korea) has created a 17.78-cm-thick (7-in) flexible liquid crystal display (LCD) that maintains its thickness when bent, keeping picture quality stable. The high-resolution LCD is sandwiched between two sheets of high-end flexible plastic that are much thinner and less brittle than current screens.

★ BIGGEST AWARD IN SCIENCE AND TECHNOLOGY

The €1,000,000 ($1,331,345; £685,629) Millennium Technology Prize is awarded every two years in recognition of outstanding contributions to world science and technology. The 2006 winner was Professor Shuji Nakamura (Japan) of the University of California, USA. His scientific achievements included the invention of blue-light-emitting diodes and the blue-laser diode.

★ THINNEST CHIP

On 5 February 2006, Hitachi Ltd (Japan) announced it had developed and verified operation of the world's smallest and thinnest chip, measuring 0.15 mm² (0.0002 in²) in area, and

★ SHARPEST MAN-MADE OBJECT

Scientists at the National Institute for Nanotechnology and the University of Alberta (both Canada) have created a tungsten needle that tapers to a thickness of just one atom. The breakthrough, announced in May 2006, should allow the construction of better super high-resolution electron microscopes. Pictured is the tip imaged by a field ion microscope.

7.5 µm (microns, or millionths of a metre) thick. The chip is thinner than paper (which is typically 80–100 microns thick), so one application could be as an "intelligent" watermark in bank notes.

★ OLDEST HUMAN DNA

A team of French and Belgian researchers have extracted DNA from the tooth of a Neanderthal child who lived in the Meuse Basin, Belgium, around 100,000 years ago. The analysis of the DNA, released in June 2006, shows that Neanderthals had a greater genetic diversity 100,000 years ago than they did by the time modern humans arrived in Europe around 35,000 years ago.

★ THINNEST MAN-MADE MATERIAL

In October 2004, UK and Russian scientists announced the discovery of the nanofabric graphene. With a thickness of just one single atom of carbon, graphene is similar to carbon nanotubes and carbon-60 "buckyball" molecules, but can exist as a single sheet of theoretically infinite size.

★ LARGEST UNDERGROUND NEUTRINO OBSERVATORY

Super-Kamiokande is a joint US-Japanese research facility located 1,000 m (3,280 ft) below ground in the Kamioka silver mine in Japan. It consists of a vast cylinder measuring 40 m (131 ft) in height and 40 m (131 ft) in diameter, which is filled with ultra-pure water. The interior is covered with 13,000 sensitive light detectors called photomultiplier tubes, which watch the water for Cerenkov light – the telltale sign that a particle has passed through the water. The men in the boat pictured bottom left are inspecting and cleaning the tubes.

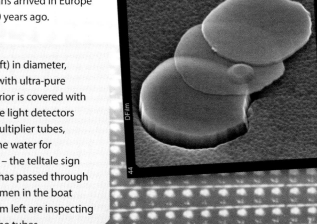

★ LARGEST HDTV SCREEN

Mitsubishi Electric (Japan) has installed a high-definition television (HDTV) screen measuring 11.2 x 66.4 m (37 x 218 ft) at the Tokyo Racecourse in Toyko, Japan, at a cost of ¥3.2 billion ($27.2 million; £14.4 million). The LED screen has a surface area of 744 m² (8,000 ft²) – equivalent in size to three tennis courts or 1,550 32-in television sets!

HIGHEST-INTENSITY FOCUSED LASER

The Vulcan laser at the Rutherford Appleton Laboratory, Oxfordshire, UK, is the highest-intensity focused laser in the world. Following its upgrade, which was completed in 2002, it is now capable of producing a laser beam with an irradiance (focused intensity) of 10^{21} watts per square inch.

★ LARGEST DIGITAL GRAPHIC

A digital graphic measuring over 929 m² (10,000 ft²) has been featured on the six bay doors of the Boeing Company in Washington, DC, USA, since 15 February 2006.

★ SMALLEST TRANSISTOR

Scientists at the University of Manchester, UK, have created prototype transistors using graphene, the world's thinnest material (see page left). Measuring just one atom thick by less than 50 atoms wide, the transistors could eventually render the silicon chip obsolete and allow the development of a brand-new type of super-fast computer chip. Their achievement was announced in March 2007.

★ MOST ADVANCED CLOAKING DEVICE

In October 2006, a team of US and UK scientists announced their creation of a device that could partially "cloak" an object from view in the microwave region of the electromagnetic spectrum. It consists of an array of 10 fibreglass rings coated with copper elements that change the direction of electromagnetic waves striking them. Placed around a copper cylinder, the cloaking device was able to deflect incoming microwaves and partially channel them around the cylinder, as if they had passed through it unaffected. This work could one day lead to technology that would hide an object from human eyes in visible wavelengths of light.

★ LARGEST FLEXIBLE E-PAPER

In 2006 in Korea, LG.Philips LCD, in co-operation with E-ink, unveiled a sheet of WXGA (wide extended graphics display) flexible E-paper with a diagonal measurement of 35.8 cm (14.1 in) and a resolution of 1,280 x 800 dpi. One possible application of such technology will be reducing the size of newspapers to a single sheet.

LG.Philips LCD makes Technology you can see!

LG. PHILIPS LCD

MAN-MADE SUBSTANCES

• **Bitterest...** The bitterest-tasting substances are based on the denatonium cation and have been produced commercially as benzoate and saccharide. Taste-detection levels are as low as one part in 500 million, and a dilution of one part in 100 million will leave a lingering taste.

• **Sweetest...** Thaumatin, also known as Talin – obtained from the arils (appendages found on certain seeds) of the katemfe plant (*Thaumatococcus daniellii*) discovered in West Africa – is 1,600 times as sweet as sucrose.

• **Darkest...** An alloy of nickel and phosphorus around 25 times less reflective than conventional black paint reflects just 0.16% of visible light. The principle was first developed by researchers in the USA and India in 1980. In 1990, Anritsu (Japan) further refined this method to produce the darkest version so far. In 2002, the National Physical Laboratory, UK, developed a new technique for the commercial manufacturing of this coating.

• **Smelliest...** The smelliest substances on Earth are the man-made "Who-Me?" and "US Government Standard Bathroom Malodor", which have five and eight chemical ingredients respectively. Bathroom Malodor smells primarily of human faeces and becomes incredibly repellent to people at just two parts per million. It was originally created to test the power of deodorizing products.

SCIENCE

★LONGEST LINEAR ACCELERATOR

The Stanford Linear Accelerator Center (SLAC) in California, USA, is a particle accelerator some 3.2 km (2 miles) long. Since beginning operations in 1966, its key achievements include the discovery of the charm quark and tau lepton subatomic particles.

The accelerator is located underground and is, according to administrators, among the world's longest, straightest objects (right). Pictured far right is the earthquake-proof Mark II Detector into which the electrons and protons are propelled in order to release subatomic particles.

★HARDEST METALLIC ELEMENT

With a Mohs value of 8.5, chromium is the hardest of the metallic elements. It is responsible for the red colour in rubies. The ★softest metallic element is caesium, with a value of just 0.2. It is soft enough to be cut with a butter knife, melts at 28°C (82°F) and explodes when dropped in water.

★LONGEST HALF-LIFE

Half-life is the measure of how long it takes an unstable element to decay. A half-life of a day means that it would take a day for half the atomic nuclei in a sample to decay into a more stable element. In 2003, scientists discovered that bismuth-209 – previously believed to be stable – in fact gradually decayed with a half-life of around 20 billion billion years – more than a billion times the age of the Universe!

DID YOU KNOW?
The diamond allotrope of carbon is the **hardest element** on Earth, with a maximum score of 10 on the Mohs scale of hardness. They are formed at least 150 km (93 miles) beneath the Earth's surface, where the pressures and temperatures are great enough to force the carbon atoms to adopt the diamond structure.

★HEAVIEST GAS

Radon has an atomic number of 222 and is chemically inert and unreactive. At room temperature and pressure, 1 m³ (35.3 ft³) of radon weighs 9.73 kg (21.4 lb) – 100 times heavier than 1 m³ of hydrogen.

★HEAVIEST NON-ELEMENTAL GAS

Tungsten hexafluoride has a density of 13.1 kg/m³ (0.81 lb/ft³) – more than 10 times heavier than air and 76 times lighter than water. It is also nearly seven times heavier than the **lightest man-made solid**, aerogel.

MOST ACCURATE VALUE FOR π (PI)

As part of a long-running project, Yasumasa Kanada (Japan) of the University of Tokyo calculated π (pi) to 1,241,100,000,000 decimal places. He broke his record of 206 billion places in December 2002 after 400 hours of computation power using a Hitachi SR8000/MPP supercomputer.

RECORD-BREAKING SOUNDS

-9.4 DB QUIETEST PLACE ON EARTH
Anechoic Test Chamber at Orfield Laboratories, Minneapolis, Minnesota, USA

100 DB LOUDEST APPLAUSE
BBC's Big Bash, at the NEC, Birmingham, West Midlands, UK, on 24–27 October 1997

108 DB LOUDEST FINGER SNAP
Bob Hatch (USA), Pasadena, California, USA, on 17 May 2000

125 DB LOUDEST WHISTLE
Marco Ferrera (USA) from 2.5 m (8 ft 3 in), Santa Monica, California, USA, on 5 March 2004

UNKNOWN DB LOUDEST NOISE
Eruption of Krakatoa, Indonesia, on 27 August 1883; 26 times the power of the largest ever H-bomb test; sound was heard 5,000 km (3,100 miles) away

93 DB LOUDEST SNORING
Kåre Walkert (Sweden), Örebro Regional Hospital, Sweden, on 24 May 1993

104.9 DB LOUDEST BURP
Paul Hunn (UK), London, UK, on 20 July 2004

110.44 DB LOUDEST CLAP
Alastair Galpin, Acoustics Testing Service, University of Auckland, New Zealand, on 18 July 2005

188 DB LOUDEST ANIMAL SOUND
Blue whales (*Balaenoptera musculus*) and fin whales (*B. physalus*)

★ NEW RECORD
★ UPDATED RECORD

RECORD-BREAKING ELEMENTS

ASTATINE (At) RAREST ELEMENT ON EARTH
Only 25 g (0.9 oz) exists naturally

GOLD (Au) MOST DUCTILE ELEMENT
One gram of gold (Au) can be drawn to 2.4 km (1 oz to 43 miles)

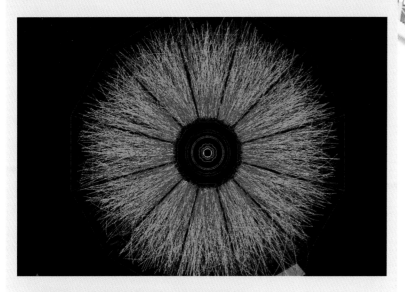

★ FIRST FORM OF MATTER

The lines in the image above are the tracks left by subatomic particles in a quark gluon plasma. The particles existed for less than 10^{-20} seconds in the aftermath of a collision between two ions of gold travelling close to the speed of light in the Relativistic Heavy Ion Collider, New York, USA. Quark gluon plasma is believed to have existed in the very early stages of the Universe, just a few microseconds after the Big Bang. In 2005, it was announced that this exotic form of matter has properties more similar to those of a liquid than a gas. The first conventional atoms of matter did not form until around 400,000 years after the Big Bang.

ELEMENTS WITH THE LOWEST MELTING AND BOILING POINTS

Helium (He) cannot be obtained as a solid at atmospheric pressure, the minimum pressure required being 2.532 MPa (24.985 atmospheres) at -272.375°C (-458.275°F). Helium also has the lowest boiling point of any element at -268.928°C (-452.070°F). For metallic elements, mercury (see below) has the lowest melting and boiling points.

★ FIRST WILDFIRE

The earliest wildfire smouldered 419 million years ago, when oxygen levels may have been considerably higher than today. Scientists from Cardiff University, UK, found evidence of a low-intensity burn, probably started by a lightning strike, while studying charred fossils of small plants found in rocks near Ludlow, UK, in April 2004.

★ LARGEST KNOWN PRIME NUMBER

A prime number is a number that can be divided only by itself and the number one – the number 13 is a "prime" example. On 15 December 2005, a team led by professors Curtis Cooper and Steven Boone (both USA) were able to generate a prime number that ran to a length of 9,152,052 digits, making it the longest ever recorded prime number.

RECORD-BREAKING TEMPERATURES

∞ – HIGHEST TEMPERATURE EVER
At the very instant of the Big Bang, 13.7 billion years ago, the Universe is thought to have had infinite temperature

2 BILLION°C (3.6 BILLION°F) – HIGHEST MAN-MADE TEMPERATURE
Achieved using the Z-Machine at the Sandia National Laboratories, Albuquerque, New Mexico, USA

15,600,000°C (28,080,000°F) – CENTRE OF THE SUN

200,000°C (360,000°F) – HOTTEST WHITE DWARF
According to Klaus Werner (Germany) of the Universität Tübingen, the glowing remnant of the dead star H1504+65 is roughly 30 times hotter than the surface of the Sun

3,414°C (6,177°F) – HIGHEST MELTING POINT AND 5,847°C (10,557°F) – HIGHEST BOILING POINT
Tungsten has the highest melting and boiling points of any element

480°C (896°F) – HOTTEST PLANET
Venus has the hottest surface of any planet in the Solar System – hot enough to melt lead!

49.2°C (120.5°F) – HIGHEST TEMPERATURE ON EARTH
Marble Bar, Western Australia, peaked during the period between 31 October 1923 and 7 April 1924

15°C (59°F) – MEAN TEMPERATURE ON EARTH

14.2°C (57.5°F) – LOWEST BODY TEMPERATURE
On 23 February 1994, Karlee Kosolofski (Canada), then aged two, survived being accidentally locked outside her home for six hours in a temperature of -22°C (-8°F)

-37.5°C (-35.5°F) – COLDEST WATER DROPLETS
Aircraft measurements of clouds over west Texas on 13 August 1999 revealed tiny water droplets that remained liquid for several minutes

-89.2°C (-128.6°F) – LOWEST TEMPERATURE ON EARTH
Occurred at Vostok, Antarctica, on 21 July 1983

450 PICOKELVIN – COLDEST MAN-MADE TEMPERATURE
Achieved by a team at MIT, Cambridge, Massachusetts, USA, led by Aaron Leanhardt (USA). A picokelvin is one million-millionth of a kelvin

-459.67°F (-273.15°C) – LOWEST POSSIBLE TEMPERATURE
The coldest that any substance can theoretically be is when there is no vibration in its atoms; aka zero kelvin. This has never been achieved

---

IRON (Fe)
MOST EXTRACTED METAL
521 million tonnes of iron were produced worldwide in 1999 from the processing of mined iron ore

LITHIUM (Li)
LEAST DENSE METAL
At room temperature, lithium has a density of just 0.5334 g/cm³

MERCURY (Hg)
LOWEST MELTING AND BOILING POINTS (METAL)
-38.829°C (-37.892°F) and 356.62°C (673.92°F) respectively

FORENSIC SCIENCE

★ FIRST FORENSIC PSYCHOLOGIST

Psychiatrists have been acting as expert witnesses since at least the mid-1840s, but the first referenced use of a psychologist called upon to testify in a court of law was that of Dr Albert Von Schrenk-Notzing (Germany) who, in 1896, drew upon his studies of suggestibility and memory recall to testify in a murder trial. His testimony related to the difficulties in accepting witness statements after the trial's intense pre-publicity – an issue that continues to affect trials today.

★ **NEW RECORD**
★ **UPDATED RECORD**

FIRST SYSTEM OF FINGERPRINTS

The earliest effective system of identification by fingerprints – the science of dactylography – was instituted in 1896 by Edward Henry (UK), an inspector-general of police in British India, who eventually became Commissioner of the Metropolitan Police in London, UK.

★ FIRST USE OF DNA PROFILING TO CLEAR A CRIMINAL SUSPECT

The world's first DNA-based manhunt took place between 1986 and 1988 in Enderby, Leicestershire, UK, during the investigation of a double rape-murder – that of Linda Mann (UK) in 1983 and Dawn Ashworth (UK) in 1986. The prime suspect, a local boy named Richard Buckland (UK), confessed to the second killing, but deoxyribonucleic acid (DNA) profiling of the victims revealed that the killer's DNA and that of Buckland did not match. Buckland thus became the first suspect exonerated using DNA profiling. In 1988, after further DNA testing, the real killer, Colin Pitchfork (UK), was sentenced to life imprisonment.

X-REF

• Check out more cutting-edge science on p.148.

• Wild about weaponry? Then turn back to p.134.

★ FIRST USE OF FORENSIC ENTOMOLOGY

According to forensic biologist Mark Benecke (Germany), the study of insects taken from crime scenes dates back to a 13th-century text book – *Hsi Yuan Lu* ("The Washing Away of Wrongs") – by Sung Tz'u (China). Called upon to investigate a fatal stabbing, Tz'u asked workers to lay down their sickles; blow flies were drawn to one sickle covered in invisible blood traces, forcing its owner to confess to the crime. (It is now known that certain blow flies lay their eggs in fresh blood.)

★ LARGEST BRAIN BANK

The Harvard Brain Tissue Resource Center at the McLean Hospital in Belmont, Massachusetts, USA, holds 3,000 brains, which are redistributed internationally for research. The bank has stored over 6,000 specimens since it opened in 1978, and, each year, typically receives 30 "healthy" brains and 240 diseased brains from patients who have suffered from neurodegenerative diseases and neuropsychiatric disorders.

MOST CRIMINALS IDENTIFIED FROM ONE ARTIST'S COMPOSITES

Since 1982, 523 criminals have been positively identified in Texas, USA, as a result of the detailed composites drawn by forensic artist Lois Gibson (USA, left). Shown above centre is an "age-progression" sketch that she created based on a photo of a suspected murderer (above left) as a younger man, which helped lead to his capture. Above right, the criminal is shown in later life.

LARGEST FORENSIC SCIENCE TRAINING PROGRAMME

Competition is extremely tough for the 16 places on the 10-week course at the National Forensic Academy in Knoxville, Tennessee, USA. Only candidates who are already employed by a law-enforcement agency can apply for a position. Three sessions are run each year, in January, May and September.

LONGEST-RUNNING BODY FARM

The "Body Farm", Knoxville, Tennessee, USA, was founded in 1971. It is a 1.2-ha (3-acre) plot of land where human bodies are allowed to decompose, under a variety of conditions, in order for scientists to study how the decay happens.

LARGEST DATABASE OF THE HUMAN SKELETON

FORDISC – or FORensic DISCrimination – is the world's most complete database relating to the human skeleton. It was established as part of the research undertaken at the University of Tennessee's "Body Farm", and allows data obtained from decomposing bodies to be analysed by forensic anthropologists. As a result, it is now possible to calculate the size, height and possibly sex and age of a victim from a single bone.

FIRST USE OF FORENSIC FACIAL RECOGNITION

Modern forensic anthropology arguably began with the work of Wilton M Krogman (USA), who popularized the use of facial reconstructions in forensic criminal investigations. By mapping tissue of varying thicknesses to cranial (skull) remains, Krogman could build a clay model closely resembling the deceased. His 1939 work *Guide to the Identification of Human Skeletal Material* helped found the discipline.

Today, computer-generated reconstructions (see right) continue the tradition.

OBJECT MOST FREQUENTLY FOUND AT A CRIME SCENE

According to the National Forensic Academy, the object most commonly found at a crime scene is a cigarette butt. However, it has been estimated that up to 30% of butts recovered are left by police attending the scene!

MOST COMMON CAUSE OF HOMICIDE

Death by "penetrating trauma" – i.e., by stabbing or shooting – is the most common cause of murder.

PERSON MOST LIKELY TO COMMIT MURDER

According to the US Department of Justice, the person most likely to commit murder is a male aged 17–30 years. Almost 90% of murders are committed by young males – in 74.6% of cases, killing another young male.

MORE FORENSIC FIRSTS

• In June 2006, Belgian and French researchers announced that they had taken DNA from the tooth of a Neanderthal child who lived in the Meuse Basin, Belgium, *ca.* 100,000 years ago – the **oldest extracted human DNA**.

• The ★**first use of DNA profiling to secure a conviction** involved a case against Robert Melias (UK), who was found guilty of rape on 13 November 1988 by DNA evidence.

• Gary Dotson (USA) was accused of raping Cathleen Crowell (UK), found guilty in July 1979, and sentenced to 25–50 years for rape and the same again for aggravated kidnapping. In 1988, DNA tests (not previously available) were conducted proving that Dotson was innocent. He was exonerated on 14 August 1988, having served eight years, in a case that marked the ★**first use of DNA profiling to overturn a conviction**.

• The ★**first use of fingerprints from a post mortem in a conviction** occurred in 1978. Police used black magnetic powder to lift fingerprints from the left ankle of a deceased female suspected of being assaulted in North Miami Beach, Florida, USA. The prints were matched to those of Stephen William Beattie (USA), who was found guilty on the basis of the fingerprint evidence and given three consecutive death sentences on 1 February 1979.

SPACE TECHNOLOGY

★ LARGEST SPACE STATION

The *International Space Station* (ISS) has been under construction since its first component, the Zarya module, was launched in 1998. The latest element to be added was the P5 Truss, on 12 December 2006, bringing the total mass of the ISS to 213,843 kg (471,442 lb). Pictured is Christer Fuglesang (Sweden), the first and only Swedish astronaut, during a spacewalk on 14 December 2006.

★ REMOTEST MAN-MADE OBJECT

Voyager 1, launched from Cape Canaveral, Florida, USA, on 5 September 1977, is the farthest man-made object from Earth. On 17 February 1998, it surpassed the slower *Pioneer 10*, which was launched on 2 March 1972. As of August 2007, *Voyager 1* is more than 15.47 billion km (9.61 billion miles) from the Sun. (See opposite page for more *Voyager 1* facts.)

LARGEST ROOM IN SPACE

The largest single habitable volume lifted into space was the NASA space station *Skylab*, which was launched in May 1973. Its main body consisted of a converted third-stage booster from a *Saturn V* rocket launcher. This cylindrical space station had internal dimensions of 14.66 m (48 ft 1.2 in) long by 6.70 m (22 ft) in diameter, giving a habitable volume of 295.23 m³ (10,426 ft³).

★ LONGEST TIME SURVIVED ON MARS BY A ROVER

The twin Mars Exploration Rovers *Spirit* and *Opportunity* touched down successfully on Mars on 4 and 25 January 2004 respectively. Since then, they have each travelled across the Martian surface, taking scientific images and measurements. As of March 2007, both Rovers are still operational. In February 2007, the *Opportunity* Rover had travelled a total of 10,000 m (32,808 ft) across the surface – some six times the distance it had been originally designed for.

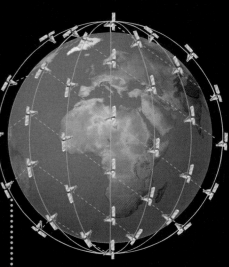

★ LARGEST PRIVATE SATELLITE CONSTELLATION

A fleet of 66 satellites in cross-linked low-Earth orbits (illustrated above) is privately owned and operated by Iridium Satellite LLC (USA). The satellite fleet, which orbits at an altitude of 780 km (485 miles), provides global communication coverage, allowing the use of a satellite telephone – and various handheld devices – anywhere on Earth, even at the poles and in the middle of the oceans.

★ FIRST FEMALE SPACE TOURIST

Anousheh Ansari (Iran) became the first female space tourist on 18 September 2006 when the *Soyuz TMA-9* capsule blasted off for a 10-day visit to the *International Space Station*. Businesswoman Ansari has had a lifelong fascination with space and is thought to have paid $20 million (£10.5 million) for the experience.

ANOUSHEH ANSARI
АНЮШЕ АНСАРИ

SPACE
adventures

FASTEST EARTH DEPARTURE SPEED

The fastest speed at which a spacecraft has ever departed from Earth is 58,338 km/h (36,250 mph). It was achieved by NASA's *New Horizons* spacecraft, which launched from Cape Canaveral, Florida, USA, on 19 January 2006, beginning a nine-year flight to Pluto and its moons. Pluto – recently downgraded to the status of a dwarf planet – is yet to be surveyed by a spacecraft.

DFilm

45
20
44
32991

★ MOST POWERFUL CAMERA TO LEAVE EARTH ORBIT

The High Resolution Imaging Science Experiment (HiRISE) is a camera on board NASA's Mars Reconnaissance Orbiter (MRO). It is capable of taking digital images of the Martian surface measuring 40,000 x 20,000 pixels. From its orbit 255–320 km (158–200 miles) above Mars, it can take images of the Martian surface showing details as small as 1 m (3 ft) across. MRO was launched on 12 August 2005 and arrived in Martian orbit on 10 March 2006.

GREATEST SPACECRAFT COLLISION

On 25 June 1997, an unmanned supply vehicle weighing 7 tonnes (15,000 lb) collided with the Russian *Mir* space station. *Mir*'s Vasily Tsibliev and Alexander Lazutkin had to work quickly to seal a breach in the hull of *Mir*'s *Spektr* module, while astronaut Michael Foale prepared *Mir*'s *Soyuz* capsule for a possible evacuation. Loss of life was avoided, but the station was left low on power and oxygen and temporarily tumbling out of control.

★ FIRST SUCCESSFUL SOLAR SAIL DEPLOYMENT

In August 2004, the Japanese space agency JAXA launched a rocket that successfully deployed two prototype solar sails in space at altitudes of 122 km (75 miles) and 169 km (105 miles) above the Earth. Solar sails are a potential new means of providing propulsion for spacecraft, using the pressure of sunlight on extremely thin reflective membranes (artist's impression above).

★ NEW RECORD
★ UPDATED RECORD

VOYAGER 1: ITS ONGOING MISSION...

Voyager 1 is now in the region of the Solar System known as the heliosheath – where the Sun's influence begins to wane. The spacecraft, travelling at around 1,000 km per minute (1 million miles per day), is expected to pass beyond the heliosheath within the next 10 years and become the first man-made object to leave the Solar System.

★ MOST RE-USED SPACECRAFT

NASA's space shuttle *Discovery* was launched on 10 December 2006 at 1:47 UCT (Universal Coordinated Time), to make its 32nd trip into space (pictured is the launch from Kennedy Space Station in Florida). Its mission (STS-116) was to deliver the *International Space Station*'s third port truss segment and to exchange crew. The flight also carried Sweden's first astronaut, Christer Fuglesang (see above left). It was the first night flight for NASA in four years. *Discovery* has been in operation since 1984.

CONSUMER TECHNOLOGY

★ HIGHEST-RESOLUTION MOBILE PHONE CAMERA

In March 2006, Samsung unveiled the SCH-B600, a mobile phone with the world's highest-resolution camera at 10 megapixels – higher than many digital cameras. The LCD can reproduce 16 million colours, and users can also watch live TV through a satellite DMB (digital multimedia broadcasting) function.

★ SMALLEST TV TUNER BOX

In October 2005, Compro Technology announced the launch of the VideoMate U900, a full-function USB 2.0 TV box shorter in length than a credit card. Despite its size of just 7.6 x 5.4 x 1.4 cm (2.9 x 2.1 x 0.5 in), it allows a PC to be used for watching TV, recording in MPEG 1, 2 and 4 formats, and video/audio capture via its USB port.

LARGEST DMB TV SCREEN

With its 25.4-cm (10-in) screen, the Samsung R7 is the world's largest digital multimedia broadcasting (DMB) television. DMB is the system used to access TV and high-quality CD sound on mobile devices such as cell phones and laptops – effectively, mobile digital television. The R7 has an aspect ratio of 16:9.

★ FASTEST HOVER SCOOTER

In January 2006, Hammacher Schlemmer & Company Inc. (USA) announced the release of the Levitating Hover Scooter. It hovers approximately 10 cm (4 in) above the ground and has a top speed of 24 km/h (15 mph). Riders control the direction by transferring their weight and modify the engine/fan speed by levers on the airboard's handlebars.

★ NEW RECORD
★ UPDATED RECORD

MOST TV SETS

The country with the most televisions is China, which had an estimated 400 million sets in 1997.

ACTUAL SIZE

★ SMALLEST CAMCORDER

Sony's HandyCam DCR-PC55 is, across its longest length, just 99 mm (3.8 in) and weighs 360 g (0.79 lb).

HIGHEST-DEFINITION SCREEN ON A TV WRISTWATCH

With 130,338 pixels, the sharpest picture achieved on a wearable television screen is the NHJ TV Wristwatch. The 1.5-in (3.8-cm) colour TV screen relies on TFT (Thin Film Transistor) technology to deliver such a high-resolution picture and retails for around $200 (£100).

★ SMALLEST MULTIMEDIA PLAYER

In August 2005, MPIO (UK) launched the MPIO-One, a 34-g (1.2-oz) media player measuring just 3.2 x 5.4 cm (1.2 x 2.1 in). It can play MPEG-4, WMV, AVI and Div-X video files (as well as MP3, WMA and OGG audio files), and has a 2.64-cm (1.04-in) OLED screen capable of displaying up to 26,000 colours.

ACTUAL SIZE

世界最大 103v型

世界最大 103v型フルハイビジョンプラズマ

LARGEST PLASMA SCREEN

A prototype of Panasonic's 103-in Plasma Display, measuring over 2.6 m (8 ft 6 in) in width, was revealed at the 2006 International Consumer Electronics Show in Las Vegas, USA, on 5–8 January 2006. It retails at around $70,000 (£36,000).

SMALLEST INSTANT CAMERA

The Polaroid PopShot, the world's first disposable instant camera, measures 16.51 x 10.79 x 6.35 cm (6.5 x 4.25 x 2.5 in) and weighs 255 g (9 oz). The PopShot camera can take 10 11.17 x 6.35 cm (4.4 x 2.5 in) colour photographs and comes with a postage-free mailing envelope that makes for easy recycling.

★ THINNEST COMPUTER KEYBOARD

The eMark Super Mobile Keyboard manufactured by Kimura Metal (Japan) is a silicone-vinyl sheet between just 1 and 5 mm (0.03 and 0.2 in) thick.

The keyboard is also spill-resistant and is so thin that it can be rolled up into a tube.

FASTEST-GROWING CONSUMER ENTERTAINMENT PRODUCT

According to Understanding & Solutions, the DVD player is the fastest-growing consumer electronics product in history. Since its launch in 1997, over 627 million units have been sold worldwide.

★ MOST SUCCESSFUL TECHNOLOGY MANUFACTURER

Hewlett-Packard Co. (USA) enjoyed sales revenues of $94.08 billion (£47.1 billion) and profits of $6.52 billion (£3.26 billion) as of April 2007. The company has a workforce of around 156,000 people.

★ DEEPEST DIVING WATCH

The deepest diving watch, the CX Swiss Military's 12,000-feet model, can function at 3,657 m (12,000 ft; 2,000 fathoms). It was made by Montres Charmex SA of Switzerland in 2006. The mechanical chronograph is a limited edition of only 365 pieces.

★ MOST POWERFUL SUB-WOOFER

The most powerful home audio sub-woofer is Eminent Technology's Model 17. It can efficiently reach frequencies as low as 1 hertz, compared with the usual lowest frequencies of around 20 hertz for regular sub-woofers. The Model 17 has to be professionally fitted in an attic or basement, which effectively becomes a giant speaker.

★ MOST EXPENSIVE WATCH

The Super Ice Cube by Chopard, Switzerland, retails at $1,130,620 (£657,188) as of 2005. It has 66.16 carats of diamonds, which includes 288 trapeze cut diamonds, 16 centre stones and 1,897 brilliant cut diamonds.

RING THE CHANGES...

• Korean electronics giant Samsung Electronics have developed a combination portable TV/mobile phone unit measuring 9.2 x 5.1 x 3.6 cm (3.6 x 2 x 1.4 in), the **smallest mobile phone TV**. The SCH-M220 provides up to 200 minutes of continuous TV viewing time.

• Currently, the world's **slimmest mobile phone** is the Samsung Ultra Edition II (below), just 5.9 mm (0.2 in) thick. The handset has a 3-mega-pixel camera and 11 hours of music play time.

ACTUAL SIZE

• The **most expensive mobile phone** was designed by GoldVish of Geneva, Switzerland, and was sold for €1,000,000 ($1,320,270; £674,310) at the Millionaire Fair in Cannes, France, on 2 September 2006.

• Samsung's (Korea) Ultra Edition 8.4 is the world's ★**thinnest 3G mobile phone**, featuring a 2-mega-pixel camera mounted in a body just 8.4 mm (0.3 in) thick.

• The **most powerful mobile-phone gun** is a .22 calibre pistol, disguised as a cell phone, which can fire a (close-range) lethal round of four bullets when numbers 5,6,7,8 are pressed in quick succession.

★ MOST FUNCTIONS ON A PENKNIFE

The Swiss Army Giant Knife 2007 is made by Wenger S.A., the makers of the Swiss Army Knife. It weighs 1.345 kg (3 lb), is 24 cm (9.4 in) long and features 87 tools – including a laser pointer, torch, whistle and cigar cutter. The knife offers 141 different functions.

ROBOTS

★ NEW RECORD
☆ UPDATED RECORD

★ SMALLEST BIPEDAL HUMANOID ROBOT

Omnibot2007 i-SOBOT measures 165 mm (6.5 in) high and is able to walk, stand up from a lying-down position and balance on one foot. It was manufactured by Takara Tomy (Japan) and demonstrated at the Toy Forum 2007 on 23 January in Tokyo, Japan.

★ OLDEST ANDROID DESIGN

There is sufficient evidence to suggest that Leonardo da Vinci (Italy) planned and sketched out a humanoid robot design around 1495. Although his sketches of the finished model have never been found, other da Vinci drawings show a mechanical knight with anatomically correct joints operated by cables and pulleys. A full-sized working replica was built by roboticist Mark Rosheim (USA) in the late 1990s to show how the "Robot Knight" worked.

★ FIRST TRUE ANDROID AVATAR

Geminoid HI-1 (above left) is a humanoid doppelgänger built by Hiroshi Ishiguro (Japan). Its innards are covered with a silicone mould of Ishiguro himself, and it can be used as his avatar – that is, using motion-capture and voice-relay systems, Ishiguro can have his robot double duplicate his movements remotely, allowing him to teach a class without needing to be there in person. Pressurized air and tiny motors are used to give Geminoid micro-movements such as blinking and fidgeting, and the chest even moves up and down as he "breathes".

Pictured above right is Ishiguro's female robot Actroid Repliee demonstrating its abilities at the Prototype Robot Exhibition in Aichi, Japan, on 9 June 2005.

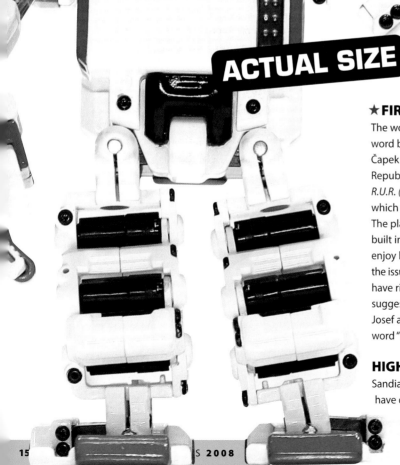

ACTUAL SIZE

pistons to jump to heights of 9 m (30 ft). They have potential applications in planetary exploration, where hoppers could be released by a probe to survey a landscape.

★ FIRST ROBOT REFERENCE

The word "robot" was introduced as a word by novelist and playwright Karel Čapek (Austria-Hungary, now Czech Republic, 1890–1938) in his play *R.U.R. (Rossum's Universal Robots)*, which premiered in Prague in 1921. The play features "artificial people" built in a factory and designed to enjoy laborious work, and explores the issue of whether or not such robots have rights. The word "robot" was suggested to Čapek by his brother Josef and derives from the Czech word "robota", meaning slave labour.

HIGHEST-JUMPING ROBOT

Sandia National Laboratories, USA, have developed "hopper" robots that use combustion-driven

FASTEST-RUNNING HUMANOID ROBOT

ASIMO (Advanced Step in Innovative Mobility) has been developed and refined by Honda (Japan) since 2000. In December 2005, Honda announced that ASIMO had been improved in order to allow it to run at a speed of 6 km/h (3.7 mph).

☆ LARGEST ROBOT COMPETITION

A total of 646 engineers, 466 robots and 13 countries took part in the 2006 RoboGames (formerly the ROBOlympics) held in San Francisco, California, USA. Events included football with re-programmed AIBO robot dogs, robo-sumo wrestling, bipedal racing and musical artistry. The USA won 28 gold, 31 silver and 21 bronze medals.

★FIRST ROBOT-STAFFED RESTAURANT

Robot Kitchen in Hong Kong, China, opened in July 2006. It has two robot staff members capable of taking orders from customers and delivering their meals to them. A third robot is being constructed that should be able to perform simple culinary tasks, such as preparing omelettes and flipping burgers.

LONGEST DISTANCE BETWEEN PATIENT AND SURGEON

Madeleine Schaal (France) had her gall bladder removed by a robot in an operating room at Strasbourg, France, while her surgeons – Jacques Marescaux (France) and Michel Gagner (USA) – remotely operated the ZEUS robotic surgical arms on a secured fibre-optic line from New York, USA, a total distance of 6,222 km (3,866 miles) apart, on 7 September 2001. The operation lasted 55 minutes and Madeleine went home after 48 hours.

★MOST ADVANCED MEDICAL MINI ROBOT

In March 2007, researchers from Japan's Ritsumeikan University unveiled a prototype robot (pictured above) measuring just 2 cm (0.78 in) long and 1 cm (0.39 in) wide, with a mass of only 5 g (0.17 oz). It is

ACTUAL SIZE

designed to be implanted into a person, after which it can travel inside the body equipped with various tools such as arms, a camera and a device to deliver medication to specific parts of the body. Previous medical mini robots only carried cameras.

CHEAPEST ROBOT

Walkman, a 12.7-cm-tall (5-in) robot, was built from the remains of a Sony Walkman for a cost of just $1.75 (£1.15) at the Los Alamos National Laboratory in New Mexico, USA, in 1996. In tests, the insect-like "junkbot", as such creations are called, struggled to get free when its legs were held – without it being programmed to do so and without making the same movement twice.

★MOST DEGREES OF FREEDOM ON A ROBOT ARM

In December 2006, OC Robotics (UK) announced it had designed and built a snake-like robot arm with 27 degrees of freedom. It is designed to be able to reach inside very restrictive enclosed spaces during the construction of large aircraft.

MOST GENDER-AWARE ROBOT

The Intelligent Earth company has developed visual gender-recognition software for its robotic head, *Doki*. Based on visual data alone, it can recognize the gender of women with an accuracy of 100%, and men with an accuracy of 96%.

LARGEST ROBOT DOG

Roboscience's RS-01 Robodog measures 82 x 67 x 37 cm (32 x 26 x 14 in) and is strong enough to lift a five-year-old child.

ROBOT HISTORY

- **350 BC** Greek mathematician Archytas of Tarentum builds a steam-driven mechanical bird.

- **1738** Jacques de Vaucanson (France) builds three life-like automata.

- **1801** Joseph Jacquard (France) builds an automated loom that is controlled by punch cards.

- **1921** Karel Čapek (Austria-Hungary) introduces the word "robot" in his play *R.U.R.* (*Rossum's Universal Robots*).

- **1962** First robotic industrial arm introduced.

- **1966** ELIZA, the first artificial intelligence program, created.

- **1989** "Genghis", the first walking robot, developed at Massachusetts Institute of Technology (MIT), USA.

- **1999** Sony releases the AIBO robotic pet dog.

- **2000** Honda unveils ASIMO, the humanoid robot.

- **2001** Cyberknife, a robotic surgeon, is cleared for use in American hospitals.

- **2005** Researchers at Cornell University, USA, build a self-replicating robot.

★FIRST ROBOT SOMMELIER

NEC System Technologies and Mie University, Japan, have developed a robot capable of tasting wine and recognizing the differences between a few dozen varieties. To "taste", the "wine-bot" fires an infrared beam through the wine and analyses the various wavelengths of light that are absorbed. A built-in speaker is used to announce the variety of wine selected.

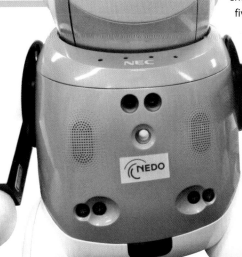

VIDEO GAMES

★ YOUNGEST PROFESSIONAL VIDEO GAMER

Born on 6 May 1998, "Lil Poison" (USA, aka Victor De Leon III) picked up a Dreamcast Controller at the age of two to play *NBA 2K*. He entered his first competition – a *Halo* tournament in his native New York – aged four, and competed in the Major League Games a year later.

By the age of seven, Lil Poison had won $2,000 (£1,162) in gaming tournaments – often competing against adult players – making him the ★ **youngest video gamer to win a cash prize**.

Despite his tender years, Lil Poison has signed an exclusive deal with gaming tournament organizers Major League Gaming, who arrange endorsement deals for gamers.

★ MOST EXPENSIVE VIRTUAL OBJECT

In October 2005, gamer Jon Jacobs (aka Neverdie) paid $100,000 (£56,000) in an auction for a virtual space station in the online role-playing game *Project Entropia*.

Described as a "pleasure paradise", the space station features a 1,000-unit apartment complex, a sports stadium, a nightclub and a shopping mall.

★ BEST-SELLING Wii GAME

Wii launch title *Wii Sports*, which came bundled with the console in most territories around the world, has sold over 2.89 million copies since September 2006.

★ HIGHEST VIDEO GAME SCORE EVER

J. C. Padilla (USA) scored 2,181,619,994,299,256,480 points playing *GigaWings2* for the Sega Dreamcast gaming console (Score Attack Mode – Stage 2) on 17 May 2004.

In contrast, the world record on Cinematronic's *Space Wars*, created in 1977, was only 19 points, a record that still stands.

DID YOU KNOW?
Dennis "Thresh" Fong (USA, b. 1977) is regarded as the ★ **first professional gamer in history**. He won every tournament he attended over a five-year period and has earned the nickname "the Michael Jordan of gaming".

★ FIRST GAMER TO SCORE 1 BILLION POINTS

On 15 January 1984, at the end of a 44-hour 45-minute marathon game of *Nibbler* at Twin Galaxies, Ottunnwa, Iowa, USA, Tim McVey (USA) had amassed an incredible 1,000,042,270 points.

The feat was made all the more remarkable as McVey had used just one quarter to achieve his record-breaking score.

★ NEW RECORD
UPDATED RECORD

★ BEST-SELLING
PLAYSTATION 3 GAME

Resistance: Fall of Man, a sci-fi first-person shooter developed by Insomniac Games (USA) and released in November 2006, had sold 1.02 million copies as of March 2007. The game was hailed as the best of the launch titles for the PS3, winning seven IGN awards in 2006 in the PS3 category (Game of the Year, Best First-Person Shooter, Best Graphics, Best Original Score, Best Sound, Best Online Multiplayer, Most Innovative Design).

★ BEST-SELLING STAND-ALONE Wii GAME

The biggest-selling stand-alone Wii title is *The Legend of Zelda: Twilight Princess*, which has sold over 1.87 million copies to date. In its first few weeks of launch, three copies of the game were sold for every four Wii purchases.

★ FIRST VIDEO GAME WORLD CHAMPION

Ben Gold (USA) became the first video game world champion when he won the North American Video Game Olympics on 8–9 January 1983. The event was later seen on ABC TV's *That's Incredible*.

★ LONGEST VIDEO GAME MARATHON

Competitors in Twin Galaxies' Iron Man Contest were offered a share of a $10,000 (£6,890) prize if they could complete 100 hours of gaming using just one quarter. James Vollandt (USA) held out the longest, with a time of 67 hr 30 min. The contest was staged from 5 to 8 July 1983 at Johnny Zee's Family Fun Centre, in Victoria, British Columbia, Canada.

> *The total prize money on offer at the World Cyber Games 2006 Championships was $462,000 (£235,937)*

Because of the attendant health risks, Twin Galaxies now sanctions very few marathons of this nature.

MOST PORTED COMPUTER GAME

Tetris, created by Alexey Pajitnov (USSR) in 1985, has been ported (translated) to more than 70 different computer-game platforms including, most recently, the XBox and numerous mobile phones.

★ MOST PARTICIPANTS IN A VIDEO GAME LEAGUE IN A SINGLE SEASON

World Cyber Games (WCG) reported that there were 1.3 million contestants in the video game league for the 2006 championships. A total of 700 players, representing 70 countries, advanced to the Grand Final in Monza, Italy. Korea were the overall league winners, with two gold medals, one silver and one bronze.

★ LARGEST ORCHESTRA FOR A COMPUTER GAME

The PlayStation2 game *Onimusha* (2001) features a soundtrack by Mamoru Samuragoch (Japan) – dubbed the "Digital Age Beethoven" – that required 203 players (the 150-piece New Japan Philharmonic Orchestra and 53 traditional Japanese instrumentalists and vocalists).

CLASSIC ARCADE HIGH SCORES*

GAME	SCORE	PLAYER	FROM	DATE
★ 1942	13,360,960	Martin Bedard	Canada	19 Nov 2006
★ Asteroids Deluxe (Tournament)	167,790	Donavan Stepp	USA	22 Aug 2004
★ Black Widow	930,100	James Vollandt	USA	1 May 1984
★ Burgertime	9,000,000	Bryan L. Wagner	USA	2 Jun 2006
★ Dance Dance Revolution	652,095,760	Takeo Ueki	Japan	8 May 2003
★ Discs of Tron	418,200	David Bagenski	USA	28 Jun 1986
★ Donkey Kong	1,049,100	Steve Wiebe	USA	23 Mar 2007
★ Donkey Kong 3	473,400	Dwayne Richard	Canada	22 Oct 2005
★ Gyruss (Tournament)	1,306,100	Richard W. Marsh	USA	22 Jun 2004
★ Hard Drivin'	219,758	David Nelson	USA	13 May 2006
★ Star Castle	9,833,940	Bob Mines	USA	14 Sep 1984
★ Mario Bros	3,481,550	Perry Rodgers	USA	2 Jul 1985
★ Top Skater (Hard/Expert)	836,733	Tai Kunag Neng	Malaysia	13 Jul 2002
★ Warlords	911,875	Peter Skahill	USA	29 Aug 1982
★ Sea Wolf	10,800	Peter Skerritt Jr	USA	3 Jun 2001
★ Space Invaders Deluxe	425,230	Matt Brass	USA	16 Sep 1982
★ Stargate	197,500	Bill Jones	USA	24 Mar 2005
★ Star Trek	123,467,525	Darren Harris	USA	8 Jul 1985
★ Time Crisis II (Singles)	1,712,400	Dennis Blechner	Germany	3 May 2001
★ Time Pilot (Tournament)	1,092,800	Kelly R. Flewin	Canada)	19 Nov 2005

* Twenty of the greatest video-game scores of all time, as selected by Twin Galaxies

GUINNESS WORLD RECORDS 2008: GAMER'S EDITION

NEW!

Every major new game reviewed

Video game fans – look out for the forthcoming Guinness World Records book **dedicated entirely to gaming**! We've teamed up with record-breaking referees **Twin Galaxies** to create the ultimate guide to **gaming records, facts and figures**, from the highest earners and best selling games to the highest-spec consoles and most powerful game engines. You'll also find all the **latest news and reviews** for all the top games. **GWR 2008: Gamer's Edition** – on sale **February 2008!**

★ HIGHEST MIND-CONTROL SCORE ON *SPACE INVADERS*

Scientists at Washington University, St Louis, USA, have devised a hands-free system of playing *Space Invaders* using brain power alone. As part of studies into brain activity, researchers attached an electro-corticographic (ECoG) grid to the brain of a teenager suffering from epilepsy. Engineers then adapted Atari software to react to stimuli transmitted through this grid, so that the unnamed volunteer could control an on-screen cursor simply by imagining the movements he would have to make to do so.

The subject reached the third screen of the game, amassing 5,000 points. This is the highest *Space Invaders* score achieved using brain power alone.

ARTS & MEDIA

CONTENTS

★ MOST HITS FROM A SOUNDTRACK IN THE US CHART SIMULTANEOUSLY

On 11 February 2006, nine tracks from the Disney Channel Original Movie *High School Musical* were simultaneously in the US Hot 100 – a world first. These included five tracks in the Top 40, the week's four highest entries, and the biggest-ever jump in the chart when "Breaking Free" by Zac Efron (main figure in white, left), Andrew Seeley and Vanessa Anne Hudgens (main figure in red, right) – all USA – rose from No. 86 to No. 4. Four tracks from the soundtrack also made the Top 10 on the Digital Download chart.

ENGINEERING

CONTENTS

LARGEST MONSTER TRUCK

Bigfoot 5, built in the summer of 1986, is one of a fleet of 17 Bigfoot trucks created by Bob Chandler (USA). It weighs a massive 17,236 kg (38,000 lb) and stands 4.7 m (15 ft 6 in) high, with 3-m-tall (10-ft) tyres. The truck is permanently parked in St Louis, Missouri, USA, where it is regularly admired by fans such as Nick Ahart (USA, below). It also makes occasional exhibitional appearances at local shows.

COLOSSAL CONSTRUCTIONS

LARGEST OFFSHORE GAS PLATFORM

The Troll A Offshore Gas Platform, located near the coast of Norway in the North Sea, is the **tallest man-made object ever moved**, standing 369 m (1,210 ft 7 in) tall – around 45 m (147 ft) taller than the Eiffel Tower. The dry weight of the gravity base structure is 656,000 tonnes (1.4 billion lb), and the platform is constructed from 245,000 m³ (8.6 million ft³) of concrete and 100,000 tonnes (220.4 million lb) of steel.

★ HEAVIEST BUILDING

The Palace of the Parliament in Bucharest, Romania, is made from 700,000 tonnes (1.5 billion lb) of steel and bronze, plus 1 million m³ (35.3 million ft³) of marble, 3,500 tonnes (7.7 million lb) of crystal glass and 900,000 m³ (31.7 million ft³) of wood.

★ TALLEST GRAIN SILO

The Henninger Turm in Frankfurt, Germany, which was originally used to store barley for the Henninger brewery, is 120 m (394 ft) tall. The building once featured a revolving restaurant but this was closed in 2002.

★ LARGEST MASONRY DOME

The concrete dome of the Pantheon in Rome, Italy – which measures 43 m (142 ft) across – has the greatest span of any dome constructed purely from masonry (that is, unreinforced stone or brick). Built by the emperor Hadrian in AD 118–128, it rises 22 m (71 ft) above its base and has a greater span than the famous domes of the great medieval cathedrals of Santa Maria del Fiore in Florence, St Peter's in Rome and St Paul's in London.

★ LARGEST HEMISPHERICAL BUILDING

The Stockholm Globe Arena in Sweden has a diameter of 110 m (361 ft), stands 85 m (288 ft) tall and has a total volume of 600,000 m³ (21 million ft³). The Globe Arena opened on 19 February 1989 and is the home ground of two of Stockholm's Elite League ice hockey teams: AIK and Djurgårdens IF.

★ NEW RECORD
★ UPDATED RECORD

★ LARGEST IRRIGATION PROJECT

The Great Man-Made River Project was initiated in 1984, with the aim of transporting water from vast underground natural aquifers to the coastal cities of Libya. To date, more than 5,000 km (3,100 miles) of pipelines have been completed, capable of carrying 6.5 million m³ (229.5 million ft³) of water per day from wells in the Libyan desert.

★ LONGEST HIGH-REACH EXCAVATOR

On 19 September 2005, Kobelco Construction Machinery Co., Ltd (Japan) announced the completion of the SK3500D excavator, which has a reach of 65.126 m (213 ft 8 in).

★ LARGEST UNOCCUPIED BUILDING

By the time construction was halted on the Ryugyong Hotel in Pyongyang, North Korea, in 1992, it had a floor space of 360,000 m² (3.9 million ft²). It had also reached its full height of 330 m (1,082 ft), making it the world's ★ **tallest unoccupied building**. At 105 storeys, the hotel is the tallest structure in North Korea, the 18th tallest building in the world and would be the world's tallest hotel if completed. Work ceased owing primarily to a lack of funding.

LARGEST HOTEL COMPLEX

The First World Hotel in Pahang Darul Makmur, Malaysia, has 6,118 rooms. The hotel, which is part of the Genting Highlands Resort, was completed during 2005. Facilities include a theme park, golf course and sky-diving simulator.

★ LARGEST HYPOSTYLE (PILLARED) HALL

The hypostyle (pillared) hall of the temple of Amon-Re at Karnak in Egypt originally had a roof supported by 134 giant columns. It is 102 m (335 ft) long and 53 m (174 ft) wide, and has a floor area of around 5,000 m² (54,000 ft²) – almost large enough to accommodate 26 tennis courts!

The temple was commissioned by the pharaoh Ramses I in 1290 BC.

★ LARGEST ABATTOIR

The Smithfield Packing Company operates the world's largest abattoir in Tar Heel, North Carolina, USA. Established in 1992, the facility can process 32,000 pigs each day.

> **DID YOU KNOW?**
> The all-suite Burj Al Arab (Arabian Tower), situated 15 km (9 miles) south of Dubai, United Arab Emirates, is the world's **tallest hotel**, standing at 320.94 m (1,052 ft) high from ground level to the top of its mast. The hotel, shaped like a sail, has 202 suites.

TALLEST STRUCTURE

The top of the drilling rig on the Ursa tension-leg platform – a floating oil-production facility operated by Shell in the Gulf of Mexico – is 1,306 m (4,285 ft) above the ocean floor. The platform is connected to the sea floor by oil pipelines and four massive steel tethers at each corner, with a total weight of approximately 16,000 tonnes (35 million lb).

★ LARGEST SURVIVING ROMAN AQUEDUCT

The Pont du Gard near Nîmes in France stands 47 m (155 ft) tall and is 275 m (902 ft) long. It was built in the late 1st century BC or the early 1st century AD and carried water across the River Gard.

★ LARGEST HYDRO-ELECTRIC PROJECT

The Three Gorges Dam in China is a massive project that will generate power for China's expanding economy, as well as helping to control flooding of the Yangtze River. The huge dam wall was completed in May 2006 and measures 2,309 m (7,575 ft) long by 185 m (607 ft) high.

LARGEST MAN-MADE FLOATING ISLAND

On 10 August 1999, the Mega-Float island was opened to the public at Yokosuka Port, Tokyo Bay, Tokyo, Japan. The steel-built structure measures 1,000 m (3,280 ft 10 in) in length, 121 m (397 ft) wide and 3 m (9 ft 10 in) deep.

WOODEN WONDERS

- The **largest wooden structure** in the world is the Woolloomooloo Bay Wharf in Sydney, Australia. Built in 1912, the wharf is 400 m (1,312 ft) long and 63 m (206 ft) wide and stands on 3,600 piles. The building on the wharf is five storeys high, 350.5 m (1,150 ft) long and 43 m (141 ft) wide, with a total floor area of 64,000 m² (688,890 ft²). It has been converted into a hotel, apartments and a marina complex.

- The ★**tallest-ever wooden structure** was believed to have been the 190-m (623-ft) Mühlacker transmission tower in Mühlacker, Germany. It was demolished in 1945.

- Although not the tallest wooden structure ever known, the 118-m (387-ft) wooden truss tower at Gliwice, Poland, is currently the ★**tallest standing wooden structure**. It was constructed in 1935 and was originally used for radio transmissions but today forms part of a mobile-telephone network.

- *Eureka* is the last of the traditional wooden-hulled side-paddle ferries that served as inland passenger vessels, connecting commuters and travellers with the railroad system in San Francisco, California, USA. It is 69 m (227 ft) long and 13 m (42 ft 8 in) wide and is currently the **largest floating wooden structure**.

- The **longest single-span self-supporting wooden structure** is the Odate Jukai Dome in Odate, Japan, which measures 178 m (584 ft) on its longest axis and 157 m (515 ft) on its shortest axis. It consists of an opaque membrane stretched over a cedar-and-steel frame constructed from 25,000 Akita cedar trees.

★ LARGEST MAN-MADE ARCHIPELAGO

Surrounded by an oval-shaped breakwater, the World Islands, 4 km (2.5 miles) off the coast of Dubai in the United Arab Emirates, are 300 small artificial islands that collectively resemble the shape of Earth's continents (artist's impression, right). When complete, the land for sale will cover an area of 9 x 6 km (5.5 x 3.7 miles), with each island measuring 23,000–86,000 m² (247,500–925,600 ft²).

ENORMOUS ENGINEERING

★ TALLEST INDOOR ICE CLIMBING WALL

The tallest indoor ice climbing wall measures 20 m (65 ft 7 in) tall and 13 m (42 ft 8 in) wide. The wall is in the O2 World building in Seoul, South Korea, and was opened on 19 November 2005.

★ LONGEST BRIDGE TUNNEL

The Chesapeake Bay Bridge-Tunnel – a series of road bridges that dip into tunnels – extends 28.40 km (17.65 miles) from the Virginia Peninsula to Virginia Beach in the USA. Its longest bridged section is Trestle C at 7.34 km (4.56 miles); its longest tunnel is the Thimble Shoal Channel Tunnel at 1.75 km (1.09 miles).

LARGEST MUD BUILDING

The Grand Mosque in Djenne, Mali, is the largest mud building in the world, measuring 100 m (328 ft) long and 40 m (131 ft) wide. The present structure was built in 1905 and was based on the design of an 11th-century mosque. Rendered annually, it is surmounted by two massive towers and inside is a forest of vast columns taking up almost half of the floor space.

★ LONGEST ROAD SYSTEM

The country with the greatest length of road is the USA, which had 6,407,637 km (3,981,527 miles) of graded roads in 2004. Pictured is a snarled spaghetti junction of roadways in Los Angeles, California, USA.

HIGHEST MOSQUE

The King Abdullah Mosque on the 77th floor of the Kingdom Centre building in Riyadh, Saudi Arabia, is 183 m (600 ft) above ground level and was completed on 5 July 2004. The Kingdom Centre, the tallest building in Saudi Arabia, dominates the skyline and is a former winner of the Emporis "Best New Skyscraper" Award.

★ LARGEST BUILDING SITE

Three palm-shaped artificial islands, built on the coast of Dubai, UAE, from 100 million m³ (3.5 billion ft³) of sand and rock, will eventually make up the Palm Island project. When finished, say the architects, each "palm" will add 60 km (37 miles) of shoreline to Dubai and increase the beachfront by 166%. *See p.195 for more.*

LARGEST DIESEL ENGINE

The 14-cylinder Wärtsila Sulzer RTA96C two-stroke diesel engine has a rated maximum output of 80,080 kW (108,920 hp), weighs 2,300 tonnes (5.07 million lb) and is 13.5 m (44 ft 4 in) tall and 27.3 m (89 ft 6 in) wide. It is designed for use in the world's largest container ships.

★ LARGEST INDOOR SKI RESORT

Ski Dubai in the desert state of the United Arab Emirates opened in December 2005 with a total area of 22,500 m² (242,187 ft²). It is covered with up to 6,000 tonnes (13 million lb) of "real" snow all year round and features a 400-m-long (1,312-ft) slope and a 90-m (295-ft) quarter pipe for trick practice.

★ LARGEST SLIDING DOORS

A pair of sliding doors fitted to the vehicle assembly building at the Japan Aerospace Exploration Agency's (JAXA) Tanegashima Space Centre in Kagoshima, Japan, are 67.46 m (221 ft 4 in) high, 26.95 m (88 ft 5 in) wide and 2.5 m (8 ft 2 in) thick. Each door weighs 400 tonnes (882,000 lb).

★ LARGEST RAILWAY SYSTEM

The USA has 227,236 km (141,198 miles) of railway lines running the length and breadth of the country.

★ NEW RECORD
★ UPDATED RECORD

★ LARGEST CYLINDRICAL AQUARIUM

The AquaDom, situated in the Radisson SAS Berlin, Germany, opened in December 2003. Sitting on a 9-m-tall (29-ft 6-in) concrete foundation, it measures 14 m (46 ft) high, 11.5 m (38 ft) in diameter, holds 1 million litres (264,000 US gallons) of salt water and is home to 1,500 tropical fish of over 50 different species.

LARGEST PALACE

The Imperial Palace in the centre of Beijing, China, covers a rectangle measuring 960 x 750 m (3,150 x 2,460 ft) over an area of 72 ha (178 acres). The outline survives from the construction of the third Ming Emperor, Yongle (1402–24), but owing to constant reconstruction work, most of the intra-mural buildings (five halls and 17 palaces) are from the 18th century.

DID YOU KNOW?
The AquaDom takes 33 tonnes (72,750 lb) of salt to reach the same salt content as the sea.

LARGEST LEVEES

The largest system of levees ever built is that around the Mississippi River and its tributaries in the USA. Begun in 1717, they now extend for over 6,000 km (3,700 miles), largely thanks to the disastrous floods of 1927 that resulted in a massive federal building program. Over 765 million m³ (1 billion yd³) of earth was used in this project.

LARGEST UNIVERSITY BUILDING

The largest university building in the world is the M.V. Lomonosov Moscow State University on the Lenin Hills, south of Moscow, Russia. It stands 240 m (787.5 ft) tall and has 32 storeys and 40,000 rooms. It was constructed between 1949 and 1953.

TALLEST DAM

The Nurek dam, on the river Vakhsh, Tajikistan, is 300 m (984 ft) high and was completed in 1980. The Rogunskaya dam, also across the river Vakhsh, was due to reach 335 m (1,098 ft) in height but the break-up of the former Soviet Union in 1991 prevented its completion.

LARGEST COMMERCIAL BUILDING

In terms of floor area, the world's largest commercial building under one roof is the flower-auction building Bloemenveiling Aalsmeer (VBA) in Aalsmeer in the Netherlands. The floor surface of the building measures 1 million m² (10.7 million ft²).

LONGEST CAR

A 30.5-m-long (100-ft), 26-wheeled limo was designed by Jay Ohrberg (USA). It has many features, including a swimming pool with diving board and a king-sized water bed.

LONGEST...

• The Kiev dam across the Dnieper River, Ukraine, was completed in 1964. It has a crest length of 41.2 km (25.6 miles), making it the **longest dam wall** in the world.

• The **longest bridge** is the Second Lake Pontchartrain Causeway, which joins Mandeville and Metairie, Louisiana, USA, at 38.422 km (23.87 miles) long.

• The railway bridge over the River Thames at Maidenhead, Surrey, UK, has a maximum span of 39 m (128 ft) – the ★ **longest-span brick arch**.

• The world's **longest road and rail bridge system** is the Seto-Ohashi Bridge in Japan, which comprises six bridge sections stretching across a total distance of 9.4 km (5.8 miles).

• The **longest wooden bridge** is the Lake Pontchartrain Railroad Trestle in Louisiana, USA. It is made of creosoted yellow pine timber and stretches for 9.36 km (5.82 miles).

• The Chiba Urban Monorail near Tokyo, Japan, is the **longest suspended monorail** train system in the world, at 15.2 km (9.45 miles). It opened on 20 March 1979, and the line has been expanded three times since then.

UNDERGROUND

LARGEST RAILWAY STATION

The world's largest station by number of platforms is Grand Central Terminal, Park Avenue and 42nd Street, New York City, USA, built from 1903 to 1913.

Its 44 platforms are situated on two underground levels with 41 tracks on the upper level and 26 on the lower. The station covers 19 ha (48 acres), and on average some 660 Metro North trains and 125,000 commuters use it every day.

★ FASTEST TIME TO VISIT EVERY STATION ON THE NEW YORK CITY SUBWAY

Kevin Foster (USA) travelled the entire New York City Subway system in 26 hr 21 min 8 sec on 25–26 October 1989.

MOST EXTENSIVE UNDERGROUND RAIL SYSTEM

The subway system of New York City, USA, has a total track length of 1,355 km (842 miles) – sufficient to stretch to Chicago, Illinois – including 299 km (186 miles) of track in yards, shops and storage.

MOST ESCALATORS IN A METRO SYSTEM

The metro subway system of Washington DC, USA, has 588 escalators, maintained by the most expensive in-house escalator service contract in North America, employing 90 technicians. One of its stations – Wheaton – has the longest escalator in America, at 75.5 m (248 ft).

UNDERGROUND RAILWAY WITH THE MOST STATIONS

The New York City Subway has 468 stations (277 of which are under ground) in a network that covers 370 km (230 miles). It opened on 27 October 1904, with 28 stations.

LEAST EXTENSIVE METRO

The shortest operating underground system is the Carmelit, in Haifa, Israel. Opened in 1959, the Carmelit is just 1,800 m (1.1 mile) long.

The only metro in Israel, the Carmelit is a funicular running at a gradient of 12 degrees. Starting at Paris Square and finishing at Carmel Central, it has only six stations.

★ LARGEST MODERN UNDERGROUND HOUSE

Microsoft billionaire Bill Gates (USA) lives in a vast earth-sheltered mansion overlooking Lake Washington in Medina, Washington, USA. The building, much of which is concealed underground, occupies 4,600 m² (50,000 sq ft) of space and was completed in 1995. Included in the £30-million ($60-million) cost of the building were 64 km (40 miles) of fibre optic cables and a team of up to 300 electricians to hook up the state-of-the-art electronics features.

LOWEST RAILWAY LINE

The Seikan Tunnel, which crosses the Tsugaro Strait between Honshu and Hokkaido, Japan, reaches a depth of 240 m (786 ft) below sea level. Opened on 13 March 1988, the tunnel is 53.85 km (33.46 miles) long. Trains stop in the middle of the tunnel for two minutes so that passengers can take pictures through the windows of panels on its walls.

★ DEEPEST SWIMMING POOL

Designed to prepare divers for underwater expeditions, the world's deepest swimming pool is "Nemo 33" in Brussels, Belgium, which stretches to depths of over 33 m (108 ft). The pool contains 2.5 million litres (550,000 gal) of springwater heated to 30°C (86°F) by an array of solar panels.

LARGEST STORM DRAIN

The G-Cans project beneath Tokyo, Japan, is designed to prevent the flooding of the city's waterways during the typhoon season, which reaches its peak during September. It consists of five circular containment silos, each measuring 65 x 32 m (213 x 104 ft), connected together by 64 km (40 miles) of tunnels, as well as a huge water-containment tank 177 x 78 m (580 x 255 ft) wide and 25.4 m (83 ft) high. The system connects to turbines that can pump 200 tonnes (440,900 lb) of water per second into the Edogawa River.

BUSIEST UNDERGROUND NETWORK

The Greater Moscow Metro has been serving the Russian capital since 1935. It has 3,135 railcars covering 159 stations and 212 km (132 miles) of track. At its peak, the system had 3.3 billion passenger journeys in a year, although by 1998 the figure had declined to 2.55 billion.

The system currently carries 8 to 9 million passengers per day, making it the world's busiest metropolitan railway system. By comparison, the New York City Subway carries 4.5 million people per day and the London Underground just under 3 million.

⭐ LONGEST UNDERSEA ROAD TUNNEL

Norway's Bomlafjord Tunnel, completed in December 2000, measures 7.93 km (4.92 miles) long.

DEEPEST ROAD TUNNEL

The Hitra Tunnel in Norway, linking the mainland to the island of Hitra, reaches a depth of 264 m (866 ft) below sea level. The three-lane tunnel was opened in December 1994.

LARGEST UNDERGROUND SHOPPING COMPLEX

The PATH Walkway in Toronto, Canada, has 27 km (16.7 miles) of shopping arcades with 371,600 m² (4 million ft²) of retail space accommodating around 1,200 shops and services. More than 50 buildings, five subway stations and a rail terminal are accessible through the complex.

⭐ LONGEST SEWAGE TUNNEL

When complete in 2019, the Chicago TARP (Tunnels and Reservoir Plan) in Illinois, USA, will involve 211 km (131 miles) of machine-bored sewer tunnels measuring 2.7–10 m (9–33 ft) in diameter. Phase one was due for completion on 1 March 2006, meaning 176 km (109.4 miles) have since been operable. The project was commissioned in the mid-1970s to better regulate flooding and sewage flow, and has cost $3 billion (£1.5 billion) so far.

⭐ FASTEST TIME TO VISIT EVERY LONDON UNDERGROUND STATION

Håkan Wolgé (pictured) and Lars Andersson (both Sweden) travelled through all 275 stations on the London Underground network in a time of 18 hr 25 min 3 sec on 26 September 2006.

ROLLER COASTERS

MOST INVERSIONS IN A ROLLER COASTER

The *Colossus* steel-track roller coaster at Thorpe Park, Chertsey, Surrey, UK, turns riders upside down 10 times during each 850-m (2,789-ft) run.

FASTEST ROLLER COASTER

Opened on 20 May 2005, *Kingda Ka* at Six Flags Great Adventure near Jackson, New Jersey, USA, has a top speed of 206 km/h (128 mph), which is reached in just 3.5 seconds.

- ★**Floorless** The 1,226-m-long (4,025-ft) *Superman Krypton Coaster* at Six Flags Fiesta Texas, San Antonio, Texas, USA, has a top speed of 112.6 km/h (70 mph).
- ★**Flying** *Tatsu*, at Six Flags Magic Mountain, Valencia, California, USA, places the rider in a face-down position and reaches a speed of 100 km/h (62 mph).
- ★**Inverted** *Wicked Twist* at Cedar Point, Sandusky, Ohio, USA, can reach 115.8 km/h (72 mph).
- ★**Shuttle-design** *Superman: The Escape* at Six Flags Magic Mountain, Valencia, California, USA, and *Tower of Terror* at Dreamworld,

Gold Coast, Australia, both of which opened in 1997, have a top speed of 161 km/h (100 mph).

- ★**Stand-up** *Riddler's Revenge* at Six Flags Magic Mountain in California, USA, has a top speed of 104.6 km/h (65 mph) and a maximum *g* force of 4.2.

TALLEST ROLLER COASTER

Designed by Werner Stengel (Germany) and built by Intamin AG of Switzerland, *Kingda Ka* at Six Flags Great Adventure near Jackson, New Jersey, USA, is 139 m (456 ft) tall.

- ★**Floorless** The *Superman Krypton Coaster* at Six Flags Fiesta Texas, San Antonio, Texas, USA, is 51.2 m (168 ft) tall.
- ★**Flying** Opened on 13 May 2006, *Tatsu* at Six Flags Magic Mountain, Valencia, California, USA, measures 52 m (170 ft) high. *Tatsu* is a Japanese word meaning "flying beast".

LONGEST ROLLER COASTER MADE OF WOOD

Beast, at Paramount's Kings Island in Kings Mills, Ohio, USA, is the longest wooden laminated track roller coaster at 2,286 m (7,400 ft). Rides reach a top speed of 104 km/h (65 mph).

- ★**Inverted** *Alpengeist*, at Busch Gardens Williamsburg, Virginia, USA, is 59.4 m (195 ft) high. *Alpengeist* is German for "Spirit of the Alps".
- ★**Shuttle-design** *Superman: The Escape* at Six Flags Magic Mountain, Valencia, California, USA, is 126.5 m (415 ft) tall.
- ★**Stand-up** Opened on 4 April 1998, *Riddler's Revenge* at Six Flags Magic Mountain in California, USA, measures 47.5 m (156 ft) tall.
- **Wood** The first hill of *Son of Beast* at Paramount's Kings Island in Kings Mills, Ohio, USA, is 66.4 m (218 ft) tall. Designed by the Roller Coaster Corporation of America and opened on 27 April 2000, it is also the world's **fastest wooden roller coaster** at 126 km/h (78.3 mph).

LARGEST DROP ON A ROLLER COASTER

- ★**Floorless** The largest drop on a floorless roller coaster measures 45.7 m (150 ft) and is found on *Medusa* at Six Flags Discovery Kingdom, Vallejo, California, USA.

- **★Inverted** Opened in 1997, *Alpengeist*, at Busch Gardens Williamsburg, Virginia, USA, has a drop of 51.8 m (170 ft).
- **★Stand-up** *Riddler's Revenge* at Six Flags Magic Mountain in California, USA, has a drop of 44.5 m (146 ft).
- **★Wood** *Son of Beast* at Paramount's Kings Island in Kings Mills, Ohio, USA, has a drop measuring 65.2 m (214 ft).
- **Steel** *Kingda Ka* at Six Flags Great Adventure, which is located near Jackson, New Jersey, USA, has a drop of 127.4 m (418 ft) – the largest drop of any steel roller coaster.

LONGEST ROLLER COASTER

Opened in 2000 – the Year of the Dragon – in Nagashima Spaland, Japan, *Steel Dragon 2000* measures 2,479 m (8,133 ft).

- **Floorless** Opened on 5 May 2000, *The Dominator* at Geauga Lake, Ohio, USA, is 1,283 m (4,210 ft) long.
- **★Inverted** *The Pyrenees* at Parque Espana-Shima Spain Village in Japan measures 1,233.8 m (4,048 ft).
- **★Shuttle-design** Manufactured by Premier Rides, *Mr Freeze* at the Six Flags Over Texas in Arlington, Texas, USA, is 451 m (1,480 ft) long.
- **Stand-up** *Riddler's Revenge* at Six Flags Magic Mountain in California, USA, is 1,332 m (4,370 ft) in length.

COASTER TYPES

Floorless roller coasters have no floors! Seats are suspended in the air around a central frame.

Flying roller coasters are rides in which passengers are suspended in harnesses horizontally beneath the coaster, parallel to the track.

Inverted roller coasters are those where the train runs under the track with upright seats hanging from the wheel carriage above.

Shuttle-design coasters have connected cars. They run to the end of a track, then back to the start, often travelling backwards.

Stand-up roller coasters are designed so that passengers stand during the ride, restrained by an upright bicycle-like seat with overhead harnesses.

★LONGEST FLYING ROLLER COASTER

The longest flying roller coaster is *Tatsu* at Six Flags Magic Mountain, Valencia, California, USA, which is 1,098 m (3,602 ft) long. Opened on 13 May 2006, it has a top speed of 100 km/h (62 mph) and reaches 52 m (170 ft) at its highest point.

OLDEST ROLLER COASTER (CONTINUOUS OPERATION)

The Scenic Railway at Luna Park, Melbourne, Australia, opened to the public on 13 December 1912 and has remained in operation ever since.

LARGEST TEMPORARY AMUSEMENT PARK

The world's largest temporary amusement park springs up around the Oktoberfest Beer Festival in Munich, Germany, each year, attracting up to 50 portable mechanical rides every October.

SPORTS

★HIGHEST CAREER EARNINGS BY A SURFER

Kelly Slater (USA) earned an unprecedented $1,462,005 (£744,098) by the end of the 2006 season. Slater also holds the record for the ★**most wins of the Association of Surfing Professionals (ASP) World Championship Tour** with eight victories (1992, 1994–98 and 2005–06), and in 2005 became the ★**first person to score two perfect-10 rides** under the ASP's two-wave scoring system.

CONTENTS

ACTION SPORTS

★ MOST BASE JUMPS IN 24 HOURS

Dan Schilling (USA) made 201 BASE (Building, Antenna, Span, Earth) jumps at the Perrine Memorial Bridge near Twin Falls, Idaho, USA, on 7–8 July 2006.

★ MOST SOMERSAULTS ON SKIS IN 10 MINUTES

Christian Rijavec (Austria) performed 29 somersaults in 10 minutes in Pitzal Tyrol, Austria, on 8 April 2006. In this record, the somersaults can be either forward (head first) or backwards (feet first).

★ MOST SKATEBOARD 360 KICKFLIPS IN ONE MINUTE

Marc Haziza (France) performed nine 360 skateboard kickflips in one minute on the set of *L'Été De Tous Les Records* in Cabourg, France, on 1 August 2005.

BASE JUMPING

OLDEST JUMPER

James Talbot Guyer (USA, b. 16 June 1928) BASE jumped off the 148-m-high (486-ft) Perrine Memorial Bridge near Twin Falls, Idaho, USA, on 2 August 2002, aged 74 years 47 days.

★ HIGHEST JUMP

The highest altitude point for a BASE jump is 6,604 m (21,666 ft), by Glenn Singleman and Heather Swan (both Australia). The daredevil duo made a wingsuit jump from a ledge on Mt Meru in the Garhwal Himalayas, India, on 23 May 2006.

★ LARGEST INDOOR BASE JUMP

Ten parachutists performed an indoor jump at the Tropical Islands Resort near Berlin, Germany, on 31 January 2005 at an event organized by the German BASE Association.

SKATEBOARDING

★ MOST CONSECUTIVE OLLIES

Ross West (UK) performed a total of 128 consecutive ollies at the Royal Bath and West Show Ground in Somerset, UK, on 10 July 2005.

★ HIGHEST WALL RIDE

Brad Edwards and Aaron Murray (both USA) rode a 2.29-m-long (7-ft 6-in) wall at the opening of The Board Gallery at the Hollywood and Highland Center in Los Angeles, California, USA, on 25 August 2006. The attempt was organized in conjunction with *Juice* Magazine, the United States Skateboarding Association (USSA) and the World Skateboarding Association (WSA).

LONGEST BOARD SLIDE

Christian Pujola Hernandez (Spain) performed a 6.5-m (21-ft 4-in) rail grind on *El Show de Los Records* in Madrid, Spain, on 22 November 2001.

★ MOST HEELFLIPS IN ONE MINUTE

Claire Alleaume (France) pulled off eight heelflips in one minute in Benodet, France, on 26 August 2005.

INLINE SKATING

HIGHEST RAMP JUMP

José Félix Henry (Spain) cleared a bar raised to 4.5 m (14 ft 8 in) on inline skates on the set of *El Show de Los Records*, Madrid, Spain, on 14 December 2001.

★ **NEW RECORD**
★ **UPDATED RECORD**

★ MOST POINTS
IN A RED BULL AIR RACE SEASON

Kirby Chambliss (USA) won a total of 38 points in the 2006 Red Bull Air Race World Series. This is the most points ever won by an individual pilot over the course of a Red Bull Air Race season.

★ GREATEST DISTANCE IN 24 HOURS (MEN)

Mauro Guenci (Italy) covered 543.5 km (337.7 miles) on inline skates on 11–12 June 2004 in Senigallia, Italy.

Guenci also holds the record for the **greatest distance skated in one hour**, at 38.63 km (24 miles).

FASTEST SPEED

On 26 September 1998, Graham Wilkie and Jeff Hamilton (both USA) reached a speed of 103.03 km/h (64.02 mph) skating downhill in Arizona, USA.

DID YOU KNOW?
The Red Bull Air Race was established in 2003. It is an international series of air races in which competitors have to navigate an aerial obstacle course in the fastest time possible.

PARACHUTING

★ HIGHEST SPEED "CANOPY PILOTING"

Jason Moledzki (Canada) completed a piloting course in 2.72 seconds in Vienna, Austria, on 25 August 2006. Canopy piloting ("swooping") is a growing and extremely dangerous activity that involves the parachutist deploying their canopy at 1,524 m (5,000 ft), before entering a course in a steep rotating dive, competing for distance, speed or freestyle manoeuvres. The **farthest swooping distance** is

★ MOST BOULDERING WORLD CUP VICTORIES (FEMALE)

Sandrine Levet (France) has won five World Cup titles in the women's bouldering competition, in 2000–01 and 2003–05.

206.85 m (678 ft 7 in), also by Jason Moledzki, at Longmont, Colorado, USA, on 15 September 2005.

★ LARGEST FREE-FLYING HEAD-DOWN FORMATION

An international team of 53 skydivers flew head-down (a very dangerous upside-down position) in formation over Perris Valley, California, USA, on 29 April 2005.

MORE TECHNICAL BOARD MOVES...

• The ★**longest coping grind** along a ramp, measuring 6.83 m (22 ft 5 in), was achieved by Micky Iglesias (Switzerland) on the set of *L'Été De Tous Les Records,* Port Médoc, France, on 20 July 2005.

• Matthias Ringstrom (USA) set the record for the ★**most consecutive front-side, front-foot impossibles**, with four on the set of *L'Été De Tous Les Records* in La Tranche-sur-Mer, France, on 26 June 2005.

• The ★**most consecutive half-cab heelflips** is 10, a feat also achieved by Matthias Ringstrom (USA), on the set of *L'Été De Tous Les Records* at La Tranche-sur-Mer, France, on 26 July 2005.

• Stefan Akesson (Sweden) maintained the ★**longest one-wheel manual (wheelie)** with a 39-m (127-ft 11-in) wheelie at the Gallerian Shopping Centre in Stockholm, Sweden, on 4 November 2006.

• Trevor Baxter (UK) cleared a bar set at 1.65 m (5 ft 5 in) to establish the record for the **highest jump from a skateboard**. He jumped off his moving skateboard and landed on it after it had passed under the bar in Grenoble, France, on 14 September 1982.

• Terence Bougdour (France) performed the **highest skateboard 540 McTwist off a halfpipe**. It measured 1.5 m (4 ft 11 in) and was achieved on the set of *L'Été De Tous Les Records*, La Tranche-sur-Mer, France, on 27 July 2005.

AMERICAN FOOTBALL

★ FIRST NFL PLAYER TO SCORE TWO INTERCEPTION RETURNS OVER 100 YARDS

The Philadelphia Eagles' Lito Sheppard (USA) became the first player in NFL history with two interception returns of over 100 yards. Both touchdown returns came against the Dallas Cowboys: a 101-yarder on 15 November 2004 and a 102-yard interception return for a touchdown on 8 October 2006.

★ FASTEST TIME TO RECEIVE 1,000 PASSES

On 10 December 2006, Marvin Harrison (USA) of the Indianapolis Colts reached 1,000 career receptions in 167 games played.
• With Colts quarterback Peyton Manning (USA), Harrison set an NFL record for the ★ most passing yardage for a quarterback and wide receiver duo, with 11,908 yards as of 2006.
• The same duo also set a record for the ★ most pass completions by an NFL quarterback and wide receiver duo, with 878 completions as of 2006.

★ MOST ARENABOWL VICTORIES

Tampa Bay Storm have won five times: in 1991, 1993, 1995–96 and 2003. The ArenaBowl has been contested annually since 1987 and is the Championship game of the Arena Football League, a version of gridiron football played indoors.

★ HIGHEST TEAM SCORE IN AN ARENABOWL GAME

The highest score recorded by one team in the annual ArenaBowl game is 69 points by the San Jose SaberCats (USA) at ArenaBowl XVIII, on 27 June 2004, when they defeated the Arizona Rattlers 69–62.

★ MOST SEASONS PASSING 4,000 YARDS IN AN NFL CAREER BY AN INDIVIDUAL

Peyton Manning (USA) of the Indianapolis Colts set an NFL record in 2006 by reaching 4,000 passing yards in a season for the seventh time in his career (1999–2004, 2006).

★ MOST WORLD BOWL VICTORIES

The most wins of the World Bowl is three by the Berlin Thunder in 2001–02 and 2004. The World Bowl has been contested since 1991, firstly as the final game of the World League of American Football in 1991–92 and then as the final game of the NFL Europe Championship in 1995–2005.

☆ LONGEST PASS COMPLETION

A record pass completion of 99 yards has been achieved on 10 occasions and has always resulted in a touchdown. The most recent was a pass from quarterback Jeff Garcia to Andre Davis (both USA) of the Cleveland Browns in a game on 17 October 2004.

☆ MOST COMBINED NET YARDS GAINED IN A CAREER

Jerry Rice (USA) gained 23,546 yards playing for the San Francisco 49ers in 1985–2000, Oakland Raiders in 2001–04, and Seattle Seahawks in 2004.

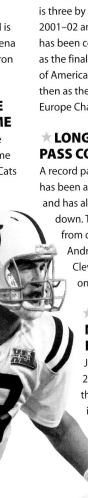

★ MOST CARRIES IN AN NFL SEASON BY A RUNNING BACK

Larry Johnson (USA, above, wearing 27) of the Kansas City Chiefs achieved the most carries in a season with 416 in 2006, surpassing the previous 410 set by Jamal Anderson (USA) of the Atlanta Falcons in 1998. Johnson rushed for 1,789 yards in the season.

☆ MOST COMBINED NET YARDS GAINED IN A SEASON

The most combined net yards gained by a single player in an NFL season is 2,690 by Derrick Mason (USA), playing for the Tennessee Titans in 2000.

☆ MOST PASS COMPLETIONS IN A CAREER BY A QUARTERBACK

Brett Favre (USA) of the Green Bay Packers completed 5,021 passes between 1992 and 2006. He also extended two of his quarterback records in 2006 by throwing for at least 3,000 yards in a season for the 15th consecutive year (see right), and by starting in his 237th consecutive regular-season game.

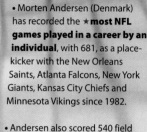

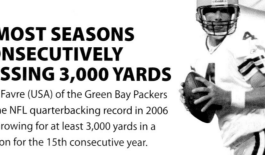

★ MOST SEASONS CONSECUTIVELY PASSING 3,000 YARDS

Brett Favre (USA) of the Green Bay Packers set the NFL quarterbacking record in 2006 by throwing for at least 3,000 yards in a season for the 15th consecutive year.

FIELD GOALS

• Morten Andersen (Denmark) has recorded the ★ **most NFL games played in a career by an individual**, with 681, as a place-kicker with the New Orleans Saints, Atlanta Falcons, New York Giants, Kansas City Chiefs and Minnesota Vikings since 1982.

• Andersen also scored 540 field goals – the **most field goals by an individual in a career**.

• Adam Vinatieri (USA) set a record for the **most field goals by an individual in a postseason career**, with 40, while playing for the New England Patriots and Indianapolis Colts since 2002.

• During the 2006 postseason, Vinatieri scored five field goals for the Indianapolis Colts against the Baltimore Ravens on 13 January 2007, the ★ **most field goals scored in a postseason game by an individual**.

• The record for the **most field goals by an individual in an NFL game** is seven and has been accomplished by four place kickers. The most recent was Billy Cundiff of the Dallas Cowboys against the New York Giants on 15 September 2003.

The other holders are Jim Bakken (USA) for the St Louis Cardinals against the Pittsburgh Steelers on 24 September 1967; Rich Karlis (USA) for the Minnesota Vikings against the L.A. Rams on 5 November 1989; and Chris Boniol (USA) for the Dallas Cowboys against the Green Bay Packers on 18 November 1996.

★ LARGEST COMEBACK IN A CHAMPIONSHIP GAME

The Indianapolis Colts overcame a 21–3 deficit and won the American Football Conference championship game over the New England Patriots 38–34, pulling off the biggest comeback in conference championship game history.

★ MOST FUMBLES IN A CAREER

Warren Moon (USA) recorded 161 fumbles playing for the Houston Oilers in 1984–1993, Minnesota Vikings in 1994–96, Seattle Seahawks in 1997–98 and Kansas City Chiefs in 1999–2000.

★ YOUNGEST PERSON TO PLAY IN THE SUPER BOWL

At 21 years 155 days, Jamal Lewis (USA, b. 26 August 1979) of the Baltimore Ravens is the youngest player to appear in the Super Bowl (2001).

★ LARGEST COMEBACK WITH UNDER 10 MINUTES LEFT TO PLAY

Vince Young (USA), playing for the Tennessee Titans, engineered the largest and most spectacular comeback in NFL history for his team, with less than 10 minutes left in the game. Having trailed 21–0 in the fourth quarter, the Titans came back and scored a 24–21 win over the New York Giants on 26 November 2006.

★ MOST TOUCHDOWNS IN A CAREER

Jerry Rice (USA) of the San Francisco 49ers, Oakland Raiders and Seattle Seahawks scored a record 208 touchdowns between 1985 and 2004.

★ YOUNGEST NFL COACH

Lane Kiffin (USA, b. 9 May 1975) was 31 years 259 days old when he signed on to coach the Oakland Raiders on 23 January 2007.

★ FIRST PLAYER WITH 20 INTERCEPTIONS AND 20 QUARTERBACK SACKS

During the 2005 season, Ronde Barber (USA) of the Tampa Bay Buccaneers became the first player in NFL history to record 20 career interceptions (28) and 20 career quarterback sacks (20), proving Barber's rare dual ability to rush the quarterback as well as defend the receivers in pass coverage.

★ MOST 100-YARD RUSHING GAMES FOR A QUARTERBACK

Michael Vick (USA) of the Atlanta Falcons holds the NFL record for the most career 100-yard games by a quarterback, with seven, through 2006.

ATHLETICS

★ NEW RECORD
★ UPDATED RECORD

MARATHON ENDEAVOURS

ACHIEVEMENT	TOTAL	ATHLETE (COUNTRY)
★ Most London Marathon wins (male)	3	Antonio Pinto (Portugal)
		Dionicio Ceron (Mexico)
★ Most London Marathon wins (female)	4	Ingrid Kristiansen (Norway)
★ Most New York Marathon wins (male)	4	Bill Rogers (USA)
★ Most New York Marathon wins (female)	9	Grete Waitz (Norway)
★ Most consecutive Hawaiian Ironman wins (male)	4	Mark Allen (USA)
★ Most consecutive Hawaiian Ironman wins (female)	5	Paula Newby-Fraser (USA)
★ Most World Road Running Championship wins (male)	1	Zersemau Tadesse (Eritrea)*
★ Most World Road Running Championship wins (female)	1	Lornah Kiplagat (Netherlands)*

*The IAAF World Road Running Championships were first held in 2006, the year of these victories.
This competition replaced the World Half-Marathon Championships*

FIVE WORLD RECORDS IN 35 MINUTES!

Jesse Owens (USA) set five records in 35 minutes at Ann Arbor, Michigan, USA, on 25 May 1935: an 8.13-m (26-ft 8.25-in) long jump at 3:25 p.m., a 20.3-sec 220 yd (and 200 m) at 3:45 p.m. and a 22.6-sec 220 yd low hurdles (and 200 m) at 4 p.m.

Earlier that day, at 3:15 p.m., he equalled another world record, with a 9.4-second 100 yd dash.

HIGHEST POLE VAULT (FEMALE)

Yelena Isinbayeva (Russia) recorded a 5.01-m (16-ft 5.2-in) pole vault in Helsinki, Finland, on 12 August 2005. On 10 February 2007, in Donetsk, Ukraine, she produced the ★ **highest indoor pole vault by a woman**, measuring 4.93 m (16 ft 2 in).

★ EARLIEST EVIDENCE OF ORGANIZED RUNNING

Historical research indicates that organized running took place in Memphis, Egypt, as long ago as 3800 BC.

★ FASTEST INDOOR 4 X 400 M RELAY (WOMEN)

A Russian team (Yulia Gushchina, Olga Kotlyarova, Olga Zaytseva and Olesya Krasnomovets) ran the indoor 4 x 400 m relay in 3 min 23.37 sec in Glasgow, UK, on 28 January 2006.

★ FASTEST 4 X 800 M RELAY (MEN)

Kenya (Joseph Mutua, William Yiampoy, Ismael Kombich and Wilfred Bungei) ran the 4 x 800 m relay in 7 min 2.43 sec in Brussels, Belgium, on 25 August 2006.

★ FASTEST INDOOR 4 X 800 M RELAY (WOMEN)

On 11 February 2007, Russia (Anna Balakshina, Anna Emashova, Natalya Pantelyeva and Olesya Chumakova) ran the indoor 4 x 800 m relay in 8 min 18.54 sec in Volgograd, Russia.

★ FASTEST 20 KM ROAD RUN (FEMALE)

Lornah Kiplagat (Netherlands) won the 20 km road run in 1 hr 3 min 21 sec in Debrecen, Hungary, on 8 October 2006.

★ FASTEST ROAD RELAY

The Kenyan team set a time of 1 hr 57 min 6 sec in Chiba, Japan, on 23 November 2005.

MOST GOLD MEDALS IN ATHLETICS WORLD CHAMPIONSHIPS

The World Championships, as distinct from the Olympic Games, were inaugurated in 1983, when they were held in Helsinki, Finland. The most golds won to date is nine by Michael Johnson (USA, left), in the 200 m (1991 and 1995), 400 m (1993, 1995, 1997 and 1999) and 4 x 400 m relay (1993, 1995 and 1999).

The **most athletics gold medals won by a woman** in the same competition is five by Gail Devers (USA) for the 100 m (1993), 100 m hurdles (1993, 1995 and 1999) and 4 x 100 m relay (1997).

★ FASTEST 110 M HURDLES

Xiang Liu (China) ran the 110 m hurdles in 12.88 seconds in Lausanne, Switzerland, on 11 July 2006.

The record for the **fastest women's road relay** is held by the People's Republic of China, with a time of 2 hr 11 min 41 sec in Beijing, China, on 28 February 1998.

★ FASTEST 1,000 KM ULTRA-DISTANCE TRACK (MALE)

Yiannis Kouros (Greece) completed the 1,000 km ultra-distance track event in a time of 5 days 16 hr 17 min in Colac, Victoria, Australia, from 26 November to 1 December 1984.

Eleanor Robinson (GB) ran the **fastest women's 1,000 km ultra-distance track event** in 8 days 27 min 6 sec in Nanango, Queensland, Australia, from 11 to 18 March 1998. The term "ultra-distance" applies to events staged over a course greater than standard and, sometimes, for events carried out under more exacting conditions than usual.

FASTEST 100 M (MALE)

On 14 June 2005, Asafa Powell (Jamaica, above left) set a new world record of 9.77 seconds for the 100 m sprint in Athens, Greece – a time that he has since matched on two separate occasions. Justin Gatlin (USA) also ran the 100 m in exactly the same time on 12 May 2006 in Doha, Qatar.

MOST WORLD CHAMPIONSHIP MEDALS WON

Merlene Ottey (Jamaica) won 14 World Championships medals: three gold, four silver and seven bronze, 1983–97.

She also holds the record for the **most Olympics athletics medals won by a woman**, with eight: three silver and five bronze, 1980–2000.

The **most medals won in the World Championships by a man** is 10, by Carl Lewis (USA), comprising eight gold, one silver and one bronze, 1983–93.

X-REF

• There's more marathon magic on p.76.

• Teamwork is sometimes the key to success – as you'll see on p.88.

• You'll find a wealth of sports stats 'n' facts from p.210 on…

• … including the GWR sports reference tables, starting on p.266.

★ MOST WORLD CUP WINS (WOMEN)

East Germany has won the International Associaton of Athletics Federations (IAAF) World Cup four times, in 1979, 1983, 1985 and 1989.

The ★ **most wins of the athletics World Cup by a men's team** is also four, by Africa in 1992, 1994, 1998 and 2002. (Both national and continental teams feature.)

★ MOST EUROPEAN CUP WINS (MEN)

East Germany won the European Cup six times, in 1970 and 1975–83. Germany has also won the title six times, in 1994–96, 1999 and 2004–05. (Held every two years from 1965 to 1993, the European Cup became an annual event in 1994.)

The ★ **most wins by a women's team** is 12, by Russia, in 1993, 1995 and 1997–2006.

OLDEST OLYMPIC MEDALLIST

Tebbs Lloyd Johnson (GB) was aged 48 years 115 days when he came third in the 50,000 m walk in London, UK, in 1948.

The **oldest female Olympic medallist** was the Czech Dana Z. Topkov (b. 19 September 1922), who was 37 years 348 days old when she came second in the 1960 Olympic javelin contest.

FARTHEST LONG JUMP

Mike Powell (USA, pictured) made a 8.95-m (29-ft 4.3-in) long jump in Tokyo, Japan, on 30 August 1991. Carl Lewis (USA) achieved the **farthest indoor long jump** – 8.79 m (28 ft 10 in) – in New York City, USA, on 27 January 1984.

★ FASTEST OUTDOOR 5,000 M (FEMALE)

Meseret Defar (Ethiopia) ran the 5,000 m in 14 min 24.53 sec in New York City, USA, on 3 June 2006.

FIRST IN THE FIELD

• On 15 August 2006, in Tallinn, Estonia, Tatyana Lysenko (Russia) achieved the **farthest hammer throw by a woman**, with a distance of 77.8 m (255 ft 3 in). In fact, the "hammer" is a metal ball on one end of a steel wire, at the other end of which is a grip. Not much good for banging in nails, though…

• The **farthest javelin throw by a man**, one of 98.48 m (323 ft 1.1 in), was achieved by Jan Železný (Czech Republic), in Jena, Germany, on 25 May 1996. And the **farthest women's javelin throw**? Turn the page…

• It's time to call the shots. Randy Barnes (USA) recorded the **farthest shot put** in Los Angeles, California, USA, on 20 May 1990, with a put of 23.12 m (75 ft 10.2 in). The **farthest shot put by a woman** measured 22.63 m (74 ft 3 in) and was produced by Natalya Lisovskaya (USSR), in Moscow, Russia, on 7 June 1987.

• Leaping ahead, on 11 June 1988 in Leningrad, USSR (now St Petersburg, Russia), Galina Chistyakova (USSR) produced the **farthest long jump by a woman**, measuring 7.52 m (24 ft 8 in). Heike Drechsler (GDR) holds the record for the **farthest indoor long jump by a woman**, with a distance of 7.37 m (24 ft 2.1 in), in Vienna, Austria, on 13 February 1988.

• One-two-three… Jonathan Edwards (GB) produced the **farthest triple jump by a man** in Gothenburg, Sweden, on 7 August 1995, with a leap of 18.29 m (60 ft 0.7 in). On 10 August 1995, Inessa Kravets (Ukraine) made the **farthest triple jump by a woman** – 15.5 m (50 ft 10.2 in) – also in Gothenburg. Fancy that: one venue, two triple records in three days!

ATHLETICS

OLDEST MARATHON

The Boston Marathon was first held on 19 April 1897, when it was run over a distance of 39 km (24 miles 1,232 yd).

John A. Kelley (USA) finished the Boston Marathon 61 times between 1928 and 1992, winning in 1935 and 1945.

FASTEST HALF-MARATHON (MALE)

Samuel Wanjiru (Kenya) ran a time of 58 min 53 sec at the Ras al-Khaimah international half-marathon in Ras al-Khaimah, United Arab Emirates, on 9 February 2007.

Elana Meyer (South Africa) recorded the **fastest half-marathon by a woman** with a time of 66 min 44 sec in Tokyo, Japan, on 15 January 1999.

★ FASTEST 50 KM ROAD WALK

Nathan Deakes (Australia, above) completed a 50 km road walk in an unprecedented 3 hr 35 min 47 sec in Geelong, Australia, on 2 December 2006.

★ FARTHEST JAVELIN THROW (FEMALE)

Osleidys Menéndez (Cuba) achieved a record-breaking throw of 71.7 m (235 ft) in the javelin event in Helsinki, Finland, on 14 August 2005.

FASTEST MARATHON

On 28 September 2003, Paul Tergat (Kenya) ran a marathon in a time of 2 hr 4 min 55 sec in Berlin, Germany.

Paula Radcliffe (UK) achieved the **fastest marathon by a woman** with a time of 2 hr 15 min 25 sec in the London Marathon, UK, on 13 April 2003.

★ FASTEST TIME TO RUN THREE MARATHONS IN THREE DAYS

Johan Oosthuizen (South Africa) ran three marathons in a combined time of 8 hr 11 min 8 sec during the Lake Tahoe Triple marathon event in Lake Tahoe, Nevada, USA, from 28 to 30 September 2006.

SHORTEST DURATION TO COMPLETE A MARATHON ON EACH CONTINENT

Tim Rogers (UK) completed a marathon on each of the seven continents in 99 days, from 13 February to 23 May 1999.

He began his "marathon" feat with the Antarctica Marathon on King Jorge Island and went on to complete a marathon in the USA (North and Central America), South Africa (Africa), France (Europe), Brazil (South America) and Hong Kong (Asia) before finishing with a marathon at Huntly, New Zealand (Oceania) over three months later.

★ SHORTEST DURATION TO COMPLETE A MARATHON ON EACH CONTINENT (FEMALE)

Noelle Sheridan (USA) set a new record for the shortest overall time to complete a marathon on each of the seven continents by a woman. She took just 208 days from 19 May to 13 December 2006.

LONGEST EVER RUNNING RACE

The 1929 trans-continental race from New York City to Los Angeles, California, USA, was 5,850 km (3,635 miles) long. Finnish-born Johnny Salo (below right) was the winner, in 79 days, from 31 March to 17 June. His time of 525 hr 57 min 20 sec (averaging 11.12 km/h, or 6.91 mph) left him only 2 min 47 sec ahead of Pietro "Peter" Gavuzzi (UK, below left).

MOST DECATHLON POINTS (FEMALE)

Austa Skujyte (Lithuania) scored 8,358 points in the decathlon event in Columbia, Missouri, USA, on 14–15 April 2005.

★ **NEW RECORD**
☆ **UPDATED RECORD**

FEATS OF ENDURANCE

- Horst Preisler (Germany) completed 1,305 races of 26 miles 385 yd (42.195 km) or longer from 1974 to 2004 – the **most marathons completed by an individual**.

- The **longest annual running race** is the Sri Chinmoy 3,100 Mile Race, held in Jamaica, New York City, USA. The fastest time to complete the race is 42 days 13 hr 24 min 3 sec by Wolfgang Schwerk (Germany) in 2002. Suprabha Beckjord (USA) is the only woman to have completed this race and is also the only person to have completed all of the 10 races held to date.

- The **most wins of the Triathlon World Championship (male)** is four, by Simon Lessing (UK), in 1992, 1995, 1996 and 1998. He has also won the **most medals overall in the Triathlon World Championship (male)** to date, with two silver medals (1993 and 1999) and one bronze (1997). The **fastest time achieved in winning the Triathlon World Championship (male)** is 1 hr 39 min 50 sec by Simon Lessing (UK) in Cleveland, Ohio, USA, in 1996.

- The **most wins of the ITU Triathlon World Championship (female)**, in the Elite Women's event, is three, all by Emma Snowsill (Australia) in 2003, 2005 and most recently in Lausanne, Switzerland, on 3 September 2006. Michellie Jones has won the **most medals in the Triathlon World Championship (female)** overall. As well as her two gold medals, she has won two silver (1998 and 2001) and three bronze (1997, 2000 and 2003). The **fastest time to win the Triathlon World Championship (female)** is 1 hr 50 min 52 sec by Jackie Gallagher (Australia) at Cleveland, Ohio, USA, in 1996.

- The **highest score in a decathlon (male)** is 9,026 points, by Roman Šebrle (Czech Republic), in Götzis, Austria, on 26–27 May 2001.

★ FASTEST HULA HOOPING
OVER 10 KM (FEMALE)

Betty Hoops (USA) ran a distance of 10 km, while continuously hula hooping, in a time of 1 hr 43 min 11 sec at the Bolder Boulder 10 km race in Colorado, USA, on 30 May 2005.

FASTEST LUNGE MILE

To "lunge", an athlete starts from a standing position and extends one leg forward, bending the other leg until its knee touches the ground. The athlete then repeats the movement with the other leg. The ★ **fastest time to lunge a mile by a woman** is 37 min 58 sec and was set by Dorothea Voegeli (Switzerland) in Dachau, Germany, on 6 November 2005.

DID YOU KNOW?
The marathon was inspired by the story (probably a myth) of Greek runner Pheidippides. He ran 34.5 km (21.4 miles) from a battlefield near the town of Marathon to Athens, to announce a Greek victory over the Persians, then died.

The record for the **fastest lunge mile by a man** is 30 min 50 sec, set by Ashrita Furman (USA) at the Sport Park in Neufahrn, Germany, on 27 October 2002.

Ashrita also recorded the ★ **fastest mile hopping on a pogo stick while juggling three balls**, in 24 min 49 sec, at the Brooklyn Promenade, Brooklyn Heights, New York City, USA, on 17 May 2006. The ★ **fastest time to hula hoop 10 km** is 1 hr 25 min 9 sec, and was set at Hechsler Park, Huntington, New York City, USA, on 12 June 2006. The holder? You've guessed it – Ashrita Furman!

☆ FASTEST TIME TO SKIP A MARATHON

The record for the fastest marathon run while skipping with a rope is 4 hr 49 min 39 sec and was set by Chris Baron (Canada) at

★ FASTEST
TIME TO HOP 100 M

Andre Miller (Barbados, far right below) hopped 100 m in 17.4 seconds during the Barbados World Record Festival at Barbados National Stadium, St Michael, Barbados, on 25 March 2006.

FASTEST BACKWARDS MARATHON

Xu Zhenjun (China, far left in the main group above) ran the Beijing International Marathon, China, backwards, in 3 hr 43 min 39 sec on 17 October 2004.

the ING Ottawa Marathon, Ottawa, Ontario, Canada, on 29 May 2005.

OLDEST MARATHON FINISHER

Greek runner Dimitrion Yordanidis ran a 26-mile marathon in Athens, Greece, on 10 October 1976, aged 98, in 7 hr 33 min.

The **oldest female marathon finisher** is Jenny Wood-Allen (UK, b. 1911). She completed the 2002 London Marathon aged 90 years 145 days in 11 hr 34 min on 14 April 2002.

☆ FASTEST JOGGLING

The record for the fastest marathon ran while juggling three objects is held by Zach Warren (USA, right), who ran the full Philadelphia Marathon – a distance of 42.2 km (26.22 miles) – while juggling three balls, in 3 hr 7 min 5 sec in Philadelphia, USA, on 20 November 2005.

AUTO SPORTS

THE LEGEND OF LE MANS

Instituted on 26–27 May 1923, Le Mans is the world's most famous endurance race. It is staged over the famous Circuit de la Sarthe course and organized by L' Automobile Club de l'Ouest (ACO).

The **most wins by an individual at the Le Mans 24-hour race** is seven by Tom Kristensen (Denmark) in 1997 and 2000–05.

★FASTEST SPEED IN TOP FUEL NHRA DRAG-RACING (FEMALE)

The highest terminal velocity at the end of the 440-yd (402-m) run by a female Top Fuel drag-racer is 531.58 km/h (330.31 mph) by Melanie Troxel (USA) at the Texas Motorplex in Dallas, USA, on 7 October 2005.

DAYTONA 500

The ★**winner of the first Daytona 500**, in 1959, was Lee Petty (USA). He reached an average speed of 218 km/h (135.52 mph), driving an Oldsmobile.

• Kevin Harvick's (USA) 0.02-second margin of victory in the 2007 Daytona 500 was the ★**closest Daytona 500 victory** since the advent of electronic scoring in 1993.

• Driving a No. 48 Lowe's Chevrolet Monte Carlo in 2006, Jimmie Johnson (USA) became the ★**first driver to win the Daytona 500, Allstate 400 and the NASCAR Nextel Cup Championship in the same year**.

The fastest lap in the Le Mans 24-hour race is 3 min 21.27 sec by Alain Ferté (France) on 10 June 1989

FORMULA ONE

Alberto Ascari (Italy) enjoyed an uninterrupted run of nine Formula One grands prix in 1952–53 driving for Ferrari, the **most consecutive Formula One grand prix victories**.

• Inaugurated in 1950, the World Drivers' Championship has been won seven times by Michael Schumacher (Germany) in 1994–95 and 2000–04, the **most Formula One World Championships won**.

• Schumacher also achieved the **most Formula One grand prix wins by a driver in a season**, with 13 victories in 2004.

• The **most Formula One constructors' World Championships won** is 14 by Ferrari in 1961, 1964, 1975–77, 1979, 1982–83 and 1999–2004.

★MOST WOMEN RACING AT A MOTORSPORTS EVENT

A total of 62 women took part in the Crash.net Formula Woman Novice Cup Challenge staged at Pembrey Circuit, Pembrey, Wales, UK, on 19–20 November 2005.

INDYCAR

Mario Andretti (USA) is the ★**only racer to have won the Indianapolis 500** (1969), **Daytona 500** (1967) **and a Formula One world title** (1978).

• Al Unser Jr beat Scott Goodyear (both USA) in the **closest finish in the history of the Indianapolis 500 race**, on 24 May 1992. The margin of victory was 0.043 seconds.

• Nigel Mansell (UK) made history in 1993 by becoming the **first rookie to win the IndyCar Championship**.

Mansell was also the 1992 Formula One World Driving Champion, making him the ★**first driver to win the IndyCar and Formula One titles in consecutive seasons**.

• In 1989, Emerson Fittipaldi (Brazil) and Patrick Racing shared winnings of $1,001,604 (£610,978), becoming the ★**first driver and team to earn $1 million in one year for winning the Indianapolis 500**.

• Sam Hornish Jr (USA) won the Indianapolis 500 with the ★**first last-lap pass** in the 90-year history of the race, on 28 May 2006. Hornish took the lead on the final lap, passing rookie Marco Andretti (USA) just before the chequered flag to capture his first Indy 500 win.

★ YOUNGEST INDYCAR WINNER

Marco Andretti (USA, b. 13 March 1987) is a third-generation driver from one of motor racing's most famous families. Aged 19 years 167 days, he became the youngest winner of a major open-wheel racing event when he scored his first career Indy Racing League victory at Infineon Raceway in Sonoma, California, USA, on 27 August 2006. Andretti beat Dario Franchitti (UK) by 0.66 seconds to win the Indy Grand Prix in Sonoma.

NASCAR

Jeff Gordon (USA) holds the record for the ★ **highest National Association for Stock Car Auto Racing (NASCAR) career earnings**, with winnings of $82,373,526 (£42,067,015) to the end of the 2006 season.
• In 2006, Denny Hamlin (USA) amassed prize money of $6,725,332 (£3,434,534), the ★ **highest single-season NASCAR earnings by a rookie**.
• The ★ **most money won from one NASCAR Truck Series race** is $93,375 (£47,685) by Jack Sprague (USA) at Daytona on 16 February 2007
• The ★ **most consecutive race wins in NASCAR** is 10 by Richard Petty (USA) in 1967.
• Ricky Rudd (USA) started 788 consecutive races during his career from 1975 to 2005, the ★ **most consecutive starts in NASCAR**.
• The ★ **most pole positions achieved in a NASCAR season** is 20 by Bobby Isaac (USA) in 1969.
• The record for ★ **most cars in a 400-mile NASCAR race** is 35, set at the 2006 Allstate 400.
• The record for ★ **most cars in a 500-mile NASCAR race** is 31 on the lead lap at the 2006 Daytona 500.
• Juan Pablo Montoya (Colombia) became the ★ **first Formula One driver to switch to racing full time in the NASCAR Nextel Cup series** in 2006.

NHRA

For a petrol-driven piston-engined car, the ★**highest speed in Pro Stock National Hot Rod Association (NHRA) Drag Racing** is 337.48 km/h (209.75 mph) by Jason Line (USA) in a Pontiac GTO at Dinwiddie, Virginia, USA, on 15 October 2006.
• The ★**most NHRA Pro Stock championships won** is 10 by Bob Glidden (USA) in 1974, 1975, 1978, 1979, 1980 and 1985–89.
• Anthony Schumacher (USA) holds the record for ★**most consecutive Top Fuel NHRA round wins**, with 21 consecutive victories in 2005 and 2006 in the US Army dragster.
• The ★**youngest NHRA Pro Stock winner** is Richie Stevens (USA, b. 27 September 1978), who won the Winston Finals in Pomona, California, USA, on 18 November 1998, aged 20 years 51 days.
• The ★**most NHRA Funny Car championships won** is 14 by John Force (USA) in 1990–91, 1993–2002, 2004 and 2006. Force is also the career leader in Funny Car victories, with 122 wins, and the season leader, with 13 wins in 1996.
• Warren Johnson (USA, b. 7 July 1943) became the ★**oldest driver to win an NHRA event**, at the age of 62 years 234 days. His record-breaking victory came at the Checker Schuck's Kragen NHRA Nationals at Firebird International Raceway, in Chandler, Arizona, USA, on 26 February 2006.

★ **NEW RECORD**
★ **UPDATED RECORD**

★ MOST NHRA TOP FUEL DRAG-RACING TITLES

Joe Amato (USA) won five NHRA championships in the Top Fuel category. His victories came in 1984, 1988 and 1990–92.

★ HIGHEST EARNINGS IN A SINGLE NASCAR SEASON (MALE)

Jimmie Johnson (USA, left and in No.48, below) won $15,952,125 (£8,146,529) in 2006. He also achieved the ★ **most consecutive wins of the Coca-Cola 600 race**, with three in 2003–05. This 965-km (600-mile) race is the longest in NASCAR.

AUTO SPORTS

★ MOST MOTO GRAND PRIX TITLES

The Moto GP classification was instituted in 2002 and replaced the motorcycle World Championship 500cc Grand Prix.

The greatest number of Moto grand prix championships won by an individual is four, by Valentino Rossi (Italy) in 2002–05.

MOTOCROSS

★ MOST ARENACROSS CHAMPIONSHIPS

Arenacross is a US indoor motocross competition. Two riders have won five championships: Dennis Hawthorne (USA), with wins in 1986–1990, and Buddy Antunez (USA), in 1997–2001.

MOTOCROSS WORLD CHAMPIONSHIP

The **most wins of the 125cc motocross World Championship** is three, by three riders: Gaston Rahier (Belgium) in 1975–77, Harry Everts (Belgium) in 1979–81 and Alessio Chiodi (Italy) in 1997–99.

• The **most wins of the 500cc motocross World Championship** is five. It is shared by Roger de Coster (Belgium), with

★ MOST 250CC MOTOCROSS WORLD CHAMPIONSHIP WINS

Joel Robert (Belgium) has won the 250cc motocross World Championship six times, in 1964 and 1968–72. Stefan Everts (Belgium, right) equalled this feat in 1995–97 and 2003–05.

victories in 1971–73 and 1975–76, and Joel Smets (Belgium), with wins in 1995, 1997–98, 2000 and 2003.

YOUNGEST MOTOCROSS CHAMPION

Dave Strijbos (Netherlands, b. 9 November 1968) won the 125cc motocross title aged 18 years 296 days on 31 August 1986.

MOTORCYCLE

MOST WORLD CHAMPIONSHIP CAREER RACE WINS

Between 24 April 1965 and 25 September 1977, Giacomo Agostini (Italy) won 122 races – 68 at the 500cc class and 54 at the 350cc class.

★ MOST SUPERBIKE TITLES BY A MANUFACTURER

In 1977–2005, Kawasaki and Suzuki (both Japan) each won nine titles. Britain's Chris Walker is pictured on a Kawasaki ZX-7RR in the 2002 World Championship at Silverstone, UK.

MOST WORLD CHAMPIONSHIP WINS BY A MANUFACTURER

Honda (Japan) won 48 World Championships in 1961–99.

MOST WORLD CHAMPIONSHIP RACE WINS IN A SEASON

Two riders have won 19 motorcycle World Championships in a season: Giacomo Agostini (Italy) in 1970, and Mike Hailwood (UK) in 1966.

MOST SUPERBIKE WORLD CHAMPIONSHIPS

Carl Fogarty (UK) won 59 races, 1992–99. He has also won the **most superbike World Championship titles**, with four (1994–95, 1998–99).

★ MOST MOTORCYCLE SIDE-CAR WORLD CHAMPIONSHIPS

Steve Webster (UK) has won an unprecedented 10 motorcycle side-car World Championships, with victories in 1987–89, 1991, 1997–2000 and 2003–04.

★ MOST SUZUKA 8 HOURS WINS BY A MANUFACTURER

Honda (Japan) provided the winning motorcycle 20 times in the Suzuka 8 Hours endurance race, in 1979–2005.

NHRA

★ MOST NHRA TITLES IN ALL CATEGORIES (FEMALE)

Angelle Sampey (USA) won 40 National Hot Rod Association (NHRA) Pro Stock motorcycle titles between 1996 and 2006.

Sampey is the ★ **first female to win an NHRA Pro Stock motorcycle championship**, winning three in a row between 2000 and 2002.

DRAG RACING

The ★ **most NHRA championships won in the Pro Stock motorbike category** is six by Dave Schultz (USA) in 1987–88, 1991, 1993–94 and 1996.
• The ★ **fastest speed achieved by a petrol-driven, piston-engined motorcycle (Pro Stock)** is 317.69 km/h (197.45 mph) by G.T. Tonglet (USA) on a Harley-Davidson on 18 March 2005, and Andrew Hines (USA) – also on a Harley-Davidson – on 19 March 2005. Both feats were achieved at Gainesville, Florida, USA.

• The ★ **fastest time to cover 440 yd on a Pro Stock motorbike** is 6.011 seconds and was achieved by Chip Ellis (USA) at Sonoma, California, USA, on 30 July 2006.

RALLYING

MOST RALLY WORLD CHAMPIONSHIP RACE WINS IN A SEASON

Didier Auriol (France) won six rally World Championship races in 1992.

MOST RALLY WORLD CHAMPIONSHIP RACE WINS

Carlos Sainz (Spain) recorded a total of 26 World Championship race wins between 1990 and 2004.

TT RACES

LONGEST MOTORCYCLE RACE CIRCUIT

The "Mountain" circuit on the Isle of Man, over which the principal TT Races have been run since 1911 (with minor amendments in 1920), has 264 curves and corners and is 60.72 km (37.73 miles) long.

★ FASTEST LAP SPEED

The Isle of Man TT circuit record for the highest lap speed is 208.33 km/h (129.451 mph) by John McGuinness (UK, riding for England) on a Honda CBR1000 Fireblade on 9 June 2006.

MOST WINS IN ONE YEAR

The greatest number of events won in one year in the TT Races is four – in the Formula One, Junior, Senior and Production categories – by Phillip McCallen (Ireland) in 1996.

MOST WINS IN A CAREER

Joey Dunlop (Ireland) recorded 26 wins at the TT races between 1977 and 2000.

★ MOST WINS BY A MANUFACTURER

The greatest number of wins by a manufacturer at the Isle of Man TT Races is 183, by Yamaha (Japan), from 1965 to 2005.

First held on 28 May 1907, the Isle of Man TT Races are the world's oldest motorcycle races

TT RACES

The year 2007 marks a century of the TT (Tourist Trophy) Races, staged in the last week of May and the first week of June. Public roads on the Isle of Man are closed off to become the race circuit – now the oldest motorcycle course in regular use – and crowds of picnickers turn out to watch the racers hurtle round the roads at breakneck speeds.

★ MOST MOTOCROSS DES NATIONS WINS

Also known as the "Olympics of Motocross", the Motocross des Nations has been contested annually since 1947.

Two teams have won 16 times: Great Britain in 1947, 1949–50, 1952–54, 1956–57, 1959–60, 1963–67 and 1994; and the USA in 1981–93, 1996, 2000 and 2005.

★ **NEW RECORD**
☆ **UPDATED RECORD**

BALL SPORTS

★ NEW RECORD
★ UPDATED RECORD

★ MOST APPEARANCES IN INTERNATIONAL HOCKEY

Jeroen Delmee (Netherlands, pictured in orange with France's Nicolas Gaillard) made a record 338 appearances for the Netherlands men's team from 1994 to 2006.

MOST AFL GAMES

The career record for most Australian Football League (AFL) games played is 426 by Michael Tuck (Australia) for Hawthorn in 1972–91.

★ MOST WINS OF THE VOLLEYBALL GRAND PRIX (WOMEN)

Brazil has won the women's volleyball Grand Prix six times: 1994, 1996, 1998 and 2004–06. Pictured is Brazil's Fabiana Claudino in the Fédération Internationale de Volleyball (FIVB) World Grand Prix in Tokyo, Japan, on 20 August 2006.

AUSTRALIAN FOOTBALL

★ MOST MATCHES WON

In the 2000 season, Essendon won 24 out of 25 matches.

HIGHEST TEAM SCORE

Geelong scored 239 (37–17) against Brisbane on 3 May 1992. Geelong also recorded the **longest winning streak**, with 23 consecutive Premiership wins in 1952–53. The **most consecutive games lost** in the AFL Premiership is 51 by University in 1912–14.

MOST GOALS

John Coleman (Australia) scored 12 goals for Essendon v. Hawthorn in the 1949 season, the **most goals scored on an AFL debut**.
• The **most goals in a season** is 150, by Bob Pratt (for South Melbourne) in 1934 and Peter Hudson (for Hawthorn; both Australia) in 1971.

CANADIAN FOOTBALL

★ MOST PASS ATTEMPTS IN A CFL CAREER BY A QUARTERBACK

Quarterback Damon Allen (USA) had achieved 9,071 pass attempts in his Canadian Football League (CFL) career to the end of the 2006 season.

He also set a new record for the ★ **most career pass completions in Canadian football** with 5,113 to the end of the 2006 season.

Finally, Allen set a new record for the ★ **most career touchdown passes in Canadian football**, with 391, to the end of the 2006 season.

Allen's CFL career began in 1985.

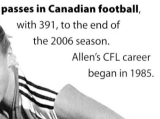

★ MOST HOCKEY CHAMPIONS TROPHY WINS

Three teams have won this trophy eight times: Germany in 1986–88 (as West Germany), 1991–92, 1995, 1997 and 2001; the Netherlands in 1981–82, 1996, 1998, 2000, 2002–03 and 2006; and Australia in 1983–85, 1989–90, 1993, 1999 and 2005. Pictured is Australia's Michael McCann, scorer of the winning goal in 2005.

★ MOST WOMEN'S HOCKEY WORLD CUP WINS

The Netherlands have won the women's hockey World Cup six times, in 1974, 1978, 1983, 1986, 1990 and 2006. Pictured in orange is the Netherlands' Maartje Goderie with Mariana Gonzalez (Argentina) in the semi-final in Spain on 6 October 2006.

★MOST TIMES TO WIN AVP BEST OFFENSIVE PLAYER AWARD (FEMALE)

The greatest number of Association of Volleyball Professionals (AVP) Pro Beach Tour Offensive Player of the Year awards won by a female player is three by Misty May-Treanor (USA) in 2004–06.

★MOST TIMES TO WIN THE AVP BEST DEFENSIVE PLAYER AWARD (FEMALE)

Holly McPeak (USA) has won the Defensive Player of the Year award three times, in 2002–04.

GAELIC FOOTBALL

HIGHEST COMBINED SCORE IN AN ALL-IRELAND FINAL

The greatest aggregate score by both teams in an All-Ireland final was 45 points, when Cork (26, 3–17)* beat Galway (19, 2–13) in 1973.

LARGEST DISCIPLINARY FINES FOR A SINGLE AFL MATCH

Following the match between the Western Bulldogs and St Kilda on 4 May 2003, disciplinary fines totalling AUS$67,500 ($49,773; £28,163) were imposed on players.

LARGEST ATTENDANCE

The Down v. Offaly final at Croke Park, Dublin, Ireland, in 1961 attracted 90,556 spectators.

HANDBALL

MOST MEN'S WORLD CHAMPIONSHIPS

Sweden has won four titles, in 1954, 1958, 1990 and 1999, as has Romania in 1961, 1964, 1970 and 1974.

★MOST WOMEN'S EUROPEAN CHAMPIONSHIPS

Two teams have won these championships three times: Denmark in 1994, 1996 and 2002; and Norway in 1998, 2004 and 2006.

The **most women's handball World Championships** won is three by East Germany in 1971, 1975 and 1978; and by the USSR in 1982, 1986 and 1990.

★MOST WINS OF THE BEACH WORLD CHAMPIONSHIPS (MEN)

The men's beach handball World Championships has been staged on two occasions, and the most wins is one, by Egypt in 2004 and Brazil in 2006.

The ★**most wins of the beach handball World Championships (women)** is one, by Russia in 2004 and Brazil in 2006.

HIGHEST SCORE AT THE HANDBALL OLYMPIC GAMES (WOMEN)

Austria scored 45 points against Brazil in 2000.

OTHER BALL SPORTS

- The record for the **most consecutive footbag kicks with two footbags** is held by Juha-Matti Rytilahti (Finland) with 68 kicks by one foot on 30 September 2001.

- The **most footbag kicks in five minutes** is 1,019 by Andy Linder (USA) on 7 June 1996.

- In 2006, England hosted the inaugural Commonwealth Korfball Championships, and went on to win it. By default, therefore, England secured the record for the ★**most wins of the Commonwealth Korfball Championships**.

- The **longest game of korfball played is 26 hr 2 min**, set by the Korfball Club De Vinken at Vinkeveen, the Netherlands, on 23–24 May 2001.

- The **largest korfball tournament** was held on 14 June 2003, when 2,571 men and women participated in the Kom Keukens/Ten Donck international youth korfball tournament in Ridderkerk, the Netherlands.

* NB: in Gaelic football records, the aggregate score is listed first. The goals and points, respectively, are given separately afterwards

BALLSPORTS

HOCKEY

★MOST GOLD MEDALS WON BY AN INDIVIDUAL (FEMALE)

Rechelle Hawkes (Australia), captain of the Australian women's field hockey team (also known as the Hockeyroos), has won three gold medals – in 1988, 1996, and 2000.

CANADIAN FOOTBALL – MOST YARDS PASSING IN A CAREER

Damon Allen (USA) threw for a record 71,590 yards during his CFL career for Edmonton, Ottawa, Hamilton, Memphis, British Columbia and Toronto between 1985 and 2006.

★ **NEW RECORD**
☆ **UPDATED RECORD**

HIGHEST SCORE IN INTERNATIONAL HOCKEY (WOMEN)

The England women's hockey team beat France 23–0 at Merton, London, UK, on 3 February 1923.

MOST WORLD CUPS (MEN)

Pakistan has won four times, in 1971, 1978, 1982 and 1994.

☆ MOST INTERNATIONAL GOALS SCORED BY AN INDIVIDUAL

The greatest number of goals scored in international field hockey is 288 by left full back Sohail Abbas (Pakistan, b. June 9, 1977) between 1998 and 2006. Sohail is a field hockey defender and penalty corner specialist.

MOST OLYMPIC HANDBALL GOLD MEDALS – WOMEN

The Danish women's team have won three consecutive Olympic gold medals, in 1996, 2000 and 2004. Pictured is Kristine Andersen (Denmark) of the 2004 winning team taking on Korea.

NETBALL

☆ MOST COMMONWEALTH GAMES TITLES

Netball has been played three times at the Commonwealth Games, first in Kuala Lumpur, Malaysia, in 1998, then Manchester, UK, in 2002, and Melbourne, Australia, in 2006, with Australia winning on the first two occasions and New Zealand the third.

★ MOST CONSECUTIVE PASSES

Pupils of Brookfield Community School, Chesterfield, Derbyshire, UK, achieved 164 netball passes in a row on 22 September 2006.

MOST INTERNATIONAL APPEARANCES (FEMALE)

Irene van Dyk (New Zealand) made a record 129 appearances at international level playing for South Africa and New Zealand between 1994 and 2005.

LONGEST MARATHON

The world's longest game of netball lasted 55 hours and was played by members of Capital NUNS netball club at the Shell Centre, Waterloo, London, UK, from 22 to 24 July 2005.

MOST EUROPEAN HANDBALL CHAMPIONSHIPS WON – WOMEN

The most European handball Championships won by a women's team is three: by Denmark in 1994, 1996 and 2002; and by Norway in 1998, 2004 and 2006. The Norwegian team is pictured in red playing against Russia on their way to winning the 2006 European Handball Championship (by 27 points to 24) on 17 December in Stockholm, Sweden.

FASTEST BALL

The fastest speed a projectile moves in any ball game is around 302 km/h (188 mph) – in jai alai, a sport that originates from the Basque areas of Spain and France. The jai alai ball is three-quarters the size of a baseball and harder than a golf ball. It is propelled through the air – and caught – using a 70-cm-long (27-in) scoop-shaped cesta basket-glove (or *xistera* in the Basque language).

OTHER BALL SPORTS

• The record for the **longest hurling hit** is a "lift and stroke" of 118 m (129 yd; 387 ft), credited to Tom Murphy of Three Castles, Kilkenny, Ireland, in a "long puck" contest in 1906.

• The **lowest combined score in an all-Ireland hurling final** is four, when Tipperary (one goal, one point) beat Galway (nil) in the first championship held at Birr, Offaly, Ireland, in 1887.

• The **most team wins of the shinty Challenge Cup** is a record 28 by Newtonmore, Highland, in 1907–86.

• The Camanachd Cup is shinty's most prestigious trophy. The **most consecutive Camanachd Cup wins by a team** is seven, by Kingussie (Scotland), from 1997 to 2003.

• The record for the **most goals scored in a Major League Lacrosse career** is 206, held by Mark Millon (USA) of the Baltimore Bayhawks and the Boston Cannons between 2001 and 2005.

• The **longest recorded lacrosse throw** is 148.91 m (162.86 yds; 488 ft 5 in), by Barnet Quinn of Ottawa, Canada, on 10 September 1892.

VOLLEYBALL

★ HIGHEST CAREER EARNINGS IN BEACH VOLLEYBALL

Karch Kiraly (USA) has won a record $3,172,461 (£1,618,938) in official Association of Volleyball Professional (AVP) Tour earnings through to the end of the 2006 season. He also won a record 148 AVP Tour titles between 1979 and 2006.

★ MOST TIMES TO WIN AVP BEST OFFENSIVE PLAYER AWARD (MALE)

The most AVP Pro Beach Tour offensive player of the year awards won by a male player is four by Jose Loiola (Brazil) from 1995 to 1998.

★ MOST TIMES TO WIN AVP BEST DEFENSIVE PLAYER AWARD (MALE)

The most Pro Beach defensive player of the year awards won by a male is four by Mike Dodd (USA) in 1994–97.

★ MOST CONSECUTIVE WINS OF THE WORLD CHAMPIONSHIP (MEN)

Italy has won the volleyball world championships three times, in Brazil in 1990, Greece in 1994 and Japan in 1998. The **most successive wins of the women's World Championships** is three by the USSR: in 1952 in the Soviet Union, 1956 in France and 1960 in Brazil.

DID YOU KNOW?
In electronically timed tests, a golf ball driven off a tee was found to have a top speed of 273 km/h (169.6 mph), compared with Jose Ramon Areitio's jai alai throw of 302 km/h (188 mph)!

★ MOST WINS OF THE EUROPEAN CHAMPIONSHIPS

The USSR men's team has won the volleyball European championships a record 12 times between 1950 and 1992. The **most wins of the volleyball European Championships by a women's team** is 13, also by the USSR between 1949 and 1991.

★ GAELIC FOOTBALL: MOST ALL-IRELAND FINAL WINS

Kerry has won 34 All-Ireland finals between 1903 and 2006. The **greatest number of successive wins in an All-Ireland Final** is four by Wexford (1915–18) and by Kerry twice (1929–32 and 1978–81). Pictured is Kerry's John Crowley (Ireland) in action against Mayo's Gary Ruane (Ireland).

MOST NATIONAL CHAMPIONSHIPS WON BY A TEAM

Changos de Naranjito won 20 championships in the Puerto Rico Men's Volleyball National League between 1958 and 2004.

BASEBALL

★LARGEST BASEBALL MITT

On display at the San Francisco Giants' home stadium in San Francisco, California, USA, this giant mitt measures 8 m (26 ft) high, 9.7 m (32 ft) wide and 3.6 m (12 ft) deep. It weighs 9,070 kg (20,000 lb).

IN A CAREER...

★ MOST STRIKEOUTS

The Major League Baseball (MLB) record for the most strikeouts in a career is 5,714 by Nolan Ryan (USA) playing for the New York Mets, California Angels, Houston Astros and Texas Rangers (all USA) from 1966 to 1993.

★ MOST CONSECUTIVE GAMES PLAYED

From the beginning of his career with the New York Yankees (USA) on 14 January 2003, Hideki Matsui (Japan) played 518 consecutive games until 11 May 2006, when he injured his wrist.

DID YOU KNOW? The baseball mitt shown above is a replica of a vintage 1927 four-fingered glove, scaled up to 36 times its actual size!

★FIRST CATCHER TO LEAD THE MAJOR LEAGUES IN BATTING AVERAGE

Joe Mauer (USA) batted .347 while playing for the Minnesota Twins (USA) in 2006.

★ MOST RUNS BATTED IN BY A SWITCH HITTER IN A SEASON

Mark Teixeira (USA) achieved 144 playing for the Texas Rangers (USA) in 2005. The National League (NL) record is 136 by Lance Berkman (USA, pictured right) playing for the Houston Astros (USA) in 2006.

MOST GAMES LOST BY A PITCHER

The pitcher who lost the most games in a career was Denton True "Cy" Young (USA), with 316 losses between 1890 and 1911 while playing for the Cleveland Spiders, St Louis Cardinals, Boston Red Sox, Cleveland Indians and Boston Braves (all USA).

★ MOST CONSECUTIVE 200-HIT SEASONS

Ichiro Suzuki (Japan) played six consecutive 200-hit seasons for the Seattle Mariners (USA) from 2001 to 2006.

★ MOST BASES ON BALLS

Playing for the Pittsburgh Pirates and San Francisco Giants (both USA) from 1986 to 2006, Barry Bonds (USA) recorded 2,426 bases on balls. Bonds' achievement also represents the record for the ★ **most intentional bases on balls in a career** – confirming that he truly is a dangerous batter.

★LARGEST BASEBALL

The largest baseball measured 3.6 m (12 ft) in diameter and went on display at the David L. Lawrence Convention Center, Pittsburgh, Pennsylvania, USA, from 7 to 11 July 2006. The ball is signed by famous players such as Ted Williams and Hank Aaron (both USA).

★ MOST STRIKEOUTS BY A LEFT-HANDED PITCHER

Randy Johnson (USA) made 4,544 left-handed strikeouts playing for the Montreal Expos (Canada), and the Seattle Mariners, Houston Astros, Arizona Diamondbacks and New York Yankees (all USA) from 1988 to 2006.

★ MOST TIMES HIT BY A PITCH

The MLB modern record (i.e. post-1900) for the most times to be hit by a pitch in a career is 282, held by Craig Biggio (USA) playing for the Houston Astros (USA) from 1988 to 2006.

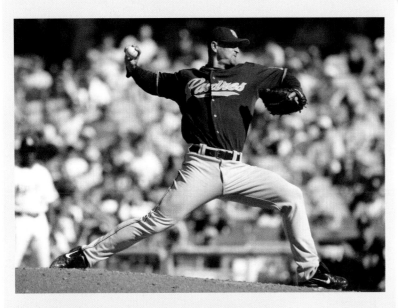

★ MOST SAVES IN A CAREER

Trevor Hoffman (USA, above) made an unprecedented 482 saves playing for the Florida Marlins and San Diego Padres (both USA) from 1993 to 2006. The record for the ★ **most saves in the American League in a career** is held by Mariano Rivera (Panama), with 413 for the New York Yankees (USA) from 1995 to 2006.

MOST HOME RUNS...

★ UNDER ONE MANAGER FROM START OF CAREER

Chipper Jones (USA) hit 357 home runs while playing for manager Bobby Cox (USA) of the Atlanta Braves (USA) from 1993 to 2006.

★ BY A SWITCH HITTER

Switch hitter Mickey Mantle (USA) hit 536 home runs playing for the New York Yankees (USA) from 1951 to 1968.

The record for **most career home runs by a switch hitter in the National League** is 357 by Chipper Jones (USA), playing for the Atlanta Braves (USA) from 1993 to 2006.

★ MOST TIMES HIT BY A PITCH IN A GAME

Several players have been hit three times by a pitch. The most recent were Nomar Garciaparra (USA), playing for the Los Angeles Dodgers (USA) on 3 July 2006, and Reed Johnson (USA, right), playing for the Toronto Blue Jays (Canada) on 29 April 2006.

★ BY A SECOND BASEMAN

Jeff Kent (USA) hit 319 home runs while playing for the Toronto Blue Jays (Canada), and the New York Mets, Cleveland Indians, San Francisco Giants, Houston Astros and Los Angeles Dodgers (all USA) from 1992 to 2006.

★ BY A LEFT FIELDER

Playing for the Pittsburgh Pirates and San Francisco Giants (both USA) from 1986 to 2006, Barry Bonds (USA) hit 698 home runs.

★ BY A CATCHER

Mike Piazza (USA) hit 396 home runs while playing for the Los Angeles Dodgers, Florida Marlins, New York Mets and San Diego Padres (all USA) from 1992 to 2006.

★ BY A DESIGNATED HITTER

David Ortiz (Dominican Republic) hit 47 home runs playing for the Boston Red Sox (USA) in 2006.

★ BY A ROOKIE SECOND BASEMAN IN A SEASON

Playing for the Florida Marlins (USA) in 2006, Dan Uggla (USA) hit 27 home runs in a single season.

★ ONLY MEMBERS OF THE "40-40" CLUB

Just four MLB players have hit at least 40 home runs and stolen at least 40 bases in the same season (the "40-40" club). The most recent was Alfonso Soriano (Dominican Republic, above) playing for the Washington Nationals (USA) in 2006.

SOLD AT AUCTION

• The **most valuable baseball bat** in the world was the one used by George Herman Ruth (aka "Babe" Ruth, USA) to hit the first home run on opening day 18 April 1923 at Yankee Stadium in New York City, USA. The bat was purchased by MastroNet, Inc. (an Illinois-based auction house in America) at an auction at Sotheby's, New York City, USA, for a record $1,265,000 (£654,694) on 2 December 2004.

• The record for the **most valuable baseball** was set on 12 January 1999 when Todd McFarlane (USA) paid $3,054,000 (£1,874,655), including commission, for a ball at Guernsey's auction house in New York City, USA. The baseball in question was the one hit by Mark McGwire (USA) of the St Louis Cardinals for his 70th and final home run in his record-setting 1998 season.

• At an auction in Dallas, Texas, USA, on 5 May 2006, Heritage Auction Galleries sold a baseball signed in 1961 by legendary baseball player Joe DiMaggio and film star Marilyn Monroe (both USA). It sold for $191,200 (£103,000) – the ★ **most valuable autographed baseball.**

• The ★ **most valuable baseball card** was a rare 1909 tobacco card, known as T206 Honus Wagner, sold by SCP Auctions in Los Angeles, California, USA, to an anonymous collector for $2.35 million (£1.19 million) on 27 February 2007.

• The glove used by legendary US baseball star Lou Gehrig during his final game on 30 April 1939 became the **most valuable baseball glove** in history when it sold for $389,500 (£236,778) at Sotheby's, New York City, USA, on 29 September 1999.

BASKETBALL

★ MOST THREE-POINT FIELD GOALS MADE IN AN NBA SEASON

Ray Allen (USA) scored 269 goals playing for the Seattle SuperSonics during the 2005–06 season. He also holds the record for **most three-point field goals made in one half of a game** with eight against the Charlotte Hornets on 14 April 2002.

★ LONGEST TIME TO SPIN A BASKETBALL ON ONE FINGER

Joseph Odhiambo (USA) span a regulation basketball continuously for 4 hr 15 min on 19 February 2006 in Houston, Texas, USA, during the NBA All-Star Jam Session.

★ MOST SUCCESSFUL FREE THROWS IN ONE HOUR

Michael Campbell (USA) managed a total of 1,197 successful free throws in one hour at the Princeton Family YMCA in Princeton, New Jersey, USA, on 21 July 2006.

★ FARTHEST BASKETBALL SLAMDUNK FROM A TRAMPOLINE

Daisuke Nakata (Japan, above) achieved a basketball slamdunk from a trampoline set 6.3 m (20 ft 8 in) from the backboard, on the set of the *Muscle Musical* show in Tokyo, Japan, on 29 December 2006. The record was matched on the same show by Shunsuke Nagasaki (Japan).

NBA

★ FASTEST COACH TO 900 VICTORIES

Phil Jackson (USA) recorded 900 victories out of 1,264 games while coaching the Chicago Bulls (1989–97) and Los Angeles Lakers (1999–2003, 2005–06). Jackson surpassed the feat that Pat Riley (USA) accomplished in 1,278 games with the Lakers (1981–89), New York Knicks (1991–94) and Miami Heat (1995–2002, 2005–06).

★ BEST THREE-POINT FIELD-GOAL SHOOTING PERCENTAGE IN A SINGLE POSTSEASON

Derek Fisher (USA) shot 61.7% from beyond the three-point line, making 29 of his 47 attempts for the Los Angeles Lakers in the 2002–03 postseason.

★ OLDEST PLAYER TO RECORD 20 REBOUNDS IN A GAME

At the age of 40 years 251 days, Dikembe Mutombo (Congo, b. 25 June 1966) recorded 22 rebounds playing for the Houston Rockets (USA) in their 108–97 victory over the Denver Nuggets on 2 March 2007.

★ FIRST ALL-STAR GAME HELD OUTSIDE AN NBA CITY

The Western Conference All-Stars defeated the Eastern Conference All-Stars 153–132 in the NBA All-Star Game, played in Las Vegas, USA, on 18 February 2007. It was the first All-Star game not held in an NBA city.

MOST...

The ★ **most consecutive three-point field goals scored** is 13, a feat achieved by two players: Brent Price (USA) for the Washington Wizards (1995–96); and Terry Mills (USA) for the Detroit Pistons (1996–97).

★ BEST THREE-POINT FIELD-GOAL SHOOTING PERCENTAGE IN A CAREER

Steve Kerr (Lebanon) is the NBA's most accurate three-point shooter. He shot 45.4% from beyond the three-point line, making 726 of his 1,599 regular-season attempts while playing for six different teams from 1988 to 2003.

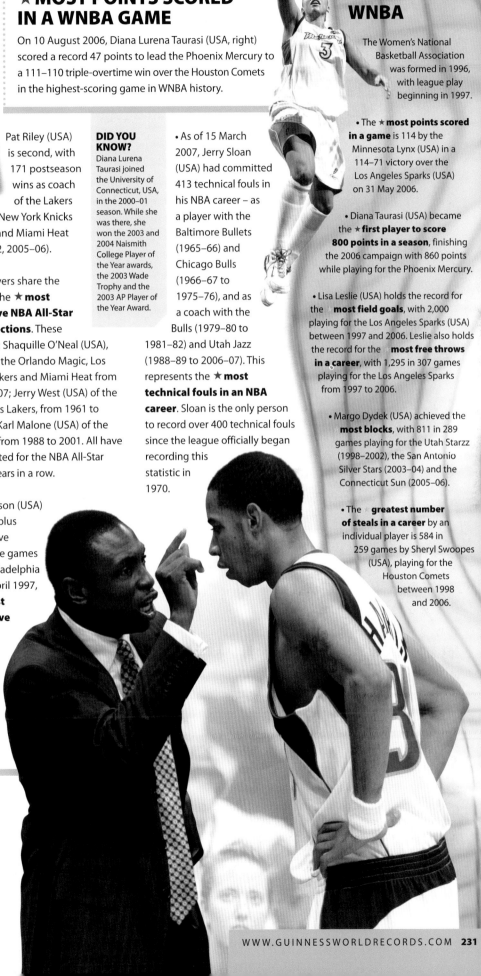

★ MOST POINTS SCORED IN A PROFESSIONAL GAME (FEMALE)

Anat Draigor (Israel) scored 136 points for Hapoel Mate Yehuda against Elitzur Givat Shmuel in Mesilat Zion, Israel, on 5 April 2006, the greatest number of points scored in a female professional basketball game.

• The Dallas Mavericks' 110–87 win over the Atlanta Hawks on 26 February 2007 gave them the record for the ★ **most winning streaks of 12 or more games in a single season**, with three. They are the first team in NBA history to achieve this feat.

• Reggie Miller (USA) scored the ★ **most career three-point field goals**, with 2,560 goals for the Indiana Pacers (USA) in 1987–2005.

• Phil Jackson (USA) has won 178 play-off games as coach of the Chicago Bulls (1989–97) and Los Angeles Lakers (1999–2003, 2005–06), ★ **the most play-off games won by a coach**.

★ FASTEST COACH TO 100 NBA VICTORIES

Avery Johnson (USA, pictured with Devin Harris) recorded 100 victories out of a record 131 games as coach of the Dallas Mavericks. The 100th win came in the Mavericks' win over the Denver Nuggets in Denver, Colorado, USA, on 31 December 2006.

★ MOST POINTS SCORED IN A WNBA GAME

On 10 August 2006, Diana Lurena Taurasi (USA, right) scored a record 47 points to lead the Phoenix Mercury to a 111–110 triple-overtime win over the Houston Comets in the highest-scoring game in WNBA history.

Pat Riley (USA) is second, with 171 postseason wins as coach of the Lakers (1981–89), New York Knicks (1991–94) and Miami Heat (1995–2002, 2005–06).

• Three players share the record for the ★ **most consecutive NBA All-Star Game selections**. These players are: Shaquille O'Neal (USA), playing for the Orlando Magic, Los Angeles Lakers and Miami Heat from 1994 to 2007; Jerry West (USA) of the Los Angeles Lakers, from 1961 to 1974; and Karl Malone (USA) of the Utah Jazz, from 1988 to 2001. All have been selected for the NBA All-Star Game 14 years in a row.

• Allen Iverson (USA) scored 40-plus points in five consecutive games for the Philadelphia 76ers in April 1997, the ★ **most consecutive games in which a rookie has scored 40-plus points**.

DID YOU KNOW?
Diana Lurena Taurasi joined the University of Connecticut, USA, in the 2000–01 season. While she was there, she won the 2003 and 2004 Naismith College Player of the Year awards, the 2003 Wade Trophy and the 2003 AP Player of the Year Award.

• As of 15 March 2007, Jerry Sloan (USA) had committed 413 technical fouls in his NBA career – as a player with the Baltimore Bullets (1965–66) and Chicago Bulls (1966–67 to 1975–76), and as a coach with the Bulls (1979–80 to 1981–82) and Utah Jazz (1988–89 to 2006–07). This represents the ★ **most technical fouls in an NBA career**. Sloan is the only person to record over 400 technical fouls since the league officially began recording this statistic in 1970.

WNBA

The Women's National Basketball Association was formed in 1996, with league play beginning in 1997.

• The ★ **most points scored in a game** is 114 by the Minnesota Lynx (USA) in a 114–71 victory over the Los Angeles Sparks (USA) on 31 May 2006.

• Diana Taurasi (USA) became the ★ **first player to score 800 points in a season**, finishing the 2006 campaign with 860 points while playing for the Phoenix Mercury.

• Lisa Leslie (USA) holds the record for the **most field goals**, with 2,000 playing for the Los Angeles Sparks (USA) between 1997 and 2006. Leslie also holds the record for the **most free throws in a career**, with 1,295 in 307 games playing for the Los Angeles Sparks from 1997 to 2006.

• Margo Dydek (USA) achieved the **most blocks**, with 811 in 289 games playing for the Utah Starzz (1998–2002), the San Antonio Silver Stars (2003–04) and the Connecticut Sun (2005–06).

• The **greatest number of steals in a career** by an individual player is 584 in 259 games by Sheryl Swoopes (USA), playing for the Houston Comets between 1998 and 2006.

COMBAT SPORTS

BOXING

LONGEST FIGHT

The longest world title fight (under Queensberry Rules) was that between light-weights Joe Gans (USA) and Oscar Matthew "Battling" Nelson (Denmark) at Goldfield, Nevada, USA, on 3 September 1906. It was ended in the 42nd round when Gans was declared the winner on a technicality.

★ MOST COUNTRIES COMPETING AT A WORLD TAE KWON DO CHAMPIONSHIPS

The most participating nations at a tae kwon do ("art of hand and foot fighting") World Championships is 114 at the 17th (10th, Women's) event held between 13 and 17 April 2005 in Madrid, Spain. Pictured are Chonnapas Preanwaew (Thailand, left) and Catherine Sheridan (Ireland) competing at the event.

YOUNGEST WORLD CHAMPION

Wilfred Benitez (USA) of Puerto Rico was 17 years 176 days when he won the WBA light welterweight title in Puerto Rico on 6 March 1976.

OLDEST CHAMPION

Archie Moore, aka "Ol' Mongoose" (USA) – who was recognized as a light heavyweight champion up to 10 February 1962, when his title was removed – was then believed to be between 45 and 48 years old.

MOST KNOCK DOWNS IN A BOUT

Vic Toweel, South Africa's first boxing world champion, knocked down Danny O'Sullivan (UK) 14 times in 10 rounds in their commonwealth bantamweight fight in Wembley Stadium, Johannesburg, South Africa, on 2 December 1950. O'Sullivan eventually retired.

★ **NEW RECORD**
★ **UPDATED RECORD**

★ MOST CONSECUTIVE WORLD MIDDLEWEIGHT TITLE DEFENCES

The most consecutive successful defences of the WBC middleweight world title is 14 by Carlos Monzon (Argentina) between 1970 and 1977. He achieved this despite being shot in the leg, in 1973, by his wife – in that year, he defended the title twice then continued boxing for four more years!

MOST KNOCK-OUTS IN A CAREER

The greatest number of finishes classed as "knock-outs" in a career is 145 (129 in professional bouts) by Archie Moore (USA, b. Archibald Lee Wright). The "Ol' Mongoose" from Mississippi fought in a career spanning from 1936 to 1963, and for almost 10 years he reigned as light-heavyweight world champion.

HIGHEST ANNUAL EARNINGS FOR A BOXER

Oscar de la Hoya (USA, pictured above left) is the world's highest paid boxer, with estimated earnings of $38 million (£22 million) in 2005, according to the *Forbes Rich List*.

TAE KWON DO

MOST OLYMPIC GOLD MEDALS WON

Ha Tae-kyung (South Korea) holds two olympic titles in men's tae kwon do – winning gold in the flyweight in 1988 and welterweight in 1992. Chen Yi-an (Taiwan) matched this record for female competitors, winning the bantamweight title in 1988 and the lightweight in 1992.

★ OLDEST AND YOUNGEST WRESTLERS TO WIN THE WWE CHAMPIONSHIPS

The **oldest wrestler to win the World Wrestling Entertainment (WWE) Championship** is Vince McMahon (USA, far left), who took the title aged 54 years 21 days on 14 September 1999. The ★ **youngest person to win the WWE Championship** is Brock Lesnar (USA, left) – he was just 25 years 44 days when he beat The Rock on 25 August 2002.

★ MOST CONSECUTIVE WORLD SUPER-MIDDLEWEIGHT TITLE DEFENCES

Joe Calzaghe (UK) – aka the "Italian Dragon" – made his 19th title defence on 14 October 2006, when he successfully beat Sakio Bika (Cameroon) in Manchester, UK, in a highly aggressive and frequently "dirty" fight.

MARTIAL ARTS

• The record for the **most sumo-wrestling bouts won** is held by *ozeki* Tameemon Torokichi (Japan), alias Raiden (1767–1825). In 21 years (1789–1810) he won 254 bouts and lost 10 to gain the highest ever winning percentage of 96.2.

• The **most competitive full-contact rounds** contested in boxing and martial arts is 6,264 by multiple record-holder Paddy Doyle (UK) from 1993 to November 2005.

• The **most full-contact kicks in one hour** is 5,545 by Ron Sarchian (USA) at Premier Fitness, Encino, California, USA, on 16 June 2006.

• The **most kumite karate titles won by an individual** is four, by Guusje van Mourik (Netherlands) in the Female Over 60 kg category in 1982, 1984, 1986 and 1988.

• The record for the **most martial arts punches in one minute** is 548, and was achieved by Mick Fabar (Australia) at the Aussie Stadium in Sydney, Australia, on 22 June 2006.

• Csaba Mezei and Zoltán Farkas (both Hungary) of the Szany Judo Sport Team completed the **most judo throws in 10 hours**, achieving 57,603 at the Szany Sports Hall, Szany, Hungary, on 1 May 2003. The lucky "victims" were 27 members of the Sport Team.

Don "The Dragon" Wilson (USA) won the **most world kickboxing titles**, taking 11 titles in three weight divisions (light-heavyweight, super light-heavyweight and cruiserweight) in 1980–1999.

★ MOST WINS OF THE WWE ROYAL RUMBLE FROM ENTRY NO. 30

The Royal Rumble begins with 30 men – two in the ring and the rest outside; at regular intervals, one wrestler after another enters the fight, and the last man standing is the winner. Although the best position to enter the fight is last, at number 30, only one wrestler, The Undertaker (USA), has won from this position. It was achieved at the 2007 Royal Rumble on 27 January.

MOST MEN'S WORLD CHAMPIONSHIP TITLES

The most tae kwon do world titles won by a man is four, by Chung Kook-hyun (South Korea). He held light-middleweight titles in 1982 and 1983, and welterweight titles in 1985 and 1987.

★ MOST PINE BOARDS BROKEN WITH FEET IN ONE MINUTE (2 PEOPLE)

Alejandro Marín and Angel Sánchez (both Spain) used moves associated with the Korean martial art tae kwon do to break a record 18 pine boards with their feet on the set of *Guinness World Records – El Show de los Records* in Madrid, Spain, on 4 June 2006.

★ FASTEST TIME TO BREAK FIVE GLASS BOTTLES

Tae kwon do expert Alberto Delgado (Spain) smashed five glass bottles with his right hand in a time of 1 min and 39 sec on the set of *Guinness World Records – El Show de los records* in Madrid, Spain, on 11 June 2006.

WRESTLING

MOST CONSECUTIVE SUMO WRESTLING WINS

The *yokozuna* Sadaji Akiyoshi (Japan), alias Futabayama, set an all-time record of 69 consecutive wins (1937 to 1939).

★ MOST WINS OF THE WWE ROYAL RUMBLE

The most wins of the Royal Rumble by an individual is three, by "Stone Cold" Steve Austin (USA) in 1997, 1998 and 2001. His consecutive wins (1997–98) is also a record, shared with Hulk Hogan (USA, 1990–91) and Shawn Michaels (USA, 1995–96).

★ MOST WWE CHAMPIONSHIPS WON

The most World Wrestling Entertainment men's championships won by an individual is seven, by The Rock (USA, aka Dwayne Douglas Johnson, right) between 1998 and 2002.

The **most WWE championships won by a woman** is also seven, achieved by Trish Stratus (USA, aka Patricia Anne Stratigias) between 2001 and 2006.

CRICKET

WORLD CUP

★ MOST WINS

With their victory in 2007, Australia won their third International Cricket Council (ICC) World Cup in a row. They also have the ★ **longest unbeaten streak in World Cup matches**, having gone 29 games without losing.

★ HIGHEST-SCORING TEST PARTNERSHIP

Between 27 and 31 July 2006, Kumar Sangakkara (287) and Mahela Jayawardene (374) scored 624 for the third wicket for Sri Lanka v. South Africa at the Sinhalese Sports Club in Colombo, Sri Lanka.

★ NEW RECORD
★ UPDATED RECORD

★ MOST RUNS IN A MATCH

Australia (377–6) and South Africa (294 all out) scored a one-day international (ODI) record total 671 runs at Warner Park, Basseterre, St Kitts, on 24 March 2007.

This included the ★ **fastest World Cup century** by Matthew Hayden (Australia), who hit 101 runs from 66 balls.

★ MOST WICKETS

Glenn McGrath of Australia has taken 71 wickets in 39 World Cup matches, including 26 in the 2007 tournament – the ★ **most wickets in a single World Cup**.

★ MOST CATCHES

Australian wicketkeeper Adam Gilchrist has held the most catches in World Cups, with 45 from 1999 to 2007. He also has the ★ **fastest World Cup final century** in 72 balls against Sri Lanka at Kensington Oval, Bridgetown, Barbados, on 28 April 2007.

★ MOST WORLD CUP RUNS

Sachin Tendulkar (India) scored a record 1,796 runs from 1992 to 2007. He also holds records for the **most runs in a single World Cup**, with 673 runs in the 2003 tournament in South Africa, the ★ **most centuries in ODI matches in a career**, with 41 from 1989 to 2007, and ★ **most ODI runs in a career,** with 14,847 at an average of 44.05.

MOST WINS OF THE CRICKET WORLD CUP (FEMALE)

The most women's cricket World Cup wins by a national side is six by Australia, in 1978, 1982, 1988, 1997, 2000 and 2005.

★ HIGHEST MARGIN OF VICTORY

India scored 413–5 to beat Bermuda (156 all out) by 257 runs at Queen's Park Oval, Port of Spain, Trinidad, on 19 March 2007. India's total was also the ★ **highest innings by a team**.

★ MOST CONSECUTIVE INTERNATIONAL WICKETS

Lasith Malinga (Sri Lanka) became the first bowler to achieve four consecutive dismissals in any form of international cricket against South Africa in Guyana on 28 March 2007.

FEWEST RUNS IN A GAME

This record stands at 73, when Sri Lanka (37–1) beat Canada (36 all out) at Boland Bank Park, Paarl, South Africa, on 19 February 2003.

INTERNATIONAL CRICKET

HIGHEST PARTNERSHIP IN A ONE-DAY INTERNATIONAL

Sachin Tendulkar and Rahul Dravid (both India) amassed 331 runs against New Zealand in Hyderabad, India, on 8 November 1999.

★ HIGHEST SCORE IN A ONE-DAY INTERNATIONAL BY A TEAM

Sri Lanka reached 443–9 against the Netherlands in a match held in Amstelveen, the Netherlands, on 4 July 2006. They also have the **highest Test score**, with 952–6 against India at Colombo, Sri Lanka, on 4–6 August 1997.

★ MOST WICKETS TAKEN IN TEST MATCHES

Shane Warne (Australia) is the leading Test match wicket-taker, with 708 wickets (average 25.41 runs per wicket) in 145 matches, from August 1992 to his retirement after the final Test of the Ashes series in 2007.

WICKET-KEEPING:
MOST CATCHES IN TEST CRICKET

Mark Boucher (South Africa) made 376 catches in 102 Tests playing for South Africa between 1997 and 2007.

MOST TEST MATCHES UMPIRED

Steve Bucknor (Jamaica) has officiated at 117 Test matches between 1989 and 2007. He also holds the record for **most World Cup finals umpired**, with five between 1992 and 2007.

★ MOST TEST MATCHES AS CAPTAIN

Allan Border (Australia) played as captain of his national side a record 93 times between 1978 and 1994. All his games as captain were played consecutively, which is also a record. He also has the ★ **most Test games played consecutively**, playing 153 consecutive games (out of 156) for Australia between 1978 and 1994.

★ HIGHEST PARTNERSHIP IN A LIMITED OVERS MATCH

Mohammed Shaibaaz Tumbi and B. Manoj Kumar (both India) put on a record stand of 721 runs for St Peter's School against St Philip's High School in Secunderabad, India, on 15 November 2006.

BATTING:
MOST RUNS IN TEST CRICKET

Brian Lara (Trinidad and Tobago) scored 11,953 runs in 232 Test innings (at an average of 52.88) for the West Indies between 1990 and 2007.

★ MOST DISMISSALS IN THE 90s IN TEST MATCH CRICKET

Steve Waugh (Australia) has been dismissed 10 times in the 90s. Such a score is unenviable as it means getting out before reaching the milestone of a century (100 runs).

★ MOST ODI MATCHES PLAYED IN A CAREER

Sanath Jayasuriya (Sri Lanka) has played 390 ODIs for his country between 1989 and 2007

★ MOST INTERNATIONAL WICKETS TAKEN

Muttiah Muralitharan (Sri Lanka) has taken 1,129 wickets playing for Sri Lanka, the ICC XI and the Asia XI between 1992 and 2007. The figure comprises 674 Test and 455 ODI wickets.

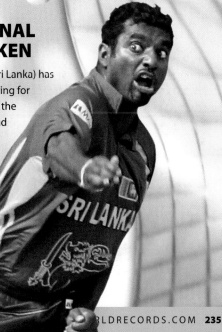

BIG HITTERS

• The ★**highest limited overs total in professional cricket** is 496–4 from 50 overs by Surrey v. Gloucestershire at the Brit Oval, London, UK, on 29 April 2007.

• At the 2007 World Cup, Herschelle Gibbs (South Africa) became the ★**first person to score six sixes in one over in an international match** against the Netherlands at Basseterre, St. Kitts, on 16 March.

• The ★**most Test match centuries in a calendar year** is nine by Mohammad Yousuf (formerly known as Yousuf Youhana, Pakistan) in 2006.

• The **highest batting average in Test cricket** is held by Sir Don Bradman (Australia), with an average of 99.94 playing for Australia in 52 Tests (6,996 runs in 80 innings) between 1928 and 1948.

• Brian Lara (Trinidad and Tobago) scored 501 not out in 7 hr 54 min for Warwickshire v. Durham at Edgbaston on 3–6 June 1994 – the **highest innings score**.

• Lara also holds the record for the **highest Test innings**, when he scored 400 not out for the West Indies v. England at the Antigua Recreation Ground, St John, Antigua, on 10–12 April 2004.

• In a Junior House match between Clarkes House (now Poole's) and North Town at Clifton College, Bristol, UK, in June 1899, Arthur Edward Jeanne Collins (UK) scored a total of 628 not out in 6 hr 50 min – the **highest ever score**.

CYCLING

★ MOST CROSS-COUNTRY MOUNTAIN BIKING WORLD CUP WINS (FEMALE)

Between 2003 and 2006, Gunn-Rita Dahle Flesjaa (Norway) won the cross-country mountain biking World Cup four times.

FASTEST ...

★ TIME TO CYCLE ACROSS AUSTRALIA – PERTH TO SYDNEY (MALE)

Richard Vollebregt (Australia) cycled from Perth, Western Australia, to Sydney, New South Wales, Australia, in 8 days 10 hr 57 min from 13 to 21 October 2006.

The **fastest time for a woman to cycle across Australia – Perth to Sydney** – was achieved by Helen Shelley (Australia). She cycled between the two cities in 13 days 2 hr 55 min from 24 April to 7 May 1999.

★ MAJOR TOUR TIME TRIAL OVER 20 KM

Rubin Plaza Molina (Spain), riding for team Comunidad Valenciana–Puerta Castalla, averaged a record speed of 56.21 km/h (34.93 mph) over a 38.9-km (24.1-mile) time trial from Guadalajara to Alcalá de Henares in the 2005 Vuelta a España (Tour of Spain), the fastest time trial achieved in any of the three major cycling tours (Italy, France, Spain).

★ MOST CROSS-COUNTRY MOUNTAIN BIKING WORLD CHAMPIONSHIP WINS (MALE)

From 2004 to 2006, the Union Cycliste Internationale (UCI) cross-country mountain biking World Championships was won three times by Julien Absalon (France). Henrik Djernis (Denmark) achieved the same feat between 1992 and 1994.

★ CYCLE JOURNEY ACROSS AMERICA (AVERAGE SPEED)

Pete Penseyres (USA) cycled coast to coast across the USA in 8 days 9 hr 47 min during the 1986 Race Across America event. He achieved an average speed of 24.78 km/h (15.4 mph) over a 5,000-km (3,107-mile) course between Huntington Beach, California, and Atlantic City, New Jersey.

The record for the ★ **fastest cycle journey across America by a woman (average speed)** was set by Seana Hogan (USA), who cycled coast to coast in just 9 days 4 hr 2 min during the 1995 Race Across America ultracycling event. She set an average speed of 22.4 km/h (13.92 mph) over a 4,686-km (2,912-mile) course between Irvine, California, and Savannah, Georgia, USA.

MOST WINS

★ CONSECUTIVE UCI CYCLING TRIALS WORLD CHAMPIONSHIPS (MALE)

Benito Ros Charral (Spain) won the Union Cycliste Internationale (UCI) men's trial World Championships three times consecutively from 2003 to 2005, the most by an individual rider.

★ CYCLO-CROSS WORLD CHAMPIONSHIPS (MALE)

Eric De Vlaemink (Belgium) won the cyclo-cross World Championships seven times, the most won by a man, in 1966 and from 1968 to 1973.

The ★ **most wins of the cyclo-cross World Championships by a woman** is three, by Hanka Kupfernagel (Germany) in 2000–01 and later in 2005.

★ FASTEST TIME TO CYCLE 10 M ON GLASS BOTTLES

Wang Jianguang (China) cycled 10 m (32 ft 9 in) on glass bottles in 29 seconds. He achieved the record using a standard bicycle on the set of *Zheng Da Zong Yi – Guinness World Records Special* in Beijing, China, on 20 December 2006.

★ MOST UCI MEN'S ROAD TIME TRIAL WORLD CHAMPIONSHIP WINS

Michael Rogers (Australia) won the Union Cycliste Internationale (UCI) Road Time Trial World Championships three times, from 2003 to 2005, the most times it has been won by an individual.

★ CROSS-COUNTRY MOUNTAIN BIKING WORLD CHAMPIONSHIPS (FEMALE)

The greatest number of cross-country mountain biking World Championships won by a woman is four, by Gunn-Rita Dahle Flesjaa (Norway), with victories in 2002 and from 2004 to 2006 inclusively.

★ TRIALS CYCLING WORLD CHAMPIONSHIPS (MALE)

Two riders have won three elite men's trials cycling World Championships: Marco Hösel (Germany) in 1999, 2002 and 2006, and Benito Ros Charral (Spain) from 2003 to 2005.

The ★ **most trials cycling World Championship titles won by a woman** is six, consecutively, by Karin Moor (Switzerland) from 2001 to 2006.

PROFESSIONAL WORLD CHAMPIONSHIP CYCLING TITLES

Koichi Nakano (Japan) won 10 World Championship Cycling titles in the professional sprint event between 1977 and 1986.

The **most World Championship cycling titles won by a woman** is 12 by Jeannie Longo (France): for 3 km pursuit in 1986 and from 1988 to 1989; road from 1985 to 1987, 1989 and 1995; track 1989; and time trial from 1995 to 1997.

OLYMPIC CYCLING MEDALS

Daniel Morelon (France) has won five Olympic cycling medals. He won two gold medals in 1968, a third in 1972, a silver in 1976 and a bronze in 1964.

TOUR DE FRANCE

Lance Armstrong (USA) won the Tour de France seven times between 1999 and 2005. He finished his last race, on 24 July 2005, in 86 hr 15 min 2 sec – clocking up another record: his average speed of 41.65 km/h (25.88 mph) beat his previous record of 40.26 km/h (25.02 mph) set in 1999.

★ MOST UCI ROAD RACE WORLD CHAMPIONSHIP WINS (MALE)

The most Union Cycliste Internationale (UCI) Road Race World Championships won by an individual is three by four riders: Alfredo Binda (Italy) in 1927, 1930 and 1932; Rik Van Steenbergen (Belgium) in 1949, 1956 and 1957; Eddy Merckx (Belgium) in 1967, 1971 and 1974; and most recently Óscar Freire Gómez (Spain, right) in 1999, 2001 and 2004.

TOUR OF ITALY

The record for the most wins of the Giro d'Italia (Tour of Italy) is five and is shared by three people: Alfredo Binda (Italy) in 1925, 1927–29, 1933; Fausto Coppi (Italy) in 1940, 1947, 1949, 1952–53; and Eddy Merckx (Belgium) in 1968, 1970, 1972–74.

TOUR OF SPAIN

Roberto Heras Hernández (Spain) won the Vuelta a España (Tour of Spain) four times – in 2000, and from 2003 to 2005 – as well as 10 stage victories. However, following a two-year suspension by the Spanish Cycling Federation (RFEC) for testing positive for the synthetic hormone erythropoietin (EPO), the 2005 title went to runner-up Denis Menchov (Russia).

CYCLING SUCCESSES

• The **longest distance cycled backwards** was set on 11 August 1985 by Alan Pierce (Australia). He cycled 100 km (62.5 miles) in reverse in Brisbane, Australia, in 4 hr 5 min 1 sec, sitting on the handlebars of a regular bicycle.

• The **highest downhill speed on a bicycle**, attained cycling downhill on snow or ice, is 212.13 km/h (132 mph). The record was set by downhill mountain bike racer Christian Taillefer (France) on a Peugeot cycle at the speed ski slope in Vars, France, in March 1998.

• The world's **largest cycling event** was the Udine Pedala 2000, held at Udine, Italy, on 11 June 2000. Organized by Italian financial services provider Rolo Banca 1473, the event attracted 48,615 cyclists who completed a circuit of 29.3 km (18.2 miles) around the city.

• The **most vertical metres cycled in 24 hours** was 18,093 m (59,362 ft) by Marcel Knaus (Switzerland) on 16–17 July 2005 in Wildhaus, Switzerland.

• The **youngest ever winner of the Tour de France** was Henri Cornet (France) in 1904, aged 19 years 350 days. He actually finished the race in fifth position, but was awarded the victory after the first four riders, Maurice Garin, Lucien Pothier, César Garin and Hippolyte Aucouturier, were all disqualified.

FISHING

★HEAVIEST BLUEFIN TUNA

On 26 October 1979, at Aulds Cove, Nova Scotia, Canada, Ken Fraser (Canada) landed the heaviest bluefin tuna ever. The immense fish weighed 678.58 kg (1,496 lb), heavier than many sharks!

★ **NEW RECORD**
★ **UPDATED RECORD**

★HEAVIEST BARRACUDA

Cyril Fabre (France) caught a Guinean Barracuda weighing a massive 45.9 kg (101 lb 3 oz). Fabre caught the IGFA world-record fish while fishing near Olende, Gabon, on 27 December 2002. Barracuda can be found in the waters of the Eastern Atlantic and can grow to a length of around 2 m (6 ft 6 in).

★FARTHEST CAST INTO A FISH BOWL

Maria Dolores Montesinos Fernández (Spain) managed to cast a weighted fly into a fish bowl with a neck diameter of 17.5 cm (6.8 in) – without the fly touching the sides of the fish bowl – from a distance of 7 m (22 ft 11 in). The record was set at the studios of *El Show de los Récords*, Madrid, Spain, on 11 December 2001.

LARGEST FISHING ROD

The largest fly-fishing rod measures 21.75 m (71 ft 4.5 in) in length, while the reel measures 1.21 m (4 ft) in diameter and 3.1 cm (1.2 in) wide. The immense rod was assembled by Tiney Mitchell (USA) at the Pirates' Landing Restaurant, Port Isabel, Texas, USA, on 12 June 1999.

HEAVIEST FRESH- AND SALTWATER FISH

SPECIES	WEIGHT	NAME	YEAR
★Albacore	40 kg (88 lb 2 oz)	Siegfried Dickemann (Germany)	1977
★Barracuda, Guinean	45.9 kg (101 lb 3 oz)	Cyril Fabre (France)	2002
★Barracuda, Hellers	2.04 kg (4 lb 8 oz)	Dan Stockdon Jr (USA)	2005
★Bass, European	9.48 kg (20 lb 14 oz)	Robert Mari (France)	1999
★Bass, meanmouth	3.88 kg (8 lb 8 oz)	Dru Kinslow (USA)	2006
★Batfish, tiera	1.92 kg (4 lb 3 oz)	Steven Wozniak (USA)	2006
★Bonito, Atlantic	8.30 kg (18 lb 4 oz)	D. Gama Higgs (USA)	1953
★Bonito, Pacific	9.67 kg (21 lb 5 oz)	Kim Larson (USA)	2003
★Bream	6.01 kg (13 lb 3 oz)	Luis Rasmussen (Sweden)	1984
★Bream, gilthead	7.36 kg (16 lb 3 oz)	Jean Serra (France)	2000
★Carp, common	34.35 kg (75 lb 11 oz)	Leo van der Gugten (Netherlands)	1987
★Carp, silver	16 kg (35 lb 4 oz)	Josef Windholz (Austria)	1983
★Catfish, giant (Mekong)	63 kg (138 lb 14 oz)	Richard Ainsworth (UK)	2004
★Catfish, redtail	46 kg (101 lb 6 oz)	Johnny Hoffman (USA)	2006
★Char, whitespotted	7.96 kg (17 lb 8 oz)	Hajime Murata (Japan)	2006
★Chub, European	2.62 kg (5 lb 12 oz)	Luis Rasmussen (Sweden)	1987
★Cod, Atlantic	44.79 kg (98 lb 12 oz)	Alphonse Bielevich (USA)	1969
★Cornetfish, red	1.05 kg (2 lb 5 oz)	Junzo Okada (Japan)	2006
★Dainanumihebi	1.25 kg (2 lb 12 oz)	Takashi Nishino (Japan)	2006
★Eel, conger	6.8 kg (15 lb)	Ryan Dougherty (USA)	2002
★Featherback, giant	9.08 kg (13 lb 6 oz)	Anongnat Sungwichien-Helias (Thailand)	2006
★Flounder, olive	11.4 kg (25 lb 2 oz)	Masayuki Jinnou (Japan)	2006
★Flounder, stone	2.6 kg (5 lb 11 oz)	Norikazu Fukinaga (Japan)	2006
★Graysby, Panama	0.9 kg (2 lb)	Karrie Ables (USA)	2006
★Grouper, areolate	0.62 kg (1 lb 5 oz)	Jean-Francois Helias (France)	2006
★Grouper, cloudy	0.63 kg (1 lb 6 oz)	Supachai Boongayson (Thailand)	2006
★Grouper, duskytail	0.85 kg (1 lb 13 oz)	Wathini "Nid" Thisami (Thailand)	2006
★Grouper, snowy	17.03 kg (37 lb 9 oz)	Jason Ferguson (USA)	2006
★Grunt, burrito	4.53 kg (10 lb)	Harold Lance Rigg (USA)	2006
★Grunt, tomtate	0.56 kg (1 lb 4 oz)	John Overton (USA)	2006
★Haddock	6.8 kg (14 lb 15 oz)	Heike Neblinger (Germany)	1997
★Hake, European	7.08 kg (15 lb 9 oz)	Knut Steen (Norway)	2000
★Halibut, Atlantic	190 kg (418 lb 13 oz)	Thomas Nielsen (Norway)	2004
★Kitsune-mebaru	2.7 kg (5 lb 15 oz)	Kouichirou Morikawa (Japan)	2006
★Korai-Nigoi	2.97 kg (6 lb 8 oz)	Junichi Inada (Japan)	2006
★Ladyfish, Machnata	7 kg (15 lb 6 oz)	Frederik Hendrikss (Denmark)	2006
★Lizardfish, wanieso	3.6 kg (7 lb 14 oz)	Harunori Kinjo (Japan)	2006

★LARGEST ICE-FISHING COMPETITION

The Veljekset Keskinen MiljoonapPilkki has been organized annually since 1997. The largest ever event took place on Lake Ponnenjärvi, Töysä, Finland, with 26,462 participants on 15 March 2003.

MOST FLY-FISHING TEAM TITLES

World fly-fishing championships were inaugurated by CIPS (Conféderation Internationale de la Pêche Sportive) in 1981. The most team titles held is five, by Italy in 1982–84, 1986 and 1992.

MOST FRESHWATER WORLD CHAMPIONSHIPS

The individual title to this competition has been won three times, by Robert Tesse (France), 1959–60, 1965; and Bob Nudd (England), 1990–91, 1994.

HEAVIEST FRESH- AND SALTWATER FISH

SPECIES	WEIGHT	NAME	YEAR
★Mackerel, atka	1.19 kg (2 lb 10 oz)	David Witherell (USA)	2006
★Mackerel, Atlantic	1.2 kg (2 lb 10 oz)	Jorg Marquard (Norway)	1992
★Mullet, striped	3.45 kg (7 lb 10 oz)	Krag Ross (USA)	2004
★Nigoi	2.45 kg (5 lb 6 oz)	Yoshiro Saito (Japan)	2006
★Palometa	0.81 kg (1 lb 12 oz)	Henry Flores Jr (USA)	2006
★Perch, European	1.5 kg (3 lb 4 oz)	Johnny Hogli (Norway)	1998
★Permit	27.21 kg (60 lb)	Renato Fiedler (Brazil)	2002
★Pike, Northern	25 kg (55 lb 1 oz)	Lothar Louis (Germany)	1986
★Piranha, black	3.175 kg (6 lb 15 oz)	Alejandro Mata (Venezuela)	1995
★Pompano, gafftopsail	1.7 kg (3 lb 12 oz)	Brett Philip (USA)	2006
★Porcupinefish, black-blotched	1.05 kg (2 lb 5 oz)	Lootjirot Panthrapat (Thailand)	2006
★Porgy, black	3.78 kg (8 lb 5 oz)	Ryushiro Omote (Japan)	2006
★Queenfish, doublespotted	2.94 kg (6 lb 8 oz)	Jodie Johnson (USA)	2006
★Ray, bluespotted ribbontail	1.43 kg (3 lb 2 oz)	Steven Wozniak (USA)	2006
★Rock cod, bluelined	0.7 kg (1 lb 8 oz)	Jean-Francois Helias (France)	2006
★Sailfin, vermiculated	1.36 kg (3 lb)	Jay Wright Jr (USA)	2006
★Salmon, Atlantic	35.89 kg (79 lb 2 oz)	Henrik Henriksen (Norway)	1928
★Sea bass, blackfin	9.66 kg (21 lb 4 oz)	Yuki Inoue (Japan)	2006
★Shark, banded (hound)	15.25 kg (33 lb 9 oz)	Takashi Nishino (Japan)	2006
★Shark, brownbanded bamboo	2.12 kg (4 lb 10 oz)	Steven Wozniak (USA)	2006
★Shark, great hammerhead	580.59 kg (1,280 lb)	Bucky Dennis (USA)	2006
★Shark, lemon	183.7 kg (405 lb)	Colleen Harlow (USA)	1988
★Shimazoi	1.85 kg (4 lb 1 oz)	Masahiko Kikuchi (Japan)	2006
★Snakehead, great	4.46 kg (9 lb 13 oz)	Jean-Francois Helias (France)	2006
★Snapper, mangrove red	11.62 kg (25 lb 9 oz)	Takuya Kano (Japan)	2006
★Sole, lemon	1.8 kg (3 lb 15 oz)	Robert Stalcrona (Sweden)	2004
★Stingray, Atlantic	4.87 kg (10 lb 12 oz)	David Anderson (USA)	1994
★Swordfish	536.15 kg (1,182 lb)	Louis Marron (USA)	1953
★Tilefish, blueline	7.9 kg (17 lb 6 oz)	Jenny Manus (USA)	2006
★Trevally, giant	72.8 kg (160 lb 7 oz)	Keiki Hamasaki (Japan)	2006
★Trout, lake	32.65 kg (72 lb)	Lloyd Bull (Canada)	1995
★Trout, rainbow	19.1 kg (42 lb 2 oz)	David White (USA)	1970
★Tuna, bluefin	678.58 kg (1,496 lb)	Ken Fraser (Canada)	1979

★HEAVIEST LEMON SHARK

On 28 November 1988, Colleen Harlow (USA) landed a lemon shark, weighing 183.7 kg (405 lb), at Buxton, North Carolina, USA, the heaviest All-Tackle IGFA record for this species. On 17 May 2006, a (174.6-kg) 385-lb lemon shark (pictured above) was caught on fly by Dr Martin Arostegui (USA) – and guided by Ralph Delph (USA) – near the Marquesas Keys, Florida, USA. IGFA officially nominated the shark as the ★ **heaviest fish ever documented on fly**.

IGFA ALL-TACKLE RECORDS

The tabulated records on these pages are sourced from the IGFA (International Game Fish Association) Freshwater and Saltwater All-Tackle Records for the largest of each species caught in any line-class category. Since its inception in 1939, IGFA has taken an active, global role in fisheries management and fish conservation.

MOST PARTICIPANTS IN A SEA-ANGLING COMPETITION

The most people to have participated in a sea angling competition is 679. The contestants were taking part in the 20th Torskfestivalen (Cod Festival) held at Öresund, Helsingborg, Sweden, which took place from 15 to 17 January 1999.

SMALLEST-EYED FLY-FISHING HOOK

The smallest-eyed fly-fishing hook was produced by Ticmco Ltd., Tokyo, Japan, on 12 June 1999. The inner diameter of the eye was 0.265 mm (0.01 in), while the outer diameter was 0.8 mm (0.03 in). The hook shank length was 3.60 mm (0.14 in).

★HEAVIEST HAMMERHEAD

On 23 May 2006, Bucky Dennis (USA) used a live-lined stingray to land a great hammerhead shark weighing 580.59 kg (1,280 lb) at Boca Grande, Florida, USA. It took Dennis and his crew almost six hours to land the record-breaking fish.

FOOTBALL

★ YOUNGEST PLAYER IN THE ENGLISH PREMIERSHIP

Matthew Briggs (UK, left) was brought on as a 77th-minute substitute for Fulham against Middlesbrough, aged 16 years 65 days, on 13 May 2007.

He was 64 days younger than the previous record-holder, Tottenham Hotspur's Aaron Lennon (UK).

UEFA CHAMPIONS LEAGUE

★ NEW RECORD
★ UPDATED RECORD

★ BIGGEST MATCH WIN

On 10 December 2003, Italy's Juventus – the most successful team in the country's footballing history – beat the Greek side Olympiakos 7–0 on their home turf at Turin.

★ FASTEST GOAL

Roy Makaay (Netherlands) scored the opening goal for Bayern Munich (Germany) against Real Madrid (Spain) in just 10 seconds in Munich, Germany, on 7 March 2007.

Paolo Maldini (Italy) took just 51 seconds to score for AC Milan against Liverpool at the Atatürk Stadium in Turkey on 25 May 2005, the **fastest goal in a Champions League final**.

The goal also made Maldini (b. 26 June 1968) the **oldest player to score in a Champions League final** – he was aged 36 years 333 days at the time.

★ MOST EXPULSIONS IN A SINGLE WORLD CUP FINALS TOURNAMENT MATCH

On 25 June 2006, a total of four red cards were awarded (two to each side) when Portugal met Holland in a World Cup match in Nuremberg, Germany.

As well as the four reds, 16 yellow cards were issued – nine to Portugal and seven to Holland.

MOST GOALS IN INTERNATIONAL FOOTBALL (MALE)

The most football international goals scored by a man is 109, by Ali Daei (Iran, in white), between 1993 and 2006.

TOP-DIVISION LEAGUE WINNERS

COUNTRY	CHAMPIONSHIP*	TEAM	WINS	DATES
Scotland	Premier League	Glasgow Rangers	51	1891–2005
Greece	Super League	Olympiakos	35	1931–2007
Portugal	Liga	SL Benfica	31	1935–2005
Spain	La Liga	Real Madrid	29	1931–2003
Netherlands	Eredivisie	Ajax Amsterdam	29	1917–2004
Belgium	Jupiler League	RSC Anderlecht	29	1947–2007
Hungary	Borsodi Liga	Ferencváros	28	1903–2004
Italy	Serie A	Juventus	27	1904–2003
Finland	Veikkausliiga	HJK	21	1911–2003
Norway	Tippeligaen	Rosenborg	20	1967–2006
Germany	Bundesliga	Bayern Munich	20	1931–2006
England	Premiership	Liverpool	18	1901–1990
Sweden	Allsvenskan	IFK Göteborg	17	1908–1996
Denmark	Superliga	Kjøbenhavns Boldklub	15	1913–1980
Ireland	Premier Division	Shamrock Rovers	15	1923–1994
France	Ligue 1	AS Saint-Etienne	10	1956–1981
Japan	J-League	Kashima Antlers	4	1996–2001
USA	MLS	DC United	4	1996-2004

* This is the current name of the top division in each country

THE CHAMPIONS LEAGUE

• The **most Champions League matches won by a team** is 70 by Real Madrid between 1992 and 2007. An unprecedented 247 goals were scored in the process.

• The **most goals in Champions League matches** is 56, by Raúl González Blanco (Spain) – for Real Madrid (1992 –2007) – and Andriy Shevchenko (Ukraine) – for Dynamo Kyiv, AC Milan and Chelsea (1994–2007). From 1992 to 2007, Raúl also made the **most Champions League appearances**: 107.

• Two players share the record for the **most appearances in a European Cup/ Champions League final**, with eight finals each. They are Paulo Maldini between 1989 and 2007 and "Paco" Francisco Gento (Spain) between 1956 and 1966. Maldini became the **oldest player to captain a Champions League team** (and the **oldest captain of a European Cup/ Champions League-winning team in a final**) when he led AC Milan out against Liverpool in Athens, Greece, on 23 May 2007. AC Milan's win that night also saw Maldini (at 38 years 331 days old) become the **oldest captain to win the Champions League** and Clarence Seedorf (Suriname) become the ★**first player to win four Champions League titles**.

★ MOST FOOTBALL TEAMS SPONSORED BY ONE INSTITUTION

Saudi Telecom sponsored the jerseys of all 12 football teams of the First Division in Saudi Arabia, in September 2006, setting a record for the most teams to be sponsored by just one institution simultaneously.

★ HIGHEST UK PREMIERSHIP ATTENDANCE

A crowd of 76,073 attended Old Trafford, Manchester, UK, for the match between Manchester United and Aston Villa on 13 January 2007. United's Michael Carrick (UK) is pictured scoring the second goal of the game.

DOMESTIC

★ MOST WIDELY SUPPORTED CLUB

Portugal's Sport Lisboa e Benfica – or simply Benfica to fans – has a record 160,398 fully paid-up members.

★ MOST WINS OF THE ENGLISH TOP DIVISION

Ryan Giggs (UK) claimed a record ninth Championship winner's medal in 2007 when Manchester United won the FA Premiership, having previously shared the record with Liverpool's Phil Neal and Alan Hansen (both UK) who have won 8 domestic titles each.

★ MOST WINS OF THE ENGLISH TOP DIVISION

Liverpool won the top division of English league football 18 times between 1901 and 1990.

In 1992, the Premiership replaced the old First Division as English football's top flight.

★ MOST CONSECUTIVE SEASONS IN THE ENGLISH TOP DIVISION

Arsenal have been in English football's top division for 81 consecutive seasons from 1920 to 2007 (excluding 1939–45, during World War II).

MOST ENGLISH PREMIERSHIP GOALS

The most goals scored in the English Premiership is 260 by Alan Shearer (UK). Shearer spent his Premiership with Blackburn Rovers (1992–96) before moving to Newcastle United in 1996 for a record fee (at that time) of £15.6 million ($22.4 million). He retired in 2006.

★ MOST PREMIERSHIP APPEARANCES

Between 1993 and 2007, midfielder and Welsh national team captain Gary Speed (UK) appeared 519 times – playing for Leeds United, Everton, Newcastle United and Bolton Wanderers.

★ MOST PREMIERSHIP MANAGER OF THE MONTH AWARDS

Manchester United's manager Alex Ferguson (UK) won 19 Manager of the Month awards between 1993 and 2007. He also holds the record for the ★**most Champions League games managed**, with 118 – a landmark passed when his team met Spain's Villareal in November 2005.

★ MOST MAJOR LEAGUE GOALS

Jason Kreis (USA) scored 108 goals in 301 games (1996 2004). Jaime Moreno (Bolivia) matched this feat, in only 203 games (1996–2007).

FOOTBALL

CONFEDERATIONS CUP COMPETITION

Every four years, the FIFA World Cup host nation and winner (or runner-up if the host nation wins) join the Confederations Cup with the champions of the six FIFA confederations: African (CAF), South American (CONMEBOL), European (UEFA), Asian (AFC), Oceania (OFC), and North and Central America and the Caribbean (CONCACAF). The tournament began in 1992 (as the biannual King Fahd Cup) and was taken over by FIFA in 1997. As of 2005, the cup is played every four years, with the next to be staged in South Africa in 2009.

★ MOST GOALS SCORED BY A GOALKEEPER

Goalkeeper Rogério Ceni (Brazil, right) scored 66 goals for Brazil's São Paulo Football Club from 1997 to 2006.

INTERNATIONAL

★ CONFEDERATIONS CUP: MOST WINS

Two countries have won the Confederations Cup (see above left) twice: France (2001 and 2003) and Brazil (1997 and 2005).

★ OCEANIA CUP: MOST WINS

Instituted in 1973 and contested by Oceania Football Confederation member nations, the Oceania Cup has been won a record four times by Australia, in 1980, 1996, 2000 and 2004.

★ CONCACAF GOLD CUP: MOST WINS

Mexico has won the Confederation of North, Central American and Caribbean Association Football (CONCACAF) Gold Cup four times, in 1993, 1996, 1998 and 2003. The Cup was instituted in 1991.

The USA has won the women's CONCACAF Gold Cup (instituted in 2000) three times – every time it has been held – in 2000, 2002 and 2006. Unsurprisingly, this gives the USA the record for the ★ **most women's CONCACAF wins**.

★ SOUTH AMERICAN CHAMPIONSHIP (COPA AMÉRICA): MOST WINS

Argentina and Uruguay have both won the South American Championship (Copa América since 1975) 14 times. First held in 1916, this Cup competition is the **oldest surviving international football competition**.

★ MOST AFRICAN PLAYER OF THE YEAR AWARDS

The African Player of the Year Award has been awarded since 1970. Three players have won three times: George Weah (Liberia), in 1989 and 1994–95; Abedi Pele (Ghana), in 1991–93; and Samuel Eto'o (Cameroon), in 2003–05.

★ MOST FIFA WORLD PLAYER OF THE YEAR AWARDS (FEMALE)

Birgit Prinz (Germany) was awarded the Fédération Internationale de Football Association (FIFA) Player of the Year Award in three consecutive years, 2003–05.

★ MOST INTERNATIONAL CAPS (FEMALE)

The greatest number of international appearances by a woman for a national side is officially 319, by Kristine Lilly (USA) in 1987–2007.

★ MOST FOOTBALLS JUGGLED

On 4 November 2006, Victor Rubilar (Argentina) juggled five regulation-size balls for 10 seconds at the Gallerian Shopping Centre in Stockholm, Sweden.

★ LARGEST FOOTBALL STICKER

A 153 x 188-cm (5-ft x 6-ft 1-in) football sticker was unveiled at Charlton Athletic's ground, The Valley, on 8 February 2007. It depicts Charlton striker Darren Bent (UK), and was created to launch FIFA's official FA Premier League 07 Sticker Collection.

LONGEST TIME CONTROLLING A FOOTBALL WHILE LYING DOWN

Tomas Lundman (Sweden) managed to keep a regulation-size football up in the air using his feet while lying on his back for 9 min 57 sec at the Gallerian Shopping Centre in Stockholm, Sweden, on 4 November 2006.

BALL CONTROL

Martinho Eduardo Orige (Brazil) juggled a football for 19 hr 30 min non-stop with feet, legs and head – without the ball ever touching the ground – at Padre Ezio Julli Gym in Araranguá, Brazil, on 2–3 August 2003, the **longest time to control a football**.

• Cláudia Martini (Brazil) juggled a football for 7 hr 5 min 25 sec in Caxias do Sul, Brazil, on 12 July 1996, the

DID YOU KNOW?
Tomas Lundman (see above) also holds the record for the **longest time to head a football**. He controlled a ball with his head, without dropping it, for 8 hr 32 min 3 sec at Lidingo, Sweden, on 27 February 2004.

longest time to control a football by a woman.
• The **longest time to keep a football in the air by using just the head while seated** is 4 hr 2 min 1 sec by Agim Agushi (Kosovo, Serbia and Montenegro, now Republic of Serbia) in Flensburg, Germany, during the Tummelum Festival, on 14 August 2005.
• Amadou Gueye (France) kept a football airborne using his chest for 30.29 seconds on the set of *L'Emission*

Des Records in Paris, France, on 7 September 2001, the **longest time to control a football using only the chest**.
• The **longest time to keep a football spinning on the forehead** is 19.96 seconds, a feat achieved by Victor Rubilar (Argentina) at the Gallerian Shopping Centre in Stockholm, Sweden, on 4 November 2006.
• Ferdie Adoboe (USA) managed 266 touches of a ball at the Schwan's USA Cup in Blaine, Minnesota, USA, on 19 July 2000, the **most football touches in one minute**.
• Jan Skorkovsky (Czechoslovakia, now Czech Republic) kept a football up while he travelled 42.195 km (26.219 miles) for the Prague City Marathon on 8 July 1990. His time of 7 hr 18 min 55 sec represents the **fastest time to run a marathon while keeping a football airborne**.

FOOTBALL TOUCHES: MOST IN 30 SECONDS BY A FEMALE

The most touches of a football in 30 seconds by a female, while keeping the ball in the air, is 155 by Chloe Hegland (Canada) in Victoria, British Columbia, Canada, on 12 December 2006. Chloe is just 10 years old, but her amazing feat (or feet?) beats the record for both men and women in this category!

LONGEST FOOTBALL MARATHON

A match played between FC EDO Simme (pictured) and FC Spiez in Erlenbach, Switzerland, on 8–9 July 2006, lasted 30 hr 10 min. The final score was 243–210 to FC Spiez. The teams played from noon on 8 July to 6.10 p.m. on 9 July.

BEACH SOCCER

An offshoot of association football, beach soccer had been played informally on beaches the world over for many years. It was not until 1992, however, that the sport's rules were formalized. Today, it is an international sport.

• The ★**most goals scored by an individual player in a Beach Soccer World Cup** is 21 by Madjer (aka João Victor Tavares), playing for Portugal at the tournament staged in Rio de Janeiro, Brazil, in 2006.

• The ★**most goals scored by an individual player in a Beach Soccer World Cup career** is 33 by Madjer, playing for Portugal at the tournaments staged in Rio de Janeiro, Brazil, in 2005 and 2006.

• The FIFA Beach Soccer World Cup has been contested twice. The record for the **most Beach Soccer World Cups** is tied, by France (the winners of the inaugural World Cup, in 2005) and Brazil (winners in 2006).

• The precursor to the Beach Soccer World Cup (organized by FIFA) was the Beach Soccer World Championships (organized by Beach Soccer Worldwide), instituted in 1995. Brazil holds the record for the ★**most Beach Soccer World Championships**, with nine victories between 1995 and 2004.

GOLF

★ MOST WOMEN'S BRITISH OPEN TOURNAMENT WINS

Karrie Webb (Australia, right) has won the women's British Open golf tournament three times – in 1995, 1997 and 2002. This record was equalled by Sherri Steinhauer (USA) with wins in 1998, 1999 and 2006.

★ HIGHEST COURSE

The Yak golf course is situated at an altitude of 3,970 m (13,025 ft) above sea level and is located in Kupup, East Sikkim, India.

★ LARGEST RANGE

With 300 individual bays, the largest golf range in the world is the SKY72 Golf Club Dream Golf Range, which opened in Joong-Ku, Incheon, Korea, on 9 September 2005. The driving range is a circle with a diameter of 358.8 m (1,176 ft) and has a total area of 269,468 m² (2,900,529 ft²).

★ LARGEST GOLF TEE

A 3.5-m-tall (11-ft 5-in) tee with a head diameter of 75.2 cm (29 in) and a shaft width of 30.2 cm (11.88 in) was made by Volvo Auto Polska and measured at the First Warsaw Golf & Country Club in Rajszew, Warsaw, Poland, on 17 September 2006.

★ LOWEST STROKE AVERAGE IN A PGA SEASON

The lowest stroke average ever achieved during a single Professional Golfer's Association (PGA) season is 68.33, by Byron Nelson (USA) during the 1945 season.

★ MOST PGA TOUR TITLES WON CONSECUTIVELY

The most golf tour titles won in a row is 11, by Byron Nelson (USA) in 1945. The run, which has since become known as "The Streak", was among a total of 18 Tour titles that Nelson won in the same year, as well as a career total of 52 PGA titles. He turned professional in 1932 and retired in the 1946 season to spend more time in Texas, where he was born.

★ MOST GOLFERS ON ONE COURSE IN 24 HOURS (WALKING)

The greatest number of walking golfers – that is, no buggies allowed – to complete a full round on the same course within 24 hours is 623, achieved by GP7 at the Shenzhen Green Bay Golf Club, China, from 24 to 25 June 2006.

★ OLDEST GOLF COURSE

The Old Links golf course in Musselburgh, Scotland, UK, is thought to be the oldest in the world. It is believed that Mary, Queen of Scots, played there in 1567, and in 1811 it became the first course to hold an all-women golf competition.

★ MOST BALLS HIT IN TWO MINUTES

With the help of Scott "Speedy" Mckinney, David Ogron (both USA) drove a record 113 balls in two minutes on the set of the *Zheng Da Zong Yi – Guinness World Records Special* TV show in Beijing, China, on 21 December 2006.

★ MOST BALLS HIT IN 12 HOURS

The most balls driven over a distance of 100 yards into a target area in 12 hours is 7,350, by Sylvain Ménard (Canada) at the Club de Golf des Erables in Gatineau, Quebec, Canada, on 1 October 2004.

★ MOST HOLES-IN-ONE BY A RYDER CUP TEAM

The European team has achieved the most holes-in-one during the history of the Ryder Cup, with six between 1927 and 2006. Over the same period, the USA team has made just one hole-in-one! Pictured is European team member Darren Clarke (UK) during the 2006 Cup, in which he scored three points in three matches, helping Europe beat the USA 18½–9½.

LARGEST GOLF FACILITY

The Mission Hills Golf Club, stretching across Shenzhen and Dongguan in China, boasts 12 fully operational 18-hole courses as of February 2007. Additional amenities include a large pro shop, a clubhouse of 27,871 m² (300,000 ft²), a ballroom, swimming pools, no less than 51 tennis courts and extensive changing rooms that can accommodate up to 3,000 guests.

★ FARTHEST GOLF SHOT

Flight Engineer Mikhail Tyurin (Russia, pictured below practising his swing on Earth) – assisted by caddy Commander Michael Lopez-Alegria (USA) – teed off during a six-hour spacewalk outside the International Space Station (ISS) on 23 February 2006. Element 21 Golf (Canada) paid an undisclosed sum for the stunt, which was permitted by the Russian space agency as a means of raising cash. NASA estimated that the ball would orbit for three days before burning up in the atmosphere – a distance of 2.2 billion yards (2.02 million km; 1.26 million miles). The Russians put their estimate at 810 billion yards (740 million km; 460 million miles)!

LONGEST PUTT

The longest recorded holed putt in a professional tournament is 33.5 m (110 ft), a record shared by Jack Nicklaus (USA) in the 1964 Tournament of Champions and Nick Price (Zimbabwe) in the 1992 US PGA.

Bob Cook (USA) sank a putt measured at an incredible 42.74 m (140 ft 3 in) on the 18th hole at St Andrews, UK, in the International Fourball Pro Am Tournament – which is not classed as a professional tournament – on 1 October 1976.

LOWEST US PGA ROUND SCORE

Gary Player (South Africa, pictured) is one of eight players to have finished a US PGA Championship round of 18 holes on just 63 shots. He achieved this record low score at Shoal Creek in Birmingham, Alabama, in 1984.
His fellow record holders are:
- **Bruce Crampton** (Australia), Firestone, Akron, Ohio, USA, 1975
- **Ray Floyd** (USA), Southern Hills, Tulsa, Oklahoma, USA, 1982
- **Vijay Singh** (Fiji) at Inverness Club, Toledo, Ohio, USA, 1993
- **Michael Bradley** (USA) and **Brad Faxon** (USA), both at Riviera Pacific Palisades, California, USA, 1995
- **Jose Maria Olazabal** (Spain) at Valhalla, Louisville, Kentucky, USA, 2000
- **Mark O'Meara** (USA) at Atlanta Athletic Club, Georgia, USA, 2001

★ **NEW RECORD**
★ **UPDATED RECORD**

MOST NATIONS REPRESENTED IN A SINGLE COMPETITION

A record 72 nations were represented at the 2000 Junior Open Championships, held at Crail Golf Club in Fife, Scotland, UK, in July 2000.

★ GREATEST DISTANCE BETWEEN TWO ROUNDS OF GOLF PLAYED ON THE SAME DAY

John Knobel (Australia) played two full 18-hole rounds on 21 May 2006: the first at The Coast Golf Club in Sydney, Australia, and the second at Forest Park Golf Club in Woodhaven, New York, USA. The distance between the two rounds was 15,982 km (9,931 miles).

★ MOST MINIATURE GOLF PLAYED IN 24 HOURS (FOURBALL)

Two teams from MGC Olympia Kiel e.V. (Germany) played 80 rounds of 18 holes – a total of 1,140 holes – of miniature golf in 24 hours at Miniaturegolfhalle in Rendsburg, Germany, on 19–20 March 2005.

GOLF TOURNAMENTS

- The ★**most Ladies Professional Golf Association Women's Championships won** is four by Mickey Wright (USA) in 1958, 1960–61 and 1963.

- The **oldest player to compete in the Ryder Cup** is Raymond Floyd (USA) in 1993, aged 51 years 20 days.

- The ★**most Kraft Nabisco Championships won by an individual** is three, by three golfers: Amy Alcott (USA) in 1983, 1988 and 1991; Betsy King (USA) in 1987, 1990 and 1997; and Annika Sorenstam (Sweden) in 2001–02 and 2005.

- The **lowest single round score at the Masters** is 63 by Nick Price (Zimbabwe) in 1986 and Greg Norman (Australia) in 1996.

- The ★**most Senior PGA Championships won by an individual** is six by Sam Snead (USA) in 1964–65, 1967, 1970–71 and 1973.

- The record for the ★**most wins of the Tradition Championship** is held by Jack Nicklaus (USA), who has won four times, in 1990–91 and 1995–96.

- The ★**most US Senior Open Championships won by an individual** is three by Miller Barber (USA) in 1982 and 1984–85.

- The ★**most Vare Trophies won by a female** is seven by Kathy Whitworth (USA) in 1965–67 and 1969–72.

ICE HOCKEY

★ FIRST PLAYER TO SCORE IN FIRST SIX GAMES

Playing for the Pittsburgh Penguins (USA) in 2006, Evgeni Malkin (Russia) became the first player in 89 years to score in his first six games.

★ FASTEST TIME TO SCORE A HAT TRICK (FEMALE)

Melissa Horvat (Canada) scored three times in just 35 seconds for Burlington 1 Bantams (Canada) against Stoney Creek (Canada) in Burlington, Ontario, Canada, on 4 March 2006.

NHL

★ LONGEST SCORING STREAK BY A ROOKIE

Paul Stastny (Canada), of the Colorado Avalanche (USA), achieved a 20-consecutive-game scoring streak, the most by a rookie. He had 11 goals and 18 assists during the streak, which began on 3 February and ended on 17 March 2007.

★ LONGEST-SERVING CAPTAIN

The longest-serving captain of any team in National Hockey League (NHL) history is Steve Yzerman (Canada), who served as captain of the Detroit Red Wings (USA) for 20 seasons from 1986 to 2006. Yzerman led the Red Wings to three Stanley Cup championships (1997–98, 2002) and had his jersey, No.19, retired in a ceremony at Joe Louis Arena in Detroit, Michigan, USA, on 2 January 2007.

★ LONGEST CONTRACT

The longest contract in NHL history is the 15-year deal given to goalkeeper Rick DiPietro (USA) by the New York Islanders (USA) on 12 September 2006. DiPietro's contract managed to top the previous longest NHL contract, a 10-year deal the New York Islanders had given to Alexei Yashin (Russia) in 2001.

EUROPEAN COMPETITION

The ★ **most ice-hockey World Championships (men)** won by a nation is four by Sweden in 1921, 1923–24 and 1932. After 1932 and until 1991, European teams could only be awarded European Championship medals.

LONGEST WINNING STREAK TO END A SEASON

The New Jersey Devils (USA) won their last 11 regular-season games of the 2005–06 season to set the NHL record for the longest winning streak at the end of a season, which ran from 28 March to 18 April 2006.

★ MOST VICTORIES IN A SEASON BY A GOALIE

The NHL record for the most victories by a goalkeeper in a single season is 48, set by Martin Brodeur (Canada) while playing for the New Jersey Devils (USA) during the 2006–07 season.

★ MOST SEVERE SUSPENSION

The NHL record for the longest suspension is 25 games, which was handed to Chris Simon (Canada) of the New York Islanders (USA). It was his punishment for a two-handed stick attack to the face of Ryan Hollweg (USA) of the New York Rangers (USA) in a 2–1 loss on 8 March 2007 at the Nassau Coliseum, New York.

★ SHORTEST NHL PLAYER

At 1.7 m (5 ft 7 in), forward Brian Gionta (USA) of the New Jersey Devils (USA) is the shortest active player in the league. The ★ **tallest NHL player** is defenceman Zdeno Chara (Czech Republic) of the Boston Bruins (USA), who is 2.05 m (6 ft 9 in).

MOST MINUTES PLAYED IN A SEASON

The NHL record for the most minutes played in a season is 4,434 by Martin Brodeur (Canada) as goalkeeper for the New Jersey Devils (USA) during the 1995–96 season.

MOST SHUTOUTS IN A REGULAR SEASON

The most NHL shutouts by a goalie in a season is 15 by Tony Esposito (Canada) for the Chicago Blackhawks (USA) in the 1969–70 season.

MOST GOALS SCORED BY A TEAM IN AN NHL SEASON

The Edmonton Oilers scored 446 goals in the 1983–84 NHL season, the most by any team. The Oilers also achieved a record 1,182 scoring points in the same season. Pictured is the Oilers' Chris Pronger (front) during the 2006 Stanley Cup, against the Carolina Hurricanes in Raleigh, North Carolina, USA.

MOST SHUTOUTS IN A CAREER

The NHL record for most career shutouts by a goalie is 103 by Terry Sawchuk (Canada). During his career, which ran for 21 years from 1949 to 1970, he played with a number of teams: the Detroit Red Wings (USA), Boston Bruins (USA), Toronto Maple Leafs (Canada), Los Angeles Kings (USA) and New York Rangers (USA).

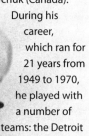

MOST CONSECUTIVE...

EVENT	TEAM/PLAYER	NUMBER	DATE
★Wins to start a season	Buffalo Sabres (USA)	10	4 Oct–26 Oct 2006
★Road wins to start a season	Buffalo Sabres (USA)	10	4 Oct–11 Nov 2006
★Games scoring a goal, NHL Team	Calgary Flames (Canada)	264	Nov 1981–Jan 1985
★Games scoring the winning goal	Newsy Lalonde (Canada)	5	Feb 1921
★Games played by an NHL defenceman	Karlis Skrastins (Russia)	495	21 Feb 2000–25 Feb 2007
★Team wins to start a season, NHL goalie	Martin Brodeur (Canada)	38	2006–07 season
★Seasons winning 30 games, NHL goalie	Martin Brodeur (Canada)	11	1995–96 to 2006–07 season
★Seasons winning 35 games, NHL goalie	Martin Brodeur (Canada)	10	1996–97 to 2006–07 season
★Seasons winning 40 games, NHL goalie	Martin Brodeur (Canada)	6	1997–98, 1999–2001, 2002–03, 2005–07 seasons

★MOST OVERTIME GAME-WINNING GOALS

The NHL play-off record for most overtime game-winning goals is seven by Joe Sakic (Canada) playing for the Quebec Nordiques (Canada) and the Colorado Avalanche (USA) from 1992 to 2006.

★FIRST CONSECUTIVE 40-GOAL SEASONS BY AN OVER 35-YEAR-OLD

By scoring two power-play goals against the Vancouver Canucks on 11 March 2007, Teemu Selanne (b. 3 July 1970, Finland) of the Anaheim Ducks (USA) became the first NHL player over 35 to record consecutive 40-goal seasons.

★FIRST PLAYER IN 400 GAMES WITH THREE TEAMS

Chris Chelios (USA) became the first player in NHL history to appear in 400 or more games for three different teams: the Montreal Canadiens (1984–90), the Chicago Blackhawks (1990–99) and the Detroit Red Wings (1999–2007).

YOUNG GUNS

• The ★youngest player to start in an NHL All-Star game is Sidney Crosby (Canada, b. 7 August 1987) of the Pittsburgh Penguins (USA). At 19 years 5 months, he was in the starting lineup for the Eastern Conference in the NHL All-Star game on 24 January 2007, becoming the youngest-ever player elected by the fans since All-Star fan balloting began in 1986. Crosby also became the ★youngest NHL player to reach 200 career points with a goal in the first period of a game against the Carolina Hurricanes (USA) on 2 March 2007. He was also the ★youngest player in NHL history with two 100-point seasons after reaching the century mark for the 2006–07 season with a goal in a 3–2 overtime win over the New York Rangers (USA) at Mellon Arena in Pittsburgh, Pennsylvania, USA, on 10 March 2007.

• At 29 years 243 days, Martin Brodeur (b. 6 May 1972, Canada), playing for the New Jersey Devils (USA), became the youngest goalkeeper to win 300 career NHL regular-season games. His 300th victory was against the Ottawa Senators (Canada) at the Corel Center in Ottawa, Canada, on 15 December 2001. At 31 years 322 days, Brodeur became the youngest goalkeeper to win 400 career NHL regular-season games. His 400th victory was an overtime win over the Florida Panthers (USA) at the Office Depot Center in Miami, Florida, USA, on 23 March 2004.

• The NHL single-season record for most goals scored by an NHL rookie is 76 goals by Teemu Selanne (Finland) playing for the Winnipeg Jets (Canada) in 1992–93. The most points scored by a rookie is 132 points, also by Selanne while playing for the Winnipeg Jets (Canada) in 1992–93.

★ NEW RECORD
★ UPDATED RECORD

RUGBY

LEAGUE

The ★ **most points scored in a National Rugby League career** by an individual player is 1,754, by Hazem El Masri (Lebanon), between 1996 and 2006, playing for the Canterbury Bulldogs (Australia).

• The ★ **most points scored in a National Rugby League season** by an individual player is 342, also by Hazem El Masri (Lebanon), playing for the Bulldogs in 2004.

• The rugby league Tri-Nations international competition was inaugurated in 1999 as a contest between Australia, Great Britain and New Zealand. Between 1999 and 2006, Darren Lockyer (Australia) and Joe Vagana (New Zealand) both scored nine tries in rugby league Tri-Nations matches, the ★ **most tries scored by a player in the history of the Tri-Nations tournament**.

• The ★ **most wins in Australia's rugby league State of Origin series** is 12 by New South Wales between 1980 and 2005.

• The ★ **most wins of the rugby league City against Country match** (played every year in Australia) is 63 by the City team from 1930 to 2006.

• The Super League is the UK's premier rugby league competition, instituted in 1996. The ★ **most Super League titles** won by a team is five, by St Helens in 1996, 1999, 2000, 2002 and 2006.

★ FASTEST TRY IN THE ENGLISH PREMIERSHIP

Tom Voyce (UK) scored a try in 9.63 seconds playing for Wasps against Harlequins on 5 November 2004, the fastest by an individual player in a Guinness Premiership match.

★ MOST WINS OF THE LANCE TODD TROPHY

The Lance Todd trophy is awarded to the outstanding player in each rugby league season's Challenge Cup Final, and has been won three times by St Helens' Sean Long (UK, right), in 2001, 2004 and 2006.

★ MOST APPEARANCES IN RUGBY UNION SUPER RUGBY FINAL MATCHES

The most Super 12 and 14 Final appearances by an individual player is eight, by Reuben Thorne (New Zealand) playing for the Canterbury Crusaders from 1998 to 2000 and 2002 to 2006.

UNION

• The ★ **most appearances in Guinness Premiership matches by an individual** is 174, by Tony Diprose (UK), between 1997 and 2006, playing for Saracens and Harlequins.

• The ★ **most tries scored in a Guinness Premiership match by an individual player** is six, by Ryan Constable (Australia) for Saracens against Bedford on 16 April 2000.

• The ★ **most tries scored in Guinness Premiership matches by an individual player** is 75, by Steve Hanley (UK) between 1998 and 2006 playing for Sale Sharks.

• The ★ **most points scored in an English Premiership rugby union match by an individual player** is 32, by Niall Woods (Ireland) playing for London Irish against Harlequins on 23 April 1998.

• The ★ **most test tries scored in rugby union test matches in one year** is 17 and was achieved by Joe Rokocoko for New Zealand in 2003 – equalling the record held by Daisuke Ohata (Japan).

• The ★ **highest attendance for a Heineken Cup pool match** is 44,100 at Parc des Princes in Paris, France, for a game played between Stade Français and Sale Sharks on 10 December 2006.

• The ★ **most Six Nations Championship wins** is four, by France, in 2002, 2004, 2006 and 2007.

• Jonny Wilkinson (UK), playing for England, scored a record 89 points in the five games of the Six Nations Championship series in 2001, the ★ **most points scored in a Six Nations season by an individual player**.

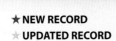

★ **NEW RECORD**
★ **UPDATED RECORD**

★ MOST RUGBY LEAGUE TRI-NATIONS TITLES

Australia have won the rugby league Tri-Nations tournament on three occasions to date, in 1999, 2004 and 2006.

• The ★ **most penalty goals kicked in a Five/Six Nations Championship match** is seven: by Simon Hodgkinson for England v. Wales at Cardiff on 19 January 1991; Rob Andrew for England v. Scotland at Twickenham, Greater London, UK, on 18 March 1995; Jonny Wilkinson for England v. France at Twickenham on 20 March 1999; Neil Jenkins for Wales v. Italy at Cardiff, UK, on 19 February 2000; Gerald Merceron for France v. Italy on 2 February 2002; and Chris Paterson for Scotland v. Wales on 10 February 2007.

• Jason Leonard (UK) has played a total of 114 times for England, the **most international appearances by a rugby union forward**. The prop was awarded his first cap in July 1990 in competition against Argentina in Buenos Aires and he won his 100th playing against France in the Six Nations Championship at Twickenham, England, in February 2003.

• The ★ **most tries scored in an international rugby union career** is 65 by Daisuke Ohata (Japan,

b. 11 November 1975). He scored three tries in his debut international on 9 November 1996, and again on 14 May 2006 in his most recent test against Georgia, breaking David Campese's (Australia) record of 64 international tries.

• The ★ **most international rugby union appearances by an individual** is by George Gregan (Australia), who competed in 127 internationals between 1990 and 2006.

SEVENS

• The ★ **most IRB Sevens Series titles** won is six by New Zealand: in 1999/2000, 2000/01, 2001/02, 2002/03, 2003/04 and 2004/05. Fiji broke New Zealand's dominance to claim their first title in 2005/06.

• The ★ **most points scored in IRB Sevens tournaments by an individual player** is 1,613, by Ben Gollings (UK) playing for England.

★ MOST POINTS SCORED IN A GUINNESS PREMIERSHIP CAREER

As of 25 February 2007, Jonny Wilkinson (UK) had scored 1,411 points for Newcastle Falcons.

He also holds the record for the **most points scored by an individual in an International Championship match**, with 35 for England (80) against Italy (23) at Twickenham, London, UK, on 17 February 2001.

★ MOST TAG RUGBY PLAYERS

On 6 July 2006, 242 players took part in the Northwich and District Primary Schools Tag Rugby Tournament 2006, at Moss Farm sports complex, Northwich, UK.

• The ★ **most tries scored in IRB Sevens tournaments by an individual player** is 165, by Santiago Gomez Cora (Argentina) between 1999 and 2007.

• The ★ **most goals scored in IRB sevens tournaments by an individual player** is 449, by Ben Gollings (UK) playing for England.

OFF THE FIELD

• The record for the ★ **longest beach rugby try** is 5.60 m (18.3 ft) and was set by Cedric Di Dio (France) on the set of *L'Été De Tous Les Records* in St Cyprien, France, on 29 June 2005.

• The record for the ★ **most consecutive passes** of a rugby ball is 262 and was organized by Wooden Spoon and the Scottish Rugby Union as part of BT Finals day at Murrayfield, Edinburgh, UK, on 30 April 2005.

• The **most rugby tackles made in one hour** is 2,670 by Aberdeen Wanderers' under-18 squad (UK) at Aberdeen Wanderers Rugby Club, Aberdeen, UK, on 10 June 2006.

• The **most World Cup titles in women's rugby union** is three, by New Zealand in 1998, 2002 and 2006. The USA and England both have one win apiece. The women's World Cup has been contested five times between 1991 and 2006.

• First held in 1997, the **most wins of the women's Hong Kong Sevens** is five by New Zealand in 1997 and from 1999 to 2002.

• The **highest rugby union goal posts** measure 33.54 m (110 ft). That is equivalent to the height of 7.5 double-decker buses stacked on top of each other! The record-breaking posts stand at the Roan Antelope Rugby Union Club, Luanshya, Zambia.

• The **largest rugby tour** was made by Ealing Rugby Club (UK) from 11 to 14 April 2003, with 264 players on a coach tour playing matches around Ireland.

• The **oldest rugby union competition**, The United Hospitals Cup, is played between teams representing hospitals in England. It was first contested in 1875.

TARGET SPORTS

TITANS OF TENPIN

The Weber Cup is tenpin bowling's equivalent of the Ryder Cup – that is, bowlers from the USA and Europe compete against each other over three days of matches. The ★**most wins of the Weber Cup** is four, by the USA, in 2000, 2001, 2002 and 2006.

★MOST TIMES TO SCORE 180 IN A PRO DARTS CORPORATION FINAL

The greatest number of maximum scores recorded in a Pro Darts Corporation final by an individual is 21, by Raymond van Barneveld (Netherlands, pictured) in his match against Phil Taylor (UK) at Purfleet, UK, on 1 January 2007.

ARCHERY

The ★**most points scored in 24 hours of shooting Fédération Internationale de Tir à l'Arc (FITA) 18 rounds** (i.e. indoor archery rounds over 18 m, or 26 ft) is 35,121 by Brian Williams and Mark Duggan (both UK) at Perriswood Archery Centre, Gower, Swansea, UK, on 18 June 2005.

• South Korea (Jang Yong-Ho, Choi Young-Kwang and Im Bong Hyun) scored the ★**most points in a FITA round outdoor recurve (team)**, with 4,074 out of a possible 4,320 in New York City, USA, in July 2003.

• The ★**most points scored in the men's individual 70 m outdoor recurve** (out of a possible 360 in a single round) is 351 by Kim Jae Hyung (South Korea) in Wonju, South Korea, on 24 October 2006.

> On 15 July 2004, archer Jeremie Masson (France) scored a record three bull's-eyes in 90 seconds

BOWLS

Alex Marshall (UK) has registered the ★**most wins of the indoor bowls World Championships**, with four titles (1999, 2003–04 and 2007).

• The ★**longest outdoor bowls marathon** lasted 105 hours and was set by 12 members of Lloyd Hotel Bowling Club, Chorlton, Manchester, UK, from 14 to 18 October 2006.

CROQUET

The President's Cup is the UK's premier invitation croquet event. Robert Fulford (UK) has achieved the ★**most wins of the President's Cup**, with six victories (1989, 1998–99, 2001–02 and 2006).

• The MacRobertson Shield (instituted 1925) is the world's top croquet team event. The ★**most wins of the MacRobertson Shield** is 13 by Great Britain (1925, 1937, 1956, 1963, 1969, 1974, 1982, 1990, 1993, 1996, 2000, 2003 and 2006).

★HIGHEST BACKWARDS TENPIN BOWLING SCORE IN A GAME

Joe Scrandis (USA) racked up a score of 175 in a single game of backwards bowling on 29 April 2006. His record-breaking feat took place at The Lanes, Fort Meade, Maryland, USA.

DARTS

Phil Taylor (UK) has won the ★**most World Championship titles**, with 13 victories, in 1990, 1992, 1995–2002 (consecutively) and 2004–06.

• Taylor also holds the record for the ★**most World Matchplay titles**, with eight wins, in 1995, 1997, 2000–04 and 2006.

• Finally, Taylor holds the record for the ★**most World Grand Prix titles won by an individual player**, with seven, in 1998–2000, 2002–03 and 2005–06.

★LONGEST SINGLES DARTS MARATHON

Stephen Lye and Mick Kinney (both UK) played a darts match that lasted 24 hours at the Summerfield Tavern, Wilmslow, Cheshire, UK, on 6–7 May 2006.

★ FASTEST TIME TO SHOOT 10 ARROWS

Luis Caídas Martín (Spain) shot 10 arrows in 1 min 7 sec on the set of *Guinness World Records – El Show de los Records* in Madrid, Spain, on 4 June 2006. Don't be fooled by the picture (left) – he shot the arrows one by one!

POOL

The Mosconi Cup is a nine-ball pool tournament contested every year by two teams of the best players from the USA and Europe. The ★ **most wins of the Mosconi Cup** is 11 by the USA in 1994, 1996–2001 and 2003–06.

• The ★ **most pool World Masters titles won** is five by Ralf Souquet (Germany) – 1994, 1996, 2000, 2002 and 2006.

• The ★ **most women's pool World Championships won** is four by Allison Fisher (UK) in 1996–98 and 2001.

• Ralph Greenleaf (USA) won the **most World Pocket Billiards Championship titles**, with 19 from 1919 to 1937.

SNOOKER

The ★ **most Masters titles won by an individual** is six by Stephen Hendry (UK), in 1989–93 (consecutively) and 1996.

★ MOST CONSECUTIVE CENTURY SNOOKER BREAKS

John Higgins (UK) achieved four consecutive breaks of 100 or more in Preston, UK, on 16 October 2005. The "Wizard of Wishaw" recorded breaks of 103, 104, 138 and 128 in his match against Ronnie O'Sullivan (UK).

DID YOU KNOW?
The ★ **youngest player to achieve a maximum score of 147 in a televised snooker match** is Ding Junhui (China) at the Masters tournament at Wembley, UK, on 14 January 2007. He was 19 years 288 days old.

• Hendry also achieved the ★ **most breaks of 100 or more in a professional career**, with 700 from 1985 to 2007.

• The final between Peter Ebdon (UK) and Graeme Dott (UK) at the Crucible in Sheffield, UK, on 1 May 2006 lasted for 74 minutes – the ★ **longest frame in a World Championship match**.

TENPIN BOWLING

The ★ **highest tenpin-bowling score in 24 hours by an individual** is 59,702 points, by Cory Bithell (USA)

at Eastways Lanes, Erie, Pennsylvania, USA, on 25–26 July 1997.

• The tenpin-bowling World Cup (instituted in 1965) is contested annually by the national champions of the Fédération Internationale des Quilleurs (FIQ). The **most wins of the tenpin-bowling World Cup** is four by Paeng Nepomuceno (Philippines) in 1976, 1980, 1992 and 1996.

• Three bowlers share the record for ★ **most World Cup tenpin-bowling titles won by a woman**, with two wins each. They are: Jeanette Baker (Australia) in 1982 and 1983; Pauline Smith (UK) in 1981 and 1993; and Shannon Pluhowsky (USA) in 2002 and 2004.

SHOOTING STARS

The first steps towards formalizing rules and regulations for shooting competitions were taken during the late 19th century. Shooting was one of the nine sports featured in the first modern Olympic Games, in 1896, and the inaugural shooting World Championship took place in France the following year. The sport's governing body is the International Shooting Sport Federation (ISSF).

You'll find a wealth of shooting records in our comprehensive sports reference section (see p. 266), but here are a few recent highlights:

• Alexei Klimov (Russia) holds the record for the ★ **men's ISSF 25 m rapid-fire pistol shot event**, with a score of 591 in, Granada, Spain, on 6 October 2006.

• On 3 August 2006, Espen Berg-Knutsen (Norway) set a new record for the ★ **men's ISSF 300 m rifle three-positions event**, with a score of 1,181 in Zagreb, Croatia.

• Thomas Farnik (Austria) holds the record for the ★ **men's 10 m air-rifle event**, with a score of 703.1 (599 + 104.1) in Granada, Spain, on 4 October 2006.

• Li Du (China) set a world record for the ★ **women's 10 m air-rifle (40 shots) event** in Zagreb, Croatia, on 4 June 2003. Her overall score was 504.9 (400 + 104.9).

• Maria Grozdeva (Bulgaria) set a world record in the ★ **women's 25 m pistol (60 shots) event** in Changwon, South Korea, on 11 April 2005. Her overall score was 796.7 (591 + 205.7).

• Sonja Pfeilschifter (Germany) scored 698.0 (594 + 104.0) in the ★ **women's rifle 50 m three-positions (20 shots) event** in Munich, Germany, on 28 May 2006.

★ NEW RECORD
★ UPDATED RECORD

TENNIS & RACKET SPORTS

WHAT'S IN A NAME?

Most historians believe tennis began in France around 800 years ago, as a game of handball played against walls or over a rope strung across a courtyard. As players served the ball, they called "*Tenez!*" ("Take this!"), which then evolved into the word "tennis".

SPEEDY SERVICE

The ★ **fastest tennis serve** measured 246.9 km/h (155 mph) and was struck by Andy Roddick (USA) in a Davis Cup semi-final on 24 September 2006.

Brenda Schultz-McCarthy (Netherlands) produced a 209-km/h (130-mph) serve in the first round of the Western & Southern Financial Group Women's Open on 15 July 2006, the ★ **fastest serve by a woman**.

★ MOST CONSECUTIVE CLAY WINS (MALE)

On 11 June 2006, Rafael Nadal (Spain) won his 60th consecutive clay-court singles match, beating Roger Federer (Switzerland) 1–6, 6–1, 6–4, 7–6 (7–4) in the French Open final.

Chris Evert (USA) holds the ★ **women's – and overall – record for most consecutive wins** with 125.

TENNIS

★ MOST CONSECUTIVE WEEKS AS WORLD TENNIS NUMBER ONE

Roger Federer (Switzerland) was ranked number-one male tennis player for 161 weeks, from 2 February 2004 to 26 February 2007.

Federer also holds the record for the ★ **most consecutive grass-court men's singles tennis-match wins**. He won his 42nd game, beating Richard Gasquet (France) 6–3, 6–2, 6–2 at Wimbledon, London, UK, on 26 June 2006.

★ LONGEST WIMBLEDON LADIES SINGLES FINAL

In terms of minutes played, the longest ladies' singles final in Wimbledon's history – indeed, one of the longest of all women's tennis Grand Slam finals – occurred on 2 July 2005, when Venus Williams beat Lindsay Davenport (both USA) 4–6, 7–6 (7–4), 9–7 in a match lasting 2 hr 45 min, at the Championships in London, UK.

★ MOST HOPMAN CUPS WON (FEMALE)

The greatest number of Hopman Cup titles won by a female player is two, by Arantxa Sánchez Vicario (Spain), playing for Spain in 1990 and 2002.

★ MOST PRIZE MONEY IN A SEASON

In 2006, Roger Federer (Switzerland) won $8.4 million (£4.3 million) from 17 tournaments.

HIGHEST ATTENDANCE

An unprecedented 30,472 people attended the Astrodome, Houston, Texas, USA, on 20 September 1973 for the "Battle of the Sexes" when Billie-Jean King beat Robert Larimore Riggs (both USA).

The record for **largest attendance at a regular tennis match** was set at the 2004 Davis Cup final (3–5 December) between the USA and Spain in Seville's La Cartuja Olympic Stadium, Spain. It was seen by about 26,600 spectators.

The ★ **largest attendance at Wimbledon for one day** was 42,457, for First Wednesday in 2002.

The ★ **largest attendance at a Wimbledon tournament** was 490,081 in 2001, when play was extended because of bad weather.

TABLE TENNIS

LONGEST RALLY

The longest table-tennis rally was played between Brian and Steve Seibel (both USA) at the Christown YMCA, Phoenix, Arizona, USA, on 14 August 2004. It lasted for 8 hr 15 min 1 sec.

★ MOST TEAM BADMINTON UBER CUP WORLD CHAMPIONSHIPS (WOMEN)

The Chinese team has won the Uber Cup (instituted 1956) nine times, in 1984, 1986, 1988, 1990, 1992, 1998, 2000, 2002 and 2004. Pictured below is team member Zhang Ning in 2006.

★ MOST OLYMPIC TABLE TENNIS TEAM GOLD MEDALS (MEN)

The greatest number of gold medals won in Olympic competitions by a men's team is six by China between 1988 and 2004. Pictured above, left to right, are China's Qi Chen and Lin Ma on their way to Olympic gold in August 2004.

MOST TEAM WORLD CHAMPIONSHIPS

The ★most women's team World Championship titles (for the Corbillon Cup) is 17, by China, in 1965, 1971, 1975–89 (every two years), 1993, 1995, 1997, 2000–01, 2004 and 2006.

The ★most men's team World Championship titles (for the Swaythling Cup) is 15, by China, in 1961, 1963, 1965, 1971, 1975, 1977, 1981, 1983, 1985, 1987, 1995, 1997, 2001, 2004 and 2006.

DID YOU KNOW?
Boris Becker (Germany) won the Wimbledon men's singles title in 1985 aged 17 years 227 days, making him the **youngest male Wimbledon champion**.

BADMINTON

★ MOST SINGLES WORLD CHAMPIONSHIPS

Five Chinese players have won singles world titles twice. Yang Yang took the men's singles in 1987 and 1989. The women's singles has been won twice by: Li Lingwei (1983, 1989); Han Aiping (1985, 1987); Ye Zhaoying (1995, 1997); Xie Xingfang (2005, 2006).

LONGEST MATCH RALLY

In the men's singles final of the 1987 All-England Championships between Morten Frost (Denmark) and Icuk Sugiarto (Indonesia) there were two successive rallies of more than 90 strokes.

★ OLDEST PERSON TO BE RANKED WORLD TENNIS NUMBER ONE

The oldest male tennis player to be ranked number one by the Association of Tennis Professionals (ATP) is Andre Agassi (USA, b. 29 April 1970), who became the highest seeded men's player on 11 May 2003, aged 33 years 13 days. He held the ranking for 14 weeks.

★ **NEW RECORD**
★ **UPDATED RECORD**

★ MOST TENNIS CLUB SINGLES CHAMPIONSHIPS (MALE)

Mike Keat (UK) won 40 consecutive championships in the men's singles at Budehaven Tennis Club Championships in Bude, Cornwall, UK, 1959–98.

★ FASTEST SHUTTLECOCK

During a Sudirman Cup match on 3 June 2005, Fu Haifeng (China) hit a shuttlecock at a speed of 332 km/h (206 mph), beating the previous record by 72 km/h (44 mph).

MOST TEAM BADMINTON WORLD CHAMPIONSHIPS (MEN)

Indonesia has won 13 men's team badminton World Championships, for the Thomas Cup: 1958, 1961, 1964, 1970, 1973, 1976, 1979, 1984, 1994, 1996, 1998, 2000 and 2002.

★ MOST WHEELCHAIR TENNIS WORLD CHAMPIONSHIPS

David Hall (Australia) has won six ITF wheelchair World Championships, in 1995, 1998, 2000 and 2002–04.

CUP GLORIES

• The Davis Cup, organized by the International Tennis Federation (ITF), is the ★**largest annual team sport competition**. The 2006 competition saw 133 countries enter – one less than the previous year. The **most wins in the Davis Cup** has been 31 by the USA between 1900 and 1995.

• The women's equivalent of the Davis Cup is the ITF's Fed Cup (originally the Federation Cup), itself the largest female annual team sporting event, with 89 countries represented in 2006. The USA has recorded the ★**most consecutive wins of the Fed Cup by an international team**, with seven victories, 1976–82.

• The Hopman Cup is an invitational mixed-team contest that has been held in Perth, Australia, every year since 1989. The ★**greatest number of Hopman Cup titles** won by an international pairing is four, by the USA, in 1997, 2003, 2004 and 2006. The **most consecutive Hopman Cup wins by a country** is two, again by the USA, in 2003–04. James Blake holds the record for the ★**most Hopman Cup titles won by a male player**, with two wins, playing for the USA, in 2003 and 2004.

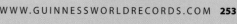

UNUSUAL SPORTS

FASTEST SANDBAG CARRYING

Peyo Mendiboure (France) carried a 80-kg (176-lb) sandbag over a 120-m (393-ft) course in 29.84 seconds on the set of *L'Été De Tous Les Records* in Argèles-Gazost, France, on 6 July 2005.

★ LONGEST-RUNNING PUMPKIN RACE

The Windsor Pumpkin Regatta and Parade in Nova Scotia, Canada, has been held annually since 1999. Competitors first parade their PVC (Personal Vegetable Craft) – giant hollowed-out pumpkins – then race them 0.8 km (0.5 miles) across Lake Pesaquid in either the motorized or paddler class.

FARTHEST DISTANCE TO HURL A HAGGIS

Alan Pettigrew (UK) threw – or "hurled" – a haggis (of minimum weight 680 g, or 1 lb 8 oz) a distance of 55.11 m (180 ft 10 in) at Inchmurrin, Argyll, UK, on 24 May 1984. The sport of haggis hurling dates back to 1977.

FASTEST SPEED FOR "WALKING ON WATER"

Remy Bricka (France) covered 1 km (0.6 miles) in 7 min 7.41 sec on the Olympic pool in Montreal, Canada, on 2 August 1989. Monsieur Bricka "walks on water" by attaching ski floats to his feet and by moving in the same way as in cross-country skiing, using a double-headed paddle instead of ski poles.

FARTHEST PEANUT THROW

On 21 February 1999, at Westfield Devils Junior Soccer Club in Launceston, Tasmania, Australia, Adrian Finch (Australia) threw a 4-mg (0.1-oz) peanut a distance of 34.11 m (111 ft 10 in).

FARTHEST NIRA (JAPANESE CHIVE) THROW

Junsuke Miyamoto (Japan) threw a nira (a type of oriental chive or leek) a distance of 11.11 m (36 ft 5 in) on 20 June 1997. Junsuke's record was ratified under the rules of "nira-tobashi" competitions held at the Sako Festival in Kochi-ken, Japan.

FARTHEST DISTANCE TO THROW A ROLLING PIN

Lori La Deane Adams (USA) threw a 907-g (2-lb) rolling pin a distance of 53.47 m (175 ft 5 in) at Iowa State Fair, Iowa, USA, on 21 August 1979.

★ FARTHEST DISTANCE TO THROW A PERSON

Juha Rasanen (Finland) threw a person weighing 60 kg (132 lb) a distance of 5.4 m (17 ft 8 in) on to a premarked mattress on the set of *Guinness World Records – El Show De Los Records* in Madrid, Spain, on 11 June 2006. In doing so, he broke his own record by over 1.5 m (4 ft 11 in).

★ LONGEST-RUNNING FINGER-WRESTLING CONTESTS

Finger-wrestling competitions known as Fingerhakeln have been staged in Bavaria, Germany, since the 14th century, when rivals competed in them for women's favours. Today, wrestlers contest various weight titles in the Bavarian Finger-Wrestling Championships held annually in Pflugdorf, near Munich. The aim is for each competitor to pull his rival across a table placed between them, using a finger lash wrapped around each contestant's digit.

★ FARTHEST WINKLE SPIT

The greatest distance for winkle spitting is 10.4 m (34 ft 1.4 in). The record is held by fisherman Alain Jourden (France), who retained the Winkle World Championship crown in Moguériec, France, on 16 July 2006 by spitting a (live) winkle 9.38 m (30 ft 9.2 in). In all, 110 competitors took part from 14 countries.

★ NEW RECORD
☆ UPDATED RECORD

LARGEST CROWD AT A CAMEL-WRESTLING FESTIVAL

A crowd of 20,000 gathered to watch 120 dromedaries wrestle at the 1994 Camel-Wrestling Festival in Selçuk, Turkey.

MOST WORLD PEA-SHOOTING CHAMPIONSHIPS

Mike Fordham (UK) won seven pea-shooting World Championships, in 1977–78, 1981, 1983–85 and 1992.

MOST ELEPHANT POLO CHAMPIONSHIPS

The Tiger Top Tuskers won a record eight World Elephant Polo

☆ FASTEST 31-LEGGED RACE OVER 50 M

Students from the Ishii Higashi Elementary School ran a 31-legged race covering a total of 50 m (164 ft) in 8.8 seconds at the school gym, in Matsuyama, Ehime Prefecture, Japan, on 16 October 2005. Thirty pupils from the sixth grade took part.

X-REF
• If you have a penchant for curious hobbies, check out our peculiar pastimes on p.86.

• Question: where can you find some truly testing Scrabble, sudoku and crossword conundrums? Answer: pp.112–113.

• Enter the Olympic Hall of Fame on p.143.

• And for the latest records in every discipline from action sports to X Games, run along to p.210…

Association Championships, in 1983–85, 1987, 1992, 1998, 2000 and 2003.

TIDDLYWINKS CHAMPIONSHIPS

Larry Khan (USA) has won the ☆ **most world singles titles of the Tiddlywinks World Championships**, with 19.

Geoff Myers (UK) has won the ★ **most world pairs titles of the Tiddlywinks World Championships**, with 12.

LARGEST WATER-PISTOL FIGHT

On 28 April 2005, 1,173 participants staged a colossal waterfight at Loyola Marymount University, Los Angeles, California, USA.

LONGEST-RUNNING PILLOW FIGHT

The World Pillow-Fighting Championships in Kenwood, California, USA, is the longest-

Nick and Alastair Benbow (both UK) ran the London Marathon three-legged in a record 3 hr 40 min 16 sec on 26 April 1998

★ LARGEST HIGH-HEELS RACE

The Glamour Stiletto Run, created by BSUR Concepting (Netherlands), takes place in cities worldwide. On 9 March 2006, 150 women ran 80 m (262 ft) through a shopping mall in Amsterdam, the Netherlands, wearing shoes with a minimum heel height of 7 cm (2.75 in). Each hoped to win €10,000 (£6,700; $12,600) of shopping money to be spent that day!

running annual competition of its kind: its 40th tournament was held on 4 July 2006. Around 100 contestants battled it out with wet, muddy pillows, sitting astride a steel pole over a mud-filled creek!

For more unusual record-breaking fights, look to the right…

MORE FIGHTING TALK

• A total of 3,745 people created their own winter wonderland at Michigan Technological University, Houghton, Michigan, USA, on 10 February 2006 with the **largest snowball fight**.

• Have you ever been asked to stop playing with your food? Clearly, no one's told the residents of Buñol in Spain. Every year, they amass around 125 tonnes (275,500 lb) of tomatoes to throw at each other on the last Wednesday of August in the Tomatina, the **largest annual food fight**.

• The **largest water-balloon fight** involved 2,849 people, who threw 51,400 balloons in the XBox 360 Water Balloon Challenge at Coogee Beach in Sydney, Australia, on 22 April 2006.

• Why eat a custard pie when it's so much more fun to throw it? On 7 October 1998, 50 people – including the band Electrasy and members of the Official Laurel and Hardy Fan Club – threw 4,400 custard pies in three minutes for the band's video of their single "Best Friend's Girl", in the **largest custard-pie fight**. And why Laurel and Hardy? Well, a total of 3,000 pies were thrown in their silent two-reeler *The Battle of the Century* (USA, 1927), the **largest custard-pie fight in a movie**. As Ollie might have said, "That's another fine mess you've got me into!"

WATERSPORTS

FASTEST 100 M BREASTSTROKE (MALE)

Brendan Hansen (USA) swam the 100 m breaststroke in 59.13 seconds in Irvine, California, USA, on 1 August 2006.

In Victoria, British Columbia, Canada, on 20 August 2006, he completed the ★ **fastest men's 200 m breaststroke** in a time of 2 min 8.50 sec.

Earlier – along with team-mates Aaron Peirsol, Ian Crocker and Jason Lezak – he had set the record for the **fastest men's short-course medley 4 x 100 m relay**, with a time of 3 min 25.09 sec in Indianapolis, USA, on 11 October 2004.

★ FASTEST 200 M BUTTERFLY (FEMALE)

Jessica Schipper (Australia) swam the women's 200 m butterfly in a time of 2 min 5.4 sec in Victoria, Canada, on 17 August 2006.

SWIMMING

FASTEST SWIMMER

On 23 March 1990, Tom Jager (USA) achieved an average speed of 8.64 km/h (5.37 mph) over 50 yards (45.72 m) in Nashville, Tennessee, USA.

• The **fastest female swimmer** is Le Jingyi (China), who achieved a speed of 7.34 km/h (4.56 mph) over 50 m on 11 September 1994.

MOST WORLD RECORDS

Ragnhild Hveger (Denmark) set 42 swimming world records between 1936 and 1942. For currently recognized events (only metric distances in 50-m pools), the **most swimming world records set by a woman** is 23, by Kornelia Ender (GDR) between 1973 and 1976.

• Arne Borg (Sweden) set 32 world records between 1921 and 1929, the **most swimming world records set by a man**. For currently recognized events, the record is 26 by Mark Spitz (USA), from 1967 to 1972.

MOST OLYMPIC GOLDS AT ONE GAMES (FEMALE)

At the 1988 Olympic Games, Kristin Otto (GDR) won six Olympic gold medals: the 50 m freestyle, the 100 m freestyle, the 100 m backstroke, the 100 m butterfly, the 4 x 100 m freestyle and the 4 x 100 m medley.

50 M

Jade Edmistone (Australia) swam the ★ **fastest women's 50 m breaststroke**, finishing in 30.31 seconds in Melbourne, Australia, on 31 January 2006.

100 M

Leisel Jones (Australia) achieved the ★ **fastest women's 100 m breaststroke** with a time of 1 min 5.09 sec in Melbourne, Australia, on 20 March 2006.

200 M

Aaron Peirsol (USA) swam the ★ **fastest men's 200 m backstroke** on 19 August 2006 in Victoria, Canada, with a time of 1 min 54.44 sec.

• The ★ **fastest women's 200 m breaststroke** record was set by Leisel Jones (Australia) on 1 February 2006 in Melbourne, Australia, with a time of 2 min 20.54 sec.

4 X 100 M RELAY

The USA (Michael Phelps, Neil Walker, Cullen Jones, Jason Lezak) recorded the ★ **fastest 4 x 100 m freestyle relay** in 3 min 12.46 sec in Victoria, Canada, on 19 August 2006.

• On 31 July 2006, Germany (Petra Dallmann, Daniela Götz, Britta Steffen, Annika Liebs) recorded the ★ **fastest women's 4 x 100 m freestyle relay**, finishing in 3 min 35.22 sec in Budapest, Hungary.

★ FASTEST 4 X 200 M FREESTYLE (WOMEN)

Germany (Petra Dallmann, Daniela Samulski, Britta Steffen, Annika Liebs) completed the women's 4 x 200 m freestyle in 7 min 50.82 sec at the European Swimming Championships held in Budapest, Hungary, on 3 August 2006.

• Australia (Sophie Edington, Leisel Jones, Jessica Schipper, Lisbeth Lenton) swam the ★ **fastest women's 4 x 100 m medley relay** in 3 min 57.32 sec in Melbourne, Australia, on 21 March 2006.

FASTEST 100 M FREESTYLE (FEMALE)

Britta Steffen (Germany) swam the women's 100 m freestyle in 53.30 seconds in Budapest, Hungary, on 2 August 2006.

★FASTEST 100 X 1,000 M RELAY (MIXED TEAM)

On 2–3 September 2006, a relay team of 100 swimmers (comprising 50 men and 50 women) took 22 hr 48 min 43.10 sec to each successfully swim 1,000 m at Volkspark, Dortmund, Germany.

DIVING

★OLDEST SCUBA DIVER

Herbert Kilbride (USA, b. 8 March 1914), a qualified PADI instructor, celebrated his 90th birthday on 8 March 2004 and remains an active scuba enthusiast.

★LONGEST SCUBA DIVE IN OPEN FRESH WATER

Jerry Hall (USA) – a Tennessee diver, not the Texan actress! – remained under water at a depth of 3.6 m (12 ft) on a submerged platform in Watauga Lake, Tennessee, USA, for 120 hr 1 min 9 sec from 29 August to 3 September 2004. In accordance with the rules, he did not surface at any time.

HIGHEST HIGH DIVE

Olivier Favre (Switzerland) recorded a dive of 53.9 m (176 ft 10 in) from a diving board at Villers-le-Lac, France, on 30 August 1987.

GREATEST HIGH-DIVE SCORE

In 2000, during the Cliff-Diving World Championships in Kaunolu, Hawaii, USA, Orlando Duque (Colombia) performed a double back somersault with four twists from 24.4 m (80 ft). He earned a perfect 10 from all seven judges and scored 159.00 points.

YOUNGEST CLIFF DIVER

In December 2005, 12-year-old Iris Alvarez (Mexico) became the youngest person – and first female – to dive 18 m (59 ft) off La Quebrada rock in Acapulco, Mexico. A person diving from the top of the cliff (at 30 m; 100 ft) would hit the water at 90 km/h (56 mph)!

★FASTEST 400 M FREESTYLE (FEMALE)

Laure Manaudou (France) swam the women's 400 m freestyle in 4 min 2.13 sec in Budapest, Hungary, on 6 August 2006.

★FASTEST 200 M BUTTERFLY (MALE)

Michael Phelps (USA) won the men's 200 m butterfly in a time of 1 min 53.8 sec in Victoria, Canada, on 17 August 2006.

He also holds the record for the **most swimming medals won by an individual at a single Olympic Games** with six golds (100 m and 200 m butterfly, 200 m and 400 m medley, 4 x 200 m freestyle and 4 x 100 m medley) and two bronze (200 m freestyle and 4 x 100 m freestyle) at the 2004 Games.

CHANNEL CHAMPS

The Brits call it the English Channel; to the French, it's La Manche ("The Sleeve"). At its narrowest – between Dover (UK) and Cap Gris-Nez (France) – this slim stretch of water separating England and France measures just 21 miles (34 km) – and to some people, that represents a challenge…

• The **first person to swim the Channel** (without a life jacket) was Matthew Webb (UK), who made the crossing in 21 hr 45 min on 24–25 August 1875.

• The official Channel Swimming Association record for the **fastest time to swim the Channel** from Shakespeare Beach, Dover, UK, to Cap Gris-Nez, France, is 7 hr 17 min by Chad Hundeby (USA), on 27 September 1994.

• For some people, once is never enough. The ★**greatest number of Channel crossings swum** is 39 by Alison Streeter (UK) from 1982 to 2000 (including a record seven in one year, 1992). The ★**greatest number of Channel crossings swum by a man** is 33 by Michael Read (UK) from 1969 to 2004.

• Different strokes for different folks: the ★**fastest crossing of the Channel using solely breaststroke** is 13 hr 31 min by Frederik Jacques (Belgium) on 16 August 2005. The ★**fastest crossing using solely backstroke** is 13 hr 22 min by Tina Neil (USA) on 9 August 2005. Finally, ★**the fastest crossing using solely the butterfly** is 14 hr 18 min by Julie Bradshaw (UK) on 5 August 2002.

★NEW RECORD
★UPDATED RECORD

DID YOU KNOW?
The ★**oldest woman to swim the Channel** was Carol Sing (USA, b. 24 August 1941), who was 57 years 361 days old when she completed the journey on 21 August 1999.

WATERSPORTS

ENTER THE DRAGON...

Dragon boats are long, thin craft fitted with dragon heads and tails and propelled by paddlers. Dragon-boat racing is a Chinese tradition, dating back some 2,500 years, but has now become a modern sport, governed by the International Dragon Boat Federation (IDBF).

The International Dragon Boat Race was instituted in 1975 in Hong Kong and is held annually. The **fastest time** to complete this 640-m (2,100-ft) course is 2 min 27.45 sec and was achieved by the Chinese Shun De team, on 30 June 1985.

The **largest dragon boat regatta** consisted of 154 dragon boats in an event organized by Wanheimer Kanu-Gilde eV in Duisburg, Germany, on 17–19 June 2005.

★ FASTEST SINGLE-SCULLS LIGHTWEIGHT-CLASS ROW (MALE)

Zac Purchase (UK) completed a single-sculls lightweight-class rowing race in a time of 6 min 47.82 sec in Eton, UK, on 6 August 2006. (This is a non-Olympic boat-class event.)

CANOEING

The ★ **longest journey by canoe or kayak** was made by Daniel Bloor (UK), who travelled 326.98 miles (526.22 km) from Tewitfield, Cumbria, to Little Venice, London, UK, from 9 June to 19 June 2006.

• Three men share the record for the **greatest number of world and Olympic titles**, with 13: Gert Fredriksson (Sweden), 1948–60, Rüdiger Helm (GDR), 1976–83, and Ivan Patzaichin (Romania), 1968–84.

• The **longest canoeing race** was the Canadian Government Centennial Voyageur Canoe Pageant and Race from Rocky Mountain House, Alberta, to the Expo 67 site at Montreal, Quebec, from 24 May to 4 September 1967. The total length of the course was 5,283 km (3,283 miles).

ROWING

The ★ **most gold medals won in the World Championships and Olympic Games** is 13 by Sir Steven Redgrave (GB) who, in addition to his five Olympic successes, won world titles at coxed pairs (1986), coxless pairs (1987, 1991, 1993–95) and coxless fours (1997–99). The rowing World Championships are distinct from the Olympic Games and were first held in 1962.

• The ★ **greatest distance rowed in 24 hours (up- and down-stream) by a man** is 263 km (163.42 miles), by Matthias Auer, Christian Klandt and Olaf Behrend (all Germany) at DRUM Rowing Club, Berlin, Germany, on 2–3 August 2003.

• Maha Drysdale (New Zealand) set the ★ **fastest men's single-sculls row** with a time of 6 min 35.4 sec, in Eton, UK, on 26 August 2006.

• The ★ **fastest men's double-sculls row** was achieved by Jean-Baptiste Macquet and Adrien Hardy (both France), with a time of 6 min 4.25 sec in Poznan, Poland, on 17 June 2006.

YOUNGEST DIVING WORLD CHAMPION

Fu Mingxia (China, b. 16 August 1978) won the women's world title for platform diving at Perth, Australia, on 4 January 1991, at the age of 12 years 141 days.

• Dongxiang Xu and Shimin Ya (both China) set a new record for the ★ **fastest women's double-sculls lightweight-class row** in a time of 6 min 49.77 sec in Poznan, Poland, on 17 June 2006.

• China (Hua Yu, Haixia Chen, Xuefei Fan and Jing Liu) set a new record for the ★ **fastest women's quadruple-sculls lightweight-class row** with a time of 6 min 23.96 sec in Eton, UK, on 27 August 2006.

• The ☆ **fastest women's coxed-eights row** was achieved by the USA (Sickler, Cooke, Goodale, Shoop, Mickelson, Francia, Lind, Davies and Whipple) with a time of 5 min 55.5 sec in Eton, UK, on 27 August 2006.

SURFING

The ☆ **most ASP Tour World Championship titles won by a woman** is seven by Layne Beachley (Australia) in 1998–2004.

• Beachley also holds the record for the ★ **highest surfing career earnings by a woman**, with $567,935 (£294,189) to the end of the 2005 season.

• Lastly, in 1998, Beachley won $75,300 (£30,000) in surfing competitions, the **highest earnings from surfing in one season by a woman**.

★ FASTEST ROW BY COXLESS FOURS (WOMEN)

Australia (Selby Smith, Lutz, Bradley, Hornsey) completed a coxless fours race in 6 min 25.35 sec in Eton, UK, on 26 August 2006.

WATER POLO

• The ★ most wins of the men's water polo World Championships is two: Hungary in 1973 and 2003; the Soviet Union in 1975 and 1982; Italy in 1978 and 1994; Yugoslavia in 1986 and 1991; and Spain in 1998 and 2001. It was first held at the World Swimming Championships in 1973.

• Since it was introduced in 1986, the ★ women's water polo World Championships has been won a record two times, by Italy (in 1998 and 2001) and by Hungary (in 1994 and 2005).

WATER-SKIING

The ★ highest score for men's barefoot water-skiing tricks is 10,880 points by Keith St Onge (USA) at the 15th Barefoot Water Ski World Championships, Adna, Washington, USA, on 17 September 2006.

• The ★ fastest women's barefoot water-skiing speed is 154.63 km/h (96.08 mph) by Teresa Wallace (USA) at Firebird International Raceway, Chandler, Arizona, USA, on 16 November 2006.

WILD-WATER RACING

West Germany is the ★ most successful men's team at the International Canoe Federation (ICF) wild-water racing World Championships, K1 class. The team has won eight titles, in 1963, 1965, 1969, 1971, 1973, 1979, 1983 and 1985.

• The ★ most individual titles won at the ICF wild-water racing World Championships is four by Vladimir Vala and Jaroslav Slucik (both Slovakia), who won the C2 events in 1996, 2000 and two titles in 2004.

The ★ most successful women's team at the ICF wild-water racing World Championships is France, who have won three titles in the K1 team event, in 1996, 1998 and 2000.

YACHTING

The ★ highest speed reached on water by a yachtsman is 48.70 knots (90.19 km/h; 56.04 mph) by Finian Maynard (Ireland) on a windsurfer at Saintes Maries de la Mer, France, on 10 April 2005. This achievement also gives Maynard the records for ★ highest speed reached under sail on water and the ★ highest speed reached on a windsurfer.

• The ★ women's record for the highest speed reached under sail on water by any craft over a 500 m timed run is by windsurfer Karin Yaggi (Switzerland), who achieved 41.25 knots (76.4 km/h; 47.4 mph) on F2/arrows at Saintes Maries de la Mer, France, on 10 April 2005.

AT THE OLYMPICS

• Two sportsmen share the record for the most canoeing gold medals won at a single Olympic Games, with three each: Vladimir Parfenovich (USSR) in 1980 and Ian Ferguson (New Zealand) in 1984.

Gert Fredriksson (Sweden) won six Olympic gold medals, from 1948 to 1960, the most canoeing gold medals won at the Olympic Games.

Fredriksson also picked up a silver medal in the 1952 Games and a bronze in the 1960 Games, giving him the record for ★ most canoeing medals won at the Olympic Games, with eight in total.

In short, Gert Fredriksson was the most successful men's canoeist in Olympic history.

• Five players share the record for most water polo Olympic gold medals, with three wins each: Britons George Wilkinson (in 1900, 1908 and 1912), Paulo "Paul" Radmilovic and Charles Sidney Smith (both in 1908, 1912 and 1920); and Hungarians Desz Gyarmati and Gyorgy Karpati (both in 1952, 1956 and 1964).

• The first sportsman ever to win individual yachting gold medals in four successive Olympic Games was Paul B. Elvstrøm (Denmark). He triumphed in the Firefly class in 1948 and the Finn class in 1952, 1956 and 1960. Elvstrøm also won eight other world titles in a total of six classes.

• The record for longest span by an Olympic competitor stands at 40 years. Of the four sportsmen who share this record, three are yachtsmen: Magnus Andreas Thulstrup Clasen Konow (Norway) in 1908–20, 1928 and 1936–48; Paul B. Elvstrøm (Denmark) in 1948–60, 1968–72 and 1984–88; and Durward Randolph Knowles (GB 1948, then Bahamas) in 1948–72 and 1988). The fourth, Dr Ivan Joseph Martin Osiier (Denmark), competed in Olympic fencing in 1908–32 and 1948.

★ FASTEST TIME TO FINISH THE IJSBA PRO-AM WOMEN RUNABOUT SLALOM COURSE

The fastest electronically timed run for an International Jet Sports Boating Association (IJSBA) Pro-Am Women Runabout slalom course is 20.06 seconds by Karine Paturel (France, pictured) on Lake Havasu, Arizona, USA, on 13 October 1995.

The ★ fastest electronically timed run for an IJSBA Pro Runabout 785 slalom course is 18.26 seconds by Minoru Kanamori (Japan) on Lake Havasu, Arizona, USA, on 14 October 1995.

WILD WEST ARTS

★ LARGEST
TRICK-ROPING LOOP (MALE)

Charles Keyes (USA) spun a rope of 34.8 m (114 ft 5 in) on 21 April 2007 at the Will Rogers Wild West International Expo in Claremore, Oklahoma, USA (see far right for more on this event), beating his previous record of 32.66 m (107 ft 2 in) set at the 2006 Expo. The secret of his success is "bodybuilding, weight-lifting, running and aerobics."

★ LARGEST
TRICK-ROPING LOOP (FEMALE)

Kimberly Mink (USA) spun a loop around her, fed to a length of 23.21 m (76 ft 2 in) – measured from the end of the extended hondo (the eye of the rope) to her marked hand position – at Jerome High School in Jerome, Idaho, USA, on 25 January 2003.

★ **NEW RECORD**
★ **UPDATED RECORD**

★ YOUNGEST
WINNER OF THE
TEXAS SKIP RACE

Cody Lamb (USA), two-time winner of the "Rising Star" award at the Will Rogers Expo (2005–06), is, at 11 years old, the youngest competitor to win the Texas skip race. Along with his mother Kim and father Dan, Cody was inducted into the National Knife Throwers Hall of Fame in Austin, Texas, USA, in 2007 as the "Western Performing Family of the Year".

★ LARGEST GATHERING
OF WILD WEST ARTISTS

The Will Rogers Wild West International Expo, staged annually in Claremore, Oklahoma, USA, by the Wild West Arts Club (WWAC), is the largest gathering of Wild West performers and competitors in the world. Each year, around 200 entrants compete across various "cowboy" disciplines (see far right) for thousands of dollars in prize money. The event was previously held in Las Vegas until moving in 2005 to Claremore, Oklahoma – home of famous movie cowboy Will Rogers (USA, 1879–1935).

MOST CONSECUTIVE
TEXAS SKIPS

Andrew Rotz (USA) achieved an incredible 11,123 consecutive Texas skips at the National Convention of the Wild West Arts Club in Las Vegas, Nevada, USA, on 11 March 2003, smashing the previous record set at 4,011. The attempt took a bone-shattering 3 hr 10 min to complete.

★ MOST TEXAS SKIPS
IN ONE MINUTE

Daniel Ledda (Spain) achieved a record 80 Texas skips in 60 seconds on the set of *Guinness World Records – El Show de los Records* in Madrid, Spain, on 11 June 2006.

★ YOUNGEST
WILD WEST ARTS COMPETITOR

At just seven years old, Maxwell William Mobley (USA) became the youngest registered entrant in a Wild West Arts event, when he participated in the youth "Wedding Ring" race, which involves running a race while maintaining a rope loop around the body.

★ LONGEST WHIP CRACK

Wild West performance artist and whip maker Adam Winrich (USA) cracked a whip measuring 65.8 m (216 ft) excluding the handle – almost as long as a jumbo jet! – in Fall Creek, Wisconsin, USA, on 24 May 2006. (To "crack", the end must be made to travel above the speed of sound, breaking the sound barrier.)

Winrich also holds records for the ★ **most stock-whip cracks in one minute**, with 272 on 18 October 2006 at the Stone's Throw bar in Eau Claire, Wisconsin, USA; the ★ **most bullwhip cracks in one minute**, with 253, also at the Stone's Throw bar; and ★ **most whip cracks in one minute with two whips**, with a total of 420 at the 2007 Will Rogers Wild West Expo in Claremore, Oklahoma, USA.

★ LARGEST MOUNTAIN-MAN EVENT

Chuck Weems (USA, above) organizes the Texas State Knife and Tomahawk Championships, a mountain-man-style throwing contest that, in February 2007, attracted a record 54 entrants (winners pictured, inset).

★ FASTEST DRAW (OPEN STYLE)

The record for the world's fastest draw has stood since 1982 when, on a given signal, Ernie Hill (USA) drew his gun from a standing position and fired a shot in a record 0.208 seconds!

WILD WEST ARTS CLUB

Guinness World Records is indebted to the Wild West Arts Club (WWAC) for the majority of the records on these pages. The WWAC is "dedicated to preserving the Western arts of trick roping, riding, shooting, whip cracking and the throwing arts", and stages the annual Will Rogers Wild West International Expo at Claremore, Oklahoma, USA.

The group – a non-profit heritage foundation – currently boasts around 600 active members from 10 countries, and celebrated its 16th year at the Expo held in February 2007.

If you wish to take part in next year's Expo, contact the WWAC on **www.wwac.com**.

★ FASTEST TEXAS SKIP OVER 100 M

Ray Kozak (USA) completed a 100-m sprint in 17.61 seconds while performing 23 consecutive Texas skips at the Warren County Middle School, McMinnville, Tennessee, USA, on 26 February 2005.

A Texas skip is a vertical loop that is repeatedly pulled from one side of the body to the other; with each pass, the roper jumps through the centre of the loop.

★ FASTEST WHIP

The whip-cracking speed and accuracy world record is held by John Bailey (USA) of Ypsilanti, Michigan, USA, who hit 10 targets consecutively with a cracking whip in 8.04 seconds at the 2007 Wild West Arts Expo in Claremore, Oklahoma, USA, on 21 April 2007.

★ MOST KNIFE-THROWING WORLD TITLES WON

Dr Michael Bainton (USA) has won four knife-throwing world championships, in 2003–05 and 2007. He is also the only thrower to make a perfect score in the impalement category at the World Championships.

WINTER SPORTS

MOST SKELETON TITLES

Alex Coomber (GB) has won four world skeleton titles: the World Cup in 2000, 2001 and 2002, and the World Championships in 2000.

BOBSLEIGH

The ★ **most wins of the women's bobsleigh World Championships** is four, by Germany, in 2000, 2003, 2004 and 2005.

• The **most individual Olympic bobsleigh medals won** is seven (one gold, five silver and one bronze) by Bogdan Musiol (GDR) in 1980–92.

SKIING

The ★ **highest recorded speed for a male skier** is 252.40 km/h (156.83 mph), achieved by Simone Origone (Italy) at Les Arcs, France, on 20 April 2006.

★MOST BIATHLON WORLD CUP PURSUIT MEDALS (WOMEN)

First held in 1997, the biathlon World Cup 10-km pursuit has seen Germany win a record six medals: two gold (most recently in 2005 by Uschi Disl, pictured), two silver and two bronze.

Germany has won a total of 14 medals in both men's and women's events, the ★**most World Cup pursuit medals won by a country**.

• The ★ **highest recorded speed by a female skier** is 242.59 km/h (150.73 mph), by Sanna Tidstrand (Sweden), also at Les Arcs, France, on 20 April 2006.

• The ★**oldest known ski** was found in a peat bog at Hoting, Sweden. It dates from *ca.* 2500 BC.

• The ★ **greatest distance skied uphill** (using fur-covered skis) in 24 hours is 14,609 m (47,929 ft), by Erwin Reinthaler (Austria) in Bad Gastein, Austria, on 11–12 March 2006.

• During the 1970s, Annemarie Moser-Pröll (Austria) achieved 62 World Cup race wins – 36 in the downhill, 16 in the giant slalom, three in the slalom and seven in the combined, giving her the record for the ★**most ski-race World Cup victories**.

★LONGEST-RUNNING SKIKJÖRING EVENT

The longest-running winter horse-racing event that requires the "jockeys" to be pulled on skis by horses is Skikjöring, which has been held annually in February since 1907. Skikjöring takes place during White Turf St Moritz, an international horse race meet on the frozen surface of Lake St Moritz, Switzerland.

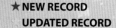

★ **NEW RECORD**

UPDATED RECORD

★ MOST WINS OF THE IDITAROD TRAIL SLED DOG RACE

The Iditarod Trail Sled Dog Race is held annually in Alaska, USA, and covers more than 1,850 km (1,150 miles). The most wins to date is five by Rick Swenson (USA, pictured) in 1977, 1979, 1981–82 and 1991.

- The ★ youngest winner of a freestyle skiing World Cup event is Anais Caradeux (France), aged 15 years 199 days, at Les Contamines, France, on 15 January 2006.
- The ★ oldest winner of a freestyle skiing World Cup event is Mike Nemesvary (UK), aged 83 years 77 days, at Angel Fire, New Mexico, USA, on 19 March 1983.
- When Annelise Coberger (New Zealand) won a silver medal in the women's ski slalom at the XVI Olympiad in Albertville, France, in 1992, she became the ★ first Winter Olympic medallist from the southern hemisphere.

SKI JUMPING

The ★ longest competitive ski jump by a man is 239 m (784 ft) by Bjørn Einar Romøren (Norway) at Planica, Slovenia, on 20 March 2005.
- Three ski fliers share the record for the ★ most ski fly World Championships, with two wins each: Walter Steiner (Switzerland) in 1972 and 1977; Sven Hannawald (Germany) in 2000 and 2002; and Roar Ljøkelsøy (Norway) in 2004 and 2006.

SNOWBOARDING

The ★ first competition for snow body-boarders was held in Switzerland in 2002.
- The ★ youngest winner of a snowboarding World Cup event is Sophie Rodriguez (France), aged 15 years 200 days, at Kreischberg, Austria, on 23 January 2004.

- Ursula Bruhin's (Switzerland) victory at Le Relais, Canada, on 17 December 2005 made her the ★ oldest individual winner of a snowboarding World Cup event, at the age of 35 years 273 days.
- Snowboard Cross was included in the Winter Olympics programme for the first time in 2006. The women's gold medal was won by Tanja Freiden (Switzerland) at Bardonecchia, Italy, on 17 February 2006, giving

MOST OLYMPIC SNOWBOARD MEDALS

Two snowboarders have won two Olympic medals each: Ross Powers (USA, above), with gold (2002) and bronze (1998) in the halfpipe; and Karine Ruby (France), with gold (1998) and silver (2002) in the parallel giant slalom.

★ MOST WORLD ICE GOLF CHAMPIONSHIPS

Since the first World Ice Golf Championship was held in March 1999 in Uummannaq, Greenland, two players have gone on to win the Championship title twice. Annika Östberg (Denmark, pictured) won in 2000 and 2001, followed by two consecutive wins by Roger Beames (UK) in 2002 and 2003.

her the record for the ★ most snowboard cross Olympic medals won by a woman.
- Likewise, Seth Wescott's (USA) victory in the men's event on 16 February 2006 gave him the record for the ★ most snowboard cross Olympic medals won by a man.

SKATE GREATS

- Natalia Kanounnikova (Russia) has the ★ fastest spin on ice skates, with a maximum rotational velocity of 308 RPM (revolutions per minute) at Rockefeller Center Ice Rink, New York City, USA, on 27 March 2006.

- The most figure-skating Olympic gold medals won by a man is three, by Gillis Grafstrom (Sweden) in 1920, 1924 and 1928. Sonja Henie (Norway) achieved the most figure-skating Olympic gold medals won by a woman, with three wins at the Winter Olympic Games of 1928, 1932 and 1936.

- The fastest time in the men's 10,000 m speed-skating event is 12 min 41.69 sec* by Sven Kramer (Netherlands) in Salt Lake City, Utah, USA, on 10 March 2007.

- The fastest time in the women's 3,000 m speed-skating event is 3 min 53.34 sec by Cindy Klassen (Canada) in Calgary, Canada, on 18 March 2006.

- The ★ oldest international speed-skating competition is the Alberto Nicolodi Trophy, organized by Sportivi Ghiaccio Trento, Trento, Italy, which had its 46th anniversary on 11–12 February 2006.

*awaiting ratification

X GAMES

HIGHEST BMX VERTICAL AIR

The highest unassisted air on a halfpipe is 5.8 m (19 ft), by Dave Mirra (USA, pictured) off a 5.4-m-tall (18-ft) ramp in San Diego, California, USA, in January 2001. Mat Hoffman (USA) achieved 8.07 m (26 ft 6 in) on a BMX from a quarterpipe ramp on 20 March 2001 in Oklahoma City, Oklahoma, USA, but was towed by a motorcycle in the run-up to the jump.

GAMES

By the late 20th century, the public profile of extreme action sports was on the rise and growing increasingly popular with a younger generation. In recognition of this, the Entertainment and Sports Programming Network (ESPN) organized the Extreme Games in Rhode Island, USA, in 1995. Nine events featured, including BMX, bungee jumping and skateboarding, and the competition attracted 198,000 spectators. In 1996, the contest was re-named X Games and the next year saw the debut of the Winter X Games.

HIGHEST ATTENDANCE AT AN EXTREME SPORTS EVENT

The 1999 ESPN Summer X Games, held in San Francisco, California, USA, were attended by a record 268,390 visitors over its 10-day duration.

★ HIGHEST ATTENDANCE AT THE WINTER X GAMES

An unprecedented 85,100 spectators attended Winter X Games 5 in 2001 at Mount Snow, Vermont, USA. This represents **the greatest attendance for any winter action sports event**.

FIRST SKATEBOARD 900

Skateboard legend Tony Hawk (USA) became the first person to achieve a "900" (two-and-a-half airborne rotations) in competition at X Games 5 in San Francisco, California, USA, on 27 June 1999. The 900 (named after the fact that the skater spins through 900°) is regarded as one of the most difficult tricks in vert skateboarding.

★ LONGEST HANDSTAND ON A SNOWSKATE BOARD

Trenton R. Schindler (USA) performed a snowskate-board handstand lasting a record 4.38 seconds at Winter X Games 11 in Aspen, Colorado, USA, on 28 January 2007.

★ LONGEST OLLIE ON A SNOWSKATE BOARD

Phil Smage (USA) performed a 3.45-m (11-ft 4-in) ollie on a snowskate board at Winter X Games 11 in Aspen, Colorado, USA, on 27 January 2007. An ollie involves lifting the board off the snow with just the momentum of your body.

★ MOST CONSECUTIVE OLLIES ON A SNOWSKATE BOARD

Phil Smage (USA) set another world snowskate record at Winter X Games 11 by achieving 14 consecutive ollies (or kickflips) on 25 January 2007.

SUMMER MEDAL WINNERS

MOST MEDALS

The most individual medals of any kind won during the history of the Summer X Games is 20 by Dave Mirra (USA), who competes in BMX Freestyle. Mirra also holds the record for the ★ **most Summer X Games gold medals won by an individual**, with 18 wins as of 2 March 2007.

SKATEBOARDING

Tony Hawk and Andy Macdonald (both USA) have each won 16 X Games skateboard medals.

MOTO X

Travis Pastrana (USA) has won a total of 11 X Games medals during his career in Moto X Best Trick, Freestyle and Step Up, seven of them gold. Moto X (Best Trick) was once also a discipline of the Winter X Games.

★ HIGHEST OLLIE ON A SNOWSKATE BOARD
The highest ollie on a snowskate board is 70.5 cm (27.75 in) by Phil Smage (USA) at ESPN's Winter X Games 11 in Aspen, Colorado, USA, on 26 January 2007.

MOST SNOWBOARD SUPERPIPE MEDALS AT THE WINTER X GAMES (MALE)
Danny Kass (USA) has won a total of four medals for Snowboard SuperPipe: gold in 2001, silver in 2003 and 2004, and bronze in 2005.

MOST INDIVIDUAL MEDALS AT THE WINTER X GAMES
Barrett Christy (USA) won 10 Winter X Games medals in a variety of snowboard disciplines between 1997 and 2001. For Slopestyle, she won gold in 1997, silver in 1998 and 1999, and bronze in 2000 and 2002; in Big Air, she won gold in 1997 and 1999, and silver in 1998 and 2001; finally, she earned a silver for SuperPipe in 2000.

★ FIRST MOTO X DOUBLE BACKFLIP

Travis Pastrana (USA) made history at X Games 12 in Los Angeles, California, USA, on 4 August 2006 by performing the first double backflip on a motorcycle – an incredible stunt for which he was awarded gold for Best Trick. The following day, Pastrana went on to pick up his third gold of the games, in the Rally event.

The **most Moto X Winter X Games medals won** is two, by five US riders: Mike Metzger, Mike Jones, Tommy Clowers, Caleb Wyatt and Brian Deegan, whose two medals (2002, 2005) were gold – another record!

WINTER MEDAL WINNERS

SKIER X

Enak Gavaggio (France) holds six Skier X medals – gold in 1999 and bronze from 2001 to 2004 and 2007.

SKIING

Tanner Hall (USA) has won a record nine Winter X Games skiing medals: a gold for Big Air, three golds and one silver for Slopestyle, and two golds and two silvers for SuperPipe Men's.

SKI SUPERPIPE

Jon Olsson (Sweden) has won four Ski SuperPipe medals: gold in 2002, silver in 2004 and bronze in 2003 and 2005. Superpipes have 5-m-high (16-ft 4-in) walls that are almost 90° vertical.

YOUNGEST X GAMES ATHLETE

The youngest-ever X Games athlete is Nyjah Huston (USA, b. 30 November 1994), who was 11 years 246 days old when he made his competition debut in the men's Skateboard Street at X Games 12, staged from 3 to 6 August 2006.

SNOCROSS

Canadian X Games competitor Blair Morgan has earned a total of eight medals for SnoCross: gold from 2001 to 2003 and 2005 to 2006, silver from 1999 to 2000, and bronze in 2004.

XTREMES OF XCELLENCE

• Ryan Sheckler (USA, b. 30 December 1989) was 13 years 230 days old when he won the Skateboard Park gold medal at X Games 9 in Los Angeles, California, USA, on 17 August 2003. This feat made him the **youngest X Games gold medallist**.

• Lindsey Adams Hawkins (USA, b. 21 September 1989) became the **youngest female X Games gold medallist** when she won the Skateboard Vert competition, aged 14 years 321 days at X Games 10 in Los Angeles, California, USA, on 7 August 2004.

• Ayumi Kawasaki (Japan) was 12 years old in 1997 when she won an X Games bronze medal in the women's Aggressive Inline Skate Vert competition. The achievement made her the **youngest X Games medallist**.

• The record for the **oldest X Games athlete** is held by Angelika Casteneda (USA), who was 53 years old when she competed in the X Venture Race in 1996. Casteneda secured a gold medal in the race, a feat that also gives her the record for the **oldest X Games medallist**.

★ **NEW RECORD**
☆ **UPDATED RECORD**

MOST GOLD MEDALS AT THE WINTER X GAMES
Two X Games competitors have won six gold medals each – Shaun Palmer (USA, above) and Shaun White (USA). Palmer won gold in Skier X (2000), Snowboarder X (1997–99), Snow Mountain Biking (1997) and Ultracross (2001). White won his golds in Snowboard SuperPipe (2003 and 2006) and Slopestyle (2003–06).

MOST SNOWBOARD SLOPESTYLE MEDALS AT THE WINTER X GAMES
Shaun White (USA) has earned five Snowboard Slopestyle medals: gold in 2003, 2004, 2005 and 2006 and silver in 2002.

MOST SKI SLOPESTYLE MEDALS AT THE WINTER X GAMES
Jon Olsson (Sweden, pictured) and Tanner Hall (USA) have each won four medals for Ski Slopestyle. Hall took gold in 2002–04 and silver in 2005. Olsson took bronze in 2002–05.

SPORTS REFERENCE

★ **NEW RECORD**
☆ **UPDATED RECORD**

ARCHERY – OUTDOOR RECURVE

MEN	RECORD HOLDER	RECORD	PLACE	DATE
30 m	Kye Dong-Hyun (South Korea)	360/17	Cheongju, South Korea	1 Sep 2002
50 m	Kim Kyung-Ho (South Korea)	351	Wonju, South Korea	1 Sep 1997
70 m	Kim Jae-Hyung (South Korea)	349	Yecheon, South Korea	24 Oct 2006
70 m Round (72 Arr.)	Im Dong-Hyun (South Korea)	687	Athens, Greece	12 Aug 2004
90 m	Jang Yong-Ho (South Korea)	337	New York City, USA	16 Jul 2003
12 Arr. Final Match	Choi Won-Jong (South Korea)	120/0	Ulsan, South Korea	18 Oct 2005
144 Arr. FITA Round	Oh Kyo-Moon (South Korea)	1,379	Wonju, South Korea	1 Nov 2000
3 x 144 Arr. FITA Round	South Korea (Jang Yong-Ho, Choi Young-Kwang, Im Dong-Hyun)	4,074	New York City, USA	16 Jul 2003
24 Arr. Final Match	China (Xue Haifeng, Jiang Lin, Wu FengBo)	229	Porec, Croatia	12 May 2006
70 m Round (3 x 72 Arr.)	South Korea (Jang Yong-Ho, Kim Bo-Ram, Oh Kyo-Moon)	2,031	Atlanta, USA	1 Jul 1996

WOMEN	RECORD HOLDER	RECORD	PLACE	DATE
30 m	Yun Mi-Jin (South Korea)	360/15	Yecheon, South Korea	27 Oct 2004
50 m	Park Sung-Hyun (South Korea)	350	Yecheon, South Korea	12 Mar 2003
60 m	Kim Yu-Mi (South Korea)	351	Cheongju, South Korea	26 Aug 2004
70 m	Park Sung-Hyun (South Korea)	351	Cheongju, South Korea	9 Oct 2004
70 m Round (72 Arr.)	Park Sung-Hyun (South Korea)	682	Athens, Greece	12 Aug 2004
12 Arr. Final Match	Song Mi-Jin (South Korea)	118	Cheongju, South Korea	13 Aug 2001
144 Arr. FITA Round	Park Sung-Hyun (South Korea)	1,405	Cheongju, South Korea	10 Oct 2004
☆ 3 x 144 Arr. FITA Round	South Korea (Park Sung-Hyun, Yun Mi-Jin, Yun Ok-Hee)	4,129	New Delhi, India	10 Nov 2005
☆ 24 Arr. Final Match	South Korea (Kim Yu-Mi, Lee Sung-Jin, Lee Tuk-Young)	226	Antalya, Turkey	9 Jun 2006
70 m Round (3 x 72 Arr.)	South Korea (Park Sung-Hyun, Lee Sung-Jin, Yun Mi-Jin)	2,030	Athens, Greece	12 Aug 2004

24 ARROW FINAL MATCH

Xue Haifeng (China, member of the record-holding team) in action at the men's archery individual event in Athens, Greece, on 16 August 2004.

ATHLETICS – INDOOR FIELD EVENTS

MEN	RECORD	NAME & NATIONALITY	PLACE	DATE
High jump	2.43 m (7 ft 11.66 in)	Javier Sotomayor (Cuba)	Budapest, Hungary	4 Mar 1989
Pole vault	6.15 m (20 ft 2.12 in)	Sergei Bubka (Ukraine)	Donetsk, Ukraine	21 Feb 1993
Long jump	8.79 m (28 ft 10.06 in)	Carl Lewis (USA)	New York City, USA	27 Jan 1984
Triple jump	17.83 m (58 ft 5.96 in)	Aliecer Urrutia (Cuba)	Sindelfingen, Germany	1 Mar 1997
	17.83 m (58 ft 5.96 in)	Christian Olsson (Sweden)	Budapest, Hungary	7 Mar 2004
Shot	22.66 m (74 ft 4.12 in)	Randy Barnes (USA)	Los Angeles, USA	20 Jan 1989
Heptathlon*	6,476 points	Dan O'Brien (USA)	Toronto, Canada	14 Mar 1993

WOMEN	RECORD	NAME & NATIONALITY	PLACE	DATE
High jump	2.08 m (6 ft 9.8 in)	Kajsa Bergqvist (Sweden)	Arnstadt, Germany	4 Feb 2006
☆ Pole vault	• 4.93 m (16 ft 2 in)	Yelena Isinbayeva (Russia)	Donetsk, Ukraine	10 Feb 2007
Long jump	7.37 m (24 ft 2.15 in)	Heike Drechsler (GDR)	Vienna, Austria	13 Feb 1988
Triple jump	15.36 m (50 ft 4.72 in)	Tatyana Lebedeva (Russia)	Budapest, Hungary	6 Mar 2004
Shot	22.50 m (73 ft 9.82 in)	Helena Fibingerová (Czechoslovakia)	Jablonec, Czechoslovakia	19 Feb 1977
Pentathlon†	4,991 points	Irina Belova (Russia)	Berlin, Germany	15 Feb 1992

* Still awaiting ratification/confirmation by the IAAF at time of going to press

* 60 m 6.67 seconds; long jump 7.84 m; shot 16.02 m; high jump 2.13 m; 60 m hurdles 7.85 seconds; pole vault 5.20 m; 1,000 m 2 min 57.96 sec

† 60 m hurdles 8.22 seconds; high jump 1.93 m; shot 13.25 m; long jump 6.67 m; 800 m 2 min 10.26 sec

WOMEN'S POLE VAULT

Yelena Isinbayeva (Russia) competes at the Norwich Union Grand Prix meeting on 22 July 2005 at Crystal Palace Athletics Stadium, London, UK. She holds both the indoor and outdoor pole vault world records.

ATHLETICS – OUTDOOR FIELD EVENTS

MEN	RECORD	NAME & NATIONALITY	PLACE	DATE
High jump	2.45 m (8 ft 0.45 in)	Javier Sotomayor (Cuba)	Salamanca, Spain	27 Jul 1993
Pole vault	6.14 m (20 ft 1.73 in)	Sergei Bubka (Ukraine)	Sestriere, Italy	31 Jul 1994
Long jump	8.95 m (29 ft 4.36 in)	Mike Powell (USA)	Tokyo, Japan	30 Aug 1991
Triple jump	18.29 m (60 ft 0.78 in)	Jonathan Edwards (GB)	Gothenburg, Sweden	7 Aug 1995
Shot	23.12 m (75 ft 10.23 in)	Randy Barnes (USA)	Los Angeles, USA	20 May 1990
Discus	74.08 m (243 ft 0.53 in)	Jürgen Schult (GDR)	Neubrandenburg, Germany	6 Jun 1986
Hammer	86.74 m (284 ft 7 in)	Yuriy Sedykh (USSR)	Stuttgart, Germany	30 Aug 1986
Javelin	98.48 m (323 ft 1.16 in)	Jan Železný (Czech Republic)	Jena, Germany	25 May 1996
Decathlon*	9,026 points	Roman Šebrle (Czech Republic)	Götzis, Austria	27 May 2001

WOMEN	RECORD	NAME & NATIONALITY	PLACE	DATE
High jump	2.09 m (6 ft 10.28 in)	Stefka Kostadinova (Bulgaria)	Rome, Italy	30 Aug 1987
Pole vault	5.01 m (16 ft 5.24 in)	Yelena Isinbayeva (Russia)	Helsinki, Finland	12 Aug 2005
Long jump	7.52 m (24 ft 8.06 in)	Galina Chistyakova (USSR)	St Petersburg, Russia	11 Jun 1988
Triple jump	15.50 m (50 ft 10.23 in)	Inessa Kravets (Ukraine)	Gothenburg, Sweden	10 Aug 1995
Shot	22.63 m (74 ft 2.94 in)	Natalya Lisovskaya (USSR)	Moscow, Russia	7 Jun 1987
Discus	76.80 m (252 ft)	Gabriele Reinsch (GDR)	Neubrandenburg, Germany	9 Jul 1988
Hammer	77.80 m (255 ft 3 in)	Tatyana Lysenko (Russia)	Tallinn, Estonia	15 Aug 2006
Javelin	71.70 m (235 ft 2.83 in)	Osleidys Menéndez (Cuba)	Helsinki, Finland	14 Aug 2005
Heptathlon†	7,291 points	Jacqueline Joyner-Kersee (USA)	Seoul, South Korea	24 Sep 1988
Decathlon**	8,358 points	Austra Skujyte (Lithuania)	Columbia, USA	15 Apr 2005

*100 m 10.64 seconds; long jump 8.11 m; shot 15.33 m; high jump 2.12 m; 400 m 47.79 seconds; 110 m hurdles 13.92 seconds; discus 47.92 m; pole vault 4.80 m; javelin 70.16 m; 1,500 m 4 min 21.98 sec

† 100 m hurdles 12.69 seconds; high jump 1.86 m; shot 15.80 m; 200 m 22.56 seconds; long jump 7.27 m; javelin 45.66 m; 800 m 2 min 8.51 sec
** 100 m 12.49 seconds; long jump 6.12 m; shot 16.42 m; high jump 1.78 m; 400 m 57.19 seconds; 100 m hurdles 14.22 seconds; discus 46.19 m; pole vault 3.10 m; javelin 48.78 m; 1,500 m 5 min 15.86 sec

ATHLETICS – INDOOR TRACK EVENTS

MEN	TIME	NAME & NATIONALITY	PLACE	DATE
50 m	5.56	Donovan Bailey (Canada)	Reno, USA	9 Feb 1996
60 m	6.39	Maurice Greene (USA)	Madrid, Spain	3 Feb 1998
	6.39	Maurice Greene (USA)	Atlanta, USA	3 Mar 2001
200 m	19.92	Frank Fredericks (Namibia)	Liévin, France,	18 Feb 1996
400 m	44.57	Kerron Clement (USA)	Fayetteville, USA	12 Mar 2005
800 m	1:42.67	Wilson Kipketer (Denmark)	Paris, France	9 Mar 1997
1,000 m	2:14.96	Wilson Kipketer (Denmark)	Birmingham, UK	20 Feb 2000
1,500 m	3:31.18	Hicham El Guerrouj (Morocco)	Stuttgart, Germany	2 Feb 1997
1 mile	3:48.45	Hicham El Guerrouj (Morocco)	Ghent, Belgium	12 Feb 1997
3,000 m	7:24.90	Daniel Komen (Kenya)	Budapest, Hungary	6 Feb 1998
5,000 m	12:49.60	Kenenisa Bekele (Ethiopia)	Birmingham, UK	20 Feb 2004
50 m hurdles	6.25	Mark McKoy (Canada)	Kobe, Japan	5 Mar 1986
60 m hurdles	7.30	Colin Jackson (GB)	Sindelfingen, Germany	6 Mar 1994
4 x 200 m relay	1:22.11	Great Britain & N. Ireland (Linford Christie, Darren Braithwaite, Ade Mafe, John Regis)	Glasgow, UK	3 Mar 1991
4 x 400 m relay	3:02.83	USA (Andre Morris, Dameon Johnson, Deon Minor, Milton Campbell)	Maebashi, Japan	7 Mar 1999
4 x 800 m relay	7:13.94	Global Athletics & Marketing, USA (Joey Woody, Karl Paranya, Rich Kenah, David Krummenacker)	Boston, USA	6 Feb 2000
5,000 m walk	18:07.08	Mikhail Shchennikov (Russia)	Moscow, Russia	14 Feb 1995

WOMEN	TIME	NAME & NATIONALITY	PLACE	DATE
50 m	5.96	Irina Privalova (Russia)	Madrid, Spain	9 Feb 1995
60 m	6.92	Irina Privalova (Russia)	Madrid, Spain	11 Feb 1993
	6.92	Irina Privalova (Russia)	Madrid, Spain	9 Feb 1995
200 m	21.87	Merlene Ottey (Jamaica)	Liévin, France	13 Feb 1993
400 m	49.59	Jarmila Kratochvílová (Czechoslovakia)	Milan, Italy	7 Mar 1982
800 m	1:55.82	Jolanda Ceplak (Slovenia)	Vienna, Austria	3 Mar 2002
1,000 m	2:30.94	Maria de Lurdes Mutola (Mozambique)	Stockholm, Sweden	25 Feb 1999
1,500 m	3:58.28	Yelena Soboleva (Russia)	Moscow, Russia	18 Feb 2006
1 mile	4:17.14	Doina Melinte (Romania)	East Rutherford, USA	9 Feb 1990
3,000 m	• 8:23.72	Meseret Defar (Ethiopia)	Stuttgart, Germany	3 Feb 2007
5,000 m	14:27.42	Tirunesh Dibaba (Ethiopia)	Boston, USA	27 Jan 2007
50 m hurdles	6.58	Cornelia Oschkenat (GDR)	Berlin, Germany	20 Feb 1988
60 m hurdles	7.69	Ludmila Engquist (Russia)	Chelyabinsk, Russia	4 Feb 1990
4 x 200 m relay	1:32.41	Russia (Yekaterina Kondratyeva, Irina Khabarova, Yuliva Pechonkina, Yulia Gushchina)	Glasgow, UK	29 Jan 2005
4 x 400 m relay	3:23.37	Russia (Yulia Gushchina, Olga Kotlyarova, Olga Zaytseva, Olesya Krasnomovets)	Glasgow, UK	28 Jan 2006
4 x 800 m relay	• 8:18.54	Russia (Anna Balakshina, Natalya Pantelyeva, Anna Emashova, Olesya Chumakova)	Volgograd, Russia	11 Feb 2007
3,000 m walk	11:40.33	Claudia Stef (Romania)	Bucharest, Romania	30 Jan 1999

• Still awaiting ratification/confirmation by the IAAF at time of going to press

★ WOMEN'S 5,000 M

Tirunesh Dibaba (Ethiopia) waves to the crowd at the Reebok Boston Indoor Games in Boston, Massachusetts, USA, after winning the 5,000 m in a time of 14 min 27.42 sec on 27 January 2007.

SPORTS REFERENCE

WOMEN'S 200 M

Florence Griffith-Joyner (USA) crosses the finish line at the Seoul Games, South Korea, on 29 September 1988, having run the 200 m in 21.34 seconds. Her record remains unbroken after nearly 20 years.

★ 4 X 800 M RELAY

The Kenyan relay team (Wilfred Bungei, Joseph Mutua, Ismael Kombich and William Yiampoy, left to right) celebrate their world record in the 4 x 800 m men's relay race in Brussels, Belgium, on 25 August 2006.

ATHLETICS – OUTDOOR TRACK EVENTS

MEN	TIME/DISTANCE	NAME & NATIONALITY	PLACE	DATE
100 m	9.77	Asafa Powell (Jamaica)	Athens, Greece	14 Jun 2005
	• 9.77	Justin Gatlin (USA)	Doha, Qatar	12 May 2006
☆	9.77	Asafa Powell (Jamaica)	Gateshead, UK	11 Jun 2006
☆	9.77	Asafa Powell (Jamaica)	Zürich, Switzerland	18 Aug 2006
200 m	19.32	Michael Johnson (USA)	Atlanta, USA	1 Aug 1996
400 m	43.18	Michael Johnson (USA)	Seville, Spain	26 Aug 1999
800 m	1:41.11	Wilson Kipketer (Denmark)	Cologne, Germany	24 Aug 1997
1,000 m	2:11.96	Noah Ngeny (Kenya)	Rieti, Italy	5 Sep 1999
1,500 m	3:26.00	Hicham El Guerrouj (Morocco)	Rome, Italy	14 Jul 1998
1 mile	3:43.13	Hicham El Guerrouj (Morocco)	Rome, Italy	7 Jul 1999
2,000 m	4:44.79	Hicham El Guerrouj (Morocco)	Berlin, Germany	7 Sep 1999
3,000 m	7:20.67	Daniel Komen (Kenya)	Rieti, Italy	1 Sep 1996
5,000 m	12:37.35	Kenenisa Bekele (Ethiopia)	Hengelo, Netherlands	31 May 2004
10,000 m	26:17.53	Kenenisa Bekele (Ethiopia)	Brussels, Belgium	26 Aug 2005
20,000 m	56:55.60	Arturo Barrios (Mexico)	La Flèche, France	30 Mar 1991
1 hour	21,101 m	Arturo Barrios (Mexico)	La Flèche, France	30 Mar 1991
25,000 m	1:13:55.80	Toshihiko Seko (Japan)	Christchurch, New Zealand	22 Mar 1981
30,000 m	1:29:18.80	Toshihiko Seko (Japan)	Christchurch, New Zealand	22 Mar 1981
3,000 m steeplechase	7:53.63	Saif Saaeed Shaheen (Qatar)	Brussels, Belgium	3 Sep 2004
☆ 110 m hurdles	12.88	Xiang Liu (China)	Lausanne, Switzerland	11 Jul 2006
400 m hurdles	46.78	Kevin Young (USA)	Barcelona, Spain	6 Aug 1992
4 x 100 m relay	37.40	USA (Michael Marsh, Leroy Burrell, Dennis Mitchell, Carl Lewis)	Barcelona, Spain	8 Aug 1992
	37.40	USA (John Drummond Jr, Andre Cason, Dennis Mitchell, Leroy Burrell)	Stuttgart, Germany	21 Aug 1993
4 x 200 m relay	1:18.68	Santa Monica Track Club, USA (Michael Marsh, Leroy Burrell, Floyd Heard, Carl Lewis)	Walnut, USA	17 Apr 1994
4 x 400 m relay	2:54.20	USA (Jerome Young, Antonio Pettigrew, Tyree Washington, Michael Johnson)	Uniondale, USA	22 Jul 1998
★ 4 x 800 m relay	7:02.43	Kenya (Joseph Mutua, William Yiampoy, Ismael Kombich, Wilfred Bungei)	Brussels, Belgium	25 Aug 2006
4 x 1,500 m relay	14:38.80	West Germany (Thomas Wessinghage, Harald Hudak, Michael Lederer, Karl Fleschen)	Cologne, Germany	17 Aug 1977

WOMEN	TIME/DISTANCE	NAME & NATIONALITY	PLACE	DATE
100 m	10.49	Florence Griffith-Joyner (USA)	Indianapolis, USA	16 Jul 1988
200 m	21.34	Florence Griffith-Joyner (USA)	Seoul, South Korea	29 Sep 1988
400 m	47.60	Marita Koch (GDR)	Canberra, Australia	6 Oct 1985
800 m	1:53.28	Jarmila Kratochvílová (Czechoslovakia)	Munich, Germany	26 Jul 1983
1,000 m	2:28.98	Svetlana Masterkova (Russia)	Brussels, Belgium	23 Aug 1996
1,500 m	3:50.46	Qu Yunxia (China)	Beijing, China	11 Sep 1993
1 mile	4:12.56	Svetlana Masterkova (Russia)	Zürich, Switzerland	14 Aug 1996
2,000 m	5:25.36	Sonia O'Sullivan (Ireland)	Edinburgh, UK	8 Jul 1994
3,000 m	8:06.11	Wang Junxia (China)	Beijing, China	13 Sep 1993
☆ 5,000 m	14:24.53	Meseret Defar (Ethiopia)	New York City, USA	3 Jun 2006
10,000 m	29:31.78	Wang Junxia (China)	Beijing, China	8 Sep 1993
20,000 m	1:05:26.60	Tegla Loroupe (Kenya)	Borgholzhausen, Germany	3 Sep 2000
1 hour	18,340 m	Tegla Loroupe (Kenya)	Borgholzhausen, Germany	7 Aug 1998
25,000 m	1:27:05.90	Tegla Loroupe (Kenya)	Mengerskirchen, Germany	21 Sep 2002
30,000 m	1:45:50.00	Tegla Loroupe (Kenya)	Warstein, Germany	6 Jun 2003
3,000 m steeplechase	9:01.59	Gulnara Samitova-Galkina (Russia)	Iráklio, Greece	4 Jul 2004
100 m hurdles	12.21	Yordanka Donkova (Bulgaria)	Stara Zagora, Bulgaria	20 Aug 1988
400 m hurdles	52.34	Yuliya Pechonkina (Russia)	Tula, Russia	8 Aug 2003
4 x 100 m relay	41.37	GDR (Silke Gladisch, Sabine Rieger, Ingrid Auerswald, Marlies Göhr)	Canberra, Australia	6 Oct 1985
4 x 200 m relay	1:27.46	United States "Blue" (LaTasha Jenkins, LaTasha Colander-Richardson, Nanceen Perry, Marion Jones)	Philadelphia, USA	29 Apr 2000
4 x 400 m relay	3:15.17	USSR (Tatyana Ledovskaya, Olga Nazarova, Maria Pinigina, Olga Bryzgina)	Seoul, South Korea	1 Oct 1988
4 x 800 m relay	7:50.17	USSR (Nadezhda Olizarenko, Lyubov Gurina, Lyudmila Borisova, Irina Podyalovskaya)	Moscow, Russia	5 Aug 1984

• Still awaiting ratification/confirmation by the IAAF at time of going to press

ATHLETICS – ROAD RACE

MEN	TIME	NAME & NATIONALITY	PLACE	DATE
10 km	27:02	Haile Gebrselassie (Ethiopia)	Doha, Qatar	11 Dec 2002
15 km	41:29	Felix Limo (Kenya)	Nijmegen, Netherlands	11 Nov 2001
	• 41:29	Samuel Wanjiru (Kenya)	Ras Al Khaimah, UAE	9 Feb 2007
20 km	• 55:31	Samuel Wanjiru (Kenya)	The Hague, Netherlands	17 Mar 2007
Half marathon	• 58:35	Samuel Wanjiru (Kenya)	The Hague, Netherlands	17 Mar 2007
25 km	1:12:45	Paul Malakwen Kosgei (Kenya)	Berlin, Germany	9 May 2004
30 km	1:28:00	Takayuki Matsumiya (Japan)	Kumamoto, Japan	27 Feb 2005
Marathon	2:04:55	Paul Tergat (Kenya)	Berlin, Germany	28 Sep 2003
100 km	6:13:33	Takahiro Sunada (Japan)	Tokoro, Japan	21 Jun 1998
Road relay	1:57:06	Kenya (Josephat Ndambiri, Martin Mathathi, Daniel Mwangi, Mekubo Mogusu, Onesmus Nyerere, John Kariuki)	Chiba, Japan	23 Nov 2005

WOMEN	TIME	NAME & NATIONALITY	PLACE	DATE
10 km	30:21	Paula Radcliffe (GB)	San Juan, Puerto Rico	23 Feb 2003
15 km	46:55	Kayoko Fukushi (Japan)	Marugame, Japan	5 Feb 2006
20 km	1:03:21	Lornah Kiplagat (Netherlands)	Debrecen, Hungary	8 Oct 2006
Half marathon	1:06:44	Elana Meyer (South Africa)	Tokyo, Japan	15 Jan 1999
25 km	1:22:13	Mizuki Noguchi (Japan)	Berlin, Germany	25 Sep 2005
30 km	1:38:49	Mizuki Noguchi (Japan)	Berlin, Germany	25 Sep 2005
Marathon	2:15:25	Paula Radcliffe (GB)	London, UK	13 Apr 2003
100 km	6:33:11	Tomoe Abe (Japan)	Tokoro, Japan	25 Jun 2000
Road relay	2:11:41	China (Jiang Bo, Dong Yanmei, Zhao Fengdi, Ma Zaijie, Lan Lixin, Li Na)	Beijing, China	28 Feb 1998

• Still awaiting ratification/confirmation by the IAAF at time of going to press

ATHLETICS – ULTRA-LONG DISTANCE (TRACK)

MEN	TIME/DISTANCE	NAME & NATIONALITY	PLACE	DATE
100 km	6:10:20	Don Ritchie (GB)	London, UK	28 Oct 1978
100 miles	11:28:03	Oleg Kharitonov (Russia)	London, UK	2 Oct 2002
1,000 miles	11 days 13:54:58	Piotr Silikin (Lithuania)	Nanango, Australia	11–23 Mar 1998
24 hours	303.306 km (188.46 miles)	Yiannis Kouros (Greece)	Adelaide, Australia	4–5 Oct 1997
6 days	1,023.200 km (635.78 miles)	Yiannis Kouros (Greece)	Colac, Australia	26 Nov–2 Dec 1984

WOMEN	TIME/DISTANCE	NAME & NATIONALITY	PLACE	DATE
100 km	7:14:06	Norimi Sakurai (Japan)	Verona, Italy	27 Sep 2003
100 miles	14:25:45	Edit Berces (Hungary)	Verona, Italy	21–22 Sep 2002
1,000 miles	13 days 1:54:02	Eleanor Robinson (GB)	Nanango, Australia	11–23 Mar 1998
24 hours	250.106 km (155.40 miles)	Edit Berces (Hungary)	Verona, Italy	21–22 Sep 2002
6 days	883.631 km (549.06 miles)	Sandra Barwick (New Zealand)	Campbelltown, Australia	18–24 Nov 1990

ATHLETICS – RACE WALKING

MEN	TIME	NAME & NATIONALITY	PLACE	DATE
20,000 m	1:17:25.6	Bernardo Segura (Mexico)	Bergen, Norway	7 May 1994
20 km (road)	1:17:21	Jefferson Pérez (Ecuador)	Paris Saint-Denis, France	23 Aug 2003
30,000 m	2:01:44.1	Maurizio Damilano (Italy)	Cuneo, Italy	3 Oct 1992
50,000 m	3:40:57.9	Thierry Toutain (France)	Héricourt, France	29 Sep 1996
50 km (road)	3:35:47	Nathan Deakes (Australia)	Geelong, Australia	2 Dec 2006

WOMEN	TIME	NAME & NATIONALITY	PLACE	DATE
10,000 m	41:56.23	Nadezhda Ryashkina (USSR)	Seattle, USA	24 Jul 1990
20,000 m	1:26:52.3	Olimpiada Ivanova (Russia)	Brisbane, Australia	6 Sep 2001
20 km (road)	1:25:41	Olimpiada Ivanova (Russia)	Helsinki, Finland	7 Aug 2005

OFFICIAL BODIES

• **IAAF** International Association of Athletics Federations www.iaaf.org

• **IAU** International Association of Ultrarunners www.iau.org.tw

• **RWA** Race Walking Association www.racewalking association.btinternet.co.uk

MEN'S 20 KM RACE (WALKING)

Jefferson Pérez (Ecuador) crosses the finishing line of the 20 km men's road walk at the IAAF World Athletics Championships in Paris, France, on 23 August 2003. He achieved a record time of 1 hr 17 min 21 sec.

★ **NEW RECORD**
☆ **UPDATED RECORD**

FREEDIVING

MEN'S DEPTH DISCIPLINES	DEPTH/TIME	NAME & NATIONALITY	PLACE	DATE
☆ Constant weight with fins	111 m (364 ft 2 in)	Herbert Nitsch (Austria)	Hurghada, Egypt	9 Dec 2006
☆ Constant weight without fins	82 m (269 ft)	William Trubridge (New Zealand)	Long Island, The Bahamas	11 Apr 2007
Variable weight	140 m (459 ft 4 in)	Carlos Coste (Venezuela)	Sharm, Egypt	9 May 2006
☆ No limit	183 m (600 ft 4 in)	Herbert Nitsch (Austria)	Zirje, Croatia	28 Aug 2006
Free immersion	106 m (347 ft 9 in)	Martin Stepanek (Czech Republic)	Grand Cayman, Cayman Islands	3 Apr 2006

MEN'S DYNAMIC APNEA				
☆ With fins	223 m (731 ft 7 in)	Tom Sietas (Germany)	Tokyo, Japan	28 Aug 2006
☆ Without fins	183 m (600 ft 4 in)	Tom Sietas (Germany)	Tokyo, Japan	27 Aug 2006

MEN'S STATIC APNEA				
☆ Duration	9 min 8 sec	Tom Sietas (Germany)	Hamburg, Germany	1 May 2007

WOMEN'S DEPTH DISCIPLINES				
☆ Constant weight with fins	88 m (288 ft 8.5 in)	Mandy-Rea Cruickshank (Canada)	Grand Cayman, Cayman Islands	29 Apr 2007
Constant weight without fins	55 m (108 ft 5 in)	Natalia Molchanova (Russia)	Dahab, Egypt	7 Nov 2005
Variable weight	122 m (400 ft 3 in)	Tanya Streeter (USA)	Turks and Caicos Islands	19 Jul 2003
No limit	160 m (524 ft 11 in)	Tanya Streeter (USA)	Turks and Caicos Islands	17 Aug 2002
Free immersion	80 m (262 ft 5 in)	Natalia Molchanova (Russia)	Dahab, Egypt	3 Jun 2006

WOMEN'S DYNAMIC APNEA				
With fins	200 m (656 ft 2 in)	Natalia Molchanova (Russia)	Moscow, Russia	23 Apr 2006
Without fins	131 m (429 ft 9 in)	Natalia Molchanova (Russia)	Tokyo, Japan	20 Dec 2005

WOMEN'S STATIC APNEA				
Duration	7 min 30 sec	Natalia Molchanova (Russia)	Moscow, Russia	22 Apr 2006

ROWING

MEN	TIME	NAME & NATIONALITY	REGATTA	DATE
☆ Single sculls	6:35.40	Mahe Drysdale (New Zealand)	Eton, UK	26 Aug 2006
☆ Double sculls	6:03.25	Jean-Baptiste Macquet, Adrien Hardy (France)	Poznan, Poland	17 Jun 2006
☆ Quadruple sculls	5:37.31	Konrad Wasielewski, Marek Kolbowicz, Michal Jelinski, Adam Korol (Poland)	Poznan, Poland	17 Jun 2006
Coxless pairs	6:14.27	Matthew Pinsent, James Cracknell (GB)	Seville, Spain	21 Sep 2002
Coxless fours	5:41.35	Sebastian Thormann, Paul Dienstbach, Philipp Stüer, Bernd Heidicker (Germany)	Seville, Spain	21 Sep 2002
Coxed pairs*	6:42.16	Igor Boraska, Tihomir Frankovic, Milan Razov (Croatia)	Indianapolis, USA	18 Sep 1994
Coxed fours*	5:58.96	Matthias Ungemach, Armin Eichholz, Armin Weyrauch, Bahne Rabe, Jörg Dederding (Germany)	Vienna, Austria	24 Aug 1991
Coxed eights	5:19.85	Deakin, Beery, Hoopman, Volpenheim, Cipollone, Read, Allen, Ahrens, Hansen (USA)	Athens, Greece	15 Aug 2004
LIGHTWEIGHT				
☆ Single sculls*	6:47.82	Zac Purchase (GB)	Eton, UK	26 Aug 2006
Double sculls	6:10.80	Elia Luini, Leonardo Pettinari (Italy)	Seville, Spain	22 Sep 2002
Quadruple sculls*	5:45.18	Francesco Esposito, Massimo Lana, Michelangelo Crispi, Massimo Guglielmi (Italy)	Montreal, Canada	1992
Coxless pairs*	6:26.61	Tony O'Connor, Neville Maxwell (Ireland)	Paris, France	1994
Coxless fours	5:45.60	Thomas Poulsen, Thomas Ebert, Eskild Ebbesen, Victor Feddersen (Denmark)	Lucerne, Switzerland	9 Jul 1999
Coxed eights*	5:30.24	Altena, Dahlke, Kobor, Stomporowski, Melges, März, Buchheit, Von Warburg, Kaska (Germany)	Montreal, Canada	1992

WOMEN	TIME	NAME & NATIONALITY	REGATTA	DATE
Single sculls	7:07.71	Rumyana Neykova (Bulgaria)	Seville, Spain	21 Sep 2002
Double sculls	6:38.78	Georgina and Caroline Evers-Swindell (New Zealand)	Seville, Spain	21 Sep 2002
Quadruple sculls	6:10.80	Kathrin Boron, Katrin Rutschow-Stomporowski, Jana Sorgers, Kerstin Köppen (Germany)	Duisburg, Germany	19 May 1996
Coxless pairs	6:53.80	Georgeta Andrunache, Viorica Susanu (Romania)	Seville, Spain	21 Sep 2002
☆ Coxless fours*	6:25.35	Robyn Selby Smith, Jo Lutz, Amber Bradley, Kate Hornsey (Australia)	Eton, UK	26 Aug 2006
☆ Coxed eights	5:55.50	Mickelson, Whipple, Lind, Goodale, Sickler, Cooke, Shoop, Francia, Davies (USA)	Eton, UK	27 Aug 2006
LIGHTWEIGHT				
☆ Single sculls*	7:28.15	Constanta Pipota (Romania)	Paris, France	19 Jun 1994
☆ Double sculls	6:49.77	Dongxiang Xu, Shimin Yan (China)	Poznan, Poland	17 Jun 2006
☆ Quadruple sculls*	6:23.96	Hua Yu, Haixia Chen, Xuefei Fan, Jing Liu (China)	Eton, UK	27 Aug 2006
Coxless pairs*	7:18.32	Eliza Blair, Justine Joyce (Australia)	Aiguebelette-le-Lac, France	7 Sep 1997

Denotes non-Olympic boat classes

★ MEN'S FREEDIVING

Herbert Nitsch (Austria) currently holds two freediving records: constant weight with fins (he dived to 111 m or 364 ft 2 in using his muscle power alone but using fins for propulsion), and the "deepest man" record (that is, a "no-limit" dive) of 183 m (600 ft 4 in), which he achieved using a weighted sled to pull him down and air-filled balloons to return to the surface.

SHOOTING

MEN	SCORE	NAME & NATIONALITY	PLACE	DATE
300 m rifle three positions	1,181	Epsen Berg-Knutsen (Norway)	Zagreb, Croatia	3 Aug 2006
300 m rifle prone	600	Harald Stenvaag (Norway)	Moscow, USSR	15 Aug 1990
	600	Bernd Ruecker (Germany)	Tolmezzo, Italy	31 Jul 1994
300 m standard rifle 3 x 20	589	Trond Kjoell (Norway)	Boden, Sweden	7 Jul 1995
	589	Marcel Buerge (Switzerland)	Lahti, Finland	16 Jul 2002
50 m rifle three positions	1,186	Rajmond Debevec (Slovenia)	Munich, Germany	29 Aug 1992
50 m rifle prone	600	This record has been achieved a total of 16 times. Most times: Sergei Martynov (Belarus) with 5.		
10 m air rifle	600	Tevarit Majchacheeap (Thailand)	Langkawi, Thailand	27 Jan 2000
50 m pistol	581	Alexsander Melentiev (USSR)	Moscow, USSR	20 Jul 1980
25 m rapid fire pistol	591	Alexei Klimov (Russia)	Granada, Spain	6 Oct 2006
25 m centre fire pistol	590	Afanasijs Kuzmins (USSR)	Zagreb, Yugoslavia	15 Jul 1989
	590	Sergei Pyzhianov (USSR)	Moscow, USSR	5 Aug 1990
	590	Mikhail Nestruev (Russia)	Kouvola, Finland	1 Jul 1997
	590	Park Byung-Taek (South Korea)	Lahti, Finland	14 Jul 2002
	590	Mikhail Nestruev (Russia)	Belgrade, Serbia & Montenegro	10 Jul 2005
	590	Jaspal Rana (India)	Doha, Qatar	8 Dec 2006
25 m standard pistol	584	Erich Buljung (USA)	Caracas, Venezuela	20 Aug 1983
10 m air pistol	593	Sergei Pyzhianov (USSR)	Munich, West Germany	13 Oct 1989
50 m running target	596	Nicolai Lapin (USSR)	Lahti, Finland	25 Jul 1987
50 m running target mixed	398	Lubos Racansky (Czech Republic)	Milan, Italy	4 Aug 1994
10 m running target	590	Manfred Kurzer (Germany)	Athens, Greece	18 Aug 2004
10 m running target mixed	391	Manfred Kurzer (Germany)	Pontevedra, Spain	14 Mar 2001
	391	Lukasz Czapla (Poland)	Zagreb, Croatia	31 Jul 2006
Trap	125	Giovanni Pellielo (Italy)	Nicosia, Cyprus	1 Apr 1994
	125	Ray Ycong (USA)	Lahti, Finland	9 Jun 1995
	125	Marcello Tittarelli (Italy)	Suhl, Germany	11 Jun 1996
	125	Lance Bade (USA)	Barcelona, Spain	23 Jul 1998
	125	Pavel Gurkin (Russia)	Americana, Brazil	10 Aug 2005
	125	David Kostelecky (Czech Republic)	Granada, Spain	5 Oct 2006
Double trap	147	Michael Diamond (Australia)	Barcelona, Spain	19 Jul 1998
Skeet	124	Vincent Hancock (USA)	Changwon, South Korea	16 Apr 2005
	124	Vincent Hancock (USA)	Rome, Italy	22 May 2005
	124	Ennio Falco (Italy)	Rome, Italy	22 May 2005
	124	Mario Nunez (Spain)	Belgrade, Serbia & Montenegro	18 Jul 2005
	124	Tino Wenzel (Germany)	Belgrade, Serbia & Montenegro	18 Jul 2005
	124	Vincent Hancock (USA)	Americana, Brazil	13 Aug 2005
	124	Erik Watndal (Norway)	Americana, Brazil	13 Aug 2005
	124	Antonis Nicolaides (Cyprus)	Dubai, UAE	22 Nov 2005
	124	George Achilleos (Cyprus)	Dubai, UAE	22 Nov 2005
	124	Jin Di (China)	Qingyuan, China	10 Apr 2006
	124	Qu Ridon (China)	Qingyuan, China	10 Apr 2006
	124	Anthony Terras (France)	Santo Domingo, Dominican Republic	28 Mar 2007

WOMEN	SCORE	NAME & NATIONALITY	PLACE	DATE
300 m rifle three positions	588	Charlotte Jakobsen (Denmark)	Lahti, Finland	12 Jul 2002
	588	Charlotte Jakobsen (Denmark)	Zagreb, Croatia	3 Aug 2006
300 m rifle prone	597	Marie Enqvist (Sweden)	Plzen, Czech Republic	22 Jul 2003
50 m rifle three positions	594	Sonja Pfeilschifter (Germany)	Munich, Germany	28 May 2006
50 m rifle prone	597	Marina Bobkova (Russia)	Barcelona, Spain	19 Jul 1998
	597	Olga Dovgun (Kazakhstan)	Lahti, Finland	4 Jul 2002
	597	Olga Dovgun (Kazakhstan)	Busan, Philippines	4 Oct 2002
	597	Olga Dovgun (Kazakhstan)	Zagreb, Croatia	29 Jul 2006
10 m air rifle	400	This record has been achieved a total of 12 times. Most times: Lioubov Galkina (Russia) with 3.		
25 m pistol	594	Diana Iorgova (Bulgaria)	Milan, Italy	31 May 1994
	594	Tao Luna (China)	Munich, Germany	23 Aug 2002
10 m air pistol	393	Svetlana Smirnova (Russia)	Munich, Germany	23 May 1998
10 m running target	391	Xu Xuan (China)	Lahti, Finland	6 Jul 2002
10 m running target mixed	390	Audrey Soquet (France)	Lahti, Finland	9 Jul 2002
Trap	74	Victoria Chuyko (Ukraine)	Nicosia, Cyprus	13 Jun 1998
	74	Chen Li (China)	Qingyuan, China	4 Apr 2006
	74	Zuzana Stefecekova (Slovakia)	Qingyuan, China	4 Apr 2006
Double trap	115	Yafei Zhang (China)	Nicosia, Cyprus	20 Oct 2000
Skeet	74	Elena Little (GB)	Belgrade, Serbia & Montenegro	17 Jul 2005
	74	Christine Brinker (Germany)	Qingyuan, China	9 Apr 2006
	74	Shi Hong Yan (China)	Qingyuan, China	9 Apr 2006
	74	Zemfira Meftakhetdinova (Azerbaijan)	Cairo, Egypt	18 May 2006

★ MEN'S 25 M CENTRE FIRE PISTOL

Jaspal Rana (India) shows his gold medal won at the 15th Asian Games in Doha, Qatar, on 8 December 2006. Rana shot a combined tally of 590 in the precision and rapid rounds to equal the world mark set by Latvian shooter Afanasijs Kuzmins (USSR) in Zagreb in 1989. Three others have also achieved this record: Sergei Pyzhianov (USSR) in 1990, Mikhail Nestruev (Russia) in 1997 and 2005, and Park Byung-Taek (South Korea) in 2002.

★ MEN'S SKEET

Skeet shooting is one of the major types of competitive shotgun shooting at clay targets. Below, Jin Di (China) competes in the men's final during the 15th Asian Games in Doha on 8 December 2006; he, and teammate Qu Ridon, scored a record 124.

SPORTS REFERENCE

☆ MEN'S 500 M LONG TRACK

Lee Kang-Seok (South Korea) skates in the second race of the men's 500 m at the 2007 ISU World Single Distances Speed Skating Championships at the Utah Olympic Oval in Salt Lake City, Utah, USA. He won the gold medal for this race on 9 March 2007.

ISU

The International Skating Union is the sport's official regulating body. For more info, visit **www.isu.org**

WOMEN'S 500 M SHORT TRACK

Evgenia Radanova (Bulgaria) skates in the women's 500 m heat at the Torino 2006 Winter Olympics in Turin, Italy, on 12 February 2006. She holds the world record for this event at 43.671 seconds.

SPEED SKATING – LONG TRACK

MEN	TIME/POINTS	NAME & NATIONALITY	PLACE	DATE
☆ 500 m	• 34.25	Lee Kang-Seok (South Korea)	Salt Lake City, USA	9 Mar 2007
☆ 2 x 500 m	• 68.69	Lee Kang-Seok (South Korea)	Salt Lake City, USA	9 Mar 2007
1,000 m	1:07.03	Shani Davis (USA)	Calgary, Canada	20 Nov 2005
☆ 1,500 m	• 1:42.32	Shani Davis (USA)	Calgary, Canada	4 Mar 2007
3,000 m	3:37.28	Eskil Ervik (Norway)	Calgary, Canada	5 Nov 2005
☆ 5,000 m	• 6:08.48	Sven Kramer (Netherlands)	Calgary, Canada	3 Mar 2007
☆ 10,000 m	• 12:41.69	Sven Kramer (Netherlands)	Salt Lake City, USA	10 Mar 2007
500/1,000/500/1,000 m	137,230 points	Jeremy Wotherspoon (Canada)	Calgary, Canada	18–19 Jan 2003
500/3,000/1,500/5,000 m	146,365 points	Erben Wennemars (Netherlands)	Calgary, Canada	12–13 Aug 2005
500/5,000/1,500/10,000 m	145,742 points	Shani Davis (USA)	Calgary, Canada	18–19 Mar 2006
☆ Team pursuit (8 laps)	• 3:37.80	Netherlands (Sven Kramer, Carl Verheijen, Erben Wennemars)	Salt Lake City, USA	11 Mar 2007

WOMEN	TIME/POINTS	NAME & NATIONALITY	PLACE	DATE
☆ 500 m	• 37.04	Jenny Wolf (Germany)	Salt Lake City, USA	10 Mar 2007
☆ 2 x 500 m	• 74.42	Jenny Wolf (Germany)	Salt Lake City, USA	10 Mar 2007
1,000 m	1:13.11	Cindy Klassen (Canada)	Calgary, Canada	25 Mar 2006
1,500 m	1:51.79	Cindy Klassen (Canada)	Salt Lake City, USA	20 Nov 2005
3,000 m	3:53.34	Cindy Klassen (Canada)	Calgary, Canada	18 Mar 2006
☆ 5,000 m	• 6:45.61	Martina Sáblíková (Czech Rebublic)	Salt Lake City, USA	11 Mar 2007
500/1,000/500/1,000 m	149,305 points	Monique Garbrecht-Enfeldt (Germany)	Salt Lake City, USA	11–12 Jan 2003
		Cindy Klassen (Canada)	Calgary, Canada	24–25 Mar 2006
500/1,500/1,000/3,000 m	155,576 points	Cindy Klassen (Canada)	Calgary, Canada	15–17 Mar 2001
500/3,000/1,500/5,000 m	154,580 points	Cindy Klassen (Canada)	Calgary, Canada	18–19 Mar 2006
Team pursuit (6 laps)	2:56.04	Germany (Daniela Anschütz, Anni Friesinger, Claudia Pechstein)	Calgary, Canada	13 Nov 2005

• Please note that these records were still awaiting ratification by the International Skating Union at the time of going to press.

SPEED SKATING – SHORT TRACK

MEN	TIME	NAME & NATIONALITY	PLACE	DATE
500 m	41.184	Jean-François Monette (Canada)	Calgary, Canada	18 Oct 2003
1,000 m	1:24.674	Jiajun Li (China)	Bormio, Italy	14 Feb 2004
1,500 m	2:10.639	Ahn Hyun-Soo (South Korea)	Marquette, USA	24 Oct 2003
3,000 m	4:32.646	Ahn Hyun-Soo (South Korea)	Beijing, China	7 Dec 2003
5,000 m relay	6:39.990	Canada (Charles Hamelin, Steve Robillard, François-Louis Tremblay, Mathieu Turcotte)	Beijing, China	13 Mar 2005

WOMEN	TIME	NAME & NATIONALITY	PLACE	DATE
500 m	43.671	Evgenia Radanova (Bulgaria)	Calgary, Canada	19 Oct 2001
1,000 m	1:30.037	Jin Sun-Yu (South Korea)	Bormio, Italy	13 Nov 2005
1,500 m	2:18.861	Jung Eun-Ju (South Korea)	Beijing, China	11 Jan 2004
3,000 m	5:01.976	Choi Eun-Kyung (South Korea)	Calgary, Canada	22 Oct 2000
3,000 m relay	4:11.742	South Korea (Choi Eun-Kyung, Kim Min-Jee, Byun Chun-Sa, Ko Gi-Hyun)	Calgary, Canada	19 Oct 2003

☆ MEN'S TEAM PURSUIT

Sven Kramer leads Carl Verheijen and Erben Wennemars as the Dutch team sets a world record at the 2007 ISU World Single Distances Speed Skating Championships in Salt Lake City, Utah, USA. They won gold for the eight-lap team pursuit on 11 March 2007 in 3 min 37.8 sec.

SWIMMING – LONG COURSE

MEN	TIME	NAME & NATIONALITY	PLACE	DATE
50 m freestyle	21.64	Alexander Popov (Russia)	Moscow, Russia	16 Jun 2000
100 m freestyle	47.84	Pieter van den Hoogenband (Netherlands)	Sydney, Australia	19 Sep 2000
200 m freestyle	1:43.86	Michael Phelps (USA)	Melbourne, Australia	27 Mar 2007
400 m freestyle	3:40.08	Ian Thorpe (Australia)	Manchester, UK	30 Jul 2002
800 m freestyle	7:38.65	Grant Hackett (Australia)	Montreal, Canada	27 Jul 2005
1,500 m freestyle	14:34.56	Grant Hackett (Australia)	Fukuoka, Japan	29 Jul 2001
4 x 100 m freestyle relay	3:12.46	USA (Michael Phelps, Neil Walker, Cullen Jones, Jason Lezak)	Victoria, Canada	19 Aug 2006
4 x 200 m freestyle relay	7:03.24	USA (Michael Phelps, Ryan Lochte, Klete Keller, Peter Vanderkaay)	Melbourne, Australia	30 Mar 2007
50 m butterfly	22.96	Roland Schoeman (South Africa)	Montreal, Canada	25 Jul 2005
100 m butterfly	50.40	Ian Crocker (USA)	Montreal, Canada	30 Jul 2005
200 m butterfly	1:52.09	Michael Phelps (USA)	Melbourne, Australia	28 Mar 2007
50 m backstroke	24.80	Thomas Rupprath (Germany)	Barcelona, Spain	27 Jul 2003
100 m backstroke	52.98	Aaron Peirsol (USA)	Melbourne, Australia	27 Mar 2007
200 m backstroke	1:54.32	Ryan Lochte (USA)	Melbourne, Australia	30 Mar 2007
50 m breaststroke	27.18	Oleg Lisogor (Ukraine)	Berlin, Germany	2 Aug 2002
100 m breaststroke	59.13	Brendan Hansen (USA)	Irvine, USA	1 Aug 2006
200 m breaststroke	2:08.50	Brendan Hansen (USA)	Victoria, Canada	20 Aug 2006
200 m medley	1:54.98	Michael Phelps (USA)	Melbourne, Australia	29 Mar 2007
400 m medley	4:06.22	Michael Phelps (USA)	Melbourne, Australia	1 Apr 2007
4 x 100 m medley relay	3:30.68	USA (Aaron Peirsol, Brendan Hansen, Ian Crocker, Jason Lezak)	Athens, Greece	21 Aug 2004

WOMEN	TIME	NAME & NATIONALITY	PLACE	DATE
50 m freestyle	24.13	Inge de Bruijn (Netherlands)	Sydney, Australia	22 Sep 2000
100 m freestyle	53.30	Britta Steffen (Germany)	Budapest, Hungary	2 Aug 2006
200 m freestyle	1:55.52	Laure Manaudou (France)	Melbourne, Australia	28 Mar 2007
400 m freestyle	4:02.13	Laure Manaudou (France)	Budapest, Hungary	6 Aug 2006
800 m freestyle	8:16.22	Janet Evans (USA)	Tokyo, Japan	20 Aug 1989
1,500 m freestyle	15:52.10	Janet Evans (USA)	Orlando, USA	26 Mar 1988
4 x 100 m freestyle relay	3:35.22	Germany (Petra Dallmann, Daniella Goetz, Britta Steffen, Annika Liebs)	Budapest, Hungary	31 Jul 2006
4 x 200 m freestyle relay	7:50.09	USA (Natalie Coughlin, Dana Vollmer, Lacey Nymeyer, Katie Hoff)	Melbourne, Australia	29 Mar 2007
50 m butterfly	25.57	Anna-Karin Kammerling (Sweden)	Berlin, Germany	30 Jul 2000
100 m butterfly	56.61	Inge de Bruijn (Netherlands)	Sydney, Australia	17 Sep 2000
200 m butterfly	2:05.40	Jessicah Schipper (Australia)	Victoria, Canada	17 Aug 2006
50 m backstroke	28.16	Leila Vaziri (USA)	Melbourne, Australia	28 Mar 2007
100 m backstroke	59.44	Natalie Coughlin (USA)	Melbourne, Australia	27 Mar 2007
200 m backstroke	2:06.62	Krisztina Egerszegi (Hungary)	Athens, Greece	25 Aug 1991
50 m breaststroke	30.31	Jade Edmistone (Australia)	Melbourne, Australia	30 Jan 2006
100 m breaststroke	1:05.09	Leisel Jones (Australia)	Melbourne, Australia	20 Mar 2006
200 m breaststroke	2:20.54	Leisel Jones (Australia)	Melbourne, Australia	21 Feb 2006
200 m medley	2:09.72	Wu Yanyan (China)	Shanghai, China	17 Oct 1997
400 m medley	4:32.89	Katie Hoff (USA)	Melbourne, Australia	1 Apr 2007
4 x 100 m medley relay	3:55.74	Australia (Emily Seebohm, Leisel Jones, Jessicah Schipper, Lisbeth Lenton)	Melbourne, Australia	31 Mar 2007

Long course swimming events are held in a pool measuring 50 m in length. This is the international standard and Olympic pool size. **Short course** swimming is done in a pool measuring 25 m. This means that a 100-m swum long course would consist of two lengths, whereas it would involve four lengths in a short-course pool. The swimmer "gains" some time because of the additional number of turns in short course, so short-course records (see p.274) are "faster" than long-course.

★ MEN'S 100 M BACKSTROKE

Aaron Peirsol (USA) competes in the men's 100 m at the 12th FINA World Championships on 27 March 2007 at the Rod Laver Arena in Melbourne, Australia. He won in a record time of 52.98 seconds.

FINA

The International Swimming Federation (FINA), based in Lausanne, Switzerland, is responsible for administering international competitions in aquatic sports. For more information, visit **www.fina.org**

★ WOMEN'S 4 X 100 M MEDLEY RELAY

Australians Lisbeth Lenton (front), Emily Seebohm, Jessicah Schipper and Leisel Jones (back, left to right) celebrate their victory in the 4 x 100 m medley relay final at the 12th FINA World Championships in Melbourne, Australia. On 31 March 2007, the Australian women's team won the 4 x 100 m medley relay gold medal and set a new world record of 3 min 55.74 sec. The USA took the silver medal in a time of 3 min 58.31 sec; China won bronze in 4 min 1.97 sec.

★ NEW RECORD
⚝ UPDATED RECORD

SWIMMING – SHORT COURSE

MEN	TIME	NAME & NATIONALITY	PLACE	DATE
⚝ 50 m freestyle	20.98	Roland Schoeman (South Africa)	Hamburg, Germany	12 Aug 2006
100 m freestyle	46.25	Ian Crocker (USA)	New York City, USA	27 Mar 2004
	46.25	Roland Schoeman (South Africa)	Berlin, Germany	22 Jan 2005
200 m freestyle	1:41.10	Ian Thorpe (Australia)	Berlin, Germany	6 Feb 2000
400 m freestyle	3:34.58	Grant Hackett (Australia)	Sydney, Australia	18 Jul 2002
800 m freestyle	7:25.28	Grant Hackett (Australia)	Perth, Australia	3 Aug 2001
1,500 m freestyle	14:10.10	Grant Hackett (Australia)	Perth, Australia	7 Aug 2001
4 x 100 m freestyle relay	3:09.57	Sweden (Johan Nyström, Lars Frölander, Mattias Ohlin, Stefan Nystrand)	Athens, Greece	16 Mar 2000
4 x 200 m freestyle relay	6:56.41	Australia (William Kirby, Ian Thorpe, Michael Klim, Grant Hackett)	Perth, Australia	7 Aug 2001
50 m butterfly	22.60	Kaio Almeida (Brazil)	Santos, Brazil	17 Dec 2005
100 m butterfly	49.07	Ian Crocker (USA)	New York City, USA	26 Mar 2004
200 m butterfly	1:50.73	Franck Esposito (France)	Antibes, France	8 Dec 2002
50 m backstroke	23.27	Thomas Rupprath (Germany)	Vienna, Austria	10 Dec 2004
⚝ 100 m backstroke	49.99	Ryan Lochte (USA)	Shanghai, China	9 Apr 2006
⚝ 200 m backstroke	1:49.05	Ryan Lochte (USA)	Shanghai, China	9 Apr 2006
50 m breaststroke	26.17	Oleg Lisogor (Ukraine)	Berlin, Germany	21 Jan 2006
100 m breaststroke	57.47	Ed Moses (USA)	Stockholm, Sweden	21 Jan 2002
200 m breaststroke	2:02.92	Ed Moses (USA)	Berlin, Germany	17 Jan 2004
100 m medley	51.52	Ryk Neethling (South Africa)	New York City, USA	11 Feb 2005
⚝ 200 m medley	1:53.31	Ryan Lochte (USA)	Shanghai, China	8 Apr 2006
400 m medley	4:00.37	Laszlo Cseh (Hungary)	Trieste, Italy	9 Dec 2005
4 x 100 m medley relay	3:25.09	USA (Aaron Peirsol, Brendan Hansen, Ian Crocker, Jason Lezak)	Indianapolis, USA	11 Sep 2004

WOMEN	TIME	NAME & NATIONALITY	PLACE	DATE
50 m freestyle	23.59	Therese Alshammar (Sweden)	Athens, Greece	18 Mar 2000
100 m freestyle	51.70	Lisbeth Lenton (Australia)	Melbourne, Australia	9 Aug 2005
200 m freestyle	1:53.29	Lisbeth Lenton (Australia)	Sydney, Australia	19 Nov 2005
400 m freestyle	3:56.79	Laure Manaudou (France)	Trieste, Italy	10 Dec 2005
800 m freestyle	8:11.25	Laure Manaudou (France)	Trieste, Italy	9 Dec 2005
1,500 m freestyle	15:42.39	Laure Manaudou (France)	La Roche-sur-Yon, France	20 Nov 2004
4 x 100 m freestyle relay	3:33.32	Netherlands (Inge Dekker, Hinkelien Schreuder, Chantal Groot, Marleen Veldhuis)	Shanghai, China	8 Apr 2006
4 x 200 m freestyle relay	7:46.30	China (Xu Yanvei, Zhu Yingven, Tang Jingzhi, Yang Yu)	Moscow, Russia	3 Apr 2002
50 m butterfly	25.33	Anne-Karin Kammerling (Sweden)	Gothenburg, Sweden	12 Mar 2005
⚝ 100 m butterfly	55.95	Lisbeth Lenton (Australia)	Hobart, Australia	28 Aug 2006
200 m butterfly	2:04.04	Yang Yu (China)	Berlin, Germany	18 Jan 2004
50 m backstroke	26.83	Li Hui (China)	Shanghai, China	2 Dec 2001
100 m backstroke	56.71	Natalie Coughlin (USA)	New York City, USA	21 Nov 2002
200 m backstroke	2:03.62	Natalie Coughlin (USA)	New York City, USA	27 Nov 2001
50 m breaststroke	29.90	Jade Edmistone (Australia)	Brisbane, Australia	26 Sep 2004
⚝ 100 m breaststroke	1:03.86	Leisel Jones (Australia)	Hobart, Australia	28 Aug 2006
200 m breaststroke	2:17.75	Leisel Jones (Australia)	Melbourne, Australia	29 Nov 2003
100 m medley	58.80	Natalie Coughlin (USA)	New York City, USA	23 Nov 2002
200 m medley	2:07.79	Allison Wagner (USA)	Palma de Mallorca, Spain	5 Dec 1993
400 m medley	4:27.83	Yana Klochkova (Ukraine)	Paris, France	19 Jan 2002
⚝ 4 x 100 m medley relay	3:51.84	Australia (Jessicah Schipper, Lisbeth Lenton, Tayliah Zimmer, Jade Edmistone)	Shanghai, China	7 Apr 2006

★ MEN'S 200 M MEDLEY

Ryan Lochte (USA) celebrates his new world record of 1 min 53.31 sec in the men's 200 m individual medley at the FINA World Swimming Championships (short course) held at the Qi Zhong Stadium in Shanghai, China, on 8 April 2006. The next day, Lochte also broke the world records in the 100 m and 200 m backstroke.

★ WOMEN'S 4 X 100 M FREESTYLE RELAY

Inge Dekker (Netherlands) swims in the 100 m butterfly semi-final at the World Swimming Championships (short course) in Shanghai, China.

At the same event on 8 April 2006, the Dutch team (also including Chantal Groot, Hinkelien Schreuder and Marleen Veldhuis) won the freestyle relay race in 3 min 33.32 sec.

TRACK CYCLING – ABSOLUTE

MEN	TIME/DISTANCE	NAME & NATIONALITY	PLACE	DATE
200 m (flying start)	9.772	Theo Bos (Netherlands)	Moscow, Russia	16 Dec 2006
500 m (flying start)	25.850	Arnaud Duble (France)	La Paz, Bolivia	10 Oct 2001
1 km (standing start)	58.875	Arnaud Tournant (France)	La Paz, Bolivia	10 Oct 2001
4 km (standing start)	4:11.114	Christopher Boardman (GB)	Manchester, UK	29 Aug 1996
Team 4 km (standing start)	3:56.610	Australia (Graeme Brown, Luke Roberts, Brett Lancaster, Bradley McGee)	Athens, Greece	22 Aug 2004
1 hour	49.7 km*	Ondrej Sosenka (Czech Republic)	Moscow, Russia	19 Jul 2005

WOMEN	TIME/DISTANCE	NAME & NATIONALITY	PLACE	DATE
200 m (flying start)	10.831	Olga Slioussareva (Russia)	Moscow, Russia	25 Apr 1993
500 m (flying start)	29.655	Erika Saloumiaee (USSR)	Moscow, USSR	6 Aug 1987
3 km (standing start)	3:24.537	Sarah Ulmer (New Zealand)	Athens, Greece	22 Aug 2004
1 hour	46.65 km*	Leontien Zijlaard-van Moorsel (Netherlands)	Mexico City, Mexico	1 Oct 2003

Some athletes achieved better distances within an hour with bicycles that are no longer allowed by the Union Cycliste Internationale (UCI). The 1-hour records given here are in accordance with the new UCI rules.

★ MEN'S 200 M TRACK CYCLING

Theo Bos (Netherlands) in action in the men's sprint during the UCI Track Cycling World Championship on 1 April 2007 in Palma de Mallorca, Spain. Just a few months earlier, on 16 December 2006, Bos had set a new world record of 9.772 seconds for the 200 m (flying start) in Moscow, Russia.

WATER-SKIING

MEN	RECORD	NAME & NATIONALITY	PLACE	DATE
Slalom	1.5 buoy/9.75-m line	Chris Parrish (USA)	Trophy Lakes, USA	28 Aug 2005
Barefoot slalom	20.6 crossings of wake in 30 seconds	Keith St Onge (USA)	Bronkhorstspruit, South Africa	6 Jan 2006
Tricks	12,400 points	Nicolas Le Forestier (France)	Lac de Joux, Switzerland	4 Sep 2005
Barefoot tricks	10,880 points	Keith St Onge (USA)	Adna, USA	17 Sep 2006
Jump	73 m (239 ft 6 in)	Freddy Krueger (USA)	Polk City, USA	29 May 2005
Barefoot jump	27.4 m (89 ft 11 in)	David Small (GB)	Mulwala, Australia	8 Feb 2004
Ski fly	91.1 m (298 ft 10 in)	Jaret Llewellyn (Canada)	Orlando, USA	14 May 2000
Overall	2,818.01 points*	Jaret Llewellyn (Canada)	Seffner, USA	29 Sep 2002

WOMEN	RECORD	NAME & NATIONALITY	PLACE	DATE
Slalom	1 buoy/10.25-m line	Kristi Overton Johnson (USA)	West Palm Beach, USA	14 Sep 1996
Barefoot slalom	17.0 crossings of wake in 30 seconds	Nadine de Villiers (South Africa)	Witbank, South Africa	5 Jan 2001
Tricks	8,740 points	Mandy Nightingale (USA)	Santa Rosa, USA	10 Jun 2006
Barefoot tricks	4,400 points	Nadine de Villiers (South Africa)	Witbank, South Africa	5 Jan 2001
Jump	56.6 m (186 ft)	Elena Milakova (Russia)	Rio Linda, USA	21 Jul 2002
Barefoot jump	20.6 m (67 ft 7 in)	Nadine de Villiers (South Africa)	Pretoria, South Africa	4 Mar 2000
Ski fly	69.4 m (227 ft 8.2 in)	Elena Milakova (Russia)	Pine Mountain, USA	26 May 2002
Overall	2,850.11 points**	Clementine Lucine (France)	Lacanau, France	9 Jul 2006

* 5@11.25 m, 10,730 tricks, 71.7 m jump
** 4@11.25 m, 8,680 tricks, 52.1 m jump; calculated with the new 2006 scoring method (slalom base reduced by 24)

IWSF

Founded in Geneva, Switzerland, in July 1946, the International Water Ski Federation is the world governing body for towed water sports. These include all sports performed on the water in which the athlete is towed by a rope attached to any mechanical propulsion device. Barefoot water-skiing operates under the umbrella of the IWSF. For more information, visit **www.iwsf.com**

★ MEN'S BAREFOOT TRICKS

At the 15th Barefoot Water-Ski World Championships held on 17 September 2006 in Adna, Washington, USA, Keith St Onge (USA) achieved 10,880 points for barefoot water-skiing tricks – the highest score ever in this discipline. He also holds the world record in barefoot slalom, with 20.6 crossings of the wake in 30 seconds.

SPORTS REFERENCE

★ **NEW RECORD**
☆ **UPDATED RECORD**

WEIGHTLIFTING

MEN	CATEGORY	WEIGHT LIFTED	NAME & NATIONALITY	PLACE	DATE
56 kg	Snatch	138 kg	Halil Mutlu (Turkey)	Antalya, Turkey	4 Nov 2001
	Clean & jerk	168 kg	Halil Mutlu (Turkey)	Trencín, Slovakia	24 Apr 2001
	Total	305 kg	Halil Mutlu (Turkey)	Sydney, Australia	16 Sep 2000
62 kg	Snatch	153 kg	Shi Zhiyong (China)	Izmir, Turkey	28 Jun 2002
	Clean & jerk	182 kg	Le Maosheng (China)	Busan, South Korea	2 Oct 2002
	Total	325 kg	World Standard*		
69 kg	Snatch	165 kg	Georgi Markov (Bulgaria)	Sydney, Australia	20 Sep 2000
	Clean & jerk	197 kg	Zhang Guozheng (China)	Qinhuangdao, China	11 Sep 2003
	Total	357 kg	Galabin Boevski (Bulgaria)	Athens, Greece	24 Nov 1999
77 kg	Snatch	173 kg	Sergey Filimonov (Kazakhstan)	Almaty, Kazakhstan	9 Apr 2004
	Clean & jerk	210 kg	Oleg Perepetchenov (Russia)	Trencín, Slovakia	27 Apr 2001
	Total	377 kg	Plamen Zhelyazkov (Bulgaria)	Doha, Qatar	27 Mar 2002
85 kg	Snatch	186 kg	Andrei Rybakov (Bulgaria)	Wladyslawowo, Poland	6 May 2006
	Clean & jerk	218 kg	Zhang Yong (China)	Ramat Gan, Israel	25 Apr 1998
	Total	395 kg	World Standard*		
94 kg	Snatch	188 kg	Akakios Kakhiasvilis (Greece)	Athens, Greece	27 Nov 1999
	Clean & jerk	232 kg	Szymon Kolecki (Poland)	Sofia, Bulgaria	29 Apr 2000
	Total	417 kg	World Standard*		
105 kg	Snatch	199 kg	Marcin Dolega (Poland)	Wladyslawowo, Poland	7 May 2006
	Clean & jerk	242 kg	World Standard*		
	Total	440 kg	World Standard*		
+105 kg	Snatch	213 kg	Hossein Reza Zadeh (Iran)	Qinhuangdao, China	14 Sep 2003
	Clean & jerk	263 kg	Hossein Reza Zadeh (Iran)	Athens, Greece	25 Aug 2004
	Total	472 kg	Hossein Reza Zadeh (Iran)	Sydney, Australia	26 Sep 2000

WOMEN	CATEGORY	WEIGHT LIFTED	NAME & NATIONALITY	PLACE	DATE
48 kg	☆ Snatch	98 kg	Yang Lian (China)	Santo Domingo, Dominican Republic	1 Oct 2006
	☆ Clean & jerk	120 kg	Chen Xiexia (China)	Taian City, China	21 Apr 2007
	☆ Total	217 kg	Yang Lian (China)	Santo Domingo, Dominican Republic	1 Oct 2006
53 kg	Snatch	102 kg	Ri Song-Hui (North Korea)	Busan, South Korea	1 Oct 2002
	☆ Clean & jerk	129 kg	Li Ping (China)	Taian City, China	22 Apr 2007
	☆ Total	226 kg	Qiu Hongxia (China)	Santo Domingo, Dominican Republic	2 Oct 2006
58 kg	☆ Snatch	111 kg	Chen Yanqing (China)	Doha, Qatar	3 Dec 2006
	☆ Clean & jerk	141 kg	Qiu Hongmei (China)	Taian City, China	23 Apr 2007
	☆ Total	251 kg	Chen Yanqing (China)	Doha, Qatar	3 Dec 2006
63 kg	☆ Snatch	116 kg	Pawina Thongsuk (Thailand)	Doha, Qatar	12 Nov 2005
	☆ Clean & jerk	142 kg	Pawina Thongsuk (Thailand)	Doha, Qatar	4 Dec 2006
	Total	256 kg	Pawina Thongsuk (Thailand)	Doha, Qatar	12 Nov 2005
69 kg	☆ Snatch	123 kg	Oxana Slivenko (Russia)	Santo Domingo, Dominican Republic	4 Oct 2006
	Clean & jerk	157 kg	Zarema Kasaeva (Russia)	Doha, Qatar	13 Nov 2005
	Total	275 kg	Liu Chunhong (China)	Athens, Greece	19 Aug 2004
75 kg	Snatch	130 kg	Natalia Zabolotnaia (Russia)	Doha, Qatar	13 Nov 2005
	Clean & jerk	159 kg	Liu Chunhong (China)	Doha, Qatar	13 Nov 2005
	☆ Total	286 kg	Svetlana Podobedova (Russia)	Hangzhou, China	2 Jun 2006
+75 kg	☆ Snatch	139 kg	Mu Shuangshuang (China)	Doha, Qatar	6 Dec 2006
	Clean & jerk	182 kg	Gonghong Tang (China)	Athens, Greece	21 Aug 2004
	☆ Total	318 kg	Jang Mi-Ran (South Korea)	Wonju, South Korea	22 May 2006

*From 1 January 1998, the International Weightlifting Federation (IWF) introduced modified bodyweight categories, thereby making the then world records redundant. This is the new listing with the world standards for the new bodyweight categories. Results achieved at IWF-approved competitions exceeding the world standards by 0.5 kg for snatch or clean and jerk, or by 2.5 kg for the total, will be recognized as world records.

WOMEN'S 69 KG CLEAN & JERK

Zarema Kasaeva (Russia) in action during the women's 69 kg weightlifting category at the Athens 2004 Olympic Games. The following year, on 13 November 2005, she broke the world record in this discipline by achieving 157 kg in the clean & jerk in Doha, Qatar.

IWF

The International Weightlifting Federation is the international governing body for the sport of weightlifting. The IWF was founded in 1905 and currently has 167 member nations. For more information about the sport, visit **www.iwf.net**

WOMEN'S +75 KG SNATCH

Heavyweight gold winner Mu Shuangshuang (China) breaks the world snatch record in the +75 kg category of the women's weightlifting. The 22-year-old lifted 139 kg at the 15th Asian Games in Doha, Qatar, on 6 December 2006 to beat the previous record by Jang Mi-Ran (South Korea) by 1 kg.

WINTER X GAMES

DISCIPLINE	MEDALS	HOLDER & NATIONALITY
Overall	10	Barrett Christy, Shaun White (both USA)
Skiing	9	Tanner Hall (USA)
Snowboard	10	Barrett Christy, Shaun White (both USA)
MEN		
Moto X	2	Tommy Clowers, Mike Jones, Mike Metzger, Caleb Wyatt, Brian Deegan (all USA)
Skier X	6	Enak Gavaggio (France)
Skiing Slopestyle	4	Jon Olsson (Sweden), Tanner Hall (USA)
Skiing SuperPipe	4	Jon Olsson (Sweden), Tanner Hall, Simon Dupont (both USA)
SnoCross	8	Blair Morgan (Canada)
Snowboarder X	6	Seth Wescott (USA)
Snowboard Slopestyle	6	Shaun White (USA)
Snowboard SuperPipe	4	Danny Kass, Shaun White (both USA)
WOMEN		
Skier X	5	Aleisha Cline (Canada)
Snowboarder X	4	Lindsey Jocobellis (USA)
Snowboard Slopestyle	5	Barrett Christy, Janna Meyen (both USA)
Snowboard SuperPipe	4	Kelly Clark (USA)

SUMMER X GAMES

DISCIPLINE	MEDALS	HOLDER & NATIONALITY
Overall	20	Dave Mirra (USA)
BMX Freestyle	20	Dave Mirra (USA)
Moto X	11	Travis Pastrana (USA)
Skateboard	16	Tony Hawk, Andy Macdonald (both USA)
Aggressive inline skate	8	Fabiola da Silva (Brazil)
Wakeboard	6	Darin Shapiro, Tara Hamilton, Dallas Friday (all USA)

⭐ MEN'S SKIING SUPERPIPE

Tanner Hall (USA) competes in the Men's Skiing SuperPipe Elimination at Winter X Games 11 on 25 January 2007. During his career, Hall has won a record nine medals for skiing: four in SuperPipe, four in Slopestyle and one in Big Air.

WOMEN'S WAKEBOARDING

Gold medallist Dallas Friday (USA) competes in the women's Wakeboarding Finals at X Games 11 in Aspen, Colorado, USA, in January 2007. Friday has won six medals in this discipline.

LONGEST SPORTS MARATHONS

SPORT	TIME	NAME & NATIONALITY	PLACE	DATE
Basketball	60 hr 3 sec	"Miyazaki 60" (Japan)	Miyazaki, Japan	16–18 Jun 2006
Billiards (singles match)	45 hr 10 min	Arie Hermans and Jeff Fijneman (Netherlands)	Oosterhout, Netherlands	12–14 Feb 2004
Bowling, tenpin	120 hours	Andy Milne (Canada)	Ontario, Canada	24–29 Oct 2005
Bowls, indoor	36 hours	Arnos Bowling Club (UK)	Southgate, UK	20–21 Apr 2002
Bowls, outdoor	105 hours	Lloyd Hotel Bowling Club (UK)	Manchester, UK	14–18 Oct 2006
Cricket	33 hr 30 min	Citipointe Church/Global Care (Australia)	Brisbane, Australia	10–11 Jun 2006
Curling	33 hr 10 min	Rotary Club of Ayr/Ayr Curling Club (UK)	Ayr, UK	24–25 Mar 2005
Football	30 hr 10 min	FC Edo and FC Spiez (Germany)	Erlenbach, Switzerland	8–9 Jul 2006
Futsal	30 hours	Max Cosi/Quinny and Christos Michael Keo teams (Cyprus)	Limassol, Cyprus	19–20 Nov 2005
Handball	70 hours	HV Mighty/Stevo (Netherlands)	Tubbergen, Netherlands	30 Aug–2 Sep 2001
Hockey (ice)	240 hours	Brent Saik and friends (Canada)	Strathcona, Canada	11–21 Feb 2005
Hockey (indoor)	24 hours	Mandel Bloomfield AZA (Canada)	Edmonton, Canada	28–29 Feb 2004
Hockey (inline)	24 hours	8K Roller Hockey League (USA)	Eastpointe, USA	13–14 Sep 2002
Hockey (street)	30 hours	Conroy Ross Partners (Canada)	Edmonton, Canada	17–18 Sep 2004
Korfball	26 hr 2 min	Korfball Club de Vinken (Netherlands)	Vinkeveen, Netherlands	23–24 May 2001
Netball	55 hours	Capital NUNS Netball Club (UK)	London, UK	22–24 Jul 2005
Parasailing	24 hr 10 min	Berne Persson (Sweden)	Lake Graningesjön, Sweden	19–20 Jul 2002
Pétanque (boules)	40 hr 9 min	Bevenser Boule-Freunde (Germany)	Bad Bevensen, Germany	22–23 Jul 2006
Punch-bag	36 hr 3 min	Ron Sarchian (USA)	Encino, USA	15–17 Jun 2004
Rifle shooting	26 hours	St Sebastianus Schützenbruderchaft (Germany)	Ettringen, Germany	20–21 Sep 2003
Skiing	202 hr 1 min	Nick Willey (Australia)	Thredbo, Australia	2–10 Sep 2005
Snowboarding	180 hr 34 min	Bernhard Mair (Austria)	Bad Kleinkirchheim, Austria	9–16 Jan 2004
Softball	95 hr 23 min	Delmar and Renmark/Drive for 95 (Canada)	Dollard-des-Ormeaux, Canada	29 Jun–3 Jul 2005
Tennis (doubles match)	48 hr 15 min	Jahrsdoerfer, Lavoie, Okpokpo, Tse (USA)	Houston, USA	13–15 Apr 2006
Tennis (singles match)	25 hr 25 min	Christian Barschel and Hauke Daene (Germany)	Mölln, Germany	12–13 Sep 2003
Volleyball (indoor)	51 hours	Bunbury Indoor Beach Volleyball (Australia)	Bunbury, Australia	18–20 Nov 2005
Water polo	24 hours	Rapido 82 Haarlem (Netherlands)	Haarlem, Netherlands	30 Apr–1 May 1999
Water-skiing	56 hr 35 min 3 sec	Ralph HIldebrand and Dave Phillips (Canada)	Rocky Point, Canada	10–12 Jun 1994
Windsurfing	71 hr 30 min	Sergiy Naidych (Ukraine)	Simerferopol, Ukraine	6–9 Jun 2003

GWR marathon guidelines are constantly updated – please contact us for information before you attempt a record.

ACKNOWLEDGMENTS

For Guinness World Records:

Chief Operating Officer Alistair Richards
Financial Controller Nicola Savage
Assistant Accountant Neelish Dawett
Finance Assistant Jack Brockbank
Contracts Administration Lisa Gibbs
Senior Vice President, Sales & Marketing Sam Fay
Senior Marketing Manager Laura Plunkett
English Language Sales Director Nadine Causey
International Sales Director Frank Chambers
Senior Brand Manager Kate White
Communications Officer Amarilis Espinoza
International Brand Manager Beatriz Fernandez
English Language Sales Executive John Pilley
Records Management (remote) Amanda Sprague
Director of Television Rob Molloy
Development Producer Simon Gold
Archiving & Production Assistant Denise Anlander
Software Manager Katie Forde
Software Engineer Kevin Wilson
IT Support Paul Bentley, Ryan Tunstall, James Herbert, Gordon Sherratt
Legal Jan Rowland, Juliette Bearman,
Barry Kyle, Amanda Richards
Human Resources Kelly Garrett, Michel Ellis
Facilities Manager Fiona Ross
GWR overseas Chris Sheedy (Australia), Angela Wu (China),
Jun Otsuki (Japan), Olaf Kuchenbecker (Germany)

Special thanks to

Jennifer Banks, Ellie Gibson, Nick Minter, Christopher Reinke, Nicola Shanks,
Nick Watson, Jimmy Weight

The 2008 book team would also like to acknowledge the following people and organizations for their help during the production of this year's edition:

82ASK (Tom, Sarah, Rhod, Paul); 4Kids Entertainment (Bob Mitchell, Brian Simmons); Pedro Adrega, FINA; Animal Planet (Mike Kane, Krishna San Nicolas); Toby Anstis; Anthrocon; Ascent Media (Suzane, Carla, Simon, Esther, Keith); Florrie Baldwin; Zoe Ball; Mike Batt; Sam and Kerri Baxter; BBC TV (Julia Cottrell, Leah Henry); Prof. Michael Besser; Luke and Joseph Boatfield; boxofficemojo.com; Nicky Boxall; Sir Richard Branson; Nikki Brin; Anna Browne; Bruntingthorpe Aerodrome; Daniel Byles; Peter Cassidy, RWA; CCTV; Sasha Cestnik; Charlton Athletic Football Club; Edd China, Cummfy Banana; Paulo Coelho; Scott Cory; David Crouch, Toyota; Davy's Wine Bar; Johnny Depp; Emmerdale; EPSN; Louis Epstein; Sian Evans, BVI, UK; Explorer's Club; explorersweb.com; Dick Fiddy; Neil Fingleton; Flix Marketing (Nic, Tam, Scott, Sharan, Jamie); Food Network (Art Edwards, Susie Fogelson, Keegan Gerhard, Tom Giesen, Allison Page); Ashrita Furman; Marion Gallimore, FISA; Jorge Garcia; Lois Gibson; Ryan Gibson-Judge; Terry Gilliam; Greenpeace; Jordan, Ryan and Brandon Greenwood; Victoria Grimsell; Debby de Groot; Ray Harper; Jan Hauge; Hayden Planetarium, New York; Gavin Hennessy; Lisa Holden, Bloomsbury Publishing, UK; Hotel Arts, Barcelona; Paul Hunn; Sue Hyman Associates; imdb.com; INP Media (Bryn, Martin); International Game Fishing Association; IWSF (Andy Harris, Gill Hill); Michael Jackson; Sarah Jackson, Consolidated, UK; Jamiroquai; Jason Joiner; Terry Jones; Joost (Aki, Dagmara, Tim); Maureen Kane; Damien Kindler; Adam Kirley; Hans Jakob Kvalheim; Murray and Ellie Lamont; Paul Landry; Orla and Thea Langton; Steve Lee; Anthony Liu; Ken Livingstone; Carey Low; Mad Macs II (Claire Bygrave, Carol & Maureen Kane, Sam Malone, David Moncur); Manda; Martyn, Acorn; MAX Entertainment, Kuala Lumpur (Alex, Faisal, Ann, Christy, Belle, Marcus); Mayor's office, Boise, Idaho; Iain McAvoy; Scotti McGowan, Liaison PR; Jan Meek; Katie Melua (Henry Spinetti, Jim Watson, Tim Harries, Denzil Daniels, Stephen Croxford); Metro (Bob Bohn, Daniel Magnus); Millbrook Proving Ground; Mino Monta; Dr Alan Morgan (Zoobiotic Ltd, Bridgend, Wales); Clare Merryfield; Muscle Musical, Japan; Kevin Myers, BBC Wales; National Forensic Academy; National Geographic Kids magazine (Rachel Buchholz, Eleanor Shannah); Aniko Nemeth-Mora, IWF; newlaunches.com; Cast of Nørd; Ocean Rowing Society (Kenneth and Tatiana Crutchlow); Liam O'Connor; Ziggy Opoczynska, National Geographic Kids UK; Kenny Ortega and the cast of High School Musical; Palace Theatre, London, Crispin Ollington and the cast of Spamalot; Michael Perham and family; Phoenix Theatre, London, Iain McAvoy and the cast of Blood Brothers; Phoenix Theatre Bar; Fabrice Prahin, ISU; Ray Quinn; R et G Productions, France (Stephane Gateau, Jerome Revon, David Bensousan, Olivia Vandenhende, Jeff Peralta); Daniel Radcliffe; Red Lorry Yellow Lorry (Kim, Rob, Guy); Lee Redmond; Annabel Sally Reid; Beth Reynolds; Martyn Richards; Hugh Robertson, MP; J. K. Rowling; RTL (Tom, Sacha); San Manuel Indian Bingo; Shamrock Farms; Gene Simmons; Fredrik Skavlan; Alan Smithee; Stage3 Media; Paul Stanley; Statoil; Julien Stauffer, UCI; Chantal Steiner, FITA; Aaron Studman; Sunstate Equipment Co.; Russ Swift; Amanda Tapping; Taylor Herring; David Tennant; Mark Thomas; Julian Townsend; Sarah Trabucci, Scholastic publishing, US; Twin Galaxies (Walter Day, Ben Gold); Dr Neil de Grasse Tyson; Kendra Voth and Smallville Productions; Jessica & Isabel Way; Steven Webb; Ellis Webster; Fran Weelen, Royal Bath and West Show; Wild West Arts Club (Chuck Weems "Walking Eagle", Joe Darrah, Matt and Max Mobley, John Bailey, "Doc"); Elijah Wood; Daniel Woods; World Puzzle Federation; X Games (Danny Chi, Lisa Fruggiero, Debbie McKinnis, Katie Moses, Marc Murphy, Kelly Robshaw); Xi Shun; YouTube; Zheng Da Zong Yi of CCTV.

In memoriam...
Julie Winnefred Bertrand (Canada, 16 September 1891–18 January 2007, world's oldest woman at time of death); Elizabeth "Lizzie" Bolden (USA, 15 August 1890–11 December 2006, world's oldest person at time of death); Maria Esther de Capovilla (Ecuador, 14 September 1889–27 August 2006, world's oldest person at time of death); Cedric (oldest pig); Florence Finch (New Zealand, b. UK, 22 December 1893–10 April 2007, New Zealand's oldest person at time of death); Moses Hardy (USA, 6 January 1893–7 December 2006, USA's oldest man at time of death); Florence Homan (USA, 18 November 1893–13 August 2006, Ohio, USA's oldest person at time of death); Camille Loiseau (France, 13 February 1892–12 August 2006, France's oldest person at time of death); Emiliano Mercado del Toro (Puerto Rico, 21 August 1891–24 January 2007, world's oldest man at time of death); Giulia Sani-Casagli (Italy, 15 September 1893–4 September 2006, Italy's oldest person at time of death); Mary Margaret Smith (USA, 7 October 1893–23 May 2006, Ohio, USA's oldest person at time of death); Emma Tillman (USA, 22 November 1892–28 January 2007, world's oldest person at time of death).

Endpapers
(left to right)
Front Page: Largest car seat; fastest text message blindfolded; youngest hole-in-one golfer (female); largest pizza commercially available; largest skateboard; fastest backwards spelling of 50 words; largest vertical blinds; largest candy dispenser; heaviest beetroot, largest collection of coffee pots; crawling - fastest mile; fastest marathon dressed as Elvis combined with fastest marathon in superhero costume (male); most linked runners to complete a marathon; climbing machine - greatest height in 24 hours (team of 12); longest dancing dragon; largest egg and spoon race; largest tankard of beer; largest Christmas cracker-pulling, largest gathering of centenarians; largest admission ticket; largest smoothie; largest salad; oldest pig; largest shopping bag; most people on space-hoppers; largest collection of board games; most apples bobbed in a minute; most vaccinations given in a working day; largest mass handshake; largest bodhran ensemble; most candles on a cake.

Back Page: Longest journey on an electric mobility vehicle (scooter); furthest distance on a snowmobile on water; most people on unicycles; longest concert by a solo artist, tunnel ball – largest game; largest parade of military motorcycles; largest canned food structure; largest secret Santa game; largest hula dance; largest human wheelbarrow race; largest card game tournament; largest ukulele ensemble; longest lacrosse marathon; longest line of floating airbeds; largest collection of converse shoes; most different dishes on display; most skips in 30 seconds; largest gathering of people dressed as Robin Hood; longest zucchini (courgette); largest skewer kebab; longest dance party; longest cricket marathon; longest card-playing marathon; longest painting; heaviest mango.

BBC radio stations involved in GWR Day:

2CR FM • BBC 3CR • BBC Asian Network • BBC Coventry & Warwickshire • BBC GMR • BBC London Live • BBC Radio 2 (Chris Evans) • BBC Radio Berkshire • BBC Radio Bristol • BBC Radio Cambridgeshire • BBC Radio Cleveland • BBC Radio Cornwall • BBC Radio Cumbria • BBC Radio Derby • BBC Radio Devon • BBC Radio Essex • BBC Radio Five Live (Anita Anand) • BBC Radio Five Live Morning Reports • BBC Radio Gloucestershire • BBC Radio Guernsey • BBC Radio Humberside • BBC Radio Jersey • BBC Radio Kent • BBC Radio Lancashire • BBC Radio Leeds • BBC Radio Leicester • BBC Radio Lincolnshire • BBC Radio Merseyside • BBC Radio Newcastle • BBC Radio Norfolk • BBC Radio Northampton • BBC Radio Oxford • BBC Radio Shropshire • BBC Radio Solent • BBC Radio Somerset • BBC Radio Suffolk • BBC Radio Swindon • BBC Radio Ulster • BBC Radio Wales • BBC Radio York • BBC Southern Counties • BBC Wales • BBC West Midlands • BCB Radio (Bradford) • BFBS • BRMB (Birmingham) • IRN • Isle of Wight Radio • LBC (London) • Leicester Sound • Radio Clyde 1 • Sky News Radio • Time FM (South East) • The Wave (Swansea)

PICTURE CREDITS

INDEX

This year's index is organized into two parts: by subject and by superlative. **Bold** entries in the subject index indicate a main entry on a topic, and entries in **BOLD CAPITALS** indicate an entire chapter. Neither index lists personal names.

SUBJECT INDEX

Most powerful
actors and actresses 166, 167
camera to leave Earth orbit 155
jet engine 206, 207
mobile-phone gun 157
particle accelerator 146
sub-woofer 157
trebuchet 134
volcano 19

Most recent
malicious use of nerve gas 132
nuclear bomb test 132

Most successful
animated movie series 169
Bond movie 169
Internet trade 161
police dog 107
technology manufacturer 157

Most valuable
baseball equipment 229
fortune cookie 129
potato 129
telephone number 129
tooth 129

Most venomous
centipede 48
mollusc 48
scorpion 73

Newest
animal phylum 43
independent country 131
mathematical constant 25
NATO force 131

Noisiest
land animal 40

Oldest
abseiler down a building 60
android robot design 158
animals in captivity 136, 138
astronaut 120
BASE jumper 212

boxing world champion 232
branding 190
deforestation disaster 31
human DNA 148, 153
Everest climber 99
family business 127
footballer 120
fossilized animal food store 42
golf course 244
hedge maze 119
iconic sculpture 177
insect 43
lakes and oceans 34
marathon 218
marathon finisher 219
marsupial 45
music acts 181
NHRA driver 221
ocean rower (female) 94
Olympic medallist 145, 217
people 67
    to give birth 66;
    to meet 287
record shop 127
roller coaster 209
rugby union competition 249
Ryder Cup player 245
scuba diver 257
service medal recipient 133
ski 262
spider 38
spider web with prey 42
tank design 206
tennis number one 253
tick 43
topiary garden 119
tree ever documented 39
TV "child" 186
winter sports athletes 263, 265
World War I veteran living 133
wrestling champion 232

Quietest
place on Earth 150

Rarest
bird of prey 39
crocodilian 44

element on Earth 150
insect 48
seashell 45
snake 40
wild cat 44

Remotest
islands 28
land from the sea 28
man-made object 154
spot from land 28
tree 51

Richest
monarch 129
people 129
reality TV host 187

Sharpest
man-made object 148

Shortest
actor in leading adult role 163
camel species 41
NHL player 246
street 53
titles 169, 189

Shortest (time)
to complete a marathon on
    each continent 218
gestation period in mammal
    38
interval between births 67
lactation period in mammal 51
radio advertisement 191

Sleepiest
mammals 39
marsupial 48

Slimmest
lizard 49
mobile phone 157

Smallest
aircraft 202
area to claim nation status 131

banknote 127
bird of prey 45
butterfly 49
cannon 135
car in production 202
centipede 39
chameleon 46
computer drives 148
crocodile 41
deer 41
dog breed 107
eye for fly-fishing hook 239
fish species 45
gap side-wheeled through
    205
geologically active body 18
horse living 104
instant camera 157
mobile phone TV 15
monkey 40
multimedia player 156
nuclear weapon 135
ocean 34
owl 38
pig species 45
planet 20
police dog 138
revolver 135
robot (humanoid) 158
rowing boat to cross
    an ocean 94
stars 16
stellar disc 16
submarine 203
transistor 149
TV tuner box 156
vertebrate 45
waist 52

Smelliest
frog 40
mammal 39
man-made substance 149
plant 44

Smoothest
solid surface in Solar
    System 21

Softest
metallic element 150

Stretchiest
skin 142

Strongest
jet stream 24
magnetic field 18
microburst 24

Tallest
champagne fountain 111
chocolate sculpture 111
Christmas tree 124
cooked sugar sculpture 111
cookie pyramid 111
dam 197
dog 107
grain silo 194
horse living 104
human being 12, 52, 64
indoor ice-climbing wall
    196
mountain 27
mountain face 27
plants 118, 119
roller coaster 208
sea stack 26
structures 195
tree living 38
twins 67
wall-eye clouds 19

Thickest
ice 32
part of Earth's crust 26

Thinnest
3G mobile phone 157
mobile phone 157
chip 148
computer keyboard 157
man-made material 148
part of Earth's crust 26

Warmest
year on record 30

Worst
jobs 121
mountaineering disaster 98
river pollution 31

Youngest
achievers 74–75
billionaire and millionaire
    128, 129
box-office no.1 star 163
boxing world champion 232
cliff diver 257
climber of El Capitan 98
galaxy 16
great-great-great-great
    grandmother 67
ice hockey player 247
incubator 49
IndyCar winner 221
marathon runners 76
motocross champion 223
NFL coach 215
NHRA driver 221
polar visitors 74, 97
Premiership player 240
professional video gamer
    162
reigning monarch 131
snooker "147" score 251
surgery patients 68
Olympic champion 145
prime ministers 130, 131
solo ocean rowers 95
solo sailor to circumnavigate
    world 101
Super Bowl player 215
survivors 80, 81
Tour de France winner 237
voting age 130
Wild West Arts competitor
    260
Wimbledon champion
    (male) 253
winter sports
    competitors 263
wrestling champion 232
X Games athlete 265

Solutions

From pp.112–13

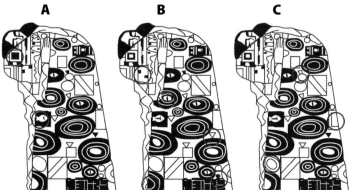

A   B   C

STOP PRESS

★ LARGEST PARADE OF MERCEDES-BENZ

A parade of 153 Mercedes-Benz cars was organized by Gargash Enterprises (UAE) with the support of their customers. The convoy started in Dubai and ended at Endurance City, Bab Al Shams Desert Resort & Spa, UAE, on 21 April 2007.

★ LARGEST PARADE OF FERRARIS

A parade of 128 Ferrari cars was organized by Ayuntamiento de Alcázar de San Juan in Ciudad Real, Castilla-La Mancha, Spain, on 5 May 2007.

★ LARGEST BUDGET FOR A WEB TV SHOW

The eight 15–20-minute-long "webisodes" of *Sanctuary*, a live-action sci-fi series created by Damian Kindler (Canada) to be released online, cost CAN$4.5 million (£2.09 million) to produce, including post-production and visual effects design. The series, starring Amanda Tapping (Canada, below), debuted online at www.sanctuaryforall.com on 14 May 2007.

★ MOST BALLOONS INFLATED IN ONE HOUR

To celebrate the 90th anniversary of the ICA shopping centres (Sweden), on 5 May 2007, a total of 32,558 participants gathered at 1,542 locations around Sweden and blew up 531,061 balloons in just an hour!

★ LARGEST HOT-POT PARTY

On 20 March 2007, the Chongqing Municipal People's Government in Chongqing, China, organized a hot-pot party for 13,612 people eating from 2,249 pots. A hot-pot consists of a simmering pot of stock at the centre of the dining table, in which food is cooked.

★ LONGEST SARI

A sari offered to Goddess Padmavathi by His Holiness Sri Sri Sri Vasanth Gurudev Shakthipeetadhipath (India), founder of Sri Parshva Padmavathi Seva Trust in Chennai, India, on 1 May 2007, measured a record 642.3 m (2,106 ft 10 in).

★ MOST ASCENTS OF MOUNT EVEREST

Apa Sherpa (Nepal) reached the summit of Mount Everest for the 17th time on 16 May 2007, the most times anyone has ever successfully climbed the world's tallest mountain. Apa first tackled Everest in 1987.

★ DOUGHNUTS: MOST EATEN IN 3 MINUTES

Lup Fun Yau ate a record six sugared jam doughnuts – without licking the lips – in three minutes. He equalled the record at *The Sun* offices in London, UK, on 2 May 2007.

★ OLDEST PEOPLE TO MEET

The highest aggregate age for two people to meet is 227 years 142 days, when Bertha Fry (USA, b. 1 December 1893) met Edna Parker (USA, b. 20 April 1893) on 21 April 2007 in Indianapolis, Indiana, USA. The meeting was coordinated by Guinness World Records' gerontology consultant Robert Young (USA).

★ NEW RECORD
★ UPDATED RECORD

★ MOST PEOPLE ON SPACE HOPPERS

The record for the most people on space hoppers is 600, all of whom bounced for one minute on the London Millennium Footbridge (aka the Wobbly Bridge), London, UK, on 15 April 2007, as part of UKTV Gold's re-branding campaign.

GAME ON

FEB 2008

GUINNESS WORLD RECORDS GAMER'S EDITION 2008

Every major new game reviewed

THE ULTIMATE GUIDE

To the World's greatest computer and videogame facts & feats

Vote for your favourite games to win a PS3* at **www.gwrgamersedition.com**

*Terms and conditions apply. See website for details.